Hellenism
Through the Ages

by

Father Dennis Michelis

Seaburn Publishing Group
P.O. Box 2085
Long Island City, N.Y. 11102
www.seaburn.com

For more information on Seaburn's Reading Group, as well as ordering, contact the
Marketing Department at: info@seaburn.com

Cover designed by CSO

Library of Congress Cat. Num.-in-Publication Data

Michelis, Dennis 2008

ISBN 1-59232-049-X

Printed in the United States of America

CONTENTS

ACKNOWLEDGEMENT

First, I wish to express my heartfelt gratitude to Mr. George Geordan who reviewed the manuscript, and all along has offered most valuable assistance and advice on many aspects of its contents.

Secondly, my sincere thanks to Miss Faye Kouvas who typed the manuscript and special thanks to Mr. Savas Magiassos for the layout and design of this book.

WHY PUBLISH THIS BOOK?

The American Foundation for Greek Language And Culture of the Tri-State Region is pleased to sponsor the publishing of this unique and excellent summary on the origins of Hellenism and its contributions to Western civilization. This book combines elements of modern and ancient Greek history with the fascinating biographies of extraordinary achievers both secular and religious who exemplify the contributions of Hellenes throughout the world. To young readers the book can be a source of pride as well as inspiration in furthering their studies of Greek history.

We hope that individuals and organizations will embrace the book and help disseminate it. The intent of the book is not financial gain, but educational and cultural enrichment. For information on ordering the book please contact Seaburn Publishers at www.seaburnbooks.com or Tri-State AFGLC at caliopey@comcast.net.

The Foundation is indebted to the specific sponsors, namely, Dr. James G. and Catherine Faller, Mr. Constantine Georgiou and Dr. Peter N. and Stella Yiannos, all of Wilmington, Delaware, whose financial and editing support facilitated the publishing of the book. In addition, the valuable help in proof reading and editing the final manuscript by Mrs. Maria George is also gratefully acknowledged. The content and format of the book remains that of the author, who, in our opinion, has done an outstanding job in depicting the Hellenic mind and expressing it in an inspirational manner.

The author concentrates on the harvest of Hellenism and, equally important, that this is a continuing process. This in spite of the heavy toll that neglect due to imposed ignorance and some unfortunate historical events have taken on the Hellenic culture; as indicated in the book by illustrations of lost treasures and description of the various periods of history and personalities.

**The Cornucopia of the Hellenic Culture is
Overflowing for All to Partake !**

FOREWORD

Presently, there are over two hundred sovereign states on the face of the earth. Some of them are extremely large, such as Russia, Canada, China, and the United States. Others are modestly large, such as France, Spain and Poland. Others such as Rumania, Portugal and Czechoslovakia are small. Extremely small countries would be Andorra, Liechtenstein and San Marino. Finally, some are tiny, consisting of only a few acres, like Monaco (392 acres), and the Vatican (109 acres). Greece is a small nation as its territory is only about 50, 966 square miles. The only American state it may compare to is North Carolina, although the latter exceeds it by 1,846 miles. Four-fifths of Greece's territory makes up its mainland, and one-fifth makes up its two thousand islands, the overwhelming majority of which are uninhabited.

Four-fifths of the total territory of Greece is mountainous. At least, twenty mountains are over seven thousand feet high. As they furrow the mainland from north to south and to a lesser degree from west to east, they form deep ravines and isolated regions. Such regions had a double effect on the people who lived in them. They kept Greece, for most of its history, divided into small states, and psychologically contributed to Greeks' traditional individualism and their love of freedom. Moreover, since the country is mostly mountainous, allowing a small portion for cultivation, its people turned to the sea. They became daring mariners and established colonies on most Mediterranean coasts seeking a better life.

Yet, despite its very limited territory, Greece has the longest history of all other European nations, and is one of the very few nations of the world that can actually claim that its history and its civilization is at least four thousand years old! What is astonishing, however, is that the people of this small country managed to lead in the intellectual, artistic and scientific foundation on which Western civilization has ever since rested. In fact, there is not a single fundamental intellectual or scientific endeavor the western man has dealt with whose origins will not be found in ancient writings of Greece.

What caused the Greek mind to assert itself so brilliantly, so admirably? As the famous British historian, Arnold Toynbee explained, "It was the successful responses the Greeks made as they tried to overcome the repeated challenges made to them by the natural and human environment."

Almost from the beginning of their history, the ever-inquisitive inhabitants of that small country enthroned reason. Unlike the people of other contemporary and preceding cultures, who, being satisfied with their mythologies and their obedience to their royal leaders, never bothered to ask questions about the complex nature around them, or about man as a social and political being, accepting everything as it was. The Greeks kept asking "Why" about everything around them. And, as they persistently strove to logically answer their "whys", they eventually formed the consummate intellectual and scientific foundation of our Western thought and science.

Twice, in its long history, Greece became a far-flung empire; first, through the conquests of Alexander the Great, and second, during Byzantine times. After centuries, both empires disappeared. It is in another "imperial venture", however, that Greece did not fail, and that is: establishing an "Empire of the mind", an empire that still has its prominence in the Western World.

This book does not purport to be a consistent history of Greece. Events pertaining to wars, political and factional strives, internecine wars, are briefly treated. The book deals with the timeless achievements of this small country's illustrious men and women in the arts and sciences.

At this point, an explanation is owed to the reader in regards to the word "Hellenism" that is used in the title of this book. This word is used to mean the Greeks and culture of over 4,000 years.

PART I

ANCIENT TIMES

1
THE GREEK PEOPLE AND THE GREEK LANGUAGE

Before we familiarize ourselves with the achievements of the people, it is pertinent that we ask: "who are the Greeks?" and "where did they come from?" Prior to the year of 2000 B.C., the people who inhabited the Greek mainland and its islands were the "Pelasgians", the "Dolopes" the "Driopes" and others. These tribes were of "Mediterranean" extraction, and like the other Mediterranean and Middle East tribes, they lived in walled hamlets or towns consisting of round or rectangular stone dwellings. They knew how to make clay pottery and house utensils and arms from copper; they worshipped female divinities and their daily sustenance was provided from farming, fishing and hunting. Moreover, all the above peoples were neither Greek nor did they speak the Greek Language.

During the third millenium, various Alpine (Central European) and Nordic (Northern European) peoples had settled in the Danube and the Rhine Valleys, a territory that stretches from modern Hungary to Belgium. The Nordics dominated the Alpines, and, among others, had imposed on them their Indo-European Languages. The tribes slowly amalgamated creating new cultures. By 1900 BC, the tribes began to break away and migrate to other countries. The Hittites crossed the Balkan Peninsula and entered Asia Minor to settle there, another group entered Italy through the Brenner Pass and settled there, other groups left Southern Germany and settled in France and Belgium, and another group left central Europe, and, after crossing the Balkan Peninsula, entered and settled in Greece. The newcomers were the "Achaeans". They were the first to bring Nordic blood into Greece and they spoke an Indo-European Language, which became the ancestor of classical and modern Greek. The Achaeans were tall, light complexioned, had blonde hair and gray or blue eyes.

The first waves of the Achaeans settled in Northern Greece. Later waves proceeded southwards and settled in the Plains of Thessaly, then in Northern Peloponnesus and then in the plains of Messenia. Eventually, those who settled in Northern Peloponnesus developed the "Mycenean Civilization" which received its name from the most prominent and prosperous city – Mycenae. One learns much about this civilization when one reads the two epics of Homer – the "Iliad" and the "Odyssey". Centuries later, the enterprising and daring Achaeans crossed the Aegean Sea, and after defeating Troy, the most prominent city in the northwestern coastal region of Asia Minor, in a war known as the "Trojan War", they established colonies, building new cities populated with people of their kind.

Having established themselves in this region which became known as "Aeolis", the enterprising Achaeans soon established commercial contacts with the Hittites who were the dominant power in Asia Minor. From Hittite records, we learn that they called the Achaeans "Ahhiyana". The Achaeans also invaded and established themselves in Cyprus, introducing the Greek Language, their pagan religion and the Greek way of life. They built new cities with "Enkomi" becoming the capital.

Yet, another country with which they traded and often raided was Egypt. From Egyptian hieroglyphic records, we learn that Egypt had been raided at least two times, specifically, in the times of Pharaoh Merneptah in 1228 B.C. and Rameses III in 1190 B.C. The Egyptians called the Achaeans "Aqaiwasha", and later "Danauna", which is the Egyptian spelling of "Danaoi", a name for the Achaeans often used by Homer.

Another major group that came and settled in Greece was the Ionians. Their place of origin is still not known for sure. They spoke the Ionic dialect of the Greek Language, and the areas they inhabited most, were the regions of Attica, Ebea and Argolis in the Peloponnese. Like the Achaeans, they too ventured to colonization. They captured most of the Cycladic Islands of the Aegean Sea and founded many cities in the central coastal region of western Asia Minor. Three large and prosperous cities were Magnesia, Priene and Miletus. The region they colonized became known as "Ionia", and to the Hittites and the other Middle Eastern peoples as "Javan" and its Greek settlers as "Javanis". In the Book of Genesis of the Old Testament Bible, Ionia is referred to as Javan. The Ionian colonization took place in the twelfth century B.C. Six hundred years later, the first Greek philosophical and scientific schools appeared in Ionia to later spread in Greece proper.

The third Greek group that came from Central Europe to inhabit Greece was the Dorians. They spoke the Greek Language, and to be more exact, the Doric Dialect. Just as Athens was the most representative city-state of the Ionian Greeks, so the Spartan was the most representative of the Dorians. Like the Achaeans and the Ionians, the Dorians after entrenching themselves in Peloponnesus, also ventured to colonization. With their ships, they conquered the Islands of Crete and Rhodes and later established colonies in the southwestern coastal region of Asia Minor where the city of Halicarnassus was the most prominent colony.

These were the three groups that, having migrated into Greece, made up the Greek people. Since each group spoke its own Greek dialect, and since these three groups after their settlement in Greece never united into one nation, but remained divided into city-states, the dialects continued to be used from the time of the invasion until the fourth century BC. During that century, however, the political supremacy of Athens and the greatness of its literature, written in the "Attic" dialect, caused the latter to become the "Koine" (Common) language of all the Greek city-states. Moreover, the conquests of Alexander the Great caused the Koine to become the "lingua franca", that is, the international language of the whole Near East, consisting of Asia Minor, Syria, Mesopotamia, Palestine, Egypt and of other countries that lay eastward. When in the first century BC the Romans conquered all these regions, they allowed the Koine to continue being the "international language".

The Greeks were also the first people in recorded history to use an alphabet consisting of both consonants and vowels. They borrowed the seventeen consonants of the Phoenician alphabet, considerably modified them, and added seven vowels, which they invented. The reason they added the seven vowels is because all prehellenic alphabets used no vowels. Thus the ancient Greeks were the first people to create a complete alphabet. In reality, the ancient Greeks had developed not one but six slightly different alphabets with each region using one. One of the six alphabets – the Chalcidic, was adopted by the Romans, becoming not only their own but of nearly all western peoples.

Along with their alphabet, the ancient Greeks also developed a grammar that eventually became the prototype and model for all three branches of the western languages, namely the Germanic, the Romance and the Slavic. Its main parts, known as adjective, pronoun, verb, adverb, preposition, conjunction, etc., will be found in the grammar of every western language.

In examining very, very briefly some of the parts of this first western grammar, we find that its nouns fall into three genders – masculine, feminine and neuter; there are two numbers – singular and plural; five cases – nominative, genitive, dative, accusative, and ablative. There are three voices for its verbs – active, middle and passive, four moods – indicative, subjunctive, optative, and imperative and seven tenses – present, imperfect, future, aorist, perfect, pluperfect and future perfect. Also, the Greek grammar has three articles – masculine, feminine, and neuter corresponding to the genders.

Finally, unlike the Latin Language which has only three participles, the ancient Greek has eleven.

It was such a varied grammar that in antiquity, in Byzantine times and in modern times it has enabled dozens of generations to fully, correctly, and precisely express their ideas in writing and through conversation, their ideas, their thoughts relative to every conceivable field.

Commenting on the above facts of the Greek Language and its excellent grammar, a contemporary linguist has remarked: "Greek is one of the most admirable instruments of communication ever devised, eminently fitted to serve as the tool both of the rigorous thinker and of the inspired poet. It is a marvelously supple and subtle language; such features as the possession of a definitive article and of numerous expressive particles, certain variations in the use of the participle, and the changes in shades of meaning attainable by shifts of word order enable it to express numerous delicate nuances with an exquisite flexibility."

Since the ancient Greeks laid the foundation of many literary, artistic, political and scientific fields that since ancient times guide the thinking and life of the western world, an astonishingly large number of Greek words will be found in every western language including the Latin which was preceded by the Greek by at least one thousand years. The borrowing was done in ancient times, in medieval times and in modern times, intensively since the Renaissance.

Our English Language has thousands of Greek words in its vocabulary. Some of these loan words have an exact transliteration such as "asthma", "paralysis", "synthesis", "analysis, "cosmos", "diagnosis", "idea", and countless more. Other loan words have had a slight change in their ultimas such as "geometry", "astronomy", "physics", "optics", "ethereal", "hexagon", "epilepsy", "arithmetic", "polyhedral", "galaxy", "chrysanthemum", "atomic theory", "atomic energy", "hydrostatics", "parallelogram", "pharmacy", and thousands of others. Finally, loan words from the Greek dictionary that have supplanted our English Language and which have been borrowed and compounded by eminent academics of every field since the Renaissance are such words as "oxygen", "hydrogen", "bibliophile", "psychology", "hematology", "telegraphy", "telephony", "geopolitics", "geodesy", "glossology", "ophidiophobia" (fear of snakes), "aechmophobia" (fear of sharply pointed objects), "heliology" (study of the sun), "potamology" (study of rivers), "limnology" (study of lakes), "spelaeology" (study of caves), "thermodynamics", "technocrat", "astronaut", "helicopter", "electron", "ballistics", "microscope", "cyclotron", and thousands of other such scientific and non-scientific words.

In his book entitled "Words", its author, Victor Stevenson, commented on the never-ending borrowing of words from the Greek dictionary to coin names of new theories, discoveries, inventions, and hypotheses wrote the following: "The debt owed to Greek by other European languages is greater than can ever be repaid. If the Hellenes could call in their verbal loans to the world, science and scholarship generally would be left almost speechless. The debt, however, goes far beyond the terminology of experts, for everyday conversation in a score of languages, and in as many professions from potter to psychiatrist, is alive with Greek words that have been so long assimilated that they are no longer thought of as Greek."

Like all other languages, Greek has also undergone an evolution. The ancient "Koine", spoken until the Fourth Century A.D., gave way to the "Modern". The Modern Greek has two versions – the "Katharevusa" (purist), whose words and grammar are classical and being such it was mostly used by academics and ecclesiastics, and the "Demotike" (language of the people), which is today's spoken language with a simplified grammar and syntax.

An element of the Greek Language that never changed is its alphabet in both upper and lower cases. Also, Modern Greek still uses 75% of the ancient Greek words.

The changes that have occurred since the introduction of written Greek more than three millennia ago are to be found in the meaning of the words and in phonology. For example, there are changes in the values of vowels and diphthongs and in accentuation. While the ancient accentuation contained elements of musical pitch that has changed into an accent of stress. Other significant changes occurred in the pronunciation of certain letters. The letter beta is no longer pronounced as "d" but as "theta". Also, the vowel "u" is no longer pronounced as the French "u" but as "e."

Today, fewer than 12 million people speak the Greek Language plus half-a-million Greeks who live in Cyprus. This is a significant reduction from ancient and Byzantine times when Greek was spoken by far more millions of people. Yet, this oldest and first language of the western world, still serves as an inexhaustible well-spring for the coining of new worlds to be applied to new inventions and ideas.

2
THE MINOAN AGE
Greece's and Europe's First Civilization

South of mainland Greece, and at the edge of the Aegean Sea, is Greece's largest island - the Island of Crete. Crete is a green island. It has many beautiful valleys and some of the highest mountains in Greece. The valleys are full of farms, orchards and fruit trees. There is little wonder why this island, from very ancient times, not only had a very large population, also developed a well-organized state with a wonderful civilization.

Archaeologists found that this island had been inhabited since the year 7,000 B.C. In the ruins, were found jars, pitchers, plates and other household items made of clay and beautifully decorated. The people raised their food by farming the rich soil and from hunting and fishing. They lived as did many others in places around the Mediterranean Sea and did not speak Greek.

By the year 1900 B.C., newcomers had settled in Crete and built new villages. Eventually these villages united under three kings whose palaces were in Knossos, Phaistos and Zacro, and many years later, the King of Knossos became the sole king of all the people who lived in Crete. With the passing of the centuries, the royal palace kept growing bigger and bigger as succeeding kings kept adding new, large rooms. This huge palace, although it was first built almost 4,000 years ago, in many aspects, was "modern".

What is really interesting about this huge building is that it had running water in its bathrooms and in other of its many rooms. At this time, no other building in the world had running water. Not even the palaces of Babylon or Egypt could make this claim.

A big pipeline brought continuously running water from nearby springs. Once in the palace, the big pipeline divided itself to as many smaller pipelines as there were bathrooms so that running water would be available all the time, whether day or night. Likewise, dirty bath and toilet refuse emptied into another pipeline, carried to another main pipeline, which in turn emptied into a nearby river. The builders of this palace were ahead of all others of that time. Running water was also visible in the garden of this palace. One could see a beautiful fountain sending its water high, just as fountains in parks are doing today. No other palace garden had such a fountain at that time.

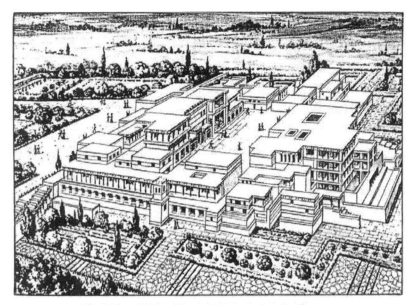

The Palace of King Minos at Knossos. Restoration.

All the rooms of the palace were brightly painted red, yellow, orange or blue colors. There were also large paintings on the walls showing beautiful flowers, birds and animals, hunting scenes, views showing everyday life, bull fighting and scenes showing towns of other countries.

The very large throne room of the palace had brightly decorated walls. The throne of the king was made of alabaster, which is stone that in appearance is similar to marble. To the right and left of the throne, were the benches on which high officials sat.

In the very large yard of the palace, the people would gather to watch wrestling matches and other games. A highlight must have been the bullfights, similar to the ones held today in Spain, Mexico, and other Latin American countries.

In 1900 through 1902, the English Archaeologist, Sir Arthur Evans, dug in the town of Knossos and found the palace buried in the earth and mostly in ruins. With the help of an English Architect, Theodore Fyfe, he was able to restore a good part of it. If one were to visit it today, one could get a good idea of how it looked at that time.

Looking at the paintings that are on the walls of the palace, we see that the ladies and the girls wore very beautiful dresses. They were ankle length and very colorful. What is interesting is that in no other country or part of the world did women dress like the women of Crete. They also wore beautiful golden earrings, necklaces and bracelets. Some of their jewelry was shaped in the form of leaves, insects or flowers.

When Sir Arthur Evans discovered the huge palace, he noticed that it had well over a hundred rooms. This did not count the many storage rooms where oil, wine, olives, cereals, and all sorts of foodstuffs were stored, in what seem to be the largest jars ever made.

Why so many rooms? The answer is that, besides the king and his family who lived in the palace, hundreds of other people also lived there. Some were his advisors and their families, the many servants, cooks and bakers, the secretaries and other professionals, teachers and the king's guards. With all these people living under the same roof, the palace resembled a town in itself.

The Minoans also left clay tablets with their writings on them. But their writing did not use the letters of the Greek alphabet. Instead they used signs, 135 in all. Each sign stood for a word and phrase, the shape of an animal, or plant, or some kind of object, or of parts of the human body. But what all these mean, we do not as yet know. They also left us the two other kinds of writing known as "Linear A" and "Linear B". They are called so because, in both the signs, there appear different combinations of thin rods. Thanks to two Englishmen (Ventris and Chadwick), who were able to unlock the meaning of Linear B, today we can read the writing of those tablets written in these letters. Tablets written in Linear A letters are still not readable.

The Minoans were also famous for being seafaring people. With their hundreds of sleek, fast and sturdy merchant ships, they traveled to every part of the Mediterranean Sea. Fierce tempests did not scare them. They were daring, strong and were very skilled in handling their ships in any kind of weather. They visited many ports and carried and sold the products of their island-nation: such as all kinds of pots to Cyprus, pots, oil and fabrics to Phoenicia, oil and wine to Egypt and fabrics and pots to Italy and Sicily. From the ports of these countries, they would buy copper from Cyprus, cereals and ivory from Egypt, marble from Northern Greece, and tin and other metals from Spain.

Such were the Minoans, the first Greeks to develop a truly great culture. As we have seen: They were very business-minded. They were very good builders of buildings and shops and had very good engineering skills. They were very industrious and progressive. They were very artistic. They loved music, dancing and the sports. And in their culture, in their society, women were equal to men. In fact, they were the first people on earth where women had equality with men.

About fifty miles north of Crete is the Island of Thera, also known as Santorini. Many rich Minoans had beautiful villas on this island and vacationed there with their families. In some of their villas, archaeologists have found some very beautiful paintings on the walls.

This island also had a very big volcano, a volcano that during the 14th century B.C. erupted so violently that it caused three-fourths of the mountain to go up in the air, while the lower part of it sank partly into the sea. Volcanologists who know much about volcanoes and earthquakes tell us that the eruption of this volcano was the greatest in man's history. It was heard throughout Europe, North Africa and the Middle East. Moreover, the sky was filled with so much smoke that the sun could not be seen for days. This eruption also destroyed nearly all the cities and towns of Crete. The beautiful palace that for whole centuries stood at Knossos was now in ruins. Many people left Crete for good and went to settle in Greece, North Africa and the Middle East.

This is how the Minoan Age came to an end, and, although afterwards, people continued to live in Crete, the homes and palaces they rebuilt were not like those of the past. Even their trading business and their ships were now a fraction of what past Minoan generations had.

The Acropolis of Mycenae. Restoration.

3

THE MYCENAEAN CIVILIZATION AND GREEK COLONIZATION

When by the fourteenth century B.C. the Minoan civilization, which, for almost six centuries had flourished in Crete, was destroyed as a result of a volcanic eruption on the nearby Island of Thera (now called Santorini), a new civilization was now flourishing on mainland Greece. Historians call it "Mycenaean", a name derived from its most powerful representative kingdom-Mycenae located in northeastern Peloponessus. Other centers of this civilization were Tiryns, Pylos, Argos, Thebes, Arni (now called Glas,) Eleusis, and Athens.

The Mycenaean civilization began in 1580 B.C. and ended in 1100 B.C. The people who developed this civilization were newcomers, and are known in history as "Achaeans". They came from northern Europe, and, when Homer referred to them in his poems - the Iliad and the Odyssey, he called them the "Fair Achaeans", apparently alluding to their very light skin and blonde or reddish hair.

When the Achaeans came to Greece, they slowly absorbed the natives who lived in the regions in which they settled. Soon they also came in contact with the Minoans who lived in Crete, from whom they learned the art of metalworking and other arts and skills.

A most obvious characteristic of all Mycenaean cities is the high protective walls that surrounded them. They were very thick, and, therefore, very difficult for attackers to pierce by battering them, and very high, thus making their scaling difficult. Another characteristic of these walls was the large and very heavy stones of which the city walls were made. They seemed to have been placed by "superhumans". Eventually, a legend was created that Cyclops had brought them to the site to build the walls, hence, their term "Cyclopean".

Mycenaean cities were usually built on high hills. This made them easier to defend. On the highest plane within the city, was the king's palace, which unlike the Minoan palaces which had three and even four floors, the Mycenaean had only two. Around the palace, whose interior walls were profusely painted with colored murals depicting mostly martial and hunting scenes, were the mansions of the king's relatives, of the wealthy, and of other prominent citizens. Farther away, were the cubical homes of the common people whose vocations were farming, fishing, hunting, metalworking, chariot making, shepherding, and etc.

The Achaeans were excellent artisans. They made beautiful pottery, on which they painted exquisit plant and animal life, magnificent artifacts made of rock crystal, precious stones and ivory as well as exquisite jewelry. Their metalworkers made beautiful drinking cups and other household utensils using precious metals whose exterior surface would often show in relief, hunting scenes, plants and even battle scenes. They had also mastered the technique of adding entaglios of gold or silver on iron, or copper knives, swords or armor.

Royal tombs were very large, round and topped by a dome. They had long entrances, and, when one entered into their spacious round and domed interior, one could not help but admire the technique of placing the stones of the dome in such a concentric way, so as to end in a round capstone.

In such tombs, the body of the king lay at the center, usually dressed in his military armor, while his face was covered with a golden mask. Around the body of the king and the queen, they would place all those objects that were most dear to them while they were living. We are very fortunate that they adhered to such a custom since so much royal jewelry, such as diadems, rings, seals, necklaces and panoply, survived. By being sealed inside the tombs, they did not disappear, as did the artifacts, which remained in the palaces, which were destroyed either by war, earthquake, or other catastrophic disaster.

The Achaeans did not limit themselves to farming and hunting. Since the fifteenth century, they took to the sea conquering Knossus in 1400 B.C., the islands of Rhodes, Kos, Cyprus and many regions in the coastal areas of Asia Minor (Turkey). In all these cities and regions, they founded trading posts, thus, carrying on a thriving trade.

From Hittite and Egyptian written records, we learn that the above Middle Eastern people held the Achaeans in high esteem. They spoke highly of them and were impressed by their power and entrepreneurial drive.

Mycenaean kings did not rule with absolutism. They had advisory committees, consisting of the most knowledgeable and wise men of their kingdom with whom they consulted and decided many matters of state. Often the king would assemble the people to announce important decisions relating to the state.

Mycenaeans used "Linear B" writing. Although Linear B writing has been deciphered, we did not learn much from the surviving tablets that were found. But, we need not worry, Homer – antiquity's greatest poet, who, in his two monumental poems – the Iliad and the Odyssey, describing Mycenaean characters, sheds ample light concerning their religion, their morals, social structure, daily life, and almost every aspect of their civilization. Moreover, when Heinrich Schleiman, the German archaeologist, conducted excavations in Troy and Mycenae in the 1870's, he brought to light, especially from the royal tombs, so many artifacts, that, putting together all these data, we have been able to reconstruct very accurately this great era of Greece's history.

Greek Colonization

Following the decline of the Mycenanean Age, and, to be more specific, between the Eighth and Sixth centuries B.C. the Greeks engaged in a vigorous colonization that took many of them to far away Mediterranean shores. Main causes of this expansionist movement were the tyrannical rule of some nobles and the proliferation of Greek population, to which the mountainous country could not provide enough food.

Owing to their traditional daring, adventurous and hard driving spirit, the Greek immigrants were able to reach and firmly plant colonies on the shores of Asia Minor and the shores around the Black Sea in the East, on the shores of North Africa, as well as on the shores of the Italian Peninsula, Sicily, Corsica, France, and Spain in the west.

Wherever the Greek colonists settled, they retained their religion, their customs, their language, and the civic structure of the mother-city. Even fire from the mother city's public hearth was brought to the colony to light the hearth of the latter. Thus, every Greek colony was like a part of Greece that had been planted in the host country. Filial ties existed between the colony and the mother-city, although the colonies always enjoyed economic and political independence.

The beneficial results of colonization were many. Greece was relieved of its overpopulation, food and useful raw material kept coming from the colonies to Greece, while oil, wine and manufactured products produced in the mother-cities were now exported in large quantities to the colonies for sale to the colonists and to the natives of the host countries. As a result, Greek merchant

The beautiful Temple of Neptune in the Greek Colony of Poseidonia, Italy.

ships dominated the Mediterranean and Greek coinage the Mediterranean markets.

Of the many dozens of Greek colonies that were founded at that time, most of them are still inhabited cities while the colony of Marseilles is presently France's second largest city, Monaco a small independent country, Naples, Italy's third largest city, and Palermo Sicily's largest city.

Of no less significance was the beneficial impact which the Greek colonies effected on the native peoples in whose lands the Greek colonists established themselves.

As the culture of the colonists was superior to that of the natives in every aspect, the latter tried to adopt those cultural aspects of the colonists. Thus, the Greek way of life, Greek technology, Greek farming and many other aspects, eventually became those of the natives.

To cite an example of the Greek colonists' impact on the people of the host lands, that of the Greek colony of Massalia (Marseilles) is interesting as well as typically representative. The colony's founding on the Mediterranean coast of France became a significant milestone in the history of the natives of that region – the Gauls. For, it was the Greek colonists who introduced the vine and the olive to the region thus laying the foundation of an agricultural industry that in the future would have far-reaching results.

The following excerpt from the writings of the Roman historian, Junianus Justinus, best summarizes the impact of the Greek colonies in France. "From the Greeks, the Gauls learned a more civilized way of life and abandoned their barbarous ways. They set to tilling their fields and walling their towns. They even got used to living by law rather than force of arms, to cultivating the vine and the olive. Their progress in manners and wealth was so brilliant that it seemed as though Gaul (France) had become part of Greece, rather than that Greece had colonized Gaul."

**Greece and Greek Colonies in
Illiria and Africa**

Greek Colonies around the Black Sea, Asia Minor, Cyprus and Egypt

**Greek Colonies in
Spain, France, and Corcica**

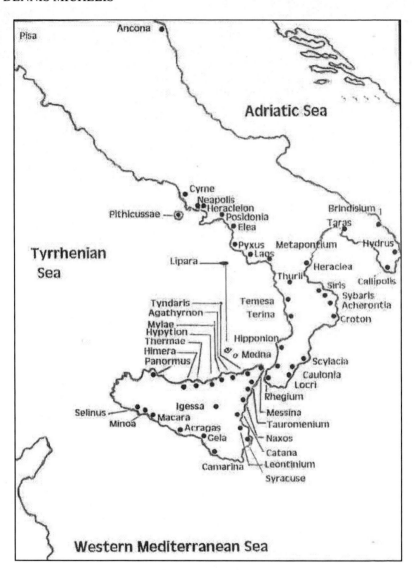

**Greek Colonies in
Italy and Sicily**

4
HOMER AND OTHER POETS

During the past 2,500 years, many famous poets were born in different countries. Ancient Israel, for example, had its King David, Rome had its Virgil and Horace, Italy had its Dante, England its Tennyson and Milton, Germany its Goethe and Schiller, America its Longfellow, and Greece its Homer, who lived twenty-eight centuries ago.

Unfortunately, we know nothing about Homer's parents and nothing certain about his birthplace. According to an ancient Greek saying, "Seven cities claimed to be his birth place - Smyrna, Chios, Colophon, Salamis, Rhodes, Argos, and Athens." Today, many experts believe that his most likely birthplace was the Greek Island of Chios. They base their claim on the fact that, for many centuries after the death of Homer, there was a school in Chios that was called "Homeridae". The Homeridae, for generations, taught poets the poems of Homer and how to sing them when they toured the various cities and towns.

By the sixth century BC, Homer's poems were introduced as regular lessons in the schools of Athens, and this move was soon imitated by the other cities of Greece. At the same time, the organizers of the great Festival of "Panathenaea", that was held in Athens every four years in honor of the goddess Athena, also introduced the recitation of Homer's poems by selected bards (poets) at the Festival.

What great poems did Homer write? He wrote two very lengthy poems - the Iliad and the Odyssey. The stories they tell and the characters they portray are so vivid and captivating that the reader becomes fascinated. But first, let us see the reason Homer wrote them.

During the eleventh century BC, the Trojan Prince, Paris, son of Priam, King of Troy, which was a small kingdom in the northwestern shores of Asia Minor (Turkey), went to Sparta. Sparta was a small kingdom on the southern mainland of Greece. He went to visit King Menelaus and his beautiful Queen Helen. One evening, Paris abducted Queen Helen and sailed off to Troy.

When King Menelaus learned that his wife had been taken away, he became so angry that he summoned the other Greek kings for the purpose of making war against Troy. They decided to capture Troy, destroy it and bring Helen back to Sparta.

After besieging the walled city for ten years, the Greeks entered the city, set fire to the houses, and finding Helen, brought her back to Sparta. This story inspired Homer to write the first of his two poems, the "Iliad". This very lengthy poem, consisting of 15,693 lines, does not relate how Paris took away Helen and caused the small Kingdoms of Greece to unite and make war against Troy. We learn all these facts from other sources. Homer tells us in his Iliad only of what happened in the last year, the tenth year of the war.

He relates, for example, how the Greeks tried repeatedly to climb the high walls of Troy and failed; how the Trojans would come out during the night and set fire to the Greek camp; how the leaders of the Greeks and Trojans held duels against each other; and, how often the Greeks quarreled among themselves. He relates all these events in such a way that, when we read them, we get the impression that these events took place not just on the tenth year of the war but throughout the ten years of the war.

Another feature that stands out in Homer's Iliad is the life-like way by which the master poet portrays his characters. For example, Agamemnon, the brother-in-law of Menelaus, is portrayed as arrogant, self-centered, yet majestic; Achilles as quick-tempered and honor-obsessed, savage in anger but, at heart, courageous and compassionate; King Nestor of Pylos as prudent, subtle but often long-winded; Odysseus conciliatory, self-controlled, resourceful; Ajax bold, magnanimous; and Diomedes as dashing and debonair.

The Trojans are also portrayed with different temperaments. Thus, Hector, King Priam's son and Paris' brother, is portrayed as valiant and affectionate; King Priam as grief-stricken but undefeated; Hecuba, wife of King Priam, always in affliction; and Andromache, wife of Hector, as a noble wife. In fact, the final parting between Hector and his wife, (Hector held a duel with Achilles and is killed by the latter), is one of the most moving scenes ever composed.

Besides the above main characters, Homer has included in the Iliad hundreds of others, both Greek and Trojan for whom the resourceful poet reserves a different temperament. This is why Homer's poems are so appealing to readers of any age and century. They are realistic, exciting, gripping, full of all kinds of human emotions that range from violence, anger or frustration all the way to peace of the mind and of the heart.

Homer's second great poem is the Odyssey. The Odyssey is a sequel to the Iliad, with Odysseus, also known as Ulysses, as the main character.

The perilous adventures of Odysseus, after the fall of Troy, are related in the 12,100 lines of this exciting poem. For ten consecutive years, Odysseus, together with his companions, survives against all odds presented to him by an angry sea and semi-barbarous people, to return to his country. But instead of returning to his home island in a few days like all the other Greek chiefs and warriors after the fall of Troy, he is delayed for ten years.

Why did such an ill fate befall Odysseus? Why did he suffer so much? According to Homer, his chief enemy was Poseidon (Neptune), the god of the sea. He was also the god who favored the Trojans above any other people. When he saw that Odysseus' trick, to have the Greeks build a huge wooden horse in whose belly a handful of Greek soldiers would be hidden so that when the Trojans would take the horse into their city as a trophy, the Greek soldiers would come out from the horse to open the city gates for the Greek Army to enter in and thus conquer Troy, Poseidon decided to punish Odysseus. During Odysseus' return, Poseidon caused fierce tempests and winds to blow his ships away from Greece so that Odysseus and his companions would find themselves in North Africa, Gibraltar, Corsica, Italy, Sicily and other faraway places.

For ten consecutive years, Odysseus kept wandering throughout the Mediterranean Sea, with his ships being tossed by fierce waves blown by winds in different directions. Wherever he and his companions landed, they would meet hostile and barbarous people, like the Cicones not far from Troy; the lotus-eaters of Tunisia; the giant one-eyed Cyclops in Sicily; the Laestrygones in Southern Corsica, who killed all his companions except those of his own ship; the enchantress Circe in Italy, who kept them hostage for a year and turned his companions to animals and then back to people; and, escaping the man-eating Sirenes. While escaping the monsters, Scylla and Charybdis in the Straits between Italy and Sicily, blown by fierce winds all the way to Giraltar and then on his return toward the Island of Malta, he lost his ship in a fierce tempest. Alone, he swam to a beach of the island where he met Calypso the queen. She offered him hospitality for seven years, and wanted him to stay there for the remainder of his life.

Odysseus, however, still longed to return to Ithaca, his home island, his Kingdom and his family. He built a raft and sailed off toward Greece. When he was nearing the Greek Island of Coercyra, a fierce tempest broke his raft and Odysseus barely managed to swim ashore.

The next day, Princess Nausica met Odysseus on the beach and took him to the palace. King Alcinous provided a ship for Odysseus thereby facilitating his return to Ithaca. After a day's journey, and ten years since he had left Troy, Odysseus at last was back on his home island.

While still on the shore, the goddess Athena, who all throughout his adventures had protected Odysseus, appeared to him and told him that many suitors of his wife Penelope had been lodging at the palace until she decided to marry one of them. But Penelope would not. Athena also warned him that, if he went to the palace as king, the suitors would definitely kill him. In order to protect him, she disguised him as a beggar. As he entered his palace, he was recognized only by his old dog and his nurse, Eurycleia, by a scar on his leg as she was washing his feet. The only one to whom Odysseus revealed himself was to his son, Telemachus, now twenty years old.

The next morning Penelope told Telemachus to announce that the suitor that would string Odysseus' mighty bow and shoot an arrow through the hand-holes of a row of axe-heads would marry her. Many suitors tried but failed. When Odysseus took the bow, he succeeded without difficulty. Instantly, he threw off his disguise, and with Telemachus and other servants, who now recognized their master, slaughtered the suitors. It was a blood bath. Penelope recognized Odysseus, and thus, after twenty years, husband and wife were reunited to live happily ever after.

This very, very briefly is the story of the Odyssey, a story that, besides its characters, tells us so much about many lands, their people, their customs, their daily vocations, about life on the sea, about the plants and animals in the different lands Odysseus visited, and the distances and the time required to sail from one place to another.

Today, by simulating his travels, it has been found that data is very accurate, as they navigated by the stars, including the many other interesting facts. Like the Iliad, the Odyssey, too, is most fascinating reading and considered classic.

What is Homer emphasizing in this great poem? He primarily emphasizes three basic ideals. First, the love of country, as Odysseus, despite ten years of wandering, a wandering very often visited by fierce tempests, was never intimidated. His burning desire to return to his homeland enabled him to overcome any cruel adversity. Second, the love of wife and family, as Odysseus was thoroughly devoted to his wife whom he loved with all his heart. His marriage to Penelope was the only one he would know throughout his life. Third, love of his people, as Odysseus loved his fellow-countrymen. He was always a fair and just ruler to them, and in return, they all loved him and were loyal to him.

From ancient times to this day, Homer's poems are of the most widely read in the world. There is not a schoolboy or college student in the world that has not heard of Homer and his two wonderful poems. In the second century BC, Aristarchus put the poems in their final order, and translations soon began to appear in Latin and other ancient languages.

During the past eighteen centuries, Homer's poems - the "Iliad" and the "Odyssey" have had the highest number of translations in nearly all the languages of the world coming second only to the Bible. This evidences their perennial and universal acceptance as World masterpieces.

Philosophers, like Plato and Aristotle, praised Homer. In fact, Plato called him "The educator of Hellas (Greece), guide for one's entire life and as the most poetic of poets and first of playwrights."

Homer inspired the ancient Greek playwrights to use his characters in their plays as he equally did so in the Roman ones. In fact, the poet Virgil modeled half his "Aeneid" on the Iliad. On the other hand, the famous Roman poet, Horace, also praised Homer's skill in narrative, plot construction and characterization beyond all other epic poets.

The great Fathers of the Church had great admiration for Homer. Achilles, Odysseus, Nausica and other characters were used as examples of virtue for Christian youth. St. Basil wrote: "All Homer's poetry is an encomium of virtue, and all that he wrote, save what is accessory, bears to this end." Other Church Fathers saw the voyage of Odysseus as a symbol of the Christian's journey through life; the Sirens, the powers of evil to which he is exposed; his ship, the church and its mast, the Cross.

Writers of the Renaissance and later eras owe much to Homer. In fact, at the beginning of the nineteenth century when there was a rise of romantic Hellenism in Europe and America, many lyric poets and novelists derived inspiration and material from the Homeric poems. Alfred Tennyson and James Joyce have written very important works on the theme of Odysseus. Nikos Kazantzakis has written a long sequel to the Odyssey in 33,333 lines. Finally, others that drew inspiration from the characters of Homer are William Shakespeare, Racine, Calderon, Dryden, Vico, Goethe, Pascoli, Giraudoux and a host of other writers.

A chain of epic, lyrist, elegist, iambic and dithyrambic poets followed Homer. We will very briefly review the most important.

Hesiod, whose highly prized poems, "The Theogony", and "Works and Days", for the most part, survived and furnish us much information about the origin of the Olympian gods and goddesses and about pastoral life in early Greece.

The Rhodian, Pisander, wrote a very long poem entitled "Heracleia". The poem earned him the honorific, "Rhodian Homer". Antimachus, who hailed from the city of Colophon, Asia Minor, was another notable epic poet. He wrote the "Thebais" - a long poem relating early legends about the royal house of Thebes, Greece.

Famous early elegists were Tyrtaeus, Memnermus and Callinus. But Theognis of Megara, Greece, surpassed all three. He also penned some very pithy maxims of practical philosophy, called in Greek, "Gnomae", and in Latin "Sententiae". Consider the following example:

> *"Fairest is righteousness, and best is health,*
> *And sweetest is to win the heart's desire."*

Alcaeus and Sappho, both from the Greek Island of Lesbos, were composers of the finest erotic poetry that has ever been composed. Sappho's love poems earned her admiration, not only by her contemporaries, but also by those who read her poems today. The highest commendation she has earned was that if Homer was "The Poet", she was "The Poetess" and "The Tenth Muse".

Stesichorus hailed from the Greek colony of Himera in southern Italy and wrote poetry to be sung by choruses. He is also the composer of a long poem, "The Sack of Ilion" (Troy). A great number of his poems deal with heroes of ancient Greek legends who lived in humble pastoral places.

Ibycus, a native of the ancient Greek colony of Rhegion, Italy, also composed poems to be sung by boys' choruses. His poems earned him much praise. Many of them have survived. Stasinius, a native of Cyprus, also wrote a very long poem entitled "Cyprian Epics".

Finally, the most famous lyrist (lyrical poet) was Pindar. He showed his genius at the age of twenty-four when a prince from Pharsalus asked him to write a poem. His masterful poem made him famous overnight, as, from now on, he became the frequent guest of kings and nobles. His poems filled seventeen books of which only four have survived.

His prolific poetic output is also diversified as it includes poems, hymns, dance songs, laudatory songs, dirges, poems sung by young girls, and "Epinikia" (songs of winners in Olympic and other such Pan-Hellenic games).

Homer

5
ORIGINATORS OF
THE OLYMPIC GAMES

Every four years, thousands of young athletes from nearly every nation of the world go to the countries that have offered to host the Winter and Summer Olympic Games.

An impressive ceremony is held on opening day. There is a parade of all the athletes in a large stadium to be followed by the lighting of a huge flame from a small torch that has been brought to the stadium by many athletes, passing the flame to one another, all the way from Olympia, Greece.

In the Winter Olympics that last for two weeks, the competition consists of skiing, ice-skating, ice hockey and other winter sports. The Summer Olympics last for two weeks, with games consisting of running, wrestling, swimming, and other such sports. They close with the Marathon Race which is twenty-seven miles long.

When and where did all this wonderful and great spectacle start?

It started in Greece, and, to be more exact, at Olympia. Olympia is located near the northwestern region of Peloponessus. In a valley surrounded by gently sloping hills covered with olive and pine trees, a valley mantled with daisies and sacred to the god Zeus (Jupiter), the first Olympic Games were held. It was also decided that the games would be held every four years with athletes from every Greek city.

For 1,370 years, the Olympics were held every four years. The last ones were held in 394 AD., in which year they were abolished by the Byzantine Emperor Theodosius.

Beautiful temples had been built in Olympia. The most impressive was the one dedicated to the chief gods, Zeus and the goddess Hera. A huge statue of Zeus, made by Phidias, was inside the temple. Like the statue of Athena, in the Parthenon of the Acropolis in Athens, which had ivory and gold, Zeus's statue also had ivory and gold. The statue was so awesome that it soon became known as one of the Seven Wonders of the World.

Another beautiful building in Olympia was the gymnasium where the athletes exercised before competing in the stadium. The stadium was very large and accommodated about 45,000 people who came here from all over Greece to watch the games. The stadium was not man-made, but rather a natural one consisting of two long and straight gently sloping sides with a curved one at one end. The games held in this stadium were foot racing, leaping, discus and javelin throwing.

There was a palaestra, that is, a large building divided into parlors, where wrestlers and boxers competed. There was also a large Hippodrome for four-horse chariot and horse racing.

The winners received no gold medals at that time. Instead, winners received an olive wreath that was placed on their heads by the members of the Olympic Committee. Sometimes, even kings were among the contestants. The first one was King Phillip of Macedonia; another was the Roman Emperor, Nero. When a winning athlete returned to his hometown, the leaders of the town tore down part of the city's wall so that the athlete could enter. The symbolism meant that when a city had such a strong man, it needed no walls.

After 394 AD., the year when the games were abolished, for 1,502 years there were no Olympic Games. Then, in 1896, they began again. The place where they were held, for the first time again, was Athens, Greece. Athens undertook to rebuild its ancient stadium in marble. The stadium seated 65,000 people. The man who had the idea to revive the Olympic Games was Pierre de Coubertin, a French Baron. He wrote to all the committees of sport to start the games once more pointing out the educational value of the sport if practiced in accordance with the ancient Greek ideals.

6
THE PERSIAN WARS

In the history of the World, the fifth century B.C. is known as the "Golden Age of Greece". Why? Because during this century Greece achieved intellectual, scientific, and artistic miracles seldom performed by other nations in history. By achieving these, she laid the foundation of nearly all aspects of our Western Civilization.

And yet, the first two decades of the fifth century BC were not as pleasant for that country as the latter decades. Why? Because during those decades a mighty empire from the Middle East tried to conquer Greece.

The mighty empire was Persia, which during the reigns of two of its kings - Cyrus and Darius, had taken over the countries that lay from the Persian Gulf extending to Asia Minor, and, in the continent of Africa, Egypt and Libya. Not satisfied with all their "grabs", Persia wanted more. In fact, the lands she wanted now to conquer were in Europe. But Greece stood in the way. It was an obstacle, an obstacle that had to be overcome.

The course of war between the two countries was the following. Long before the Persians had conquered Asia Minor, many Greek people had left Greece and had moved to Asia Minor seeking a better life. They lived in many cities, which, in fact, they had founded. But when the Persians conquered Asia Minor, the Greeks did not want to live under the new conquerors. They wanted to be free just as they had been. So, with the help of the two cities of Greece, namely, Athens and Eretria, they revolted. In fact, they marched against the City of Sardis - seat of the Persian administrator, and burned it.

When King Darius was informed of the city's ill fate, he decided to punish not only the Greek cities that had revolted, but also Athens and Eretria in Greece, those who had helped them. In 492 B.C., he sent a large army under General Mardonius into Northern Greece. At the same time, a large fleet followed the army by the sea. When the fleet reached the peninsula of Athos, a fierce storm sank most of the ships. Embarrassed and ashamed, Mardonius and his army went back to Persia.

King Darius was now furious. He was adamant in his desire to punish Athens and Eretria. So, in 490 B.C., he sent a new army transported on six hundred ships that sailed to Eretria. After destroying the city, the fleet took the army to the Plain of Marathon, a coastal plain some twenty-six miles northeast of Athens. Here, eleven thousand Athenian Soldiers waited to fight fifty thousand Persian Soldiers.

Miltiadis, the Athenian general, stationed his men not far from the beach where the Persians had landed. When the battle began, the Athenians slowly surrounded the Persians, and, after a fierce battle, the Athenians won. In the end, six thousand Persians lay dead against only one hundred and ninety-two Athenians. Moreover, the Athenians had also captured six

Persian warships. In panic, the Persians rushed to their ships in order to escape being captured, and   had their ships take them to the coast of Phaleron that was near Athens. Their objective was to destroy Athens. When they arrived at Phaleron, the Athenian Army was awaiting them. Afraid of another defeat, the Persians sailed back to their country.

More furious then ever, King Darius was determined to try again, but his death prevented him from doing this. His son, however, Xerxes, who now became king, vowed to definitely punish the Athenians. In 480 B.C., with an army of half a million, the Persians marched into northern Greece, while his fleet, consisting of one thousand and two hundred ships, followed by sea. Never before had such a great army and powerful fleet been ordered to move against a small country.

In the face of such a great danger, the leaders of the various small states of Greece, without "losing their cool", met together to see how they could stop such a formidable foe. Their decision was simple. Leonidas, the King of Sparta, with three hundred soldiers, was assigned to guard the very narrow pass at Thermopylae, through which the Persian Army was to pass. Themistocles, the admiral of Athens, would then align his fleet in the Straits of Salamis, a narrow strait between the coast of Attica and the coast of the Island of Salamis.

When the Persian army, numbering at half a million, approached the narrow pass of Thermopylae, it was forced to stop. King Xerxes then sent a soldier to tell King Leonidas to hand over their weapons. Proudly, King Leonidas answered, "Come and get them". In other words, you will have to fight in order to get them. Feeling insulted, Xerxes ordered his men to attack. But no Persian soldier was able to pass. Xerxes kept ordering more and more attacks, but all of them failed with thousands of Persian dead and lying on the ground.

Then, unfortunately, something happened that turned the tide in favor of the Persians. A shepherd by the name of Efialtes showed the Persian King a path from the other side of the mountain that led behind the line of the Spartans. The Persians followed the path, and, in no time, they had surrounded the Spartans. Seeing that death was very near, the three hundred Spartans fought to the last man. And, by putting up such a gallant fight to the end, they showed how much they loved freedom and their country. When the Persian Wars ended, Simonides, a famous poet, composed the following epigram to be engraved on their mass grave:

"Tell the Lacedaimonians, O, passer by,
that here, obedient to their words, we lie."

From Thermopylae, the Persian Army marched to Athens only to find an empty city. They set fire to the homes and destroyed the temples that were on the citadel of the Acropolis.

When the Persian Fleet arrived near Athens, the Persian admiral, having been informed that the Athenian Fleet had lined up in the Straits of Salamis to do battle, proceeded toward the straits. Knowing that his ships outnumbered the Greek Fleet by four to one, he was confident that victory would be his.

Minutes before the two fleets clashed, one of the Greek commanders shouted, "Sons of Greece, rise up and free your fatherland! Free the women and children, the seats of your ancestral gods, the graves of your forefathers! Nothing less is at stake in this battle!"

Then, when the Persian admiral ordered his ships to attack, Themistocles, the Greek admiral, by maneuvering skillfully, rather ingeniously managed to surround most of the Persian warships with the result being that he sent the Persian ships to the bottom of the straits. For the mighty Persian Fleet, it was a humiliating disaster. For the small Athenian Fleet, it was a series of events of eternal glory. More importantly, that stunning naval victory won on September 11, 480 B.C, saved Greece. The Persians were now stranded in a hostile, enemy land. Xerxes, in shame and boiling with anger, ordered most of his army to return to Persia.

Persian presence on Greek soil had by no means ended yet, for Xerxes had left a force of three hundred thousand in Thessaly - a region in central mainland Greece with orders to do battle against Greeks in the spring of 479 B.C. The battle was fought at Plataea, and there, a Greek Army of seventy thousand was able to completely rout the enemy, thus administering yet another humiliating defeat to the Persian Army. Those of the Persians who survived the battle returned to Persia in shame.

Such were the two first decades of the fifth century B.C. The ancient Greeks never saw so great a threat to their freedom and their country as when mighty Persia set out to punish and conquer them. Yet, even in the face of s o great a danger, when the greatest and mightiest nation on earth was marching against them, the Greeks did not lose heart. Trusting in their intellect and planning to determine the best possible way to defend their small country, and trusting in their strength to fight as never before, they performed a miracle. They made themselves one of the greatest legends of human history.

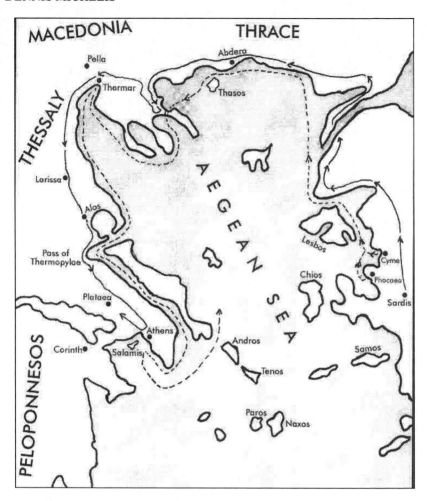

THE CAMPAIGN OF XERXES AGAINTS GREECE
→ March of the Persian Army
‐ ‐ ► Route of the Persian Fleet

7
THE ROAD TO DEMOCRACY

During the millennia that preceded the birth of Christ and for centuries, thereafter, the nations of the world were ruled by absolute monarchs. Whether they were kings or emperors, their decrees and their orders were the law of the land. No subject had the right to object, criticize, or disobey the monarch's order. If any of them did, punishment would soon follow.

Early Greece's cultures showed the same pattern. During the Minoan and Mycenaean Ages, the kings of the small Greek states had absolute power over their subjects. Until the sixth century B.C., the Athenian city-state had the same type of government.

But, in the Athenian city-state, such authoritarian leadership was not to last forever. A new form of government would originate in this tiny country; a government that in the future would become the most common in nearly all the industrially and technologically advanced nations. This novel, this original form of government was "Democracy", (Rule by people).

Initially, democracy did not appear as we know it today. In its place of origin, Athens, it appeared germinally in the sixth century B.C. and reached its full development in the fifth century B.C.

The sixth century B.C. was not an auspicious time for the people of Athens. The land owning and powerful hereditary aristocracy held nearly all the governmental departments. Legislative and judicial bodies were in the hands of elite citizens. The commoners and the poor had no representation. Moreover, during this difficult time most small farmers lacked capital. They would borrow money from the rich by mortgaging their lands. As in most cases they were unable to redeem their loans and their farms would be confiscated by the rich. And so, the large estates of the wealthy kept growing while the small farmers kept losing their land.

The situation of the free laborers was worse. Unable to meet the needs of their families with their limited earning, they borrowed from the wealthy at high interest, pledging themselves as repayment. Since most of them were unable to redeem their loans, their creditors would automatically claim them as their slaves with the right to sell them. And so, a class of free laborers was gradually transformed into a class of slaves.

Such a state of affairs (whereby the rich became richer, farmers kept losing their farms, and the free workers were becoming slaves) if continued, would definitely lead to civil unrest and civil war. Realizing the danger, the people started searching for a wise and capable politician who, when given a free hand, might avert the coming internal strife.

Solon, the son of Execestides, was the man of the hour. He was the scion of a noble and wealthy family, had received a very good education, and, early in life became a merchant and managed to earn considerable wealth. Despite all this, Athenians respected him more for his wisdom. In fact, they were convinced that only Solon, a highly cultivated citizen already known for his prudence, justice and love for all his compatriots, would be able to diffuse the crisis and prevent the imminent civil strife.

There are three fragments from his writings, which well-bespeak of his noble political thinking. They are:

1. "Law and order make rough things smooth, stop insolence, weaken violence, with the growing blooms of sin, straighten crooked judgments, calm arrogant deeds, stop deeds of dissension, and stop the anger of painful strife; through law and order, all men's affairs are suitable and prudent."

2. "Society is well-governed when the people obey the magistrates, and the magistrates obey the laws."

3. "To make a state durable, the magistrates must obey the laws, and the people the magistrates."

When, in 594 B.C. Solon became "Archon" of Athens, he immediately turned his attention to the people who had lost their farms and those who had become slaves. Believing that, "That is the most perfect government under which the wrong to the humblest is an affront to all," he inaugurated his leadership with legislation that aimed to rehabilitate his unfortunate compatriots.

His measure that brought relief to countless compatriots was called "Seisachtheia" (shaking off of burdens). He declared that all mortgages and debts of the debtors were cancelled, and that all those who had become slaves for debt were free again. Needless to say, this measure put an end to serfdom in the Athenian state.

To pave the way for democracy, Solon promulgated certain measures. He organized the Athenian citizenry in four classes according to property. They were: the "Pentacosiomedimni", that is, "500 – bushel men" because they produced that amount of grain, the "Hippeis" who produced 300 bushels of grain, the "Zeugitae" who produced at least 200 bushels of grain and all other citizens were the "Thetes" whose annual income was less than 150 bushels.

Of the above four classes of citizens, only those who belonged to the upper three could vote for the election of responsible officials, and only the first class enjoyed the privilege of being elected to the highest offices. Thus, the citizens who belonged to the class of "Thetes" did not as yet enjoy the right of electing or being elected to the high offices of state administration.

Despite the above conditions, the foundation of true democracy had already been laid. Solon, by making the highest offices of the land available to people of property, did away with the old system whereby high officials and even those of the highest rank had to be nobles or aristocrats.

Solon also founded the following administrative and judicial institutions. The "Ecclesia" was an assembly of people where all the citizens would gather to pass laws or chose magistrates. Thus, the magistrates, who were the highest officials, were elected by the people. The "Heliaea", a popular court consisting of 6,000 citizens, was the highest court with powers to adjudicate not only the highest officials of the Athenians, but also of archons. In ancient times, in no other nation could a magistrate or high official be tried before a peoples' court for misconduct, or for handling badly his responsible high duties. Only in Athens would such a truly democratic trial be conducted. The third governmental institution that Solon founded was the "Boule" also known as "Council of 400" whose members were drawn from the four Athenian tribes. Each tribe was represented by 100 members. Their duty was to prepare the agenda for the "Ecclesia" whose function was to pass the laws.

Finally, other important measures which proved very beneficial to the common people that Solon initiated were: his limiting of the area of land that could be owned by a citizen. This was a measure that prevented the growth of very large estates. His changing of the coinage weights and measures, thus making them identical to those of Euboea which were more widely used in the Greek colonies, thus contributing to the boosting of Athenian trade. His encouraging of foreign, skilled craftsmen to come and settle in Athens for the purpose of promoting the various industries. His granting freedom to citizens who had no heirs to will their property as they desired instead of willing it to the next of kin as the hitherto law required. His introduction of trial by jury. He decreed that the sons of those who were killed in battle should be educated by the state. And lastly, he permitted any citizen to indict another for a crime, so that the citizens would become more conscious of their civil responsibilities.

The above are only seven of the innumerous measures that he legislated for the benefit of the Athenian citizenry. Solon sought to put an end to the monopoly of power and influence the old noble and aristocratic families held over Athenian politics. He was quite successful in his efforts and thus administrative and magisterial power passed to citizens who were not nobles. We may, therefore, rightly regard Solon as the "Founder of Democracy."

Unquestionably, Cleisthenes, who decades later became archon of Athens, was a worthy successor of Solon. He was a prominent Athenian citizen – the son of Megacles and Agariste, both of whom were members of the famous Alcmaeonidae family. Cleisthenes was also a maternal grand-uncle of Pericles.

Cleisthenes' achievement lies in the reorganization of the Athenian state's citizen body. He substituted ten tribes for the old four, and divided the entire area of Attica, which was the area of the Athenian state, into 139 local units called "Demes" (townships). This new division of the urban and rural population into ten tribes and 139 Demes took the interest of the citizens away from the old clans and religious affiliations and provided the political system with a new electoral basis. From now on, the citizens would be interested in the politics of their local demes and especially those centered in Athens.

Cleisthenes made the Ecclesia (assembly of people) the most powerful political body of the state with members who were citizens from every tribe and deme and were over twenty years of age.

He increased the number of the members of the Boule (council) from 400 to 500 with fifty from each tribe, its members were elected by lot, and the fifty members of each tribe were in charge of all affairs for thirty-six days.

He also introduced "Ostracism" (ten year exile) of any high official, even an archon, whose conducting of his duties was detrimental to the state.

Cleisthenes' reforms greatly increased the opportunity of every Athenian citizen to assume public service. With him, the democratization of the Athenian city-state greatly expanded and was firmly established. It now remains for Pericles to put the finishing touches on this inestimable contribution of Greece to the world.

8

THE PERFECTOR OF DEMOCRACY

In all of human history, fewer than a handful of men have been blessed to have their name associated with their country's reaching a peak of excellence in all human endeavors.

Pericles, the leader of Athens, is one of those very few illustrious men. When historians refer to the Golden Age of Athens, or of Greece, they also refer to it as "The Age of Pericles".

He is more than worthy of such a supreme honor. Actually, it has been accorded to him during the past twenty-five consecutive centuries, because what was achieved by his compatriots during his thirty year leadership, history has rarely duplicated. It was a time when the human spirit burst forth with superhuman creativity – a creativity that since that remote time has had very few near parallels.

Pericles was born to a noble Athenian family in 495 B.C. His father Xanthippus – a prominent Athenian, became famous when in 479 B.C., he led Athens to victory over the Persians at Mycale. The defeat of the Persian Army convinced King Xerxes that any future attempt to invade European Greece would be futile. Agariste, his mother, was the daughter of an Alcmeonidan aristocrat and very influential Athenian.

Being the scion of an aristocratic and financially well-to-do family, Pericles received a very good education. His teachers were the thinkers Zeno and Anaxagoras. The latter taught him natural philosophy, refutation and rhetoric. Since he was determined to enter the political arena, he pursued rhetoric with fervor.

He was only five years old when the Battle of Marathon was fought between the invading Persians and the Athenians with the latter emerging as victors, and he was fifteen years old in 480 B.C. when the Persians led by King Xerxes again invaded Greece hoping this time to conquer it. Needless to say that the heroic resistance of the three hundred Spartans at Thermopylae to delay the advance of the Persians towards Athens, a delay that gave time to the Athenians to prepare their fleet to meet the Persian one in the Straits of Salamis, and the burning of the City of Athens and its Acropolis (Citadel), must have greatly impressed the young teenager. Little did he know then, that thirty-two years hence as supreme leader of Athens, it would be that he would begin the reconstruction of the citadel with buildings of such magnificence that to this day they have been objects of profound admiration.

In 463 B.C., young Pericles felt that he was ready to enter the Athenian political arena. One of his first acts was to join in the prosecution of Cimon – a leading conservative politician who favored and vigorously advocated friendly relations with Sparta – a traditional antagonist of Athens. With the help of Ephialtes – a leading liberal politician, Pericles was able to obtain an ostracism (temporary exile) of Cimon, an event that much disturbed Athens' wealthy citizens who began to sense that their political clout would soon slip from their hands and be transferred to the less privileged citizenry.

Pericles' skillful and shrewd initial political maneuverings and eloquent, persuasive speeches, which earned him the sobriquet "Olympian", soon earned him the respect and admiration of his fellow countrymen. As a result, by 454 B.C., they elected him to the highest government office – the office of "Strategos" (General). Actually, ten candidates were annually elected to the office of generalship. But Pericles always ranked as first among the ten – a position that made him the highest leader of the land. Thereafter, as his prestige grew steadily, he was re-elected many times to this office, and from the year 443 until his death in 429 B.C., he was elected to fifteen consecutive terms.

The office of strategos involved military as well as political responsibilities. Although Pericles distinguished himself more as a politician than as chief military commander, he nevertheless showed successful leadership in many land and sea battles against Sparta and its allies. In one of his victorious expeditions he was past sixty.

Describing the wise generalship of Pericles, the ancient Greek biographer Plutarch in his book entitled "Parallel Lives", wrote: "In his generalships he was especially famous for his caution. He never willingly undertook a battle that involved great risk or uncertainty, nor did he envy or emulate those who took great risks, won brilliant success, and were admired as great generals. He always said to his fellow-citizens that as far as it was in his power they would live forever and be immortals."

From the above, it becomes evident that Pericles' generalship was one of restraint. He was never eager to risk his armies to win a victory at any cost. Rather, he was calculating and rational, and whenever he perceived that there was a chance to settle the problem with his enemy diplomatically he would devote himself entirely to exhaustive negotiations.

As is universally acknowledged, it was in the exercise of his political responsibilities that this most famous statesman enshrined his name and his fame in history.

Since the beginning of the Fifth Century B.C., Cleisthenes, a maternal uncle of Pericles, had introduced a democratic government to Athens. While before Clesthenes' democratic reforms, court and government positions were always occupied by aristocrats, actually they were their monopoly. After Cleisthenes' reforms, members of the courts and of the other government's positions could now be occupied by members belonging to all other social classes.

But even after these reforms, the highest government and court positions were not available to the poor classes. As the poor classes were not as educated as the aristocrats, and as the poor did not have the funds to support a run for election, and if elected, to close their small business for a year, or stop working in their vocation in order to serve their city, lest such a move would definitely deprive themselves and their families of the necessary sustenance, it was evident that Cleisthenes' democracy was a limited and a deferential one. It was a democracy that did not consider every citizen capable to serve in the highest offices, but it was an effort to gain more participation.

It was this shortcoming in the democracy of Cleisthenes that the genius of Pericles sought to correct. Under his skillful leadership and persuasive arguments, he made the limited Athenian democracy a full and all-embracing democracy. How did he solve the problem? By what means did he correct the shortcomings of his country's democratic system?

The answer was very simple. He introduced salaries. If a poor man could not run for public office because his family would be deprived of the necessary income for its sustenance, then, he insisted, that the state ought to recompense this poor but competent man to serve his country while his tenure lasted. Only in this way would every citizen of the democratic state be given the opportunity to serve his country and thus claim that every citizen is equal before the law. It was felt that failure to enact state payment to the public officials would result in less than a full and true democratic society. The bill he introduced passed and thus the first fully democratic state in the history of mankind came into being.

Praising the incalculable importance of this political achievement, which in the history of political science represents a most significant milestone, Pericles, in a funeral oration that he delivered during the "Peloponnesian War" (433-404 B.C.), said:

"We live under a form of government which does not emulate the institutions of our neighbors; on the contrary, we are ourselves a model which some follow, rather than imitators of other peoples. It is true that our government is a democracy because its administration is in the hands, not of the few, but of the many; yet while as regards the law, all men are on an equality for the settlement of their private disputes, as regards the values set on them, it is as each man is in any way distinguished that his is preferred to public honors, not because he belongs to a particular class, but because of particular merits; not gain on the ground of poverty is a man barred from a public career by obscurity of rank, if he but has it in him to do the State a service. And not only in our public life are we liberal, but also as regards our freedom from suspicion of one another in the pursuit of everyday life...we are obedient to those in authority and to the laws, and especially to those laws which are ordained for the succor of the oppressed and those which, though unwritten, bring upon the transgressor a disgrace which all men recognize...we have provided for the spirit many relaxations from toil, we have games and sacrifices regularly throughout the year, and homes fitted out with good taste and elegance; and the delight we each day find in these things, drives away sadness. And our city is so great that all the products of the earth flow in upon us, and ours is the happy lot to gather in the good fruits of our own soil with no more home-felt security of enjoyment than we do those of other lands."

Establishing full democracy was not Pericles' only achievement. Being an ardent patriot and lover of his city, he had a grand vision. His vision was to make Athens: "The educator of Greece", that is, a city whose cultural, artistic and architectural aspects would serve as ideal examples for all other Greek cities. He desired his city to be the leading, the principal pace setter in all aspects of Greek creativity. Thanks to his ever-driving energy and skillful forcefulness, his vision materialized, winning for himself and his beloved city universal eternal admiration.

Using superb persuasive oratory, he would introduce to the Council successive bills to receive authorization to rebuild the temples of the Acropolis that since 480 BC, when the Persians had sacked the city, lay in ruins. He also introduced bills to receive authorization to beautify the city with new civic and government buildings that would make Athens the exquisite architectural showcase not only of Greece, but also, of all the known world. He succeeded in passing all the bills, and what was then built, has been admired and to a large extent emulated since.

Using funds from the Treasury of the "Delian League" – a league consisting of many cities in Greece and western Asia Minor, which paid annual tribute to Athens for military protection by the latter, he began the rigorous reconstruction.

The Parthenon was first to be built on the hill of the Acropolis – a temple dedicated to goddess Athena, patroness of the city. It took ten years to complete, and, when its last architectural members were put in its place, it was the most majestic and beautiful structure ever built in antiquity. It was the "crown" of the hill on which it was built, and, at the same time, the "crowning achievement" of all ancient architecture.

Construction of other temples followed, like the "Erechtheum" which was a temple dedicated to Athena and Neptune, the temple of "Athena Nike" (Athena the Victorious), and the impressive "Propylaea" – an elaborate entrance, and elaborate gateway to the Acropolis. On the southern slope of the hill, the "Odeum" was built. It was a concert hall where during the Panathenaic Festival and on other occasions, musical and choral performances were held. Simultaneously, other civic and government buildings were built in the "Agora" (Market Place) adding a fresh and hitherto unimaginable beauty to the old city. Needless to add, that this twenty year building program created jobs for a very large number of the population whose long employment brought them great prosperity.

Five hundred years later, when Plutarch saw the above mentioned structures, he wrote the following comment in his book: "Parallel Lives of Illustrious Greeks and Romans" one of which was that of Pericles.

"For this reason the works of Pericles are all the more admired and respected; they were created in a short time for all time. Each one of them, in its beauty, was even then at once an antique; but in the freshness of its vigor it is, even to the present day, recent and newly wrought. Such is the bloom of perpetual newness, as it were, upon these works of his, which makes them look untouched by time, as though the unfaltering breath of an ageless spirit had been influenced in them."

The same author, in expressing the fervor that had taken over the craftsmen who worked to build the magnificent temples wrote: "As the works went up, towering over others in their greatness and inimitable in their beauty and grace, the workmen contended with one another to surpass themselves in the beauty of their craftsmanship."

Pericles' tenure was also graced by the presence of many intellectuals. To mention the most important, they were the philosophers Anaxagoras, Socrates and Plato, the historians Herodotus and Thercydides, the playwrights Aeschylus, Sophocles, Euripides, and Aristophanes and a galaxy of other thinkers. Their scintillations touched upon every social, psychological, moral, theological, aesthetic, artistic, legal, natural, political, and anthropological question or subject and became the basis of our western philosophical and scientific thought.

In view of all the above, there can be no doubt that the Athenian State differed radically from such states and cultures as the Egyptian, the Assyrian, the Summerian, the Babylonian, the Syrian, the Hebrew, the Indian, the Chinese, and those of Central America – societies that existed before and after the Athenian. For while the Athenian society fashioned by Pericles in the Fifth century B.C. consisted of a free, dynamic, creative, and democratically-minded citizenry, the other societies were dominated by powerful kings and a caste of priests, who used a difficult system of writing that only very few scribes could master. They had rigid hierarchical systems, professional standing armies and a citizenry ready to obey whatever the king decreed.

In 431 B.C., a war broke between Sparta and Athens. It was to last for twenty-seven years resulting in the defeat of Athens. Pericles did not precipitate the war, but he could have prevented it. Certain actions that he took against the allies of the Spartans so strained the relations between the two traditionally antagonistic Greek states, that war became inevitable. Briefly, these are the vents that darkened the hitherto illustrious career of Pericles.

In 433 B.C., Athens contracted a defensive alliance with Corcyra and later ordered the citizens of Potidaea to raise their fortifications and to no longer receive magistrates from Corinth, which was the most important ally of Sparta. Later, Pericles issued a decree ordering the inhabitants of the nearby city of Megara – an ally of Sparta, to stop trading with the cities that were allied to Athens. These three provocations so strained the relations between Athens and Sparta that negotiations failed to resolve the differences.

At this point, Sparta declared war against Athens. This lasted until 404 B.C. In history, the war is known as the "Peloponnesian War" – a war that, besides taking a heavy toll among the combatants, also took a heavy toll of the civilian population.

Pericles, knowing that the Athenian Army was no match to the Spartan, devised a strategy whereby he would not meet the Spartans on land to do battle. On the other hand, knowing that Athens' superiority lay in its navy, he used the navy to control the seas and harass the allies of Sparta in the Peloponnesus. He also ordered the population of the entire region of Attica to come into the City of Athens and lodge behind the city's fortification walls. Food sent by Athens' allies would arrive by sea to the port of Piraeus which was connected with Athens by the Long Walls which secured its safe transport to Athens without Spartan interference.

But when so many thousands of citizens crowded the city and the city and the wide fortified road that connected Athens and Piraeus, a plague broke out which claimed the lives of thousands of citizens as well as the life of Pericles, his sister and his two legitimate sons in 429 B.C.

What kind of private life did Pericles have? His first marriage produced two sons before ending in divorce. Then, in 445 B.C., he met Aspasia who had come from the City of Miletus of Asia Minor. She was a bright, very well read woman that thrilled the Athenian intelligentsia with her wits and loose morals. When she met Pericles, the two became very close friends, and, for fifteen years thereafter lived as husband and wife, producing a son whom they named Pericles.

Pericles had great admiration for the theater. But, the poor could not attend its performances since they could not pay the entrance fee. Pericles, after introducing a bill to the City's Council, received authorization to institute the "Theoric Fund" – a treasury that would pay the entrance fee of any poor Athenian citizen to the theater. And so, thanks to this measure, the poor could now attend any play they wished.

Such was the life of the most illustrious Athenian statesman whose name became synonymous to the Golden Age of his beloved state. Although his behavior was rather pompous, throughout his public life he enjoyed a reputation of absolute incorruptibility. He was a genuine patriot, always proud of his city, its democratic political system, and its possessing the noblest culture. Endowed with a rational mind and with oratorical powers that few men have matched in history, he could sway the electorate of his country to approve expensive projects, rare policies and most any issue.

Throughout the centuries, historians have always praised him. We end this brief biographical account with the following one written by Thucydides, a contemporary historian of Pericles. "Pericles, because of his position, his intelligence, and his known integrity, could respect the liberty of the people and at the same time hold them in check. It was he who led them, rather than they who led him."

Pericles

9

THE ATHENIAN AGORA

Many cities in the U.S. and in other countries of the world are divided into many square blocks with each block containing many houses. Since the city is divided into square blocks, the streets appear to criss-cross each other. Civic buildings such as the courthouse, the city-hall and others are usually in the center of the town while in other sections there may be squares and parks.

Athens, having been founded in very ancient times, had no square blocks. Cities consisting of square blocks, criss-crossing streets and squares, appeared for the first time in Greece during the fourth century B.C. and the architect who must be given credit for designing such a new and orderly city was Hippodamus. In the history of man, he is the first architect to devise such a plan- a plan still followed today. This also makes him the world's first city planner. He designed the port city of Piraeus that is seven miles away from Athens in this new plan, and most cities that were built afterwards followed his plan.

Aside from the large and beautiful temples on the Acropolis and the public buildings of Athens, the homes of the people were generally small. They had one or two floors, three to seven rooms, and in the middle of the home was a small courtyard. They were built of stones and the walls in order to render them more beautiful, were painted red. The dining room was the largest room in the house. Since most ancient Greek people did not eat at a table as we do, but reclining in beds, the dining room had to be large enough to contain from five to seven beds. The beds were always placed alongside the walls.

Today in America and around the world, a large variety of meals are cooked and a large variety of pastries are baked. In ancient times, people did not have such a variety. They would rarely eat meat because it was very expensive, but they would eat fish often, which was less expensive. Most of their meals were vegetables, and what they ate most was bread. With their meals, they also drank wine. A variety of fruits such as figs, grapes, apples, pears and other kinds were also consumed at lunches and dinners. When a man wanted to have a big dinner party at his home, he would go to the market and find a caterer who would prepare and supply everything. He would suggest what is seasonal and would even supply extra cooks and waiters if the dinner party was to be attended by many guests. He would even supply a band and dancers if requested. All the meals would be prepared at the home of the host.

At the age of six, boys would start attending school. Girls received their education at home. Boys would attend school from age six to fourteen. The school day was long, usually from sunrise to sunset. The pupils learned how to read and write, to do arithmetic and to recite the two poems of Homer

- the Iliad and the Odyssey by heart. Learning how to play the lyre and the double pipes was also part of the pupil's education, as music always accompanied the recitation of poetry. Physical exercise was included as well.

When young men reached the age of seventeen or eighteen, they could obtain higher education in the Philosophical Schools of the city run by the various philosophers. If they wished to specialize in a profession or vocation, they could take the required courses from a notable professor or vocational in the residence of the instructor.

The Agora was a very wide and open space that lay close and to the north of the hill of the Acropolis. The Agora was a combination of market and Civic Center and it was flanked on all four sides by impressive marble public buildings whose beautifully fluted columns gleamed as white as snow. The west side was arrayed by such government buildings as the "Royal Stoa (Portico)", which served as a court of inquests, the "Stoa of Zeus Eleutherios (liberator)", "The Theseum", which was one of the most beautiful temples of the city, and which has survived to this day almost intact, the "Archives building", where official state documents were kept along with registers of births, marriages, deaths and property titles and where certificates were issued to inquirers, the "Council Building", where council members drafted the laws that subsequently would be voted into laws by the "Assembly of the People" on the hill of the "Pnyx", and the "Tholos", a round building with a conical roof where seventeen executives of the Council had their dinner at public expense. In the Tholos, the State's official weights and measures were kept.

Behind the government buildings and within a "stone's throw" was the smith's section where the ironsmiths, coppersmiths, goldsmiths, silversmiths, and others made all kinds of metallic products such as jewelry, tools, doctor's instruments, weapons, etc. Near that section, was also the potter's section where pots, dishes, bath tubs, and beautiful vases of all shapes and for all kinds of purposes were made.

The south side of the Agora was mainly flanked by a large square building - the "Heliaia", a law court adjudicating misdemeanors. To the left and adjacent to this court house was a long stoa that served as offices for judges. Next to this building was a public fountain, and next to it, the State Mint where beautifully engraved coins were minted. All Athenian coins were the same. On the obverse side was engraved the head of goddess Athena, and on the reverse was engraved an owl- Athena's sacred bird.

The East Side of the Agora was flanked by two large buildings, namely the "Pantainos Library" and the "Stoa of Attalos". Pantainos was a very wealthy Athenian who had contributed the cost of this beautiful library, which in the history of man, is the first public library. Diagonally behind this library, the Roman Emperor Hadrian contributed the cost for another library, much larger than that of Pantainos, which also had a spacious garden with trees under whose shade people could sit and read. Both libraries opened at sunrise and closed at twelve noon. Books which were in the form of scrolls could not be taken home. They could be used by the reader within the library premises until twelve noon, at which time he had to return them to the library clerk at the desk. The library of Hadrian had 100,000 scrolls.

The "Stoa of Attalos" was a two story, long building with a double row of columns in its upper and lower front. In the rear, it had twenty large rooms on each floor. The Stoa had been donated by King Attalos of the Kingdom of Pergamos in Asia Minor. As a young prince he had studied in Athens, and, when he became a king, he demonstrated his gratitude to the city that had been his "Alma Mater." Merchants and all kinds of professionals rented the rooms of this state-owned stoa. The Stoa was built in the second century BC and stood for four hundred years until its destruction by the "Herulians" – a barbaric horde that raided Athens in the middle of the third century AD. Between 1952-1956, it was completely rebuilt, thanks to a most generous donation of the Rockefeller Family.

The building that dominated the northern side of the Agora was the "Stoa Poikele" (Painted Portico). It was a large building with beautiful Doric columns in its front. On its three walls, hung large paintings, reminding the Athenians of past military victories such as those at Marathon and Salamis that had secured them their freedom. The Stoic thinker, Zeno, frequently lectured here.

When Greece was conquered by Rome in 146 B.C., Roman emperors and nobles, who had great respect for Athens for being a beacon of Letters and Arts, they too, endowed Athens with beautiful buildings. M. Agrippa donated the "Odeion" (Concert Hall), a very imposing structure erected in the middle of the Agora with its façade facing north. Caesar Augustus built a large and spacious market to the right of Hadrian's Library, and Emperor Antoninus Pius donated the "Nymphaion" – a most beautiful fountain adorned with sculptures next to the mint.

Two more beautiful buildings that lay beyond the eastern limits of the Agora were the so called "Tower of the Winds", an octagonal building for measuring time internally by a water clock, and externally by eight sundials whose hour lines were engraved on the upper part of its eight sides. A hydraulically powered device consisting of a disc divided in 365 sections, indicating the days of the year, pointed the exact date. Finally, a metallic weather vane on top of the building pointed the direction of the blowing wind.

Behind the Market of Caesar Augustus was the "Agoranomeion" (Market Inspection Bureau), the first of its kind in the history of man. The government officials who worked there set the prices on the various edibles and commodities that were sold in the market, and, daily, made sure to spot check the merchants and shop keepers lest the latter used weights and measures that did not match those of the Bureau.

Finally, vertical stone markers indicated the limits of the Agora whose area was considered "sacred", while water clocks located in many areas of the Agora indicated the time.

Southeast of the Agora, and within walking distance, was a low hill called "Pnyx". The hill was quite flat at the top, and, at a vantage point, was a platform. This area was used by the "People's Assembly" to enact the laws that the People's Council had drafted at the Council Chamber located at the Agora. Under normal circumstances, 6,000 Athenians would assemble on the Pnyx to vote on new laws and other matters concerning their city. Athens was the first true democracy.

South of the Agora and almost in the middle of the city of Athens there is a hill 230 feet high. It is flat on its top, and when viewed from above, its shape reminds one of the platform of an aircraft carrier. The north, south and east slopes are very steep. But the western slope has a gentle incline. From very ancient times it has been called "Acropolis", an ancient Greek word meaning "High City" or "Citadel".

When the Persians conquered Athens in 480 B.C., they destroyed all the old temples on the Acropolis. Now Pericles decided to rebuild them. For this purpose, he summoned to Athens the best architects and sculptors from various parts of Greece to make designs for the new temples. The architects were the famous Ictinus and his assistants Callicrates and Mnesicles. Phidias, the most famous sculptor, would be in charge of all the statues that would be placed in the temples. Alcamenes and Agoracritos were his main assistants, while eighty other unknown sculptors also worked on the many statues.

When one ascended the hill of the Acropolis using the staircase on the west side, nearing the top one would see the small but very beautiful temple of "Wingless Victory". The temple is of the Ionic order, and to this day, it has survived almost intact. Callicrates was the architect.

The much larger square building to the left was the "Pinacotheca" (Art Gallery). The most beautiful paintings done by the leading Greek artists hung on its four walls. What is important about the art gallery is that it is the first and oldest in the world.

When we pass through the beautiful and impressive "Propylaea" (Gateway), designed by the architect Mnesicles in the Doric order, the first thing that would attract our attention would be a statue of the goddess "Athena Promachos" (Champion). In her right hand she holds a large shield and a long spear whose tip could be seen from as far as Cape Sunion.

Further to the left and on the northern side of the Acropolis, is another beautiful temple called the "Erectheum", dedicated to the gods Neptune and Erechtheus and the goddess Athena. It was designed by Mnesicles in the Ionic Order. The building exhibits grace and delicacy and its honeysuckle ornamentation running all around the four sides of the building blends ideally with its Ionic architectural order. What is unique about this building is its "Caryatid Porch" on the south side. Here we see stately maidens supporting the roof.   Instead of columns, the architect preferred statues depicting maidens supporting the roof.

On the north side of the Acropolis and to the left of the Erectheum was a small temple with a walled enclosure called the "Pandrosion".   When the Athenian youths reached the age of eighteen, they would come to the enclosure and therein they would recite an oath pledging to always be loyal, responsible citizens and

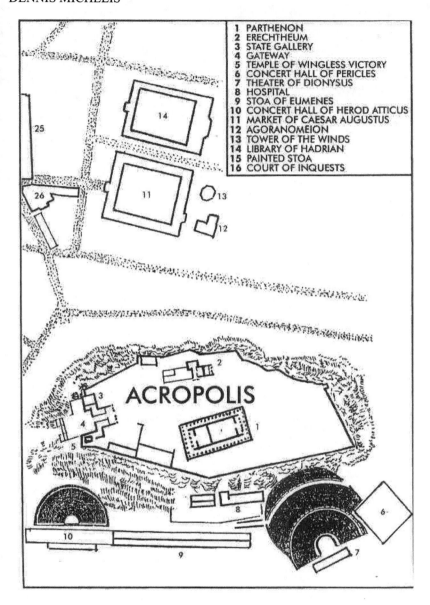

Map of the Acropolis of Ancient Athens

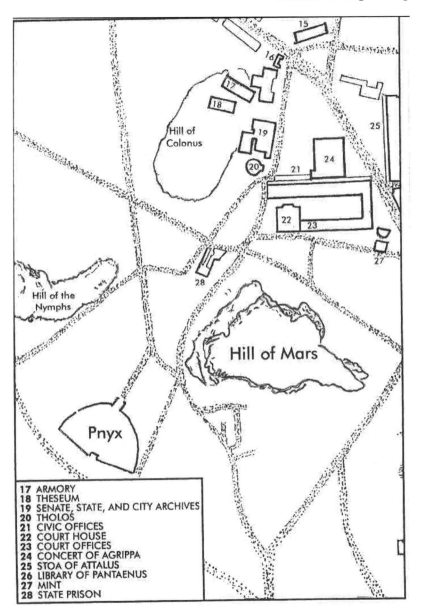

17 ARMORY
18 THESEUM
19 SENATE, STATE, AND CITY ARCHIVES
20 THOLOS
21 CIVIC OFFICES
22 COURT HOUSE
23 COURT OFFICES
24 CONCERT OF AGRIPPA
25 STOA OF ATTALUS
26 LIBRARY OF PANTAENUS
27 MINT
28 STATE PRISON

Map of the Agora of Ancient Athens

defenders of their country. This masterful oath, the first of its kind in the history of man, read as follows:

"I shall not dishonour the sacred arms I bear; I shall never desert my fellow-soldiers; I shall fight in the defense of my country and her sanctuaries; I shall hand on to posterity, to the best of my strength and with all my comrades' help, a city in no way diminished but rather made greater and more powerful. I shall obey the magistrates, the laws now in force, and those that may duly be enacted henceforward; if any person attempts to subvert them, I shall use all my strength, and the assistance of all men, to prevent this. I shall honour the cult of my ancestors. To this oath I ask the following divinities to bear witness: Aglauros, Hestia, Enyo, Enyalios, Ares, Athena Areia, and Zeus."

Looking south and across the Erechtheum is the largest and most beautiful temple on the Acropolis – the "Parthenon". (A detailed description of this temple is given in the next chapter).

A general view of the Acropolis. Restoration.

Other buildings on the Acropolis were the temple of Broraunian Artemis (Diana) and the "Chalcotheke" – a building for storing weapons in time of peace. Both these buildings were on the south side of the Acropolis and between the Gateway and the Parthenon.

At the foot of the south slope of the Acropolis were the "Theater of Dionysus", used for dramatic and comedic plays, the "Aesculapeum", which was a hospital, and the "Theater of Herodes Atticus" used for musical and choral performances. Linking the two theaters was the long "Stoa (Porch) of Eumenes". Eumenes like Attalos was a king of Pergamos. Like Attalos, he too as a young prince had studied at Athens and regarded it as his "Alma Mater". To show his gratitude, he paid the cost of this beautiful and expensive building.

Northwest of the Acropolis, rises the "Arios Pagos" (Hill of Mars). In ancient times, it was used as the Supreme Court adjudicating cases of high crimes that required the death penalty. Since this law court had the power to impose the death penalty, it could not be located in the Agora since it was regarded as a sacred area.

Finally, for the promotion of athletics, which, in ancient Athens as elsewhere in the ancient Greek world received so much attention, there were "Gymnasia", used for daily exercises and a very large marble stadium that could accommodate more than forty-thousand spectators. The stadium was another gift of the very wealthy Athenian citizen, Herodes Atticus, to his native city.

In no other city of the ancient world would contemporary twenty-first century man identify so much of the basics of his lifestyle and civic structure of his society as in Athens. Because, only in this avant-garde city of the Western World were there public schools for young children and schools of higher specialized learning, athletics, professional entertainment, annual festivals, concerts, and most of all, a democratic system of government that offered its citizenry free speech and direct representation (not representative as in our times), in its State's Council, People's Assembly, the Law-Courts and other branches of Civil Service. In an ancient world dominated by autocratic royal rulers and dictators, the Athenian City-State was an exception, a haven whose society passionately sought a free civic life, the riches of free reasoning and the creation of man-made beauty through sculpture, painting and architecture.

10
ANTINQUITY'S PERFECT STRUCTURE

In one of his writings, Cicero wrote: "Nothing is harder to find than perfection." He was absolutely right! Perfection is a rarity, "in extremis". Of the countless things man has made throughout his existence on earth, only a handful can be found to be truly perfect. Aeschylus' dramatic trilogy, "The Oresteia", in whose text not one word or character needs to be added or deleted, or Mozart's opera "The Magic Flute" in whose musical score not a single note is superfluous, would qualify.

The perfect edifice that will be described and analyzed both architecturally and artistically in this chapter is the Parthenon – antiquity's only perfect building, if not of all time.

The Parthenon – a temple dedicated to goddess Athena -patroness of the city of Athens, was built on the hill of the Acropolis. It was the largest and most beautiful among many other temples that were built on the same hill during the fifth century B.C. and during the Administration of Pericles, known in history as the "Golden Age of Greece". Since that time, the Parthenon has been the envy of the civilized world, for rarely before and since, has man worked with such zeal and persistence to create such a perfect and sublime masterpiece. The only creative age that came close, but did not quite equal it, was the High Renaissance in Italy in the early sixteenth century.

Who were the men that drew the architectural and artistic designs of so ambitious a project? They were the famous architect lctinus and his assistant Callicrates, Phidias the most famous sculptor and his main assistants – the sculptors Alcamenes and Agoracritus. Interestingly, contemporary art critics by having discerned slight almost imperceptible differences in the treatments of the sculptures and friezes that adorned the temple have come to the conclusion that some seventy-five to eighty other unknown sculptors must have been engaged in their making.

Since high quality white marble was abundant on Mt. Pentelicon situated some eight miles away, it was inevitable that the Pathenon would be built of this high quality stone in its entirety. The marble would be quarried from an area of the slope quite high from the plain below, would then be given the shape specified by the architect near the spot where it was extracted and, after being loaded on a wooden sled, it would slide down the slope on a stone covered path all the way to the plain. At the terminus, it would be loaded onto a large cart drawn by at least sixteen horses and transported the eight mile distance to the foot of the hill of the Acropolis. The cart would then be pulled upward on a wide ramp that led to the top of the hill. The pull was done by sixteen horses descending on the ramp. At the top of the ramp, many pulleys eased the pulling strain of the horses considerably.

When the various architectural members of the temple – column drums, rectangular blocks, slabs, and all sorts of marble pieces, which numbered thirteen thousand in all, began arriving at the top of the Acropolis, they would be given the final polishing. When ready, they would be lifted by cranes that were equipped with many pulleys to the designated place. The lifting of column drums was done by looping ropes around the four projections of each drum. Needless to add, that hundreds of skilled and unskilled workers from Athens and other parts of Greece were engaged in the construction.

The architectural style chosen for this temple was the Doric. The Doric Style dictates that all lines of a building are straight. Ironically, however, in the Parthenon not a single line is absolutely straight! Each line, whether belonging to a column or to some other long component, is slightly curved causing it to appear straight to the observer.

The Parthenon was the largest Doric temple in the Greek world to be completed, and to have been built entirely of marble. Other Greek temples' architectural components employed were limestone, sandstone or other kinds of stone. Commencement of construction occurred in 447 B.C., and was completed by 437 B.C. But, its sculptured embellishments took an additional five years requiring carving and placing upon the designated places. In 437 B.C., the colossal statue of Athena was installed in the temple's interior and, with this event, the dedication ceremonies took place.

The size of the Parthenon is large. Its stylobate (top step of a three stepped base on which the columns and the walls of the temple rest) is 228 by 104 ¼ feet, in other words, a ratio of nine to four. The three high steps of the base stretched the entire length of all four sides. Because such a large platform, when viewed from a distance, would appear to the eye to be sagging in the middle, thereby spoiling the beautiful aesthetics of the temple, the architect made it subtly convex on all four sides. On the two long sides, the platform rises slightly towards the center by four and a half inches, and the short sides of the platform (façade and back) rises two and a half inches. This almost imperceptible convexity causes the platform to appear absolutely straight. If we were to extend the long and short arcs of the platform on both sides so as to form two circles, the long arc's circle would have a diameter of seven miles and one hundred and sixty feet. The short arc's circle would have a diameter of two miles and three hundred feet.

Fluted, white columns of the Doric Style ring around the temple supporting the roof and allow a wide enough walkway between the colonnade and the walls of the temple. There are eight columns on the façade and eight on the back. Each of the long sides has seventeen columns. Each column's diameter at the base is six and one-fourth feet. Its height is thirty-four feet. Curiously, the ratio of the length to the height of the façade and of the back of the temple is again nine to four as is the length and width of the temple. In order for the columns to seem straight, as the Doric Style dictates, they were made to bulge about an inch at a third of the height from the base up. This very slight bulging made the column lines look straight.

None of the temple's forty-six columns stand vertically, although they appear to stand so to the spectator. They all lean very slightly inward. Moreover, the columns of all four sides, besides leaning inward, also lean ever so slightly toward the center of the side. Thus, if we were to extend imaginary lines from the top, they would all meet at one imaginary point at an altitude of one mile and a half thus forming an imaginary pyramid. This causes the Parthenon to be a "truncated Pyramid". Also, the spaces of the intermediary columns, as we move from the central columns to the corner ones, become smaller and smaller, although these differences are not easily perceived by the spectator. Finally, describing the columns, the four corner ones are thicker than the intermediary. The reason for being so is because these columns are the only ones viewed against the sky – a background that to the human eye has a diminishing effect on their width. To correct this optic deficiency, the architect made them a little wider thereby compensating the loss.

The entablature, the superstructure above the columns, like the stylobate, is also curved. It too rises toward the center with the same deviational ratio as the stylobate. The upper part of the entablature bears "Tiglyphs" alternating with "Metopes". The triglyphs are vertical projecting, grooved members painted blue. The metropes, ninety-two in all, are the spaces between the triglyphs and bear reliefs.

The reliefs of the metopes of the front side of the temple depict scenes from the "Gigantomachy", that is, the battle of the gods against the giants. Those of the long southern side depict scenes from the "Centauromachy", that is, the battle of the Lapiths and Centaurs. Those of the back side of the Temple (the western), depicts scenes of "Amazonomachy", that is, the war between Greeks and Amazons. And, those of the long, northern side of the temple depict scenes from the sack of Troy. The background of the metopes was painted red. In this way, the painted figures of the projecting reliefs could be seen clearly from below. The figures of the metopes display such a variety of poses and attitudes that monotony is prevented.

The sculptures of the pediment of the front of the temple which faces east, showed the birth of Athena. The sculptor Agoracritus carved most of the female statues of this pediment. There were eighteen statues depicting gods and goddesses in the eastern pediment. The statues of western pediment, nineteen in all, show the contest between Athena and Poseidon for the possession of Athens.

Judging the artistry of all the pedimental statues, art critics have classed them among the most majestic in the whole history of art. Although they have suffered damage, their undamaged parts reveal a mastery of sculpting which has never been surpassed. For example, the intricate drapery folds rest on the figures in such a way that reveal the masses of the human forms they cover. In some of them, the folds are done with such delicacy that they create the illusion of a transparent garment. Also, the various poses of the figures – shown in reclining, sitting or standing positions, reveal the sculptor's complete mastery of the techniques required to create such positions. Two thousand years later, Michelangelo would strive hard to achieve such a mastery.

On the upper section of all four sides of the exterior wall of the temple, and when viewed from the outside behind the colonnade, ran the world-famous frieze which was carved in low relief. It depicts the annual "Panathenaic Procession". This was an annual festival in which Athenian youths marched to the Acropolis to accord honors to Athena – the patroness of their city.

The frieze which, as mentioned above, extended on all four sides, had a total length of 525 feet. Each of the many fragments that made up the frieze had height of three feet and three inches. Four hundred human figures and two hundred animal figures have been carved on the fragments that make up the frieze. The drapery of the figures was painted in different colors. The faces of woman were left white, those of the men were somewhat darker, and the background of the frieze was blue.

The starting point of the depicted procession is the southwestern corner of the temple. The one procession would run the western, northern and eastern half of the sides of the temple, while the other procession would run the southern and the eastern half of the sides of the temple. Thus, both processions would converge on the eastern side where the gods and goddesses were depicted sitting and conversing.

The entire frieze is undoubtedly one of the most famous artistic masterpieces in the world. Both human figures and animals have been carved with the utmost care. Cavalcades, elders, sacrificial animals, chariots, jar-carriers all appear to be moving. Handsome, robust youths, some holding and others riding their horses, some in the foreground and others in the background are all masterfully depicted in a variety of poses. Young maidens, some carrying jars and other canisters full of fruits, and others simply participating in the procession, all appear with superbly serene faces and a dignified gait. The rich folds of their garments, when hit by sunlight, create a most pleasing alternate succession of light and shade.

As the frieze receives no light from above because the roof of the temple extends to the colonnade, the only light that reaches it is the one reflected from the walkway below. Yet even this reflected light was enough to make the figures clearly visible. Another factor that added to their clear visibility was the red background which made the colored figures stand out.

In the temple's interior stood the forty foot tall statue of Athena. It stood on a rectangular pedestal whose height was ten feet. The four sides of the pedestal carried reliefs of human figures and animals. The majestic and overwhelming statue of the goddess was made entirely of wood and was faced with ivory and gold. The face, neck, arms and toes were faced with ivory. The garment, shields, spear, helmet and statuette of Nike, which she held in her right hand, were faced with gold.

Two-hundred and twenty pounds of gold were required for the guilding of this gigantic statue. The value of the gold was seven hundred talents. The sum represented a tremendous cost, when

The gold and ivory statue of the
goddess Athena in the Parthenon.

compared to the three talent cost of a single trireme (ancient warship). Thus, the cost of the statue's guilding was equivalent to the cost of the two hundred and thirty-three triremes. Incidentally, the number of warships of Athens' fleet was three hundred.

This, very briefly, was the Parthenon – a masterpiece of ancient Greek architecture and sculpture, the crowning aesthetic achievements of Pericles' "Golden Age". Constructional precision, ideal dimensional relationship of its architectural components, optical refinements to prevent visual distortions, wonderful sequential figural carvings on its frieze and metopes, pedimental statuary of superb execution, and, in its interior, a gigantic statue of unparalleled magnificence, it is these unique features that made this temple perfect, and consequently, an object of admiration in all subsequent centuries. One must say that never before, and perhaps since, has mathematics, geometry and artistic creativity collaborated so closely so as to produce an architectural and artistic specimen that would be perfect at all times.

For nearly nine hundred years, the Parthenon was a temple dedicated to Athena. Then, in the early years of the fifth century, it was converted to a Byzantine church and was dedicated first to the Wisdom of God and then to the Most Blessed Virgin Mary. In 1204, it became a Catholic church, and, in 1456 when Athens was conquered by the Turks, it was converted into a mosque.

During the capture of Athens by Fancesco Morosini and the Venetian Army in 1687, as Venetian cannons were relentlessly bombarding the Acropolis, which now served as a Turkish fortress, on September 14, 1687, a shell went through an opening of the roof of the temple and ignited the gunpowder that was kept in a storage area below. The explosion caused the central part of the temple to collapse, and caused irreparable damage to many fragments of the frieze and the metopes.

Between the years 1881-1883, Lord Elgin, then Ambassador of England to Constantinople, obtained a "Firman" (authorized permission) from the Turkish sultan, and removed the frieze from the east side, from the north and south sides that had not collapsed, and from what he could salvage from broken fragments that lay on the ground. He did not extract the fragments from the western side. He also removed most of the pedimental sculptures from both pediments and transported everything to London. In London, he displayed them for an extended period at an exhibition hall, and thousands of English and continental Europeans came to see them. Later, he sold them to
the British Government, which placed them among the permanent collections of the British Museum.

Many British and non-British literati directed scathing remarks toward Elgin for extorting the sculptures from their rightful place. Most scathing of all was the English poet Byron's, who wrote: "Quod non fecerunt

Goti, fecerunt Scoti," meaning: "Scots rushed in where Goths feared to tread."

Also, eight fragments of the frieze are now in the Museum of Louvre in Paris, France, and one is in the National Museum of Copenhagen, Denmark.

It is most unfortunate that, of the originally 525 feet long frieze only 335 feet are in existence.

Many architects from all over the world have visited the Parthenon in the past and continue to do so today. Some in the past conducted measurements to unravel the secrets of this perfection, and others came to admire it despite its sad, ruinous state. Of those who conducted measurements, Penrose's are the most accurate.

Nowadays, annually during the summer, millions of tourists ascend the Hill of the Acropolis to view the Parthenon.

When Le Corbusier – who is recognized as France's 20th century most notable architect, and who together with Frank Lloyd Wright and Germany's Walter Gropius, ushered in modern architecture visited the Acropolis to see the Parthenon, commented in one of his writings: "There is nothing to equal it in the architecture of the entire world and all the ages; the plastic modulation of the Parthenon is flawless, ruthless. Its austerity goes beyond what we are accustomed to, and the normal potential of man."

American philosopher, Ralph Waldo Emerson who never visited this perfect temple, nevertheless offered an equally laudatory comment: "Earth proudly wears the Parthenon as the most precious gem upon her zone." It is a most apropos comment for a human creation that will forever represent perfection.

The Parthenon of Athens. Restoration.

11
THE PURSUIT OF WISDOM

Just as democracy, mathematics, geography, historiography and many like intellectual and scientific pursuits were the brainchild of the Greek mind, so was philosophy.

Philosophy, a word invented by the thinker Pythagoras means "lover of wisdom". More broadly, it is a systematic inquiry into the ultimate principles and laws of all things. Thus, the philosopher searches into the reason and nature of things, investigates phenomena and assigns rational causes for their existence.

Although philosophy was originated by the Greek mind, ironically, the first philosophical schools did not appear in Greece proper but in Greek colonies. They first appeared in Ionia (Western Turkey), then in southern Italy, and then in Greece. Be that as it may, all the ancient philosophical inquirers were Greeks, and what they achieved was astonishing. They searched painstakingly for the ultimate reason of every natural phenomenon, of man as a political, ethical, and societal being, of his limited span of life, his soul and the hereafter, and most importantly of God – His nature and relation to the world. All these fundamental quests were attacked brilliantly, and what resulted from these inquiries was a plethora of answers. In the process, they laid the foundations of many types of thought, of reasoning about the things they were investigating, and thus, the reasoning systems they developed are followed to this day.

As mentioned previously, the first philosophical schools appeared in the Greek colonies in Ionia, hence, the "Ionian School." The representatives of this school did not turn their attention to man, but to the cosmos, the universe. Why is there a universe? What caused its creation? Of what elements does it consist? How did life begin? It was mostly such kind of questions that they asked, and some of the answers at which they arrived are still valid today.

The first Ionian philosopher was Thales (620-546 B.C.), born in the Greek colony of Miletus. He was also an astronomer and to a lesser extent a physicist. He taught that all things are made of water, a conclusion he may have arrived at by seeing moisture in the air and in the extensive alluvial regions of his country. That water is present not only in the sea, but in the atmosphere, under the surface of the earth, and in the bodies of all living things. Today's science would fully agree with Thales. Even the sun consists mostly of hydrogen. Thales was not far from the truth. He also believed in one God, because in all his dicta, he refers always to one God, never to many.

Anaximander (b. 610 B.C.) was also a native of Miletus and a disciple and an associate of Thales. He taught that the originating principle of all things is the "Infinite", rather the "Unlimited". By these two terms, however, he did not mean infinite space, but minute particles of matter that perennially coagulate forming all material things and then they dissolve again. Anaximander also anticipated Darwin, for he taught that life first appeared in the sea in the form of fish. Later, they came ashore, threw off their scales and assumed the shapes of all animals.

Anaximenes, a native of Miletus and associate of Anaximander was the third major representative of the Ionian School. He taught that the principle, the essence of all material things, is the "Air". The "Air" is a substance and is also endowed with life. The air's thinning and thickening causes the elements of fire, water, clouds, winds, and earth.

The Pythagorean School

Pythagoras, a native of the Greek Island of Samos, in 530 B.C. journeyed to Italy and founded a philosophical school in the Greek colony of Croton. His school was rather an ethico-religious society governed by a set of rules. Members recognized one another by secret signs, dressed simply, fed on a restricted diet, remained celibate, and would refrain from disclosing the doctrines of their school.

Pythagoras taught that numbers are the essence and basis of all things, like of musical harmonies, stellar movements even of abstract ideas. He taught the doctrine of the "Transmigration of the Souls", meaning by this, that if a man was a moral person in this life, he would attain a higher status in the hereafter. If not, his soul would become a lower creature. Pythagoras is also credited with the invention of the musical scale consisting of seven notes. Finally, he taught that the supreme goal of man is to become godlike.

The Eleatic School

Like the Pythagorean School, the Eleatic School was also located in Italy, and to be exact, in the Greek colony of Elea. Its founder was Xenophanes (572-480 B.C.), who was born in Colophon of Asia Minor and came to Italy in 546 B.C. Xenophanes attacked the gods in Homer's poems as figments of poetic imagination. He taught that God is one, eternal, unchangeable, unmoved, sublime and spiritual. He is also everywhere present, and governs the world through his mind. In one of his writings, he wrote that: "People in their effort to represent God, they make him as they themselves are: the black man as black and flat-nosed, the Thracian as red-haired and blue-eyed, and if horses and oxen could paint, they, no doubt, would depict the gods as horses and oxen. People also ascribe to the gods mental characteristics, which are human. They do not understand that God is 'All eye, all ear, all intellect?'" Indeed, what an advanced theology Xenophanes had devised!

Other prominent representatives of the Eleatic School were Zeno and Melissus.

Later Ionian Philosophers

Heraclitus (535-475 B.C.), a native of Ephesus, is the first prominent representative of this school. His best known and most characteristic doctrine was that "Everything is in a state of flux." To illustrate his most cardinal point, he would say: "you never enter into the same river because its water continuously flows." He was absolutely right. Change is present in all things. There are constant changes in the nebulae, the stars and on our earth. In geologic time, the continents of the earth imperceptibly drift, coastlines very slowly change, volcanoes create new mountains, and evolution has changed all living things. Thus, nothing is permanent on earth, and if our senses tell us that they are permanent, they deceive us.

Regarding the creation of the world, Heraclitus taught that everything came from fire. By fire, however, he did not mean the flames that result from combustion, but rather invisible warm matter which is endowed with life. Everything, even water and earth, come from that warm invisible substance.

Anaxagoras (500-430 B.C.), a native of Clazomenae of Asia Minor, spent the greater part of his life in Athens. He was a close friend of Pericles, and, among his disciples he counted the famous playwright, Euripides. His main contribution to Greek philosophy, rather to the philosophy of the world, was that God is Mind. In fact, God is distinguished from all other things, because by being Mind, he is simple (mind alone is pure), it is self-ruled, it has "all knowledge" about everything and has "Supreme power over all things".

The Atomistic School

The founder of this school was Leucippus, born in Miletus. Very little is known about him. Democritus (b. 460 B.C.), however, is the best representative of this school.

Democritus believed that the universe, the earth, and every living and non-living thing on it, is composed of atoms. In number, the atoms are infinite, and being very, very tiny, they are indivisible. The reason they cannot be further divided is because, being extremely small, they contain no void. He believed that plants and animals sprang from moist earth. He regarded man as being the most admirable creature. He claimed that man's organs, which he describes in every detail, have marvelous adaptations and perform special functions. Permeating the entire body of man is the soul, which is corporeal, composed of the finest atoms. The soul is the noblest part of man, and his moral excellence is his crowning glory. Democritus, being a thorough materialist, did not believe in God.

The next school that dominated Greek intellectual activity was the "Sophists". Their philosophy will be treated in our next chapter.

The Stoics

During the late fourth century and the subsequent centuries, two more philosophical schools would dominate ancient Greek thought – the "Stoics" and the "Epicureans".

The founder of the Stoical School was Zeno (350-258 B.C.), born in Cittium, Cyprus. At first, he was a merchant. But, due to losing his ship, with all its precious cargo in a storm resulting in Zeno losing most of his wealth, he decided to become a philosopher. To realize this goal, he came to Athens, and attended for a time Plato's Academy, and by 310 B.C., he founded a school of his own. As the "Painted Porch", in Greek "Poikile Stoa", was the place where he usually lectured, his school became known as the Stoic.

What is startling in the theology of Zeno is his teaching that God, the human soul and the world are all material. Even the qualities of objects, emotions, virtues, and vices, they too, are corporeal. Life cannot come from non-living matter. It takes God to effect such a transition. The world has a soul and its soul is God Himself, who also sets the world into motion. God is Providence, and as such, watches with providential care every part of the world, and thus maintains a good moral and physical condition. Thus, everything in nature is rational and good.

He taught that the soul of man is part of the divine soul, and that a virtuous life is conformity to nature. Wisdom, he contended, consisted mainly in knowing all about life. He regarded passions as indications of a sickly soul; therefore, passions must be uprooted. He did not regard sicknesses, earthquakes, afflictions, and other unfortunate happenings as evil. Assaults and crimes on fellow humans, as well as errors that cause troubles on others were recognized as evil deeds.

Stoicism became quite popular among the Greeks as well as among inhabitants of countries of the Middle East, where many Stoic thinkers appeared. Later, Stoicism became a very popular philosophy in Rome, also. Well known Romans such as Cicero, Seneca, Varro, Quintus Sextius, Celsus, Epictetus, and the emperor-philosopher Marcus Aurelius, were of the most eminent followers of Stoicism.

Zeno taught for fifty-eight consecutive years, lived simply and ate little. He died at the age of one hundred.

The Epicureans

Epicurus (342-270 B.C.), was a native of Athens, but grew up in the Island of Samos. In 305 B.C., he returned to Athens, and, at the age of thirty-six, founded the Epicurean School. He wrote three hundred books, but most unfortunately, only fragments survived, along with some letters and his will.

Epicurus followed Democritus' materialistic theories about the world and about the atoms. He believed that the human soul is also material, therefore, after death, it too dissolves. It follows, that with the soul being mortal, the Epicurean has nothing to fear from death.

The attainment of happiness must be the goal of every mortal man. Happiness is also freedom from pain, or from fear, which is mental suffering. Like Stoicism, Epicurianism also spread in the countries of the Middle East and in Rome, where it gained many followers. In Rome and in Italy, famous Romans, like Lucretius, Pomponius, Atticus, the poets Horace and Pliny, were ardent followers of Epicurianism.

These very briefly, were the main philosophical systems of ancient Greece – idealism, realism, materialism, stoicism and epicureanism. During the past twenty-five centuries, they have been the foundations of Western thought, which eventually, "as the world becomes smaller" and Western modes of thought slowly become accepted by the non-Western world, may become universal.

Just think for a moment how their systems have become our systems. The Greek Orthodox Religion has been influenced by Platonism, our Western science has been based on Realism, some people develop stoical, apathetic attitudes on life, while Europe and America have been following the materialistic views of Democritus causing America to be, at present, the most materialistic country in the world.

In the next three chapters, the three greatest philosophers will be treated in some detail.

12
THE FIRST MAN-CENTERED SAGE

A prominent philosophical school during Athens' "Golden Age" (5th century B.C.) was that of the "Sophists". Etymologically, the word "sophist" meant a wise man. Sophists went about from city to city seeking to gather young men around them who, for a certain fee, would receive "sophistic" instruction which would eventually help them immensely in the field of public relations.

At the core of the sophists' philosophy was the doctrine that "there is no objective truth" and that "man is the measure of all things". And since there is no objective truth but only what each individual pronounces as true, then what the sophists' disciples had to learn was that disputative process whereby that would make the bad look good, the unjust look just, the ugly look beautiful, the worse look better and vice versa. But in order to win at a disputation, the sophists stressed that one ought to have readiness of exposition and presentation of arguments in a specious manner.

Most prominent sophists during the Golden Age were: Gorgias, Protagoras, Hippias, and Prodicus. They enjoyed much respect by the common people who failed to discern how wrong the sophists were in believing that there is no objective truth. But the day arrived when their gross fallacy was revealed and the man who single handedly stood against them was a humble Athenian commoner- Socrates.

Socrates, the son of Sofroniscus who was a sculptor and of Phaenarete, a midwife, was born in Athens in the year 469 B.C. When he grew up, he followed his father's art, and married Xanthippe with whom he had three children.

Regarding his education, we must assume, that during his childhood and early adolescence, he was taught the standard curricula of the times: writing, reading, arithmetic, etc. As far as pursuing higher education, that, he did not do, for, as we learn from Xenophon's "Symposium", he styled himself as a self-taught philosopher. The fact is that he possessed extensive knowledge of the doctrines of many of his predecessors such as Parmenides, Heraclitus, Anaxagoras and the "Atomists".

In Plato's dialogue, the "Apology", we are told that the gods had revealed to Socrates that he was to spend his life in Athens, and that his mission would be the moral and intellectual improvement of himself and of his contemporaries. Conforming to this "divine" revelation, Socrates, at the age of forty, quit working as a sculptor, and devoted the remainder of his life teaching his fellow Athenians to always strive to morally improve themselves. He was so devoted to this mission that he never sought public office, and the only time he interrupted his instructive missions was when he took part in the campaigns of Athens against Potidaea and Delium. Oddly, those were the only times that he went beyond the walls of his native city.

Unlike the sophists who always collected fees for their instruction, Socrates never accepted remuneration. Moreover, while the sophists taught in schools, Socrates taught in the Agora (Market place), in the gymnasia, and wherever he found people eager to listen to him. As for his character, in Xenophon's "Memorabilia", we have the following description: "No one ever heard or saw anything wrong in Socrates; so pious was he that he never did anything without first consulting the gods; so just that he never injured anyone in the least; so master of himself that he never preferred pleasure to goodness; so sensible that he never erred in his choice between what was better and what was worse. In a word, he was of all men the best and the happiest." Despite such a sterling character, however, Socrates was not without traducers who claimed, that he was uncouth in speech and manner, coarse, arrogant, impious, to mention a few.

Every so often, Socrates spoke of a heavenly voice which in the crises of his life revealed to him guidance and advice from above. He was a very religious man, and no doubt, whenever he heard the "divine voice" it must have been the voice of his consciousness.

Socrates never wrote down anything about his own life or of the things he taught. What we know about his life and teachings is derived from the dialogues of Plato, the "Clouds" – a comedy by Aristophanes in which the famous comedic playwright pokes fun at the great philosopher, the "Memorabilia" of Xenophon, and from Aristotle, who among others, tells us the names of his parents, of his wife and children.

Right from the beginning of his career as a philosopher, Socrates set himself against the sophists. Against their arrogant claim that they "knew everything", Socrates would respond with a now world-known saying, "One thing I know, that I know nothing." Then engaging them in conversation, he would eventually prove to them that they did not know everything. Also, against their claim that there is no objective truth and, therefore, there is only individual opinion, Socrates, by using the "Inductive Process" which he called "Maieutic" after his mother's profession (she was a 'Maia'– ancient Greek for midwife), through question and answer, he would arrive at the objective truths thus proving to the sophists how wrong they were.

Contrary to his fellow Athenians who believed in many fictitious gods, Socrates believed in one God who was all-wise (a supreme Mind), and all-good ruler of the world. Furthermore, he held that God's existence is shown by the providential order in nature, and by the universality of the belief in Him. Thus, in no way did he believe in mythology that was replete with foolish and immoral tales of the non-existing gods and goddesses of Olympus and which he regarded as a mere invention of the poets and poetesses.

Socrates also strongly believed in the immortality of the human soul. In fact, the concluding paragraphs of Plato's dialogue entitled

"Apology", strongly attest to Socrates' belief in the hereafter. Moreover, Socrates taught the soul is man's self, the seal of character and intelligence. Its expressions are what make us wise or foolish, good or bad.

Until Socrates made his appearance as a philosopher by the middle of the Fifth century B.C., most philosophers occupied themselves with the cosmos, the universe- its origin, the elements it consisted of, its purpose, its end. Socrates turned the attention of philosophy away from the universe and concentrated on man and his conduct in life. This turning point, affected by Socrates twenty-five centuries ago, is still adhered to. Man, his purpose for being here, his destiny, and his role in society are still the main preoccupation of today's thinkers. Man is still the pivotal entity of philosophical study and reflection.

To the all-important and fundamental question "Which is man's supreme good in this life?" Socrates answered "happiness", and by happiness he did not mean a happiness that depends on external conditions and accidents of fortune, but a "eupraxia", a well-being which is conditioned by good action.

Since, as was mentioned previously, the soul is the seat of our intelligence that causes all our actions, it logically follows that our happiness depends directly on the goodness or badness of our soul. The soul's good actions make a man happy. Not when a man possesses wealth, health, and every conceivable material comfort is he actually, truly happy, but when his soul knows how to use these advantages rightly. If they are wrongly used, then they become means of misery.

Thus, happiness becomes attainable in an individual when his soul becomes fully knowledgeable of the right, the good actions it must take at every circumstance. If this is not done, if wrong actions are taken as a result of the soul's inadequate knowledge, the individual becomes unhappy. "Eutuchia"- happiness always depends on "Eupraxia" - good action, in both cases taken by the soul.

The same principle, that of a fully knowledgeable soul for right action and good conduct, Socrates also emphasizes as an indispensable qualification for any ruler of people. Great knowledge of what is good, what is truly beneficial for his people, will cause the politician, the ruler of a people, to take the right action and thus make his subjects and himself happy. His administrative "eupraxia" will be the "royal" science of governing, the foundation of all statesmanship. This is why Socrates always emphasized that the leader of a people ought to have high intellectual qualifications of the good, so that when put into action, it always results in the well-being of his citizenry.

Socrates had great love for his country. This is attested by the following statement that he made to his disciple, Crito, when the latter visited him in his prison on the morning of the day of his death. Socrates stated: "Your country is more precious and more revered and is holier and held in higher esteem among the gods and among men of understanding than your mother and all your ancestors."

Finally, another basic dictum that he emphasized was "know thyself". But how does one get to know himself? Socrates states that one is led to know himself through repeated self-examination. Through this mental reflection on the inward self, the individual discovers his mistakes, his flaws, the inadequacies of the goodness of his soul and by deciding to hereafter avoid them, he ennobles, he increases the goodness of his soul.

In retrospect, in all of man's history, few people have thought so nobly and have made themselves a living example of moral improvement as did Socrates. As one person put it briefly and eloquently - "know yourself", this is the sum of all philosophy. From the consideration of the objective world (nature) we must turn to the study of the subjective (self). Thus "philosophy from heaven descended to the low-roofed house of man."

Socrates

13
THE MOST SUBLIME IDEALIST

During the last quarter of the fifth century BC, and to be more exact, in the year 427 B.C. A boy was born to the aristocratic family of Aristo and Perictione who lived in Athens and who they named Aristocles. To the world, he became known as Plato – a nickname meaning "wide" on an account of his wide shoulders. Through his father, Plato could trace his lineage back to Codrus, the last noble king of Athens. Through his mother, Plato could trace his lineage back to Solon, who was Athens' lawgiver.

While still a very young man, Plato aspired for a political career. But for two factors that later intervened, he was kept from statesmanship. They were, his mother's relation with two of the thirty tyrants presently ruling Athens, and the execution of Socrates, the philosopher and his teacher. The unjust execution of his teacher utterly disgusted the young aristocrat.

During his childhood and adolescence, Plato showed great interest for learning. The two fields that seemed to interest him most were philosophy and mathematics. He developed a sharp mathematical mind and possessed such an interest in mathematical and geometrical problems, that when later in his life he founded a philosophical school, above its entrance, an inscription read: "none ignorant of geometry should enter this house." His other prime interest was philosophy. Of all Greek philosophers who lived before him, the ones who influenced him most were Heraclitus, Pythagoras, and more than any other, Socrates, becoming his disciple at the age of twenty.

Following the execution of his beloved mentor Socrates, Plato left Athens and traveled to Egypt and southern Italy and Sicily where Greek colonies abounded. On his return to Athens in 387 B.C., he founded his own philosophical school in a house outside the city and near a gymnasium and park dedicated to the hero Academus. The Academy, the name by which Plato's school became known was derived from Academus. In this famous school of the ancient world, Plato taught for forty consecutive years until his death in 347 B.C.. He died at the age of eighty.

Plato wrote thirty-six dialogues, that is, their text has been written in question and answer form – a style invented by Plato. Moreover, his dialogues are written in a language so remarkable for its grace and beauty. Some of his dialogues are brief and others are written in two books of about four hundred pages each. With the exception of the dialogue entitled "Timaeus", which deals with cosmogenetical (creational) subjects all other dialogues like the "Republic", "Protagoras", the "Banquet", "Gorgias", "Phaedo" and the others deal with theological subjects. They are replete with such deep and novel insights that, since the remote time they were written, have never ceased to inspire, fascinate and challenge human minds of all times who find them timely.

Plato's theology greatly differs from that of his fellow countrymen. Unlike the latter, who believed in the Olympian Pantheon which consisted of twelve fictional gods and goddesses, Plato believed in one God of whom he conceives as the Absolute Good. In various dialogues he extols his wisdom, his all-including knowledge and his power. God is also supremely perfect. He is the absolute truth and lying is absent to Him. He exercises over all things a providence which orders and governs everything for the best. Since, according to Plato, God is invisible and intangible, he would not hesitate to often criticize his fellow countrymen for attributing anthropomorphic notions to their fictional divinities.

Plato not only believed in the existence of one God, he even advanced three arguments in favor of the existence of God. The first argument is the "teleological", one which holds that since there is order and design in all living and non-living things on earth as well as harmony in the entire universe; these prove the existence of a rational God. The second argument is known as the "efficient cause". According to this argument, Plato contends that all things cannot proceed from matter but from reason, which, being immaterial, preceded matter. It is reason therefore that is the cause of all material motion and of all the processes of matter. His third argument is that of "common consent". Through this, he teaches that, since all peoples on earth have always believed in gods this universal belief proves the existence of God.

In his dialogue entitled "Symposium", Plato discusses the essence of the beautiful. He claims that the essence of the beautiful is harmony, symmetry and order. He also contended that art ought to have for its object the realization of the beautiful. Hence, art should never aim at flattering the regular tastes of the wicked and the base. If Plato lived in our times, he would have certainly condemned most of today's artistic creations. A good artist, therefore, should try to make his artistic creation as beautiful as possible, reworking it many times until it would approach the ideal prototype that he has in mind.

Plato's views on education are most constructive. The aim of education, he contends, ought not only to be the freeing of a child or of a young man from ignorance, but simultaneously to form in him, a good, a noble character. When a child or a young man learns arithmetic, reading, and poetry, this is "ecpedeusis" (education). When a child or a young man is taught the virtues, such as justice, honesty, truthfulness and a host of others, Plato calls this learning "morphosis". When the state or the polis (city) sees to it that such a combination of learning is imparted simultaneously into the mind and soul of every student, then that state or polis (city) actually imparts an all around learning to its youth. They acquire the knowledge of things that they will use in their professional or vocational life, as well as the knowledge of right and wrong so that by choosing the right, they will always have good relations with their fellow men. Plato was also the first thinker to suggest that the state have a philosopher that will act as "minister of education".

Thus Plato's theories on education are not only invaluable, they also are ever-timely.

In his dialogue entitled "Phaedo", Plato discusses two yet fundamental questions, namely, "Is man free to choose the Good?" and "Is the grave the end of life?" To the first question Plato answers that all men are endowed with free will and therefore are free to choose the good, and choose anything else only through ignorance or error. He answers the second question by affirming that since every single human being possesses an immortal soul which unlike the body which being material, is destructible, the soul, being immaterial, is indestructible. Furthermore, in heaven, the virtuous soul will be rewarded, while the wicked one will be punished.

In his dialogue entitled "Crito", Plato discusses another fundamental issue, the issue whether an unjust law ought to be obeyed. In answering this question, Plato uses as an example Socrates, his teacher. Socrates has been unjustly sentenced to death by the Athenian Supreme Court. His disciples, with the approval of the jailers, had all agreed to help him escape on the night before his execution. When his disciple, Crito, comes to prison to take him away, Socrates flatly refuses to escape on the grounds that such an act on his part would go against anything he had taught during his life- love and devotion to country, and obedience to its laws. And so, Plato's answer to this fundamental question is laws are made to be obeyed. They might even be wrong, but as long as those laws are in effect, they should be observed.

Scholars have found gems of Platonic thought in all his dialogues. They do, however, all agree that the "Republic" and the "Laws" are his greatest.

It is in the "Republic" where Plato asserts most clearly his theory of ideas that is so characteristic of his philosophy. In this book, and to a lesser degree in his "Laws", Plato asserts that people should concern themselves with the search for truth. Since truth is perfect and eternal, however, it will not be found in the material world, the world of sights and sounds, and which we perceive through our senses. This material world that surrounds us is imperfect and continuously changes. Any search, therefore, to find truth in such a world would be futile. Only through our minds, through our reason, through dialectical (question and answer) discussion, will we be able to discover those eternal truths that represent the immutable and eternal true knowledge. Thus, by a process that begins within a material world, through reasoning, we are led to the world of ideas that represent the truth such as the ideal counterparts of justice, beauty, courage, goodness, fortitude, etc.

To illustrate this process, Plato uses an ingenious allegory- the allegory of the "Cave". Imagine some prisoners, chained in a dark cave, seeing only shadows on one of the cave's walls that they take for real. Imagine also that one of these prisoners is able to free himself from the chains and after climbing a steep slope, eventually finds himself in the bright sunlight and also sees the sun which he correctly interprets as the true source of heat and light. But when he returns to the cave and tells his inmates of his amazing discovery, none will listen to him since they have experienced only the shadows in the cave.

What Plato is trying to say through this allegory is that all of us, from the time we are born, live in a like cave filled with shadows and illusions, and thus remain in a state of apathy and ignorance. But the minute we decide to get out of it, we have a way to learn the truth. When we use the steep slope that represents the dialectical method (the question and answer method), this process will lead us to the truths we wish to know.

In the Republic, Plato proposes an ideal state consisting of three classes of people - rulers, soldiers, and workers. But it is not this utopian state that is significant in this Platonic dialogue. What really is enlightening are the many topics that he treats in its text, topics that are still intriguing as well as fascinating.

A fundamental notion that Plato expounds in this book is that every human being ought to be judged for his own worth, for what he can accomplish for his own good and the benefit of his fellow men and not because of his particular background. If an adolescent shows a proclivity toward becoming an engineer, or a carpenter, he should be availed the educational or vocational means to realize this goal. If the son of a doctor does not want to follow in the steps of his father, but instead wishes to become a musician, he should never be coerced by his father to study medicine. He should be given all the encouragement to become a good musician.

In the same book, Plato boldly champions equal rights and duties for women. He claimed that although women were by nature inferior in muscular strength, nevertheless they are endowed with the same talents and potentialities in all fields of human endeavor. Since Plato's time, how long, indeed, it took the world to realize this eminent Athenian thinker's foresight.

Finally, in the same book, Plato proposes the idea that rulers (he calls them kings) of states ought to be philosophers. Only when future rulers, he contended, have pursued intensive philosophical studies and thus have gained much knowledge of many aspects of human life and of the state as an organic social entity, will they be able to govern it wisely and beneficially. It is unfortunate that to this day many countries of the world are still governed by rulers whose education is mediocre or even less than that. What perhaps is even more ironic is that none of the constitutions of the countries of the world contains a clause requiring its leader to have superior education.

Since Plato's death twenty-four centuries ago, a very large number of ancient, medieval, and modern ecclesiastical and secular thinkers have been influenced by the Athenian thinker's idealism.

After his death, and more specifically from the fourth century BC to the fifth century AD, notable thinkers, such as Speusippus, Xenocrates, Arcesilaus, Plotinus, Hypatia, and Proclus would continue his idealism. Moreover, Platonic ideas would find their way into the text of the Old

Testament deuterocanonical book, "The Wisdom of Solomon". Also, the first century AD eminent Jewish philosopher and theologian, Philo, was a great devotee of Plato.

Early Christian Church Fathers such as Clement of Alexandria, Origen, St. Basil, St. Gregory of Nazianzus, St. Gregory of Nyssa, St. Ambrose of Milan, and the greatest Father of Western Christendom, St. Augustine, were likewise greatly influenced by the lofty idealism of Plato.

In early Middle Ages, scholastic theologians in Western Europe, men such as John Scotus Erigena, St. Anselm, Otto of Tournai, Abelard, and St. Bonaventure were greatly influenced by Plato, as was equally influenced the notable Jewish philosopher Salomon Ben Gabirol (b. Malaga, Spain).

With the coming of the Renaissance, Byzantine refugee scholars from Constantinople, Pletho Gemistus, Bessarion George Scholarius and many others would cause a rebirth of interest in Platonic studies, making Platonic scholars of the eminent Florence intellectuals, Pico and Francesco della Mirandola, Marcilio Ficino, and Lorenzo Valla.

Since the Rennaissance some of the greatest minds of the Western world have been Platonists – men like Rene Descartes, George Berkeley, Immanuel Kant, Gottleib Leibniz, Georg Wilhelm Freidrich Hegel, Ralph Waldo Emerson, Josiah Royce, and Alfred North Whitehead.

Extolling the philosophy of Plato, which, when carefully scrutinized, lifts us from the sordid world of material things to a world of exalted types and ennobling ideas, Joubert wrote: "Plato....puts light into our eyes, and fills us with a clearness by which all objects afterwards become illuminated. He prepares us, fashions us, and makes us ready to know all. The habit of reading him augments in us the capacity for discerning and entertaining whatever fine truths may afterwards present themselves. Like mountain air, it sharpens our organs and gives us an appetite for wholesome food."

Plato

14
THE MOST PROFOUND REALIST

Greece's other philosopher who is of equal stature to Plato was Aristotle. Like Plato, his mentor, he too is one of the greatest in all of human history. He was so profound a thinker that the influence of his philosophy and scientific ideas in the Western World lasted more than two thousand years. Most of his philosophical and scientific principles are still valid today, and indisputably, they will continue to be valid well into the distant future.

Aristotle, the son of Nicomachus and Phaestis, was born in the small town of Stagira in 358 B.C. His father descended from the family of Asclepiadae and was physician to the Macedonian King Amyntas II. His mother was from Chalcis.

At the age of eighteen, Aristotle went to Athens, where for the next twenty years, he attended the lectures of Plato at the Academy. Throughout this long time, Aristotle was a diligent and attentive pupil, and as expected, part of his later philosophy had been influenced by that of his venerable teacher.

In 343 B.C., Aristotle was summoned by King Phillip of Macedon to become the tutor of his son, Alexander, who was then thirteen years old. Needless to say, that the influence that Aristotle had on his young pupil was not only great, but also lasting. When young Alexander, at the age of twenty-three, set out on his campaign against the Persian Empire, reaching with his armies as far away as India, Aristotle asked his former pupil and now King of Macedonia to send him any new plant or animal that he would find in the lands he would conquer. These he would investigate scientifically thus creating a broader picture of the living things of the natural world.

About the year 335 B.C., Aristotle returned to Athens and there he established a philosophical and scientific school which he named "The Lyceum". It was located on land that now is on the eastern side of Athens' National Garden. He taught in Athens until the year 323 when he withdrew to Chalcis, his mother's hometown, where he died a year later.

Aristotle was a voluminous writer. He wrote four-hundred treatises, of which, most unfortunately for the world, only fifty survived, that is, only one-eighth. His treatises, whether philosophical or scientific all bear the mark of his erudition, clarity of thought, logical exponation, acute observation and ingenuity. The treatises are divided into five different categories. There are "Logical" treatises such as the "Analytica Priora" and "Analytica Posteriora"; "Metaphysical" treatises, "Physical" treatises that deal with nature, the weather, the heavens, the plants, and the animals; "Psychological" treatises that deal with the soul, the senses, feelings, memory, reminiscence, life, and death; and finally, "Ethical" treatises such as the "Nicomachean Ethics", the "Politica" and others.

As for the character of the famous teacher, he was noble, high-minded, thoroughly earnest, devoted to truth, courteous to his opponents, faithful to his friends, and kind to his slaves. To put it in a few words, a true intellectual gentleman.

The theology of Aristotle did not acknowledge many gods and goddesses but rather one God, the object of all desire, pure mind, immutable, eternal and simple. He arrived at the conviction that there is only one God by observing movement in all things in heaven and on earth. In fact, he contended, that although motion is perpetual, there cannot be an infinite series of movers and moved. In time pre-eternal, there must have been One, which being unmoved, caused motion to all other things. This prime mover unmoved is God. He set the whole universe in motion while He Himself remained unmoved. Moreover, Aristotle believed God is supreme intelligence, and His life, is contemplative thought. He takes interest in human affairs and created the world out of nothing, for everything is possible with God.

In his psychological treatises, Aristotle contended that each human being has a soul which is inseparable from the body, and the set of all aspects of human behavior such as thinking, feeling, sensing, and many other aspects. In some of his psychological writings, Aristotle contends that the soul, and to be more exact the intellect, is immortal.

In his moral treatises, Aristotle advances the doctrine that the supreme good of man is happiness. The ancient Greek word which he uses to define happiness is "Eudaemonia" which actually is more akin to well-being to welfare. But, how is this well-being to be attained? He answers: "When man lives a life of virtue."

Aristotle divides the virtues into two categories: the moral and the intellectual. The moral virtues are temperance, justice, courage, friendship, magnanimity, liberality, and truthfulness. Actually, these virtues are mean states between want of ambition and over-ambition. Modesty is the mean between shamelessness and bashfulness. The intellectual virtues are science, art, practical wisdom, intuitive reason, and theoretical wisdom. Through these virtues, man arrives at the life of contemplation of truth which is the highest activity.

The "Politica" of Aristotle contain the novel and very interesting political theories of Aristotle. His basic principle is that man is by nature a "social being." Man cannot live alone. He will find happiness and fulfillment only as a member of human society. Aristotle was also able to discern that man's social life begins in the family which historically preceded the state. As for the state, he emphasizes that the latter not only must see that the family remain intact, it must also seek to promote anything that contributes to the advancement and development of its citizens.

Aristotle had included in his political theories 158 different constitutions of ancient Greek cities. Unfortunately, of this large number of constitutions only one survived - that of Athens. We are fortunate for such a survival because Athens' constitution is a masterpiece of constitutional drafting.

According to Aristotle's political theories, there are three forms of government: monarchy, aristocracy and the republic. Of the three forms, the best is aristocracy, not of wealth, nor of birth, but of intellect.

Aristotle's sharp intellect was also able to accurately pinpoint the corruptions into which the above three forms of government may degenerate. Monarchy can easily degenerate into tyranny, aristocracy into oligarchy where wealth becomes a qualification for office, and republicanism into disorganized democracy. Mob rule, Aristotle taught, is a bad manifestation of democracy. However, if its citizenry has diversity, constitutional democracy may qualify as the ideal form of government.

An intellectual area that Aristotle developed very broadly was his "Logic". The primary reason that induced him to develop this area was to help him accurately describe reality, especially in his scientific investigations. To achieve this, Aristotle introduced ten categories. They are: substance, quantity, quality, relation, place, date, position, state, action, and passivity. Using Pericles as an example, the categories would analyze him as follows: substance - man, quantity -five and a half feet tall, quality - white, relation - married, place - Athenian, date - 450 BC, position - sitting, state - sober, action - making eloquent speeches, passivity - died during the Peloponnesian War.

Aristotle also uses the terms "substance" and "accidents" to describe all existent things. The substance is the very essence of a thing and it is independent and ontologically ultimate. The accidents are the various properties of the substance and inherent in it.

In medieval times, this distinction between substances and accidents was applied by the Christian theologians on many dogmas of the Church. To cite two basic examples, the Old Testament God was transfigured into the primary substance entirely independent of the rest of the created world and devoid of accidents. In fact, two early modern philosophers, Descartes and Spinoza, believed that God is the only being that can truly be called substance. The other fundamental dogma on which Aristotle's distinction between substance and accident was applied was the sacrament of the Holy Eucharist (Holy Communion). When the priest prays for the sanctifying Grace of the Holy Spirit to change the offered gifts of bread and wine into the Body and Blood of Christ, the substance of the bread and the substance of the wine do transform themselves into the Body and Blood of Christ. But, the accidents, such as color, taste, weight, and others, remain the same.

In his theories about art, Aristotle analyzes the different ways by which man creates artistic works. Whether man paints or sculpts, he looks at his environment for subjects. During the process of painting or sculpting a certain object or theme, the artist must not resort to slavish imitation of the prototype. He must try to execute it freely. More specifically, he can paint or sculpt a certain object making it look like the original; or, he can make it look more beautiful, or he can just make it appear as it ought to be based, of course, on his own judgement.

Aristotle's views on drama are classic. Consider for example, his definition of tragedy that has held to this day. It reads: "It is an imitation of an action that is serious, complete, and of a certain magnitude...in the form of action not of narrative; through pity and fear affecting the proper purgation of these emotions." As for the component parts of tragedy, Aristotle holds that these are six, namely: plot, character, philosophical content, proper expression, choral music, and staging. He also emphasizes the fact that every play must have a well-integrated plot and the text must always be well written and comprehensive.

Aristotle, as was previously mentioned, besides being a philosopher was also a scientist of the highest repute. As such, he was able to compile in his scientific writings an enormous number of scientific facts concerning the life, anatomy, reproduction, and other biological aspects of plants, animals, and man, and wrote extensively on geology, meteorology, space, and similar subjects which will be discussed in the chapter under the heading "Greek Science".

Aristotle's impact on subsequent philosophical and scientific thinking has been phenomenal. In all of man's history, the men who were able to match Aristotle's influence on whole generations for two millennia have been extremely few. He is still the master in our twenty-first century on many philosophical and scientific aspects as he was in the remote past in which he lived. Since his death, countless philosophers and scientists have carried and transmitted the intellectual torch that he lit.

Throughout the remainder of antiquity in Greece and in other ancient countries, famous thinkers such as Theophrastus in Athens and Alexandria, Dicaearchus and Aristoxenus in Italy, Eudemus in Rhodes, Demetrius, Strato, Proclus, Aristarchus of Samos, Hieronymus of Rhodes, Aristo, and Hermippus were his early successors.

In Hellenistic Times, Carneades of Panaetius, Posidonius of Rhodes, Diodorus of Tyre, Nicholaus of Damascus, and Boethus of Sidon were among the most prominent Aristotelians.

From the 2nd century AD to the sixth, Aristotle's thought would influence such great men of science as Ptolemy, the greatest geographer of antiquity; Eudoxus, the ancient astronomer; Galen, the most eminent physician; and the notable philosophers Porphyry, Proclus and Simplicius, to mention only a few.

During the Byzantine Period (330 AD - 1453) Aristotle's thinking would influence St. John of Damascus, one of the greatest theologians of our Orthodox Church, Patriarch St. Photius - the theological, literary and philosophical genius of the ninth century, the notable philosopher, Michael Psellus, and others. Notable thinkers and theologians outside the Byzantine Empire that would heavily feel the impact of his thought were the two famous Arab philosopher-physicians Avicenna of Bokhara and Averroes of

Cordova, Spain, and, in the West, one of the greatest Catholic theologians, St. Thomas Aquinas of Italy, St. Albert the Great of France, and Theodoric of Freiberg, Germany.

During the Rennaissance, Byzantine thinkers such as George of Trebizond, Theodore of Gaza, John Argyropoulos - Bishop of Florence, and Cardinal Bessarion would stress his philosophy on the universities of Northern Italy, while at the same time, Marsilius of Padua, Thaddeus of Parma, G. Fracastoro, P. Gassendi, and, in England the eminent philosopher, Francis Bacon, would do likewise.

In the eighteenth century, the "Politics" of Aristotle would exert much influence on Cajetan, Bellarmine and Suarez on the founders of International Law - Vitoria and Grotius of Holland, the British jurist, Blackstone, the British thinkers John Locke, Edmund Burke and John Acton, and, in France, the eminent philosopher Montesquieu, whose political philosophy on the division of powers influenced Thomas Jefferson.

In the nineteenth and twentieth centuries, Aristotle's thought would impact the nationalistic movements of France, Italy, and Germany, the notable scholars Herder, Brentano, Zeller and others while at the same time university presses would be printing the "Corpus Aristotelicum" in countless editions. More recently, the German scholar W. Jaeger would publish a monumental book on Aristotle's philosophy, while in Britain his thought would influence the Oxford scholars W. Ross, G. Mure, I. Barker and Alfred North Whitehead as well as the Welsh Bertrand Russell.

Summing up the invaluable contributions of Aristotle's philosophic and scientific realism, William Turner wrote: "the basic ideas of his philosophical system have become the commonplaces of education; they have found their way into the vocabulary of our everyday life, and have impressed themselves indelibly on the literature of Western Civilization. If Plato built a philosophical structure beautiful in its outline and perfect in its symmetry, Aristotle laid the foundation of his philosophy deep on the rock bottom of experience, and although all the joints of the fabric are not equally secure, the care and consistency with which the design is executed are apparent to every observer. If Plato had been called the 'Sublime,' Aristotle must be called the 'Profound', - a title which when applied to a philosopher, should be the expression of higher praise; for wisdom is of times nearer when we stoop than when we soar."

15
ORIGINATORS OF HISTORY

If we examine the written records of events of all the prehellenic cultures, we will notice that the vast majority of them revolve around their kings. They are brief, if not very brief, and what they usually describe are their ascent to the throne, who were their royal consorts, how many children they had, if they governed well- and this is stated in one or two lines, if they fought in a war, whether they won or lost, and finally, at what age and when they died. It goes without saying that such records are not history in the proper sense.

History, as is defined today, "is a record of all that happens". A world of difference then exists between the very brief records of the prehellenic cultures and of the histories that are recorded today. History today seeks to encompass a very wide range of events that occur within a nation or between nations. The progressive or regressive march of a nation, the literary, scientific, and artistic achievements made in every area, the wars fought by its people against those of another nation, what caused the wars and what was their aftermath, the leaders of that nation, conservative or liberal, successful or unsuccessful in their leadership and what effects these had on their citizenry, what caused an unprecedented advancement on a certain age and a regression in another, this is real and well rounded historical writing; and such kind of historical writing, like so many other intellectual fields, originated in Greece.

Herodotus

Cicero called him "The Father of History," an accolade synonymous with him ever after. Quintilius, referring to his style of writing, said that it is "sweet, pure, and flowing". Longinus said that he was "the most Homeric of historians". Dionysius, a countryman of his prefers him to Thucydides and declares that his writings "combine in an extraordinary degree excellences of sublimity, beauty and the true historical method of composition."

Herodotus (484-425 B.C.) was born in Halicarnassus - a Greek colony located on the western coast of Asia Minor (Turkey). At the time of his birth, his native city and all of Asia Minor were included in the Persian Empire. He was the son of Lyxos and Rhaeo, both upperclass citizens. During his formative years, he received a very good education, becoming quite proficient in the Iliad and Odyssey of Homer, the epics - "Cypria" and "Epigoni" and was also quite knowledgeable about the works of Hesiod, Alcaeus, Sappho, Aesop, Phrynichus, Aeschylus, Pindar and others.

As a young man, he traveled to more countries than any of his contemporaries. He visited all of Asia Minor, the Island of Cyprus, the Aegean Islands of Rhodes, Delos, Paros, Thasos, Samothrace, Crete, Samos,

Cythera and Aegina. He traveled the long and tiresome trip from Sardis to Susa, the capital of the Persian Empire, and visited Babylon which is located in modern southern Iraq, the cities of Tyre in Syrian Palestine and Egypt where he stayed a long time. While in Egypt, he went up the River Nile, all the way to Assuan. He also visited Thrace, the Island of Zakynthos, located on the western shores of Greece, and from there, he sailed west to visit the Greek colonies of Sicily and southern Italy. If we measure the distances, they are about three thousand and four hundred miles back and forth.

He kept extensive records of all the places he visited thus contributing immensely to our knowledge about the history, customs, morals, taboos, religions, political systems, commerce, products, monuments, and other cultural aspects of the places he visited. His descriptions of the countries he visited are quite detailed and vivid. He especially admired the architectural achievements of the Egyptians, like their pyramids, and, in his records has preserved for us the most extensive description of mummification that was practiced in Egypt. Thus, his written record is not only historical, but also geographical, archaeological, anthropological and sociological. Rightly then, he was recently accorded an additional title, "Father of Ethnology".

His massive records, besides containing historical material of the countries he visited, also contained an invaluable record of the wars between Persia and Greece. Alexandrian historians, who divided his entire record into nine books, naming each of them after each of the nine muses, reserved the entire ninth book to exclusively include his detailed accounts relating to the wars between Persia and Greece.

Herodotus' accounts deal much with men. Attributing historical events not to abstract causes, but as the works of man. His books are replete with descriptions of human characters that played major and even minor roles in wars as well as in the cultural developments of their respective countries.

The clash between Greece and Persia is described in many details. Numbers of the opposing armies, battlefields, strategies, the generals on both sides, all these military aspects have been recorded in detail. Since objectivity was a basic characteristic in Herodotus' historical writing, he does not hesitate to state that the Persians were chivalrous and even brave. Finally, the Battle of Thermopylae, the Naval Battle of Salamis where the Greek Fleet sank the Persian, the latter three times the size of the Greek, and the Battle of Plataea, where the final stroke was given the Greek defenders against the Persian invaders, are all vividly described.

Remarking on Herodotus' technique, a contemporary historian wrote: "Stories are the stuff of which he wove his book, but he arranged them carefully in a brilliant pattern. This perhaps is the reason why, as a recent writer has observed, Herodotus is enjoyed most by children and philosophers."

Thucydides

He was a master historian admired by many. The ancient literary critics of Alexandria admired his mastery of the beautiful Attic dialect which he used in all of his work. Ancient Athenian orators attempted to model their speeches after the ones Thucydides included in his history, while famous Roman historians and orators such as Sallust, Cornelius, Nepo, Cicero, and Quintilian, not only held him in high esteem and admiration, but copied his style in their own writings.

Thucydides (460-399 B.C.) was born in Athens. His father, Olorus, owned an estate in Thrace, which included a mine in Mount Pangaeus. Since his father was an aristocrat, Thucydides received an excellent education. His mentors were the sophist Anaxagoras in philosophy, and Antiphon in rhetoric.

In 424 B.C., and at the age of forty-six, Thucydides was appointed general to defend the region of Thrace, located in north eastern Greece, against the encroaching Spartans with whom Athens was presently at war – the well known "Peloponnesian War". Thucydides, having made miscalculations, failed to defend Amphipolis, a leading city in Thrace and an ally of Athens, resulting in its being conquered by the Spartans. As for Thucydides, he was exiled. When this internecine war ended in 404 B.C., Thucydides did not return to Athens. He continued to live in Thrace until his death in 399 B.C. From the time of his exile until his death, he wrote his monumental history, "The Peloponnesian War", a historical masterpiece that since the remote time of its composition has always been highly admired.

What caused him to write such an exhaustive work? In the word of a contemporary historian, "He believed that what happened once was sure to happen again under the same circumstances, and, after thinking out the story to satisfy him, he wrote his book in order that others might calculate intelligently the consequences of their decisions." He calculated that a history written soberly, dispassionately and full of true facts, would be, to future leaders and generals, "a possession forever".

His massive historical record is divided into eight books. The first, after a general introduction, enumerates the causes of the Peloponnesian War. The second, third, and fourth books describe the first nine years of that terrible internecine war, each containing three years. The fifth book describes the tenth year, followed by the interval of the "Insecure Peace". The sixth and seventh books deal with the Sicilian Expedition and the eighth book deals with the so-called "Decelean" and "Ionian" War.

Thucydides took great pains and the utmost care in gathering and then writing his material. As he admits: "As to the deeds done in the war, I have not thought myself at liberty to record them on hearsay from the first informant or on arbitrary conjecture. My account rests either on personal knowledge or on the closest possible scrutiny of each statement made by others. The process of research was laborious, because conflicting accounts were given by those who had witnessed the several events, as partially swayed or memory served them."

About a fourth of his record consists of speeches. They are given in pairs, representing the opposing views regarding a situation or a question arising in the process of the war, so that it be finally voted before the Assembly. Referring to the speeches, the author wrote: "as to the speeches made on the eve of the war, or in its course, I have found it difficult to retain a memory of the precise words which I have heard spoken; and so it was with those who brought me reports. But I have made the persons say what it seemed to me most opportune for them to say in view of each situation; at the same time I have adhered as closely as possible to the general sense of what was actually said." The only speeches that are quoted verbatim are those of Pericles who was the leader of Athens at the initial years of the war. Thucydides was present at the place of the Assembly when Pericles was delivering them, and thus they are the only ones that have been recorded verbatim.

Thucydides was the very first historian to reflect deeply on the consequences of the warring parties. Like a sociologist rather than a historian, he sees the horrible consequences of that internecine conflict, such as the destruction of houses making their inhabitants homeless - an unbearable situation until the family finds another home, the scorching and destruction of farms and orchards, which, besides being the source of food of whole populations, are also a source of livelihood to the owner, the killing of married combatants depriving their families of their most important members- the bread winner, the poverty that befalls the defeated party as a result of being forced to pay war indemnities to the victorious one, the demoralization and promiscuity that result especially on the defeated, and finally, the abandonment of the destroyed land and cities by large numbers of families in search of other places. When one looks at the results of the wars that have happened since then by the reoccurrence of the horrific situations so accurately noticed above, Thucydides' observations were not only correct, but also "classic", ever-timely.

Some call Thucydides "The Philosopher of History", and others the "First Sociologist". He was both.

Herodotus and Thucydides were not the only ancient Greek historians. They were followed by the well-known Xenophon, who, besides writing his masterful "Anabasis" (March of the Ten Thousand), wrote other genres of literature. Theopompus of Chios and Polybius were others.

Herodotus

16
ORIGINATORS OF
THE MAKE BELIEVE WORLD

In our times, professional entertainment comes to us in different ways. It comes through live stage shows that may be either dramatic or comedic; it comes through orchestral or choral performances that usually take place in concert halls; it comes in the form of opera which is a melodrama staged in opera houses; it comes through the motion pictures that are projected on the screen, through the radio, and finally, through television.

Where did all these originate, and how? Like so many other cultural aspects that are characteristic of our Western Civilization, professional entertainment originated in Greece. There, in the fifth century B.C., plays that were tragedies (serious plays) and comedies were staged for the first time in open theaters. Moreover, what is amazing is the fact that not many years after the first plays were staged, Greek playwrights were writing some of the finest plays ever written.

Ancient Greek drama did not originate spontaneously. It grew from the Dithyramb - collections of hymns originally written by notable poets celebrating different aspects of the life of god Dionysus- his birth, marriage, death, etc. Dithyrambs were composed in elevated style and were sung by choruses consisting of twelve, to twenty singers who sang to the music of a flute. The performances were held at the annual Festival of Dionysus, which, in Athens, was observed toward the end of March, and enjoyed great popularity.

Very early in the fifth century B.C., the poet Thespis, who composed dithyrambs, introduced an innovation. In order to rest his troop, which besides singing, also danced, he would come forward at intervals and would recite poetry that narrated different aspects of the life of the god Dionysus, such as his birth, marriage, death, rebirth, etc. Thus, by now, we have the chorus plus an actor. Years later, Aeschylus added a second actor whom he called "hypocrites" (answerer), who would answer to the playwright's spoken parts. Still later, Sophocles added a second hypocrite (answerer) and, by this addition, the drama had been finally developed. Henceforward, theatrical plays whether tragedies or comedies would consist of a chorus and two actors

Simultaneously, with the appearance of a full-grown tragedy and comedy, there also appeared the "Satyr plays". These were shorter plays, which included three actors and a chorus dressed as satyrs, and their theme was always a severe, caustic and critical condemnation of some notable person.

Ancient Greek plays were not staged daily or seasonally as in our times, but at intervals, and especially at the celebration of very important festivals. In Athens, where ancient drama developed to the highest form, some twenty plays written by five playwrights would be performed for five consecutive days. Initially, dozens and dozens of plays would be staged before a state commission of theater critics in a hall. The critics would select twenty plays that formed five "Tetralogies" written by five playwrights. Each playwright wrote one tetralogy, that is, three tragedies and one satyr play. He would then be assigned one of the five days to stage his tetralogy.

Performances would start early in the morning and would last until almost sundown. When all twenty plays had been performed, the priests of the god Dionysus, who was the patron god of drama, would select the winning playwright on the sixth day. Thus, from five playwrights whose tetralogies had been performed, only one would emerge as the victor.

In the presence of thousands of spectators, who, on the sixth day, would fill the theater, the winning playwright would be given an olive wreath to wear on his head. The wreath was sort of an "Oscar", and then he would lead his actors and his chorus to a dance. The producer, an affluent citizen who had contributed the cost of the chorus's training, costumes, etc. of the winning playwright, would also receive an "Oscar". His trophy consisted of an iron tripod on whose marble base his name was carved. The cost of the producer's monument was the responsibility of the state. Sometimes the producer's monuments were made of marble. One such marble monument has survived and still stands in a small square of the old "Plaka" district in Athens. It is known as the "Monument of Lysicrates".

Ancient Greek theaters were not free standing buildings, but were always settled on slopes of hills. They consisted of rows of stadium-like seats that curved a little more then halfway around the circular acting area, which was called the "orchestra." Beyond the circular orchestra and facing the audience, was the "Skene" (stage). Initially, it was used by the actors as a dressing room, but eventually its facade that looked over the stage began to resemble the facade of a public building. Although in the early years of the fifth century the stage was on the same level as the orchestra, in later years, the stage was elevated by a few feet. The orchestra was occupied by the chorus, consisting of twelve to fifteen men, while the stage was occupied by the actors. The stage was also equipped with a crane used to lower to the stage an actor who portrayed a god.

Actors were always male persons interpreting both male and female roles. They all wore masks appropriate to the character they were portraying. In tragedies, they wore high platform shoes in order to make them more visible to spectators who sat in the higher tiers of seats. The masks, which they wore, besides denoting their roles, also rendered another advantage to the actor or chorus member. The masks amplified the human voice and thus their words or songs could be heard quite clearly by spectators who sat far away.

Citizens of Athens, who could not pay the entrance fee in order to watch a performance, could obtain free tickets from the "Theoric Treasury"-

a treasury founded by Pericles. Thus, almost all Athenians, whether rich or poor, could attend the theater.

According to an article written by Basil Angelicopoulos which appeared in a Sunday supplement of the Greek newspaper "Daily", and which had been based on the findings of Paola Clancio Rossetto and Giusepina Pisani – researchers of ancient Greek and Roman theaters, referring to the number of Greek theaters, it is reported that the ancient Greeks built 190 theaters in Greece and in other countries in which they had either established colonial cities or in ones that had been conquered by Alexander the Great.

Specifically, there are 103 theaters in Greece, forty-six in Turkey, twenty-four in Italy, four in Albania, three in Libya, two each in the countries of Cyprus, Iraq and Ukraine, and one each in the countries of Egypt, Lebanon, Afghanistan, and Iran.

Of the 103 ancient theaters located in Greece, a number of them have, during the twentieth century, undergone partial restoration to prevent further collapse or deterioration. Three of them which received adequate restoration are used today for the staging of ancient Greek plays. They are: the theater of Epidaurus in southern mainland Greece, the theater of Dodona in the region of Epirus in northwestern Greece and the theater of Philippi in the region of Macedonia of northern Greece.

In addition to the 103 theaters that were built in Greece during the Classical and Hellenistic periods, the Romans built thirty more. Best known of the Roman theaters in Greece are those of "Herod Atticus", built on the southern slope of the Hill of the Acropolis, and the Roman theater of the City of Patra. Both of these have been restored and are frequently used for the staging of ancient Greek plays and musical concerts.

What is enduring, however, about ancient Greek theater - architecture is its amphitheatrical shape which in modern times has been copied countless times when modern outdoor amphitheaters have been built for cities, on campuses, or in other places.

Playwrights developed the plots of their tragedies from Greek myths that abounded in the books of Homer, Hesiod, and the other epic poets. Tragedies were always serious plays and were grouped in three works called "Trilogies". Thus, in order to see the whole drama, one would have to view all three tragedies. To the trilogy, a satyr play was appended that related to the theme of the trilogy, thus making it a "tetralogy".

Ordinarily, the main character was a god, a hero, a king, a queen, or some other notable person. But the main character was not a perfect person, but one who was usually confronted by a difficult moral choice. His struggle against adverse, inimical circumstances usually ended in giving in, and as a rule, to his or her death. Each tragedy consisted of a series of dramatic episodes that were recited by the three actors. The choral odes were sung by the chorus, whose members sang and danced to musical accompaniment.

Comedies were less serious plays and caused spectators to laugh. The structure of the comedy was much like that of the tragedy and its characters were common people living or deceased. Like the tragic playwrights, the comedic playwrights also presented their comedies in trilogies. No satyr play followed a comic trilogy.

The satyr play always followed the performance of a tragic trilogy. It was always a short, comic play based on a Greek myth and always had a relevance to the tragic trilogy that preceded it. Its chorus consisted of twelve to fifteen men and their apparel made them appear as half-men, half animals. They had the ears, tail, and legs of some animal, preferably a horse or a goat, and in their human aspects, they appeared, if young, as young men, if old, as bearded, bald persons with protruding bellies. On the stage, they danced and sang wildly, made all kinds of eroticisms, used foul language, and often appeared naive.

When at the beginning of the fifth century B.C., the drama evolved from the Dithyramb, and many playwrights began writing tragic or comedic trilogies and satyr plays. The following are those whose names and number of plays which they wrote and have survived. We must, however, bear in mind that the list that appears below, is not an exhaustive one. There have been many more playwrights who wrote dramatic works and whose names and works were unfortunately lost.

The oldest known Greek playwright was Thespis, who added an actor to the Dithyrambic chorus. As mentioned previously, with this innovative addition, the actor would recite the dramatic episodes while the chorus would sing the choral odes. Thus, to Thespis, we owe the formation of the primitive form of drama.

A younger contemporary of Thespis was Phrynichus, who won first prize in 511 B.C. We only know the titles of two of his plays - the "Fall of Miletus", in which he won his first prize, and the "Alcestis".

Contemporaries of Phrynicus included Choerilus, who wrote one hundred and sixty tragedies and satyr plays, and won thirteen first prizes, and, Pratinas, who wrote fifty tragedies and thirty-two satyr plays. Plato, not the philosopher, was another famous playwright of tragedies. Of the works of the above three playwrights, only very few fragments have survived.

Then there followed the now very famous Aeschylus, Sophocles, Euripides, and Aristophanes. Each of them will be treated separately in the later text.

Cratinus was a younger contemporary of Aristophanes. He wrote twenty-one comedies. In many of them he poked fun at Pericles. His comedy "Pytini" was selected winner over the "Clouds" of Aristophanes.

Eupolis wrote his first comedy when he was seventeen. He wrote seventeen comedies in all and won the first prize seven times. Only very few fragments of his works have survived. Epicharmus, born in the island of Cos, wrote thirty-five comedies. Unfortunately none have survived.

Other famous playwrights include the two sons of Aeschylus, Bion and Ephorion and the son of Aeschylus' sister, Philocles. Philocles won over Sophocles when the latter was staging his "Oedipus Rex". Philocles' most famous plays are those that comprise the tetralogy "Pandonis." Other tetralogies include: "Irigone," "Nafplios", "Oedipus", "Oeneas", "Priam", "Penelope", "Philoctetes" and many others. Timothy was another famous playwright who won over Sophocles. We only know the titles of two of his plays - "Alcmaeon" and "Alphesibia".

Other famous playwrights were Menander who wrote one hundred and eight comedies. We possess a very large number of fragments of five of his comedies thus were able to reconstruct them in almost their entirety. Astydamas wrote two hundred and forty tragedies, Iophon, the son of Sophocles wrote fifty tragedies; Ariston, the out-of-wedlock son of Sophocles, won many prizes. Euripides, the nephew of Euripides, wrote many plays and staged his uncle's plays. Alexis wrote two hundred and fifty comedies, Antiphanes wrote two hundred and fifty comedies. Critas, Sophron and Theognis were other noted authors.

Judging from the above number of playwrights and plays, we must admit that it is a rare phenomenon of history that a numerically small people were able, in little more than a century, to produce such a prolific output of plays.

FOUR GIANT PLAYWRIGHTS

Aeschylus

The first of the great Athenian playwrights was Aeschylus (524 - 436 B.C.). He was born to a noble family that lived in Eleusis, a town near Athens. In 490 B.C. and at the age of thirty-six, Aeschylus fought at the historic Battle of Marathon against the Persian invaders. Ten years later, when he was forty-six, he again fought against the Persians on their second invasion of Greece. This time he fought at the famous Sea Battle of Salamis. These two participations remained indelible in his mind. Moreover, being a genuine patriot, he always felt proud of the fact that the small army and fleet of his small city-state, Athens, was able to win against a numerically far superior foe - the Persian Empire.

At past thirty, Aeschylus turned playwright. He pursued that literary career during the remainder of his life, and, as present critics claim, the quality of his tragic plays could only be rivaled by William Shakespeare. During the forty-four years of his writing career, Aeschylus wrote ninety plays, or more than twenty tetralogies. In 484 B.C., he won his first prize. In fact, he won first prize thirteen times.

Unfortunately, of the ninety plays that he wrote only few survive. They are: "The Suppliants", "The Persians", "The Seven Against Thebes", "Prometheus Bound", and his famous trilogy - the "Oresteia", consisting of the "Agamemnon", "The Libation Bearers", and the "Eumenides" (The Furies). The Oresteia is the only trilogy that has survived. All the other trilogies written by Aeschylus and the other dramatists have been lost.

Aeschylus was a highly imaginative and a very religious person. In one of his earliest plays, the "Persians", we see not only his imaginative mind but his novel way of presenting his plot.

The "Persians" is the only historical play that has survived. It was produced in 472 B.C., and its plot deals with the naval victory of the Athenian Fleet over the Persians in 480 B.C., that is, eight years earlier. Today, if a playwright would write a play of such subject matter, he would extol the bravery of the Greek crews and marines, as well as the clever strategy of Themistocles, the supreme commander of the Greek fleet. As for the Persian defeat, that would be described in gloated verse. But he chose not to do that, and here is Aeschylus' most unexpected approach.

The story unfolds and ends not in Greece but in far away Persia. The action takes place first in Susa, capital of the Persian Empire, and then at the tomb of King Darius away from the palace. The Queen-mother Atossa, wife of the deceased King Darius is surrounded by Persian nobles who have assembled in the palace anxiously awaiting news of King Xerxes' military and naval expedition to Greece. The delay of hearing news causes them to suspect that something terrible must have happened. The chorus of elders is also worrying. They too suspect that another defeat, like the one that had happened at Marathon ten years earlier, has happened again.

As the play progresses, a messenger arrives announcing the total military and naval defeat of the Persian army and navy. Hearing of such catastrophic news, all bemoan the terrible loss of their great army and navy. In another scene, the Queen Mother is shown by the tomb of King Darius, and there, the ghost of the great king appears to reveal to her that what happened to their son, King Xerxes, was a punishment imposed by the gods for his excessive arrogance. In the remainder of the play, Xerxes appears weeping over his unbelievable defeat. When he asks about his generals who had taken part in the expedition, he learns that they were all killed. The play ends showing all departing to return to the palace in utmost desperation.

In this play, Aeschylus portrays Xerxes as the symbol of a man who, being drunk with power, leads his subjects to destruction. When prudence ceased to guide his decisions and actions, and in its place an immense and excessive self-confidence, self-reliance and arrogance took over, his mind was unable to recognize reality. This led him and those who followed him to destruction.

"Prometheus Bound", is another great tragedy. It is one of the three plays that make up the "Prometheia". The two other plays were lost. Briefly, the plot deals with Prometheus' punishment for defying Zeus by stealing fire from heaven out of friendship for humankind. He is bound on a crag of Mt. Caucasus where a vulture comes every day to eat from his liver, which regenerates during the night. In the end, Zeus and Prometheus reconcile and the latter is set free.

Over the centuries, this play has exerted more influence than any other of Aeschylus. The Romantic Age adopted this play as a symbol of heroic revolt against tyranny. Shelley's masterful poem, "Prometheus Unbound", written in 1820, represents the culmination of the Romantic Movement against tyranny.

In the opinion of most current critics, the "Oresteia" is Aeschylus' masterpiece, a trilogy that might well claim preeminence in the world's dramatic literature. It won a first prize when first performed in 458 B.C. Very briefly its plot is as follows.

King Agamemnon, commander of the Greek forces in the Trojan War, returns triumphantly to Argos, only to be murdered with his concubine - the Trojan prophetess Cassandra. The murderers are Agamemnon's wife, Clytemnestra, and her lover Aegisthus. After the perpetration of their crime, they take over the throne.

The second play shows how, twenty years later, the perpetrators are slain by Clytemnestra's son, Orestes, urged on by his sister, Electra. As the drama unfolds, Orestes'reluctance to commit the deed is contrasted with Clytemnestra's earlier eagerness for Agamemnon's sacrifice of their daughter, Iphigenia. Orestes' mental suffering after the murder is contrasted with Clytemnestra's gloating joy. At the end of this play, Orestes flees in madness, pursued by the Erinyes (Furies), which symbolize the spirits of retribution.

The third play shows how Orestes goes to Athens at the bidding of the Delphic Oracle to stand trial for matricide, with the god Apollo as his defender and the Erinyes as his accusers. He is acquitted by the vote of Athena, who then appeases the Erynies, converting them into "Eumenides" (kindly ones), by welcoming them to Athens and assuring them that their function of retributive justice is to be the state's foundation.

In expressing his criticism on the Oresteia, Richmond Hathorn author of "Tragedy, Myth and Mystery" wrote: "The 'Oresteia' is generally acknowledged to be the most impressive monument in all dramatic literature for its scope and complexity, for the careful elaboration of its symbolic myth, for its reinforcement by an unusually rich system of imagery, and for its weighty ethical and theological themes. It broaches, for the first time in the history of human thought, such themes as the meaning of suffering 'Man learns by suffering,' the necessity of a unified conception of god Zeus, whoever you are - by that name I shall call you - for you are all I have to call upon,' and the mystery of justice involving as it does the penetration of human reality by the divine."

Since the remote time of Aeschylus, many playwrights around the world sought to rewrite this supreme drama in their own words and stage it in period dress. Three recent ones would include Germany's Gerhart Hauptmann, who is expressing his despair over the Second World War in his epic "Die Atriden-Tetralogie" (The Atrides' Tetralogy), using the Oresteia as a foundation; America's Eugene O'Neal in whose trilogy "Mourning Becomes Electra", the ancient Oresteia reappears under a different guise in Puritan New England; and, T.S. Eliot, who in his masterful work "Murder in the Cathedral," Oresteia's chorus echoes again.

Aeschylus, whose mind thought deeply into the mysteries of passions and suffering, ever-present in human life, noticed that his native language lacked the kind of words he needed to accurately express his feelings and emotions. He solved the problem by coining one hundred Greek words, thus contributing to the enrichment of the Greek Language.

He died at Gela, a Greek colony in Sicily, where he had lived for two years prior to his death. In 470, at the request of King Hieron, King of the Greek colony of Syracuse, Sicily, he wrote and staged his last play, "Aetnea" in honor of Aetna, a new city founded by Hieron.

Prior to his death, Aeschylus wrote his own epitaph. Astonishingly, he does not want to be remembered as a great dramatist but as a Marathon fighter. The epitaph read:

"This tomb the dust of Aeschylus does hide
Euphorion's son and fruitful Gela's pride;
How famed his valor Marathon may tell,
And long-bearded Medes, who knew it all too well."

Sophocles

Sophocles (496- 406 B.C.), the son of Sophilos, was born in Colonus, a suburb of ancient Athens. Since his father was a rich armourer, he secured for his son the best education available at that time. Sophocles was born in 496 B.C., and was too young to witness the war between his people and the Persians at Marathon (490 B.C.), and was still an adolescent preventing participation in the Sea Battle of Salamis in 480 B.C. When the victory of Salamis was announced, he led the victory dance of the young men.

As a grown man, Sophocles enjoyed many blessings. He was rich, pious, handsome, good tempered, pleasure loving and witty. He was living a happy and serene life. It is amazing that a man such as he, who during his life had never known adversity, was able to write "Oedipus", a play in which his protagonist by that name met with the most horrible sufferings imaginable.

Sophocles loved Athens. He was a true patriot, and, besides writing plays, sought to serve his city in very high functions and positions. Needless to say, that in all the positions he served, he served worthily, earning the friendship of many political leaders such as Pericles, Cimon, Nicias, and other prominent citizens. He married Nicostrate, and, of the marriage, four children were born. One of them, Iophon, wrote many plays, and a grandson of his, after the death of his grandfather, staged his tragedy, "Oedipus the King", was preceded in death by Euripides, a younger colleague. To honor him, Sophocles introduced, in the theater, his chorus in mourning apparel and without garlands.

Following his death, he was buried in a family tomb located at Dekeleia, a place eleven miles distant from Athens. The citizenry of Athens, the city he so loved, decided to erect a statue of him in the Theater of Dionysus, an act that was the greatest honor for a playwright. Centuries later, Emperor Nero ordered that the statue be carried to Rome. Today, it is in the Vatican Museum along with hundreds of other Greek sculptural masterpieces.

During his long life, a life over ninety years, Sophocles wrote one hundred and twenty-three plays. He won eighteen first prizes, a very high score, and never did he get a third prize. He won his first prize in 468 B.C. when he was twenty-eight years old, introducing the tetralogy "Triptolemus", a patriotic play about a local Athenian hero. His antagonist was Aeschylus. Sophocles also founded a school of drama, which he named, "Troup of Muses".

The heroes of his plays are presented as neither "supermen" as in Aeschylus plays, nor as wicked men and women full of passions and weaknesses as in Euripides' plays. His poetry, likewise, was neither grandiloquent like that of Aeschylus, nor prosaic, like that of his younger Euripides. He always presented his heroes as ideal characters without extravagance. Even though they are presented as making mistakes, there is still something noble about them. They invariably show dutifulness and inflexible decisiveness. They all seem to possess an attachment to a personal destiny.

Sophocles did not draw his themes entirely from mythology, as did Aeschylus. He raised the number of the chorus' members from the twelve to fifteen, added a third actor on the stage, was the first to add scenery on the stage, and a crane to lower and lift the god who would descend to the stage to solve a complicated plot.

Of the hundred and twenty-three plays that he wrote, most unfortunately, only few survive as well as fragments from a satiric play. The titles of the surviving plays are: "Ajax", "Antigone", "Oedipus King", "Electra", "Philoctetes", and "Oedipus on Colonus". Also, some four hundred verses survived from his satiric play, "Ichnutiae", ninety verses from the tragedy, "Euryplyos", and twenty-five verses from his tragedy, "Society of Achaeans".

Of all the plays of Sophocles, his "Oedipus the King" and his "Antigone" are the best.

"Oedipus the King" is a play based on the sufferings of King Oedipus, the King of Thebes and descendant of Cadmus, the founder of the royal line. The royal house of Cadmus is doomed to misfortune because it has offended the gods. Oedipus, heir to the power and the woes of this stock, is driven unwittingly to committing two dreadful sins. He murders his father and marries his mother, thus fulfilling the prophecy. He suffers unspeakable agony of mind when he learns what he has done, and his children inherit the curse. His mother–wife hangs herself upon hearing that Oedipus was her son, and Oedipus blinds himself. His two sons, Eteocles and Polyneikes kill each other in civil war, and his daughter Antigone is buried alive. The whole family is ruined. Thus, the point that Sophocles is trying to make is that even a good man cannot escape the laws of fate.

In another drama entitled "Oedipus on Colonus", Oedipus dies calmly and with dignity. He is assured that all is well, for he has neither willed nor desired the terrible things he has done. Through all of this, he has been a helpless fool of fate.

"Antigone" is his other masterpiece. Very briefly the theme is as follows: King Creon, who now rules Thebes, having succeeded Oedipus, has decreed that no one is allowed to bury Polyneikes, the son of Oedipus and brother of Antigone who rightfully aspired to take the throne from his brother, Eteocles. Polyneikes must remain unburied to be eaten by vultures and scavenging animals. Antigone, abhorring such a royal decree, asked her sister, Ismene, to help her bury her brother. Ismene, afraid of the severe consequences, refuses to collaborate. Antigone, believing that the laws of God are above those of men, buries her brother. Creon orders that she be buried alive. Haemon, who is her lover and son of King Creon, tries to intercede for her. He then forces his way into the tomb, finds her dead, and slays himself.

J. B. Bury, a notable British scholar of ancient Greek civilization, reflecting on Antigone's decisiveness to bury her brother, wrote the following comments in his classic, "History of Greece". "In his 'Antigone', Sophocles took as the motive to the deep and difficult question of political and ethical science- the relation of the individual citizen to the state. What shall a man do if his duty of obedience to the government of his country conflicts with other duties? Are there any obligations higher than the loyalty to the laws of his country? Sophocles answers that there are such - for instance, certain obligations of religion. He justifies Antigone in her disobedience to the king's decree. The motive lends itself to dramatic treatment, and never has it been handled with such consummate care as by him who first saw its possibilities. But it is worth observing that the Antigone, besides its importance in the history of dramatic poetry has a high significance in the development of European thought, as the first presentation of a problem which both touches the very roots of ethical theory and is, in daily practice, constantly clamoring for solution."

Such was Sophocles, one of the greatest playwrights of all time, a gentleman, a deep thinker, a man who through his plays, sought to teach his spectators that harmony in life is indispensable - harmony with the gods, with the state, and with fellow men.

Euripides

People who watched his plays at the theater called him the "philosopher of the stage", and after the performance, on going home, delighted in singing the lyrics of his plays, Aristotle called him, "The most tragic of all playwrights". Socrates never missed the premier performances of his plays, and for six hundred years after his death, his plays were of the most performed. William Shakespeare held him in very high esteem and emulated the ancient master's philosophical style. Milton profoundly admired him, and Goethe asked, "Whether all the nations of the world since his time have produced one playwright worthy to hand him his slippers."

And yet, this ancient playwright, whose plays are still performed today, despite the high praise he received posthumously, of twenty-two competitions that he entered during his lifetime, won only four first prizes? Why such an injustice?

Euripides, although a younger contemporary of Aeschylus and Sophocles, never showed any eagerness to follow the established, idealized patterns his predecessors had to the gods, the heroes and the other characters of their plays. Being a very close friend of Socrates, Protagoras, and Prodicus, who as sophists questioned many theological, moral, social, political concepts and taboos of their times, he too did the same. He too saw, and began to present, on the stage, gods and heroes no longer as ideal persons but sharing the same passions, weaknesses and moral flaws of ordinary people.

Euripides was a deep psychologist, and as such, imbued his plays with accurate psychological analyses of the problems that plagued mankind. His plays are full of discussions of deep moral issues, asking what good conduct is, and what the good life is. As a contemporary critic rightly observes, "They are full of paradoxes calculated to arouse skepticism about moral standards and they seek to inspire the audience with broader and more humane sentiments. He makes the Homeric heroes appear not as idealistic heroes but as brutal murderers while the only admirable persons in the plays are the villagers of the chorus who, with consternation and horror, watch the terrible deeds of their 'betters'." Such kinds of plots naturally often shocked the Athenian audience. But that's what happens when the playwright is a rationalist and a daring critic of all established institutions and beliefs.

Euripides (485-406 B.C.), the son of Mnesarchus, a well-to-do farmer and of Clito, was born in the town of Phyla in central Attica. Upon deciding to become a playwright, he moved to the nearby Island of Salamis, and, instead of settling in a house, he selected a cave overlooking the sparkling blue sea, and there he lived and wrote his plays. In the cave, he also had his books, comprising one of the largest private libraries ever owned in antiquity. We must not, however, think that Euripides spent his entire life in the cave. As the Island of Salamis was only a "stone's throw" away from Athens, he would very frequently go to Athens to spend much time with his close friends – Socrates, Pericles, and the sophists, Protagoras, Anaxagoras and others. Euripides was not a recluse.

He wrote ninety-two plays, that is, twenty-three tetralogies. Unfortunately, only eighteen survive, plus hundreds of fragments of his lost plays. The fact that the number of his surviving plays is three times that of each of his two predecessors is no doubt an indication of the popularity Euripides enjoyed posthumously.

His surviving plays are, "Cyclops" (a satyr play), "Alcestis", "Medea", "The Children of Heracles", "The Trojan Women", "Electra", "Helen", "Iphigenia Among the Taurians", "Ion", "The Phoenician Women", "Orestes", "The Bacchae", "Iphigenia in Aulis", "Hecuba", "The Suppliants", "Hippolytus", "Andromache", and "Heracles". We may glimpse at some of his ideals in the very brief analysis of two of his plays that follow.

In 415 B.C., Euripides staged his "Trojan Women," which was an extraordinary tragedy. Its theme is the capture of Troy by the Greek Armies and the cruel fate that befell the women of the defeated city. As the play begins, we see the captured women coming out of their huts, while a Greek herald announces to them how they will be distributed among the conquering leaders. Cassandra, the daughter of King Priam, and the priestess of the palace, is to become a slave and the mistress of Agamemnon. The news shatters her mother, who is Queen Hecuba. But, Cassandra is not that devastated. Being a seer, she foresees in a vision, that in the near future, both she and Agamemnon would be dead. Another character that stands out in this opening scene is Andromache, who has been assigned as a slave in Neoptolemus. She appears planning on how to win the favor of her captors to allow her child, Astyanax, to return to Troy and rebuild it. But when the herald returns, he announces to her that the Greek leaders have decreed that the child must die. Critics agree that this particular incident is the most harrowing in all Greek tragedy.

Another scene shows Menelaus longing to kill Helen but dares not. Moreover, the playwright shows Menelaus as miserable as the captive women, and astonishingly, more contemptible. In the next scene, the dead body of the child is brought to the stage bedecked with flowers to be buried by his grandmother, Hecuba.

In the following scenes, Hecuba is presented as crying to the gods, who do not care at all, then to the dead, who although they love and care, they cannot help, and then, in utmost desperation as she looks at her beloved city still burning, she contemplates to hurl herself into the flames. Somehow, she is held back. At this time, a tower collapses, and a trumpet sounds calling the women to go to the ships. Brooding, they go off to slavery.

This masterful play is an indictment against slavery. Euripides abhors the decision of his victorious countrymen to make slaves of conquered women. He even presents goddess Athena, who, during the war was on the side of the Greeks, now turns away from them in disgust. Rarely, in another play, do we see the horrors of war, the fatuousness of military glory, and the inhumane hideousness of slavery pictured more powerfully. Euripides depicted these with supreme mastery.

"Medea", another masterpiece of his, is the grim story of a revengeful woman. Very briefly, this is its plot: Jason, leader of the Argonauts, having gone to Colchis, a coastal town on the Black Sea in order to obtain the Golden Fleece, now returns with it, bringing also with him the Colchian princess, Medea. The two settle in Corinth and for many years live happily. Then, Creon, King of Corinth, who has no son to succeed him to the throne, suggests to his daughter, Glauce, that she marry Jason. Jason welcomes the unexpected offer and tries to convince Medea that marrying the princess would mean a more secure and happy life for her, their children and for himself.

But Medea will not accept any of this. Enraged by his desertion of her, she decided to seek revenge. First, she succeeds in killing Jason's future bride by sending her a robe steeped in burning poison, and which, when the innocent bride put it on, died in agony together with her father who tried to save her. Then Medea, overcoming a long struggle over her maternal love, and finding her passion overcoming her reason, dares commit the most abhorrent crime, the killing of two children.

In the last scene, Medea appears high on a winged chariot which her grandfather, the sun god, has provided, gloating over the horror and misery she had wreaked on Jason, while the latter burns in anger, not being able to punish her for her crimes.

In discussing this legend, early Greek thinkers could not see any worthy moral point in this story. But, Euripides, using clever textual exponation, makes Medea a heroine, and Jason a contemptible cad. Euripides sees Medea as a woman who, even though a barbarian, nevertheless, is a human with feelings, character and rights, qualities which Jason ought to recognize and fully respect. As we can see, for Euripides, a woman is not inferior to man. Actually, he has as much sympathy and respect for any female human being as he has for a male one. For Euripides, any woman, Greek as well as non-Greek, has an innate dignity, hence he raises her to the same high level as that of the man.

In 408 B.C., at the invitation of King Archelaus of Macedonia, Euripides left Athens and went to Pella to live at the king's palace as his guest during the remainder of his life. He left his three sons in Athens. One of whom undertook to stage the plays of his father.

As mentioned earlier, hundreds of fragments belonging to lost plays have been recovered. As some of them are quite extensive, they give us the opportunity to fairly reconstruct the plots of the lost plays. Others, however, are few and short, and cannot help us in this effort.

Assessing Euripides' contribution to the evolution of Greek drama, J.B. Bury, in his "History of Greece", wrote, "He does not acquiesce, like the older playwrights in the ways of the gods with men; he is not content to be a resigned pessimist. He will receive nothing on authority; he declines to bow to the orthodox opinions of his respectable fellow countrymen, on such matters as the institution of slavery, or the position of women in society. He refuses to endorse the inveterate prejudice, which prevailed even at Athens in favor of noble birth. But perhaps nothing is as significant as his attitude to the contempt, which the Greeks universally felt for other races than their own. Nowhere is Euripides more sarcastic than when, in his 'Medea,' he makes Jason pose as a benefactor of the woman whom he has basely betrayed, on the ground that he has brought her out of an obscure barbarian home, and enabled her to enjoy the privilege of living in Greece."

During past centuries, playwrights tried to imitate Euripides in the plots of their period adaptations. To mention a few, there were France's Corneille and Racine. In fact, Racine had read Euripides' dramas in the ancient Greek Language and among other plays, which he modeled after the ancient master in his famous "Sarah Bernhardt." Germany's Goethe, who wrote his "Iphigenie;" Hugo Von Hoffmanstahl's "Elektra," later made into opera with music, by Richard Strauss, Heiner Muller's "Philoktetes" and "Medea" and in America, T.S. Eliot's "Alcestis" and Tony Harrison's adaptations of "Medea", and the "Trojan Women" are some.

As we can see, Euripides, although an ancient playwright, his ever-timely plays included contemporary concepts and issues that can rightly be called "modern."

Aristophanes

Aristophanes, the son of Philippus and Zenodora, was born in Athens in 445 B.C. His parents belonged to the landed aristocracy, a class with which Aristophanes always identified.

From adolescence, he showed great interest in the theater, especially in writing comedies. In this field, he later excelled by making himself the greatest comic dramatist of ancient times and one of the greatest comic playwrights of all time.

In all his comedies, he burlesques mythological concepts and caricatures everyday life. He also uses obscene abuse against contemporary politicians and other prominent citizens of Athenian society. His comedies are saturated with coarse invective, conservative prejudice, a kind of animosity toward urban society, irresponsible lampoonery and frequent buffoonery. He uses sharp satire to attack current trends in education, music, philosophy, literature, science, politics, and, of course, the personalities behind these innovations. And since he finds wrong in people of nearly all walks of life, it naturally follows that one must not look to the present to find ideal characters but must look to the past.

Edith Hamilton, a twentieth century scholar of Greek history and culture, in her book entitled, "The Greek Way", thus sums up Aristophane's work, "In the comedies, all the life of Athens is there: the politics of the day and the politicians; the war party and the anti-war party; pacifism; votes for women, free trade, fiscal reform, complaining taxpayers, educational theories, the current religious and literary talk - everything, in short, that interested the average citizen. All was food for his mockery. He was the speaking picture of the follies and foibles of his day."

He wrote fifty-five comedies. Unfortunately, only eleven are extant. Of others, we have only fragments. A very brief analysis of his extant comedies will give us some idea of those he attacked.

His comedy, the "Acharneans", deals with the fancy of a militant pacifist who carries out a private peace for himself with the Spartans who presently are at war with the Athenians. He does not take into account that the Athenian State, of which he was a citizen, was still at war. In reality, the comedy expresses the playwright's aversion toward the "Peloponnesian War", already ten years in progress.

His comedy, "The Knights", is directed against Cleon, a radical demagogue who is supposedly supplanted by Agoracritus, a sausage peddler, and who is more vile and ignorant than Cleon himself.

In his comedy, "The Clouds", the playwright unleashes a gross invective against the philosopher Socrates whom he grossly caricatures. In the play, old Strespsiades, who is deeply in debt, hears that he seeks out the philosopher in his "Thought Factory", where he finds him suspended high in a basket so as to escape all earthly influences and devote himself to heavenly matters. After much foolery, Socrates is found to be a corrupter of youth and his school is burned down.

In his "Wasps", the playwright satirizes the juries, which, influenced by the lawyers' persuasive oratory, or from Cleon's insistence, convict whomever they accuse.

By his comedy, "The Birds", Aristophanes tried to discourage the disastrous Athenian expedition to Sicily. The birds, who actually are the Athenians, are persuaded by a certain Peithetaerus to construct a utopian celestial city, the Cloudcuckootown. In time, Peithetaerus is even able to force the gods to cede to him all their prerogatives. The city in the air is taken as an escape motif from contemporary Athens, but the irony of it is, that the city becomes a second Athens and achieves not merely imperial but universal supremacy. The "Birds", is one of the funniest plays of Aristophanes. Behind that veneer of fun, however, one can discern Aristphane's feeling of the decay that was coming upon Athens.

"Lysistrata" (Demobilizer), is another attack against war. He presents the women of Greece plotting to bring peace by denying their husbands sexual relations during the war's duration. In the end, a peace is arranged between Athens and Sparta. The men regain their wives while a double chorus of Athenians and Spartans sing hymns to peace.

The "Thesmophoriagusae", is a licentious portrayal of women celebrating Demeter's (Ceres') festival. It ends with a satire against Euripides for exhibiting misogyny (woman hating) in his tragedies.

In "The Frogs", he shows the god Dionysus descending to Hades (underworld), to search for a tragic playwright since those on earth are worthless. A contest is declared between Euripides and the winner Aeschylus, who is brought temporarily to earth. As for Euripides, he is summarily dismissed.

In "Ecclesiazusae", we have a satire on communistic theories. The women of Athens take over the "Ecclesia" (popular assembly), and declare all property to be in common and to be distributed according to need. Actually this comedy, is parodying Plato's political theories in his book, "The Republic".

In his last extant play, entitled, "Plutus" (Greek for wealth), he tells how Plutus, the blind god of wealth, regains sight with the help of Aesculapius, god of medicine, and how Plutus, after his recovery, visits only honest men, a situation saturated by comic episodes.

From the extant plays, it becomes apparent that Aristophanes was a highly intelligent man and one who knew the Athens of his time very well. What is ironic, however, is the fact that his mocking was considered a compliment, and if the mockery came in a friendly spirit, the compliment was high indeed.

His comedies are still performed today for their themes are as timely today as they were twenty-five centuries ago. Moreover, comic playwrights of all times stage his plays in period style.

17
THE STRUGGLE FOR ATTAINING IDEAL BEAUTY

Since that very remote time when mankind first appeared on earth, people of all races and countries have nourished the arts. Cave men painted crude drawings in the caves where they lived; primitive societies all have left us painted or sculptured specimens, as have done ancient medieval and more recent cultures and civilizations. We may safely conclude that art has gone hand-in-hand with man's march in time.

Nineteenth century French poet and art connoisseur Theofile Gautier wrote: "All passes. Art alone enduring stays to us." How right he was. No matter which country we visit, its past, now and then, be it in the form of some architectural ruin, or in the form of artifacts and paintings orderly and chronologically arranged in its museums, will appear before our eyes.

Until the end of the eighteenth century, the word art had a very broad meaning. It included all branches of academic learning, what we call "industrial arts", "mechanical arts" and, of course, what we call "fine arts". As of the nineteenth century, however, whenever people use the word art, they mostly mean architecture, painting, sculpture and music. In this chapter, we will not be concerned with music since it belongs to the performing arts, but with architecture, painting and sculpture - three arts which the ancient Greeks elevated to the highest and noblest aesthetic levels.

Ancient Greek Architecture

Architecture, which is the art of building, goes back before the appearance of Greek civilization. The colossal pyramids and other monuments of the ancient Egyptians, the grandiose palaces and temples of such Middle-Eastern countries such as Sumeria, Assyria, Babylonia, Persia, Palestine, Phoenecia, and the Hittite Empire, all preceded the architectural undertakings of the ancient Greeks. So, what is peculiar to Greek architecture that made subsequent human generations esteem it, admire it, and copy it more than any other architecture of antiquity?

It was its beauty - a beauty that was due to ideal relationships between the height, width and length of the building, plus linear almost imperceptible refinements of its columns, foundations and superstructure as well as ideal arrangement of its sculptural adornment.

Ancient Greek architecture is divided into three stages, namely Minoan and Mycenaean, Classical, and Hellenistic.

Minoan and Mycenaean

In both Minoan and Mycenaean architecture, the houses of the people were like cubes, and some of them had two or even three floors. They also had windows on their walls. Some had a courtyard adjacent to the house.

In both the Minoan and Mycenaean architecture, it was the king's palace that was the largest and most beautiful building. It had many large and beautifully decorated rooms on three floors. There were many staircases leading from outside to the entrances, and many staircases from one floor to another. Another feature of these palaces was the many columns which supported the eaves of the porches, or the eaves of the inside and outside staircases. The columns were of wood and they were always painted red. The columns were always narrower at the base and wider at the top. Actually, they were a section from the trunks of trees that had been cut off from the stump, freed from its branches, the surface made smooth, painted red and then set upside down to support the roof of the porches or the roofs of the staircases. Their red color always stood in sharp contrast to the walls that were painted a cream color.

Minoan and Mycenaean cities, whether large or small, had no temples for the gods and goddesses. The only temple of the city was always contained within the palace. It was a large hall with a statue of a god or a goddess in it. The king was also the archpriest of all the people. It was he who officiated in all the religious ceremonies. Minoan architecture always provided spaces for pipes that brought water into the palace and for sewers for drainage.

Classical Architecture

Greek classical architecture began to appear by the seventh century B.C. in Greece, Asia Minor, Southern Italy, North Africa, in all the towns and cities which the Greek colonists had founded.

From the eighth century to the sixth century B.C., the institution of royalty began to disappear in the ancient Greek world, and be replaced by leaders, who, like kings, would govern with the help of a few advisors. Along with the kings, naturally, the palaces began to disappear, as the leaders who replaced the kings were content to live in their own homes. But while palaces disappeared, the temples which, during the Minoan and Mycenaean times were part of the palaces, did not disappear. They became individual structures. Moreover, up to now there was only one temple in a given city.

It was during this period that classical Greek architecture developed the three well-known styles of columns for its buildings - the "Doric", the "Ionic" and the "Corinthian". While we do not know the names of the architects who developed the Doric and the Ionic columns, we know the name of the one who designed the Corinthian. It was Callimachus, an architect from Corinth. One day, as he was visiting his mother's grave at the cemetery, he noticed an overturned basket lying on the ground nearby. Around it, thorn leaves had grown profusely. This sight so appealed to him, that he sketched it, and decided to introduce it as a third designs of a column's capital. In fact, what he did was to take the trunk of an Ionic column and top it off with his new "Corinthian Capital", and so, the third style of Greek column came to be the "Corinthian Column". Soon the Corinthian column became popular, and centuries later, it was adopted by the Romans who used it far more than the Doric or the Ionic.

The Doric column appears sturdier as it is wider than the other two, and its capital is made up of a round marble piece topped by a square one. The Ionic is a very slender column and its capital resembles two volutes. All three columns have fluting running from the top to the base, and these flutings, when struck by sunlight, created an appearance of alternating light and shade. That makes the columns look sturdier, more solid and more graceful.

The houses in classical times were not large. They were mostly small, occasionally with two floors, and their rooms were around a central courtyard. There were very few windows on the exterior walls. Most of the windows opened to the central courtyard.

It was the temples and public buildings, such as the theaters, courts, archives, and council houses, which were large and beautiful. They were built of white marble, with colonnades and other sculptural and decorative embellishments. It was the temples, however, that were the most beautiful buildings, as architects and sculptors sought to decorate their exterior by adding statues on the pediments, and friezes inside or outside the upper part of their walls. Statues, friezes and some of the ornaments of the upper part, above the columns of the temple, were painted with red, blue, or yellow colors, and the contrast of these colors, with the blue sky above and the white columns and walls from below, produced a most beautiful contrast to the eye.

Since that time, the beautiful temples and public buildings of the classical Greek architecture have been imitated throughout the world. We see Greek architecture dominating the style of most state capitals and public buildings in state capitals and cities of the United States, as we see it dominating the most beautiful monument and government buildings of our nation's capital.

Hellenistic Architecture

While the temples and administration buildings of classical times were rather small, in the centuries that followed the conquests of Alexander the Great, both temples and administrative buildings became large. Temples were now almost three hundred feet long and one hundred and fifty feet wide, and some of them would have as many as one hundred columns, each sixty to seventy feet high, to support the roof. Examples would be the temple of Zeus in Athens, of Hera on the Greek Island of Samos, of Diana at

Ephesus, Asia Minor that was regarded as one of the seven wonders of the ancient world, of Apollo at Didyma, Asia Minor, and of Serapis in Egypt and others. When Rome became the mistress of nearly all Mediterranean countries in building new temples and public buildings in all these lands, she copied the Hellenistic style's design and large size.

Ancient Greek Sculpture

When in 1508, Pope Julius asked the most famous Renaissance sculptor Michelangelo, to paint the ceiling of the Sistine Chapel at the Vatican, the latter answered: "But Your Holiness, I am a sculptor." By this answering to the Pope, he was expressing his dissatisfaction for being asked to paint and not to sculpt. As sculpting is a much higher art than painting, requiring far more care, exactness and skill of execution, Michelangelo felt demoted.

Today, most sculpture critics agree that this top Renaissance sculptor was perhaps the only one whose superb sculptures could match those executed by the ancient Greeks.

The making of statues extends far back in time. Egyptian, Assyrian and other Middle Eastern statues go back to the twenty-fifth century B.C. But all these statues are not beautiful. They all look stiff, their faces always look frontward, their hands are mostly united to their bodies, and their feet almost always appear united.

But with the coming of the ancient Greeks, we see an unprecedented change, as well as progress into all the aspects of this so difficult and exacting art. The love of beauty that the ancient Greeks sought to achieve in every intellectual and artistic activity spurred them to such persistent efforts, that in the end, their goal to be able to make human statues, replicating any bodily position and being ideally beautiful, was achieved. It was a triumph that human generations have been admiring to this day. Greek sculpture has remained unexcelled.

When the ancient Greeks began to make statues, they made them of wood and their appearance was like those made by the ancient Middle Eastern people. In later centuries, they began to make statues in bronze and of marble, and from the classical period on marble was mostly used.

With the passing of the centuries, Greek sculptors, by learning to shift the axes of the hips, of the shoulders and the angles of the head, were able to eliminate the "archaic rigidity" of the original statues. Moreover, by adding light drapery with folds and head coiffure on their female statues, was another significant step toward naturalism.

More naturalistic changes were achieved during Classical Times (480-323 B.C.). Statues can appear in pacing position, arms can appear taut or bent, the face can be made to look dignified, and, if pain had to be expressed, that also could be effected by a furrowing of the forehead and a slight parting of the lips. In statues depicting women, the drapery also underwent changes. Instead of running in vertical, parallel, heavy folds from shoulders to ankles, it would break by the thrusting forward of the relaxed thigh. Many sculptors, who wished to reveal parts of the body beneath the drapery, would make the latter to appear thin - a process requiring great skill. Also, during this period, the hair was made to appear in simple strands of short flat curls.

Famous sculptors who appeared during the Classical Times were Phidias, who, with Alcamenes and Agoracritos, carved the sculptures that adorned the pediments of the Parthenon Temple on the Acropolis as well as its frieze. Another famous sculptor was Polyclitus of Argos. Besides making beautiful statues, he wrote "Canon" pointing out the proper proportions of the members of the ideal human body. Thus, according to his canon, in the ideal human body, the head must be one-eighth of its total height, the torso three-eighths, and the legs, four-eighths. Many sculptors followed his canon, and the statues they made were true masterpieces.

Friezes (figures in relief) became very common in classical times. They were used for the embellishment of temple walls, of parapets on which temples were built, and on statue pedestals. The human and animal figures that were carved on the panels projected only two inches outwards. The flat background was usually painted blue or red. The themes of these friezes were either religious processions or battles. Human figures, particularly those depicting battle scenes, would be presented crossing their legs, or weapons, and their bodies would show such contortions and stances that the frieze would appear as a harmonious whole. Friezes also adorned the gravestones set over the graves of cemeteries. Deceased persons would appear with eyes looking down, or wandering, while still live persons in normal positions.

Statues and friezes made during the Classical Times show the gods and goddesses with faces serene and completely devoid of the troubles that plague mankind. They appear as though they are aloof of the world below them- a world for which they hardly care.

During the Hellenistic Times, that began in the late fourth century B.C. and continued on to Roman Times, Greek sculptors achieved what Greek sculpture had not achieved thus far.

During this creative period, sculptors, after studying human anatomy, were able to replicate it in their statues, plus being able to replicate any human emotion. Thus, Hellenistic statues all exhibit in a masterful way and in detail all the contortions of the human musculature as they appear in a relaxed, tense, pacing, violent, fighting condition, or in some athletic engagement. They also studied closely every contortion of the musculature of the human face. This, in turn, enabled them to depict in marble all kinds of emotions and psychological attitudes expressed by the face such as laughing, crying, anger, pain, spite, joy, sorrow, resignation, drunkenness, youth, or old age.

Hellenistic sculptors also introduced "two firsts" in Greek sculpture. They were the first sculptors to make statues of children, depicting them in all their everyday typical attitudes. To this day, their creations remain unexcelled masterpieces. The other first they introduced was that of female statues personifying cities as well as intellectual, musical and other human activities. Thus, we have female statues representing Antioch, Alexandria, and other cities, and female statues representing knowledge, wisdom, courage, justice, music, and wealth.

Very famous Hellenistic sculptors were Lysippus, who was the sculptor of Alexander the Great, Praxiteles, Scopas, as well as the sculptors that belonged to two famous schools: the "School of Pergamos", and the "School of Rhodes". The sculptors of the School of Pergamos made countless statues for their great city, and, when commissioned by King Eumenes to embellish the large "Altar of Zeus" with a frieze depicting the "Battle of the Olympian Gods Against the Giants", they created a masterpiece. Viewing the human emotions and tensions expressed in the faces and bodies of the giants, the spectator is unforgettably impressed by the dynamism, the power, the pain and the knowledge of the forthcoming doom so uniquely expressed by the sculptors. The Altar of Zeus is now in Berlin, Germany.

From the "School of Rhodes", we have such world-known fine statues as the "Nike of Samothrace" by Pythocritus. It is now in the Louvre Museum of Paris, the "Laocoon" by Polydoros, Agesandros, and Alexander, now in the Vatican Museum, and the world renowned "Aphrodite of Milos", is in the Museum of Louvre.

With the possible exception of Michelangelo, whose artistry came close to that of the ancient Greeks, no other sculptor of any age and country could emulate their perfection in this so difficult field. To this day, they remain the greatest sculptors.

Ancient Greek Painting

Painting, which is the art of forming figures or objects in colors on canvas/or on another material surface, is a very ancient art. The ancient Egyptians, Assyrians and Babylonians, for example, had numerous kinds of landscape or home life scenes in their palaces, and scenes from the lives of their gods and goddesses in their temples. And, when an Egyptian pharaoh built a pyramid that would serve as his tomb after his death, the walls of the pyramid's funerary chambers were full of paintings.

The ancient Greeks also had paintings in their homes, their temples and their public buildings. But the ancient Greeks, who have made a name in world history for having pioneered many new things, regarding painting, pioneered a state-supported institution that since it first appeared in Athens in the fifth century B.C. has been emulated by every major city around the world - the "Public Gallery". The public gallery of Athens was located on the Hill of the Acropolis to the left of the entrance of the citadel, and there, the finest paintings of ancient Greek artists were exhibited. In this way, all the people could see them and admire them.

Prehellenic cultures and civilizations painted their human or animal figures as seen from the side, profile. The Egyptians, on the other hand, when presenting human figures, would paint the face seen in profile, the chest frontally and the feet in profile. Needless to say, that using three poses to present the same human body was both awkward and unnatural.

When the ancient Greeks, and more specifically the Minoans, who lived on the Island of Santorini, as well as the Mycenaeans who lived on mainland Greece, started filling the walls of their palaces and their homes with paintings, most of the figures appeared in profile. With the passing of time, however, they were able to do in painting what they had done in sculpture. Goaded by naturalism, they sought to eventually enable themselves to paint humans, animals, plants and objects as they appear in nature.

By the fifth century B.C., their human figures could be painted at any angle, just as artists paint human figures today. Thus, a human figure could be painted as seen frontally, diagonally, sideways, and from the rear. And so, thanks to their persistent efforts, humans, animals, and country scenes could now be depicted exactly as they appear in reality.

The most famous ancient Greek artists whose genius helped them to achieve naturalism in their paintings include the following: in the fifth century, the artists who distinguished themselves were Polygnotus from the Island of Thasos, who painted a very large painting in the "Stoa Poikile" (Painted Portico) of Athens, showing the sack of Troy; Zeuxis from Heraclea of Southern Italy, who specialized in panel pictures rather than murals and who perfected the use of shading applied by all artists ever since; Apollodorus of Athens, who first invented and applied light and shade in the themes of his paintings, thereby rendering pictorial illusion later perfected by Zeuxies; Agatharchus of Samos, who was famous for stage scenery and for using geometrical perspective to achieve illusion of depth; Panaenus of Athens, who painted in the Stoa Poikile a large painting depicting "The Battle of Marathon"; and, Parrhasius of Ephesus, very famous for portraying strong emotions and all kinds of psychological states.

In the fourth century B.C., the most famous painters were Pausias of Sicyon who was the first painter to fully master the "Encaustic Technique" (pigments mixed with hot wax) which became an important medium of Greek and Roman painting, and the first in the history of art to introduce the painting of vaulted ceilings - a novelty that has been pursued ever since, and last but not least, the most famous of all ancient Greek artists Apelles from the Island of Cos. Apelles became the court painter of Phillip and Alexander. In his paintings, he used four colors and always applied a special black glaze on his paintings which rendered the colors to appear very brilliant. No other painter could match Apelles' graceful human figures. He had also completely mastered the "Technique of Chiaroscuro" (correct disposition of light and shade in painting). He painted superb pictures of Phillip and Alexander, "Aphrodite Rising from the Sea", for the Temple of

Aesculapius at Cos and which Augustus brought to Rome and put in the Temple of Caesar, and "Calumny".

It is most unfortunate that none of the aforementioned master artists' paintings have survived. The only ones that survived are the very ancient ones made by the Minoans in Crete and in Santorini. Also, many of the wall paintings made by Greek artists in Rome, Pompeii, Herculaneum and other Italian cities have survived. They are noted for their wonderful perspective and they are very graceful and very elegant.

Other places where Greek artists painted beautiful natural scenes and other themes, were those made on the walls of the homes of Alexandria, Cyrene, Jerusalem, Antioch, Ephesus and many other leading cities of the Middle East.

We also have an idea of how ancient Greek wall murals appeared by looking at the small but very beautiful paintings made on the surfaces of the thousands of ancient Greek vases that have been found during excavations. Every aspect of daily life is beautifully and masterfully depicted. Other vase decorations include athletic, battle, mythological and theatrical scenes. As for the vases themselves, they are of the most graceful pottery that man has ever made.

Ancient Greeks also liked to have the floors of their homes decorated with different scenes made not by paint but in mosaic. Some of the floors exhibit intersecting mosaics of different colors in various geometrical formations, others exhibit intertwining plant arrangements in bright colors, and others depict aviary, animal or aquatic species. Still others exhibit zodiacal or other symbolic figures.

Finally, another artistic field in which the ancient Greeks excelled was jewelry. Whether made of gold or silver, they were masterpieces of design and craftsmanship. Even the tiniest of them, be they earrings, bracelets, necklaces, cameos, rings, pyxes (small boxes), or other such items, the engravings or incrustations on them are always expertly delineated. The eye needs not strain itself to perceive the design. And all this most delicate craftsmanship was achieved without the aid of magnifying glasses.

No wonder, Greek art in all its genres, has been admired and imitated to this day. Its ideal creations will forever delight and inspire all generations.

The Tombstone of Hegeso
at the Ceramicus Cemetery of ancient Athens

18
FIVE WONDERS

Of the many wondrous structures that were built in antiquity, such as, temples, palaces, city walls, bridges, tunnels, aqueducts and other like structures, seven were singled out as "wonders". What qualified them to be included in this exclusive grouping was primarily their great size, which ordinarily caused an overwhelming impression on the beholders.

Of the seven wonders, two were built by non-Greeks. They were the Pyramid of Cheops, which was built by the Egyptians, and the Hanging Gardens of Babylon, built by the Babylonians. The remaining five were built by the ancient Greeks, and they are: "The Pharos (Lighthouse) of Alexandria", "The Colossus of Rhodes", "The Mausoleum of Halicarnassus", "The Statue of Zeus", and "The Temple of Artemis (Diane)" at Ephesus.

We will now consider each of these wonders, in detail, beginning with the Pharos of Alexandria.

The City of Alexandria which had been founded by Alexander the Great shortly after he had conquered Egypt in 332 B.C., soon grew to be one of the most prosperous cities in the ancient world. Besides being the new capital of Egypt, Alexandria also had a very large harbor, actually the largest harbor in the Mediterranean. As ships came every day from other lands into the harbor by the dozens, King Ptolemy felt that his very busy harbor ought to have some kind of a very visible landmark that would point to ships afar the location of the harbor.

After pondering for a long time, he came upon a completely novel idea – a mechanism that up to now did not exist – a lighthouse. And, with this in mind, he authorized the construction of the first, and unbelievably, the largest and tallest lighthouse ever.

Sostrates, a leading architect of his kingdom and contemporary of Euclid – the "Father of Geometry", was selected to prepare the designs and supervise the construction. Sostrates accepted the challenge, prepared the necessary blueprints and construction began in 290 B.C.

The lighthouse was to be built at the eastern end of the Island of "Pharos", overlooking the entrance to the harbor. The name of the island is a contraction of the noun Pharaoh (Eg. for king). Eventually, the name of the island became, in the Greek Language, synonymous to lighthouse. The island is some four thousand feet away from the mainland coast, with which it is connected by a causeway.

The lighthouse had three levels - a square one at the bottom, an octagonal one in the middle and a round one at the top. A ramp and circular stairs led from the bottom to the top, where the light was to be. They both wound about a wide central shaft, in which firewood was raised by a hydraulic lift.

On top of the round structure of the lighthouse, the light that was produced by the burning of firewood was directed by an immense polished bronze mirror to different points of the horizon. It could be seen by mariners sailing thirty miles away. During the night, they would see the light, and, during the day they would see the smoke.

The overall height of the lighthouse was four hundred and fifty feet, more than four-fifths of the height of the Washington Monument (555 ft.) in Washington, D.C. When built, it was the tallest building of its time, and to this day, the first and tallest lighthouse ever built.

Constructing such a tall structure twenty-three centuries ago, one admires the daring spirit of the architect and his hundreds of workmen. No doubt, for the lower section of the structure, sophisticated cranes and other lifting devices were used. But when the height of its walls rose significantly, it would be safe to assume that much of the stone for the upper levels of the Pharos was hauled up via the spiral ramp inside the building. White marble faced the exterior wall from top to bottom.

A structure of such dimensions and height naturally filled the heart of the architect Sostrates with justifiable pride, and he wanted to carve his name on the foundation. But King Ptolemy II, who then ruled Egypt, wanted only his name to be carved on it. Sostrates, who was a very clever man, had the inscription: "Sostrates, son of Dexiphanes of Knidos, on behalf of all mariners to the savior gods," chiseled on the foundation. He then covered the inscription with plaster on which he chiseled the name of the king. Many years later, as the plaster aged, cracked and fell off, it revealed the inscription of Sostrates.

For fifteen centuries, the lighthouse of Alexandria stood firmly on its ground sending its light to mariners afar. Although it suffered damages in 365 AD, and 1308 AD, it continued its task until it collapsed in 1326 AD. Today, most of its architectural members are strewn at the bottom of the harbor of Alexandria.

**The Lighthouse of Alexandria
One of the Seven Wonders of the
Ancient World**

Today, thousands of lighthouses are on the coasts of the earth sending their light to mariners far off at sea. Yet, none of these lighthouses has the height or the architectural grandeur of the Pharos of Alexandria.

No wonder the ancients included it among the Seven Wonders, and to this day, their judgment has been honored.

The Colossus of Rhodes

In 305 B.C., Demetrius, the King of Syria decided to punish the people of Rhodes for having deserted him in his unsuccessful expedition against Egypt which then was ruled by the Ptolemies. In that year, he sailed with his army on a large fleet consisting of two hundred and fifty ships to conquer Rhodes. The conquest of the island was easy, but he was unable to capture Rhodes, its capital. Although he had at his disposal the most ingenious siege machines, among which was a siege tower one hundred and thirty feet high, designed by the Athenian engineer Epimachus, a tower consisting of stories and equipped with many powerful catapults that hurled large stones against the city walls, his siege ended in failure. He withdrew, having earned instead the somewhat sarcastic epithet, "Besieger", by which he is known in history.

The people of Rhodes, believing that during the siege the sun-god "Helios", the patron god of their city, had come to their aid, decided to build a colossal statue, as a token of gratitude. It would stand close to the water of the harbor.

The Rhodians selected the famous sculptor Chares who was from Lindos, to design and make such a statue that was to exceed the height of one hundred and ten feet, making it almost the same size as the Statue of Liberty on Ellis Island in New York Harbor. When the design was drawn, it called for a standing male figure whose raised right hand held a torch. Construction commenced in 294 B.C.

The statue's exterior was made of bronze plates which Chares cast in sections, beginning with the feet. The statue would stand on a three stepped base. The bronze "skin" would be held by dowels that were firmly fastened on an iron armature that was inside the hollow interior of the statue. The hollow core of the armature was also filled with blocks of stone in order to permanently secure the upright position of the statue against strong winds and slight earthquakes.

As the statue's upward construction took form, the siege tower which Demetrius had used to capture the City of Rhodes and had left there after his withdrawal, would now be used by the workmen to add the materials to the higher levels of the statue to its completion. The statue's gradual height rose only six to eight feet per year until it was completed in 226 B.C.

It took sixty-eight years for this colossal statue to be built, and when it was finished, it became the pride of the prosperous maritime city that funded its construction. It was a magnificent statue unequaled in size by any other statue of the ancient world.

Unfortunately, the Colossus of Rhodes stood in its place for only fifty years. In 176 B.C. a violent earthquake toppled it, causing it to fall and lie crumbled on the ground.

Although short lived, history still remembers it and will always remember it as one of the greatest achievements of antiquity especially when we consider that man so long ago lacked the machinery and tools that are available today.

The Mausoleum of Halicarnassus

When in 353 B.C., Mausolus, the satrap (governor) of Caria the southwestern district of Asia Minor (Turkey), died at Halicarnassus, the capital of Caria, his wife Artemisia decided to build a most splendid tomb in his memory. This magnificent tomb, unrivalled in size, design and artistic sculptural décor, has given its name to all subsequent large and imposing tombs. We call them "Mausoleums".

As Artemisia's Asiatic domain lacked noted architects and sculptors to undertake the designing and sculptural decoration of such an ostentatious funerary monument, Artemisia sought the services of Greek architects and sculptors.

Satyrus and Pythis became the architects. Their designs not only fulfilled Artemisia's expectations, they also made history. Briefly, the shape of the most magnificent tomb was as follows: A five stepped marble platform formed the base on which a marble podium one hundred and twenty-five by one hundred and five feet rested. Above the podium rose a beautiful Ionic colonnade consisting of thirty-six fluted columns that surrounded a cela. Above this beautiful colonnade, which measured eighty by one hundred feet, rose a stepped marble pyramid of twenty-four steps. Crowning the pyramid was a rectangular marble pedestal on which a quadriga (chariot drawn by four horses) with King Mausolus and Artemisia in the chariot, formed the very apex of the whole structure. The overall height of the tomb was one hundred and forty-eight feet.

Five famous Greek sculptors undertook the exterior sculptural embellishment of this imposing monument. They were Scopas, Bryaxis, Leocharis, Timotheus, and Praxiteles. They were the best of their time.

Two superb friezes appeared on all four sides of the monument. The frieze which belonged to the colonnade and ran on all four sides of the episteleum (above the columns), depicted the battle of Greeks and Amazons. It was carved by Scopas, and being the product of such a consummate sculptor, was superb. The human figures, many of them in oblique positions, appear either pushing forward or drawing back, thereby making the battle scene quite dramatic. The figures were cut deeply so that they could be seen clearly by spectators who viewed them from ninety feet below. The high quality marble for this dramatic frieze had been imported from the nearby

Island of Cos. The other frieze that ran on the upper part of all four sides of the podium had as its theme the battle of the Lapiths and Centaurs – a well-known theme of ancient Greek Mythology. Elegant statues of famous personages stood in the spaces between the columns of the colonnade. It is disheartening that of this superb artistic embellishment, only a few fragments from the friezes, the statues of the colonnade, the statues of King Mausolus and Artemisia and broken structural members of this monument survived. Sir Charles Newton – the British archaeologist, who discovered them in the middle of the nineteenth century, sent them to the British Museum in London as part of its prized, permanent collections.

The large surfaces of this imposing monument had been faced with blue limestone and with white marble. Construction was completed many years later.

Artemisia must have paid a mythical fortune for such a tomb. However, by employing the finest architects and sculptors of her time, she succeeded in three things. She built a fabulous tomb for her husband, one of the Seven Wonders, and secured the noun "Mausoleum" in most languages of the world.

The Statue of Zeus

In northwest Peloponnesos, and not far from the Ionian Sea, is a most beautiful valley surrounded by low green hills covered with pine trees. The valley, too, abounds with pine trees and all sorts of green foliage.

This serene green setting is known to the world as Olympia – birthplace of the Olympic Games, first held in 776 B.C.

In 1875, German archaeologists were the first to come here to conduct excavations. They uncovered the "Heraeon", (Temple of goddess Hera), which they restored; the priceless statue of Hermes (Mercury), a genuine work of Praxiteles; the stadium where the ancient Olympics were held; countless objects of all kinds, the gymnasium, foundations and parts of many temples, and among others, the largest temple of this site – the Temple of Zeus (Jupiter).

This fine temple in the Doric Order had been designed by the architect Libon, and in ancient times was considered to be one of the finest, not only in Greece, but in the then known world. The metopes of the temple, like those of the Parthenon in Athens, depicted mythological scenes. When many of them were unearthed by the German archaeologist, they were in a bad state. But, the beautiful statues that adorned the eastern and western pediments of the temple were found to be in good condition. There were twenty-one in the east pediment, and twenty-two in the west pediment.

Nearly all of these pedimental sculptures were found, and the archaeologists, using Pausanias' second century description of Olympia as a guide, were able to restore these masterful sculptures in the museum in the exact order in which they had appeared on the pediments in ancient times.

The east pediment sculptures represented Zeus presiding over the sacrifice that preceded the famous chariot race of Pelops and Oenomaos for the hand of Hippodamia, which Pelops won by cheating. The west pediment sculptures were found to show a serene Apollo overseeing the fighting of Lapiths and Centaurs on either side of him.

In 430 B.C., the Athenian sculptor Phidias, unquestionably the most famous sculptor of his age, came to Olympia to carve the statue of Zeus, intended to be placed inside the cella of the temple that bore this name.

Before Pheidias began construction of the chryselephantine (gold and ivory) statue of the father of the Olympian gods and goddesses, he bought a large building that was near the temple to use as his studio. Here, he designed and carved the masterpiece of his life.

The size of the seated statue was forty-three feet high, and its wooden framework was covered with ivory and gold. The statue rested on a 3.3 foot marble base. If the statue had been presented standing, it would have been fifty-nine feet tall. In his right hand, Zeus was shown holding a Nike, that is, a winged victory (symbol of triumph in the Olympic Games).

The majestic statue of Zeus
in his temple at Olympia.

In his left hand, he held a scepter, denoting his sovereignty, being king of the gods and goddesses of Olympus. On the top of the scepter, was an eagle – the very emblem of Zeus.

The face, the hands, the chest, and feet were shown in ivory. Gold was used over his robe and sandals. Also, a beautiful floral design, depicting lilies, had been carved into his clothing while on his head lay a beautifully carved olive wreath.

The massive body of the god sat majestically on an elegant and elaborately carved throne made of ebony and ivory. The throne was additionally decorated with precious multicolored stones. One, after observing the throne, could rightly admit that it too, was a magnificent work of art.

The feet of the god rested on a large footstool that was also carved elegantly. In front of the stool was a black marble basin which was used to collect the olive oil that was poured over the statue, not for ceremonial reasons, but as a necessary measure to prevent the ivory from cracking. Also, before the throne was a large sunken rectangle on the floor, which also contained oil. Most likely its purpose was to reflect the majesty of the statue.

Pausanias, who visited Olympia and the temple, recorded that, whoever entered the temple, and came face-to-face with the majestic statue, would remain spellbound. Pheidias had done his best! The statue did emanate a supernatural impression. It was the masterpiece of his life.

There survives an ancient saying regarding the majesty of this statue, which reads: "Either Phidias climbed Mt. Olympus and saw Zeus, or Zeus must have appeared in all his magnificence in a dream of Pheidias."

Today, this magnificent masterpiece of the greatest sculptor of antiquity does not exist. Only the Temple of Olympia exists with some of its columns restored. The bedding on the floor, on which the pedestal of the statue lay, and the sunken rectangular pit still remain.

Between the years 37-41 A.D., the Roman Emperor Caligula tried, without success, to remove the gigantic statue to Rome. In 462 A.D., it was carried off to Constantinople. But, a few years later, a great fire that destroyed a good portion of the city also destroyed the statue forever.

One can say again: "What an irremediable loss." Had it survived, today, it might have been a priceless possession of the Museum of Olympia, or the Athens National Museum.

The Temple of Artemis

During the last two centuries before the birth of Christ, the City of Ephesus, located on the western coast of Asia Minor (Turkey), had become a large and prosperous city. In fact, when the Romans conquered Asia Minor and the other countries of the Middle East, they made Ephesus the capital of the Province of Asia, and improvised the title of "Asiarch" for the governor of the Province.

From the time of its founding, Ephesus was the center of the worship of the goddess Artemis (Diana) – a goddess, which in Asia, was not associated with hunting as in Greece, but with fertility. Hence, her temple was always the largest and most beautiful of the city. Elaborate ceremonies took place in it annually, attended by countless pagan pilgrims from many other cities. Ephesus always prided itself in being the goddess "Neocoros", that is, its custodian.

During the long history of Ephesus, the Temple of Artemis had been destroyed four times. The fourth time, a fire set by a pyromaniac, whose sole purpose was to have his name included in history, destroyed most of the temple. Herostratus set the fire and is still remembered. In 333 B.C., Alexander the Great conquered Asia Minor. He ordered that the temple be rebuilt larger in size and in adornment more magnificent than ever.

The architect selected to design and to oversee the construction of a temple, never so immense, was Dinocrates. The new temple was to be rectangular in shape four hundred and twenty-four by two hundred and twenty-four by two hundred and twenty feet. It was to be the largest Hellenic temple in existence. It would be surrounded by one hundred and twenty-seven Ionic columns each being sixty feet tall. An unusual feature of the thirty-six frontal columns was the beautifully sculptured ornamentation on their two lower drums. It was an innovation apparently conceived for the first time by the master architect.

The huge quantities of marble required for the construction of so large a temple came from seven miles away. Interestingly, as the massive blocks weighed forty tons each, their transportation from the quarry to the site of construction presented, at first, an awesome problem that had to be solved.

Dinocrates, who had dared to undertake so awesome a project, was no ordinary architect. After pondering over the problem, he found the solution. The column drums were fixed with central pivots within a wooden frame so that they would roll like huge rollers. Teams of oxen would then haul them from the quarry to the place of construction. As for the other rectangular blocks that would be used for the building of walls, or as other structural members, the same principle would be applied. Each end of the block would be encased within a massive wooden wheel, and then a team of oxen would drag them to their destination.

The temple was surrounded on three sides with a beautiful peristyle of Ionic columns, while in front of its façade, stood a massive and beautifully carved altar for the sacrifices.

Inside the temple, the statue of the goddess was presented not as an elegant and beautiful huntress accompanied by a gazelle, a common theme in Greek sculpture, but shaped as a mummy and adorned with extravagant symbols of fertility, such as eighteen breasts over the chest and garlands of small fruits and rows of animals over her body all the way down to her toes. Around her head, was a wide halo on which were carved winged creatures and heads of lions, bulls and goats, suggesting that she was the protectress of creatures of the field. She wore a round hat carved to look like the city's wall with three gates. Her hat symbolized her guardianship of the city.

Three openings on the roof of the temple allowed abundant light to enter into the interior of the cella. One of the openings was structured above the statue in order to illuminate it adequately.

Besides being a temple dedicated to Artemis, the temple also served as a safety deposit vault for all Asia Minor and other Middle Eastern countries. Among the inestimable treasure stored in its vault, were many priceless masterpieces by Praxiteles and other famous Greek sculptors as well as priceless paintings made by the greatest ancient Greek artist, Apelles. Among other statues, was one depicting Alexander the Great on a horse – a masterpiece for which the sculptor received twenty gold talents.

On the epistelium that ran above the columns on all four sides of the temple, ran a masterfully carved frieze. On the pediments, dozens of statues depicted scenes from the life of the goddess. The statues, due to their distance of seventy to eighty feet from those who looked at them from below, were large so that the details of their physical configurations, drapery and the like, could be clearly visible.

Such, very briefly was the fifth Greek wonder of the ancient world designed, built and adorned by master Greek architects, sculptors and artists. Although a huge structure, its beautifully fluted, unusually tall sixty-foot Ionic columns, rendered them slender. This feature greatly minimized the bulkiness of the temple making it appear most pleasing aesthetically.

19
ANCIENT GREEK SCIENCE

When long, long ago man appeared on earth, while looking at the many things around him, he must have been filled with wonder. With the passing of millennia, how did the ancient peoples try to explain the presence and workings of the natural things by which they were surrounded? The answer is: with legends, with myths, so imaginative, delightful and varied among the Egyptians, the Babylonians, the Assyrians, the Hittites and many others.

But with the coming of the Greeks, everything would change. And, here is why. When the ancient Greeks began to look at the same things the peoples before them had seen for hundreds or thousands of years before, they would not use their poetic fancy and mythology, but they would ask the most important questions: Why? How? To what aim?

Why, for example, do the stars move in circular orbits and are so shining at night? What is the basic stuff of which all things are made? Why does a river flow? Thus, in their effort to answer correctly and intelligently the whys and hows, the scientific method was born. The purpose of science as we know it today had been laid.

Although ahead of them lay a difficult road, thanks to their persistence in trying to unravel the mysteries of nature, in the end they were successful. The answers they gave to the whys and hows of natural things are our answers today.

A very basic question people have asked for centuries is: "What is the basic stuff from which all things are made?" Almost twenty-five centuries ago, Democritus, who was born in northern Greece, gave the answer. He wrote, "Everything that we see and touch is made up of atoms, atoms that are extremely tiny and therefore we can neither see them nor touch them, nor divide them anymore." Because they cannot be further divided, he called them "Atoms"- a Greek word meaning "Indivisible".

Thus, whether we have fire, water, air, a stone, a cloud, a star, an animal, anything – they are all made of extremely tiny atoms. And, what Democritus said so long ago, today's scientists all over the world agree. So, Democritus became the "Father of Atomic Theory".

Archimedes was another great, ancient Greek engineer and inventor. He was born and lived in the ancient Greek colony of Syracuse, Italy, and the following are some of his inventions. He designed and built for King Hieron, the King of Syracuse, engines of war that terrified the Romans. Those engines delayed the Romans from taking over the city by three years. He also designed and made a large burning mirror, which set the Roman ships on fire.

He invented the water screw to empty water from ships. His water screw was also used in Egypt to drain the fields after the annual floods caused by the Nile River. He said once: "Give me a place to stand, and I will move the earth." By this saying, he meant that a very great weight could be moved by a very small force. When King Hieron asked him to give an example, Archimedes made a very large crane. At one end of the crane, he placed a ship loaded with all its crew, and on the other end he asked the king to press the long bar with his hands. It is said, that at the other end, the ship was raised. He also invented the "Helix" for launching great ships into the sea and for conveying very heavy loads.

Some of his inventions added to the conveniences of life, such as watermills and automatic door openers. Others were for entertainment, including fountains adorned with automatically moving figurines, and an "automatic theater" in which the figures performed their parts through five complicated acts. We can imagine the wonder experienced by the spectators of such mechanical and not romantic performances. He also discovered the natural law of "Hydrostatics". In other words, the reason a body, a thing floats in water.

Ctesibius was another famous engineer. He designed and built many fine "water clocks".

Heron distinguished himself as a famous geometer and writer on mechanical and physical subjects. In one of his books, he describes how to make siphons, fire engines, water organs, and his most important discovery - the use of the "force of steam". He thus anteceded the Scottish engineer and inventor of the modern condensing steam engine by 1,800 years! Other inventions of this distinguished, ancient Greek scientist included a "barulcus" (weight lifter), consisting of a screw and a pulley that could lift very heavy loads, and the "dioptra," an instrument used for land surveying. It is equivalent to our modern theodolite.

Heron wrote many books on mechanics, geometry, and even mathematics. The list includes the following Greek titles: "Automatopoietice", "Belopoeica", "Cheiroballistra", "Mechanics", "Pnewmatica", "Metrica", "Stereometrica", "Geodaesia", and "Catoptrica".

"Helepolis", meaning "Destroyer of City", was the ancient Greek name for mobile siege towers used by the Greek Armies of the fourth and third century B.C. The towers were forty to fifty feet tall; they had four to six floors, each floor equipped with two large catapults for the purpose of throwing darts or big stones against the walls and the defenders of the besieged city. Some of the towers also carried drawbridges on the top floor enabling the soldiers to make assaults on the ramparts of the besieged city.

The largest siege tower constructed in ancient times was the one used by Demetrius, surnamed "The Besieger", during the siege of the city of Rhodes. It was designed by Epimachus of Athens, a very famous military engineer. The tower had nine floors; it had a square base of twenty-seven feet and a height of 130 feet. Like other such siege towers, it was self-propelled by a capstan and a belt drive on its bottom floor, manned by many men.

During the seventh century B.C., the increase of population of the capital of the Greek Island of Samos necessitated the supply of more water. To solve this problem, King Polycrates hired Eupalinus, who was the most famous hydraulic engineer of his time.

As the water source was on the other side of the mountain that rose midway between the city and the source, Eupalinus drove a 4,200 foot tunnel through the mountain for conveying the water supply to the city. The tunnel was eight feet by eight feet. What is amazing about the construction of this tunnel was that Eupalinus had two crews begin digging on the two opposite slopes of the mountain aiming to meet at the center. After many weeks of digging, the two crews met at the predetermined point without any deviation.

Medicine and Pharmacy

Ways to cure sick people go back to at least 3,000 years before Christ was born. But these "therapeutic" ways were not scientific. Actually, they were a blend of magic spells and herbal concoctions.

Scientific medicine and pharmacy, as we know it today, began in Greece almost 500 years before Christ was born. In fact, the first man who made medicine and pharmacy sciences, was Hippocrates. That is why, to this day, he is called "The Father of Medicine".

Today, we know the names of 550 ancient and Medieval Greek doctors and pharmacists. These people lived at some time between the fifth century B.C. and the fifteenth century AD; but as we can imagine, there were thousands more of them during those two thousand years. In fact, most of the therapeutic methods that they developed, and most of the drugs that they invented, were still in use until three hundred years ago.

Hippocrates was born on the Greek Island of Cos during the sixth century B.C. When he became a physician, he invented a different way to cure people. Instead of using magic and spells, he began using "diagnosis", that is, a careful examination of the pathological symptoms of the sick person to find out what caused him pain, and thus, what drugs ought to be administered for the latter's recovery. He also kept records of every case he treated in order to benefit his students. And so, he made medicine a science.

The following represents a modicum of the numberless things that he discovered in reference to sicknesses. He found out that: all sicknesses have natural causes; physical exercise, diet and water cure and can keep a man healthy; drugs strengthen the body to fight the sickness; most of the body is made up of water; and, that a smaller amount is made up of solids, such as bones, teeth and nails. He documented the detail of certain sicknesses, like cancer, tuberculosis, epilepsy, lung sicknesses, and various epidemics, and he prescribed listening, touching, and observation for the diagnosis of a sickness and noticed that listening is very important for diagnosing breathing problems.

As a surgeon, he used surgery for eye cataracts, mutilation for gangrene, and skull perforations for brain or head injuries. He studied the growth of the embryo all the way to birth. He wrote fifty-eight medical books, each divided into lesser ones, dealing with hundreds of medical subjects. No wonder that this most famous Greek physician is recognized in the entire world as "The Father of Medicine".

He wrote an oath to be taken by doctors about to start the practice of medicine - the well-known "Hippocratic Oath." This oath, which is an extremely brief summary of medical ethics as conceived by Hippocrates, is taken today by all doctors upon completing their medical studies. Below is the oath.

"I swear by Apollo the physician, and Aesculapius, and Health, and All-heal, and all the gods and goddesses, that, according to my ability and judgement, I will keep this Oath and this stipulation - to reckon him who taught me this Art equally dear to me as my parents, to share my substance with him, and relieve his necessities if required; to look upon his off spring in the same footing as my own brothers, and to teach him this art, if they shall wish to learn it, without fee or stipulation; and that by precept, lecture, and every other mode of instruction, I will impart a knowledge of the Art to my own sons, and those of my teachers, and to disciples bound by a stipulation and oath according to the law of medicine, but none to others. I will follow that system of regimen which, according to my ability and judgement, I consider for the benefit of my patients, and abstain from whatever is deleterious and mischievous. I will give no deadly medicine to anyone if asked, nor suggest any such counsel; and in a like manner I will not give to a woman pessary to produce abortion. With purity and with holiness I will pass my life and practice my Art. I will not cut persons laboring under the stone, but will leave this to be done by men who are practitioners of this work. Into whatever houses I enter, I will go into them for the benefit of the sick, and will abstain from every voluntary act of mischief and corruption; and, further from the seduction of females or males, of freedom and slaves. Whatever, in connection with my professional practice or not, on connection with it, I see or hear, in the life of men, which ought not to be spoken of abroad, I will not divulge, as reckoning that all such should be kept a secret. While I continue to keep this Oath unviolated, may it be granted to me to enjoy life and the practice of the art, respected by all men, in all times! But should I trespass and violate this Oath, may the reverse by my lot!"

Another famous ancient Greek physician was Herophilus who hailed from the city of Chalcedon, Asia Minor. He studied medicine in Alexandria, Egypt and there he spent his life.

A very brief list of the many anatomical parts of the human body that Herophilus painstakingly observed and thereafter described in his books would include: The optic nerve and the three membranes of the human eye, the liver, the pancreas, the arteries and veins. He noticed that the arteries are six times wider than the veins; he recognized the brain as the central organ of the nervous system and as the seat of intelligence; and, he divided the nerves into motor and sensory (moving and feeling). And, he examined in detail nearly every part of the human body, which he lucidly and accurately described in the ten books he wrote. As a result of all the above anatomical investigations and correct recognition of each function, he earned the most deserving honorific, "Father of Anatomy".

Erasistratus hailed from the Greek Island of Kea and was yet another famous ancient Greek doctor. The workings of the human body became the chief interest of his multiple investigations. To mention very few, they include: his admirable discovery that the blood carries air from the lungs to all the parts of the human body; his studies of the brain as the center of thought; his discovery that the roots of the nerves begin at the brain and the spinal cord; his accurate description of the optic and auditory (hearing) nerves; and, last but not least, his detailed study of the human heart, whose valves he was the first to discover and describe, as well as his marvelous discovery of the "hair like vessels" that join the arteries with the veins. The above, and the very many other observations that he made, are described in the seventeen books that he wrote. For all this fruitful work, he rightly earned the honorific, "Father of Physiology".

Galen, born in the City of Pergamum, Asia Minor, was also a very famous ancient Greek doctor. He studied medicine in Alexandria, Egypt, spent part of his life in his native city, and, later went to Rome, where he became the personal doctor of two Roman emperors.

Besides being a famous medical practitioner, Galen was also a keen observer of the human body. Some of his observations were: that the living body has no useless organs; that air is very important to life; that sickness can be caused from inside as well as outside the body; that sickness can be hereditary and contagious; and, when a person becomes sick, his weaker organs are affected first. He studied and wrote a very detailed and accurate description of the human heart. He also invented many drugs, and surprisingly, many of his salves for wounds, known today as "Galenicals", are still prepared by pharmaceutical companies around the world. Amazingly, Galen, found time to write 400 books of which only eighty survived.

Gynecology, a branch of medicine specializing in female diseases and symptoms, also had its beginning in ancient Greece. In fact, of the many gynecologists of antiquity, Soranus was the most famous. He was a native of Ephesus, Asia Minor, and lived in the second century AD. He studied medicine in Alexandria, and practiced in Alexandria and Rome. Some of his contributions include: the invention of instruments to examine women patients; he described many abnormal diseases; he described such sicknesses as lethargy and paralysis; and, discovered the causes of fever.

He wrote twenty-six books that deal with hundreds of symptoms and causes. Today, he is regarded as the greatest gynecologist and pediatrician of antiquity.

Pharmacy

The list of ancient Greek pharmacists who discovered drugs is very large. Here we will describe only one, the greatest, Dioscorides Pendanios. He was so famous, that today he is regarded as the "Father of Pharmacy". He was born at Anazarva, Asia Minor and studied pharmacy at Tarsus, also in Asia Minor, and birthplace of famous apostle, Saint Paul. At that time, Tarsus was the center of botanical and pharmaceutical studies. He spent most of his life in Rome and served as an army doctor.

He wrote nine books dealing with drugs and one "On Eyes". His most famous book, however, was the "Matteria Medica". It contains 1,000 prescriptions (813 from plants, 101 from animals and 102 from minerals), and 4,740 medical applications. But what is amazing, is that his book, became the standard book of pharmacists for 1,600 years.

Biology

Biology, the science that methodically examines all living things, that is plants and animals, originated in Greece. And since that time, it has been divided into two major classifications, namely, Zoology, the study of animals, and Botany, the study of plants.

Zoology

Anaximander, an ancient Greek thinker who lived in the city of Miletus, Asia Minor, in the sixth century BC, considering the question on where animals came from and how they evolved, wrote: "The first living things appeared in water. The animals that live on land came from fishes." According to Anaximander then, life began in the oceans and then spread to dry land.

Empedocles, likewise an ancient thinker who was born and lived in the Greek colony of Acragas, Italy, wrote: "Ever since living things appeared on earth, they evolve, however, only the fittest, the strong survive." Empedocles was the first man in history to teach what we call today "Survival of the Fittest".

Aristotle, the very famous ancient Greek thinker and scientist, was the first scientist to study systematically and classify many living creatures of all kinds – fish, birds and animals. He wrote a most admirable work on zoology entitled, "History of Animals", consisting of ten large books. In these books, he gives us a very detailed account of the structures and habits of each animal, bird and fish, and furthermore, he attempts to classify them according to their structures. He also divides all animals known to him in two main categories- those which have blood and those which do not. Those which have blood include four footed animals, the birds and the fish. To those, which do not have blood, belong the shellfish, the soft shelled and the insects.

He describes seventy-five different kinds of mammals, that is, animals which give birth to live offspring, 200 different kinds of birds, 128 different kinds of fish, eighty-three different kinds of insects, twenty-one different kinds of amphibians, eighteen different kinds of crustaceans, ten different kinds of cephalopods and forty different kinds of shellfish.

In his book entitled "The Organs of Animals", Aristotle examines with great detail the anatomical structures of animals. In another book entitled "About the Birth of Animals", he describes the organs of animals that deal with the birth of offspring. Finally, in another book entitled "The Movements of Animals", Aristotle describes how animals that live in a certain region for many generations, adapt to that environment, and move very efficiently in that environment.

For all the above contributions and many others to these sciences, Aristotle has rightly earned the title, "Father of Zoology".

Botany

The first scientist that can truly be called a botanist, that is, an expert on plants, was Aristotle.

Before Alexander the Great began his campaigns against the Persians, Aristotle asked him to take with him scientists who knew about plants, to select different and unusual plants that grew in the countries he was to conquer, and send them back to him. In this way, his plant collection would increase considerably, and so, with the foreign plants that he would receive, he would be able to make comparisons of their structures and classify them into families. Alexander obeyed his wise mentor, and when he began his campaigns, he took with him many knowledgeable men of many scientific fields, among which were many who knew about plants.

The result was that those experts, during the campaigns all the way to India, kept picking plants that did not grow in Greece and sending them to Aristotle. And so, Aristotle found himself to be the richest possessor of plants, which he could examine and classify. He planted all his plants in a very large garden, and hired people to take care of them daily. He used these plants for instruction. Finally, he wrote a large book entitled "On Plants", a book considered as the first systematic one written on Botany.

Theophrastus, a student of Aristotle and his successor as head of the "Lyceum", (as the School of Aristotle was called) went further than his master in promoting the Science of Botany. He had studied methodically this science, and now, he sat down to write the most systematic and thorough book written in ancient times.

Actually, he wrote two works. The first one is entitled "On the History of Plants", consisting of nine books, and the other is entitled "On the Causes of Plants", consisting of six books. Together, these excellent works are considered the greatest contribution to botany in ancient times.

Moreover, these books became the standard books of botanists from the third century B.C. to the fifteenth century AD, in other words, for 1,800 years!

In describing the plants, Theophrastus goes into detail. All the members of each plant stem, leaf, flower, fruit, and what have you, are all analyzed. Moreover, even though these books were written eighteen centuries ago, their descriptions are strikingly modern. As to the number of plants described in his books, they are 500 growing in Greece, North Africa, and Middle Eastern Countries, all the way to India.

He divided all plants into "trees", "bushes", "sticks", and "grasses", categories according to their roots, into evergreen and deciduous plants and trees, into straight growing, long stemmed and suckers, into hard, soft, etc. He describes in great detail fifty different kinds of forest trees, the longevity of trees and their sicknesses; he examines the stick-like kind of plants, the quality of wood, and reflects on the different kinds of areas where plants prefer to grow.

Finally, Theophrastus coined many botanical terms, all of which are used today, and emphasized that every plant has a certain area on which it grows. For all his contributions to this science, Theophrastus rightly earned the title, "Father of Botany".

Geology, Geography and Exploration

During our life, as we look at mountains, hills, rivers, and other natural features around us, we tend to believe that these never change. The truth, however, is that nothing remains the same - slowly but surely everything changes. The ancient Greek thinker Heraclitus, whose basic doctrine was "Everything Changes", was the first man in history to observe this.

Slow changes that take thousands or millions of years occur on all the continents of the earth. Shorelines change, mountains erode and consequently lose height, other mountains grow higher, where oceans existed millions of years ago we now have land, as in the case of our central states, and vice versa. New islands appear as a result of volcanic eruptions, mineral rocks change, like dolomite into marble, and coal into diamonds, and so forth.

The first man who noticed that land had risen from the sea was Aristotle. Walking one day on a very narrow path along a precipitous coast of Asia Minor, he noticed thousands of seashells embedded in the rocky slopes. He concluded that "The coastline had risen above the surface of the sea taking with it the shells." He was absolutely right. He was the first scientist in history to explain what happened in many places of the earth. Many other ancient Greek scientists after Aristotle, having seen seashells many miles inland from the coastline, were correct in concluding that, in the past, that land was the bottom of the sea.

Aristotle also explained why earthquakes happen and volcanoes erupt. In one of his books, he wrote: "Earthquakes happen due to pressure of hot air passing with difficulty through natural canals deep in the earth. If the heated air cannot pass, then, as soon as it finds a soft spot on the surface of the earth, it erupts, thus creating a volcano."

Anaximenes conceived another theory concerning the cause of earthquakes. He wrote: "Inside the earth are caves. When a very large rock falls from the ceiling to the floor of the cave, its tremendous weight causes vibrations on the earth's surface, which may be called a regional earthquake."

Strabo, by looking at the shape of certain islands, said: "Those islands that look like conical mountains were created by volcanoes." He was the first to notice it, and his explanation was correct. It was also an ancient Greek scientist who correctly observed and stated that: "The larger the river, the higher its source on a mountain."

What causes wind to blow? Why is it that in some areas the wind is hot and in others cold? Aristotle was the first scientist to explain why. He wrote: "When air warms up in a certain region because of sunlight, it becomes thinner and begins to rise up to higher levels of the atmosphere. When that happens, the cold air from another region, most likely from the sea, rushes in to fill the region where the warm air rises. And so, we have cold air blowing."

What causes tides and ebbings at coastlines? Two and a half millennia ago, Pytheas, an astronomer-mariner, explained this event. He wrote: "Tides and ebbings are due to the tremendous magnetic pull that the moon exerts on the earth." He was correct!

How big is the earth? How many thousands of miles is its circumference? That was a most difficult question. No ancient Greek mariner had sailed around the earth to keep record of the mileage, as sailors knew only the Mediterranean Sea, a little of the Atlantic Ocean north and south of the Straits of Gibraltar, and a little of the Indian Ocean. No one knew that there was a Western Hemisphere and a Pacific Ocean, the largest on earth. So, such a question seemed unanswerable.

Eratosthenes was an eminent ancient Greek geographer and astronomer who hailed from the ancient Greek colony of Cyrene, located on the Libyan coast of North Africa. He had studied geography and astronomy and became director of the largest library of his time - the Library of Alexandria. He wrote many books, but the most important were his geographical ones. Glimpsing into his writings, we learn the following: He believed the earth was round, he was the first to mark maps with lines of longitudes and latitudes still in use today; he invented the zones of the earth such as Tropical, etc., still in use today; his examination of the tides of the Atlantic and the Indian Ocean convinced him that these two were connected, and then correctly concluded that all the land on the earth was surrounded by water; and, he believed that one sailing from Spain south on the Atlantic and around Africa would reach India. He also believed that sailing west on the Atlantic one would eventually reach India.

His greatest achievement was his computation of the circumference of the earth to 24,857 miles. He arrived at this result by placing a sundial in Syene, which is located south of Alexandria, and another one in Alexandria. He then determined the position of the sun from these two points, and with the angle these formed, he computed the earth's circumference.

Explorations

Today, when we talk about famous explorers, the names of Christopher Columbus, Prince Henry of Portugal, Vasco de Gama, Magellan, and John Cabot, immediately come to mind. The ancient Greeks were also daring explorers having traveled to faraway unknown lands where no other man had gone.

The city of Massalia, better known as Marseilles, was the first ancient Greek colony on the Mediterranean shore of France. It was founded in 600 B.C., and to this day is still a thriving city of commerce and industry. It was the birthplace of two very notable ancient Greek explorers: Pytheas and Euthymenes.

The only information that we have of Euthymenes is that he sailed a total of 5,000 miles.

His explorations took place in 500 B.C. exploring the West coast of Africa beginning in Marseilles and ending in the estuary of the River Senegal. Unfortunately the book that he had written describing the details of his voyage entitled "Periplus" did not survive.

The other "Massaliote" (i.e., Greek native of Massalia), was Pytheas. He was not only an experienced navigator, but an expert mathematician and astronomer as well.

According to a no longer credible hypothesis of past historians, the tin trade monopoly was in the hands of the Carthaginians who controlled the Straits of Gibraltar.

Around 300 B.C., the merchants of Massalia offered to furnish Pytheas with a ship. His proposed mission was to sail to Britain known as the "Tin Islands" to find the exact source of tin, thus, breaking the Carthaginian monopoly. Pytheas and his crew of men accepted this great challenge.

As they left Massalia, they sailed along the Mediterranean coast of France and Spain passing the Straits of Gibraltar. They were not spotted by the Carthaginians. They turned north and kept sailing along Spain and France only stopping periodically to get provisions. The crew arrived at the small island of Ushant which is the westernmost tip of Armorica (now Brittany). Pytheas having known Massalias' latitude used his gnomon to measure the height of the sun and was able to calculate how far north he had traveled.

From that island, he sailed across the English Channel reaching Cornwall landing at the westernmost region presently known as Land's End. Cornwall was the region where tin was being mined. Thus, Pytheas had found the source of the desired metal. Upon this discovery, he recorded how tin was mined and processed in his log. He noted that after the tin was processed it was shipped to the island of Island of St. Michael. And from there it was loaded onto ships and carried to its destination.

Pytheas continued along the coast of Britain arriving eventually at Scotland. During this journey, he recorded in his log the many customs and behavior of the ancient inhabitants of Britain. He even recorded his impressions of the British countryside down to the very way that they cultivated their land. He again, as before, took measurements of the height of the sun to gage how far north he had gone, reaching the Shetlands.

While in Scotland he heard of a place "Thule", which was located at the outermost region of the earth. The prospect of setting foot at the farthest point so intrigued him that he continued his venture.

Up to this point, past historians agree that Pytheas sailed this route. As to the location of Thule, their opinions vary. There is question of whether the Orkney Islands, the Shetland Islands or even Trondheim in Norway is the actual location of Thule. It is unknown.

After this northernmost journey, Pytheas returned to Massalia via the eastern coast of Britain. Stopping at Helgoland he discovered amber, a gem that was greatly prized by the jewelers of Massalia.

Barry Cunliffe, a professor of European archeology and history at Oxford University, describes a different route and destination of Pytheas' journeys. His recent publication entitled "The extraordinary Voyage of Pytheas the Greek" writes that Pytheas was not offered a large ship by his compatriots to discover the source of tin and amber. Instead he traveled alone on ordinary vessels that he could board in Massalia and took other vessels from his stopovers in distant harbors. He did not travel around the coasts of France and Spain; rather he boarded a river vessel on the River Aude in the Southern Mediterranean coast of France. From there he traveled into the hinterland of France. He traveled by foot until he reached the River Garonne then rode a river vessel to Bordeaux. From there he sailed to Cornwall, the source of tin. Leaving Cornwall, he sailed onward to Scotland.

It was in Scotland that he heard about the "Ultima Thule" the land that was beyond the Orkney, the Shetland and Faroe Islands. The trip would take six days. It was evident now that his destination would be the Island of Iceland. Upon arrival to Iceland his vessels dropped anchor. After a few days they set out for a day's trip further north. It was then that he recorded in his log, the "congealed sea", which was actually drifting ice. It was coming from the arctic. The fog was so thick that Pytheas could hardly distinguish between the sea and the sky as he fought the unbearably cold wind. Faced with such harsh conditions, Pytheas decided to turn back to Massalia.

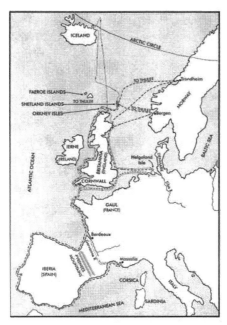

--- PAST HISTORIANS' HYPOTHETICAL ROUTES OF PYTHEAS
···· BARRY CUNLIFFE'S PROPOSED ROUTE.

Journey of Pytheos

Pytheas sailed along Britain's eastern coast eventually stopping at the Island of Abalus (Helgoland). After that he reached the estuary of the River Elbe still being a keen observer and recording how the natives lived in that region. He noticed that the Island of Abalus was the source of Amber. Thus, he became the first Mediterranean to give us written records of the early inhabitants of Germany. He then traveled from Bordeaux to the estuary of the Aude River via the River Garone as not to circumnavigate Spain.

Upon his arrival to Massalia, Pytheas wrote a book entitled "On the Ocean". In this book he recounted details of his voyage and his impressions of the people of Northern Europe and the lands that they inhabited. Unfortunately his accounts were not well received by the academia. They sounded too unrealistic. With the passing of time, the original book and its copies were lost and only fragments of it survived. The fragments that did survive were due to various geographers, astronomers and historians who included these articles in their books. Pytheas' accomplishments went almost unknown. But, today scientists have revised their opinions. Not only do they believe that his observations were accurate as far as science is concerned, but they are most enlightening.

Pytheas, the intrepid navigator-astronomer scored many firsts. They are as follows:

- He was the first to record the unusually high tides in the Atlantic off the coast of France and correctly attributed them to the magnetic pull of the moon.
- He was the first to notice that while approaching the Arctic Circle the celestial North Pole had no stars contrary to the then current belief that it was occupied by the star Polaris.
- He was the first man to accurately estimate Britain's circumference at 4,000 miles and was correct in declaring that its shape was triangular.
- He was the first to furnish us with written records of Britain's and Germany's original inhabitant's behavior.
- He was the first man to record the names Britain as "Pretannike" and its people "Pretanni". Many years later they were changed to Britannia and Briton.

He also traveled probably more than 14,000 miles.

In conclusion, Pytheas was not only a very experienced navigator, but he was also a top-notch astronomer whose astronomical measurements have been proven to be correct.

Pytheas' statue along with that of his compatriot Euthymenes have been placed in two niches in the upper façade of Marseilles' Stock-Exchange. Also his discoveries of the sources of tin and amber must have brought immense revenue to Marseilles' metal and jewelry industries.

Some other daring ancient Greek explorers were Pytholaus, Leon and Charimortus. They explored the coast of Eastern Africa.

One of the first scientists to sound the western Mediterranean Sea was Posidinius. He found that the sea south of Sardinia was 6,000 feet deep. Another explorer, Megasthenes, discovered the Ganges River of India and the island of Ceylon, which he named Taprobane.

It is written that Pytheas was the Greek explorer who went the farthest westward. It is said that Alexander was the Greek explorer who went the farthest eastward reaching the Malayan Peninsula (Laos, Malaya and Vietnam). He entered the threshold of the South China Sea. He also named the Malayan Peninsula "The Golden Peninsula".

The geographer and mapmaker, Claudius Ptolemy, who lived during the second century AD in Alexandria, made the first complete Atlas of the then known world. His atlas consisted of twenty-six maps showing the lands that extended from Ireland to the Orient. In showing Ireland, he named a city "Eblana" which today is Dublin, the capital of Ireland. He also named England's two most important headlands: "Land's End" in the southwest, and the "Lizard" in the southeast.

In addition, he indicated the exact distance between the Lizard and France. On one of his maps that shows Egypt, he placed correctly the source of the River Nile, including Mount Kilimanjaro, the highest mountain in Africa, Kenya and the Pamirs. He also included the Malay Peninsula and mentioned the City of Sinoi, which today is called Hanoi. His atlas contains 8,000 names of places, mountains, rivers, lakes, seas, cities, etc, and was regarded as the best for 1,000 years.

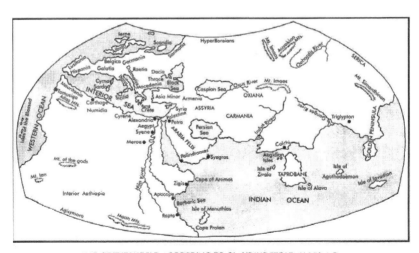

MAP OF THE WORLD ACCORDING TO CLAUDIUS PTOLEMY 150 A.D.

Astronomy

Ancient peoples were very interested in the stars. While some of them found it enough to make all kinds of fanciful stories about them, others like the Babylonians and Egyptians, took a more serious look at them, wondering about their nature, movements, etc.

With the coming of the Greeks, however, the stars became objects of intensive study as they tried to answer all the whys and hows about their origin, purpose and like questions. As their investigative process was a very methodic one, they created yet another science – Astronomy.

In the sixth century B.C., Thales of Miletus devised a method of figuring out when the next eclipse of the sun would occur. The eclipse happened on May 28, 585 B.C. Thales was also the first astronomer to discover that the light of the moon is not her own, but rather reflected sunlight.

Anaximenes discovered why eclipses happen. He correctly attributed the eclipse of the sun to the passing of the moon before it, and the eclipse of the moon to the earth's shadow falling on the first.

Parmenides answered the basic question of "What the stars are made of". He was correct in stating, "That all stars in the sky are balls of fire like our own sun."

Pythagoras was the first thinker to teach that the earth is not flat but a sphere. One day, looking at the eclipse of the moon, he noticed that the shadow of the earth falling upon it was like an arc. This phenomenon convinced him that the earth was spherical.

In the fifth century B.C., Empedocles discovered that, "The earth does not rest on any solid surface, but floats in space. An empty space surrounds the earth."

Ecphantus was the first astronomer to discover that, "The earth revolves around its axis in twenty-four hours."

Phaenos, a native of Athens and a notable astronomer, was able to measure the length of the year to be 365 days and six hours. Although he did not have at his disposal the accurate instruments that we have today, his calculation was very close to the accurate which is 365 days, five hours, forty-eight minutes and forty-six seconds!

During the third century B.C., the astronomer Aristarchus, a native of the Greek Island of Samos, made a novel discovery. He discovered, "That the volume of the sun is many times greater than that of the earth." In turn, this fact led him to the conclusion, "That the earth revolves annually around the sun in a circle."

When Aristarchus announced his theory, his fellow astronomers and the common people thought that such a theory was too radical. It was absurd for people, who all their lives felt that they lived on an earthly-firm ground, and watched the sun rise in the east, and after moving across the sky set in the west, to accept such a theory as sound. And so, Aristarchus' brilliant and absolutely correct theory remained only in his books.

Almost eighteen centuries later, the Polish Astronomer, Nicholas Copernicus, after reading Aristarchus' Theory, and after making many observations on this subject, finally announced the hard-to-accept fact that the sun and not the earth is the center of our solar system.

The first century Greek astronomer and mathematician, Sosigenes, who lived in Alexandria, Egypt, was asked by the Roman Emperor Julius Caesar to devise a calendar to be used throughout the Roman Empire. Sosigenes made the calendar, and his calendar was followed by the Western World until the fifteenth century AD. It was known as the Julian calendar, after the name of Julius Caesar, who asked for it. After being in use for 1,500 years, it was replaced by the "Gregorian Calendar," in use since the fifteenth century.

Indisputably, the most famous ancient Greek astronomer and one of the greatest astronomers of all time, was Hipparchus. He was a native of Nicea, Asia Minor, but spent most of his life on the Greek Island of Rhodes and Alexandria. Hipparchus was a genius for his milestone discoveries in Astronomy and their veracity are still honored today. Below are some of them.

He was the first astronomer to introduce trigonometry to astronomy, a geometrical field that helps the observer to calculate their distances of stars and their magnitudes.

He invented the "Dioptra", an instrument for measuring the diameter of the sun and the moon, as well as, two kinds of "Astrolabes" – the plane and the spherical. The plane astrolabe has the observer to compute the required triangulations, and, the spherical one, which consists of many metallic cycles, aids the observer to accurately determine the exact position of the desired star. Until the invention of the telescope, which occurred in the seventeenth century, Hipparchus' astrolabes were the main instruments of astronomers.

A very significant discovery that Hipparchus made in connection with the earth's rotation was the "Precession of the Equinoxes". Very briefly, it is an effect connected mainly with a gradual change of the direction of the Earth's axis of rotation. Hipparchus, using the shadow of the Earth on the moon during a lunar eclipse, was able to observe changes in the position of the Earth's axis. These changes were caused by a wobble, much like a spinning top, which is due to the gravitational pull of the moon and sun on the Earth's equator.

A milestone discovery this genius astronomer was able to make was his calculation of the "Mean Distance" of the moon from the earth. After careful observations and computations, he arrived at the correct figure of 240,000 miles. Coincidentally, this figure is equal to the diameter of the earth (8000 m) thirty times over.

Contrary to other astronomers and philosophers, who held that the stars' existence is perennial, Hipparchus taught that the stars' existence is not endless. Stars, he taught, have a beginning and an end, they form, they exist for a long time and finally they expend all their luminosity and then disintegrate. In this aspect, he was up to date.

Finally, another significant contribution was his cataloguing of 1080 stars whose position he fixed with the utmost accuracy. Moreover, he divided all the stars into six classes of brightness, or magnitudes. To the first class, belong the brightest stars and to the sixth, the faintest ones.

Hipparchus wrote many books on astronomy, some of which bear the titles "Constellations", "the Monthly Movements of the Moon", "The Duration of the Month", "the Duration of the Year", and others. Unfortunately, only the content of those that Claudius Ptolemy included in his famous astronomical compilation entitled "Syntaxis", has survived. The others perished.

The next and last brilliant ancient Greek astronomer was Claudius Ptolemy. He was born in the town of Pelusium of Lower Egypt in 108 AD, and died in Canobus in 168 AD. He spent nearly all his life in Alexandria.

Ptolemy, a very learned man in geography, mathematics, and astronomy, plus an assiduous compiler of knowledge amassed by his predecessors on all three above-mentioned fields, in reality lacked the ingenious approaches that Hipparchus used to answer the difficult workings of celestial phenomena. Nevertheless, we should not underestimate his methodic geographical, mathematical and astronomical compilations which preserved for posterity an invaluable body of knowledge on which subsequent generations would expand.

His astronomical "monument" to posterity was his "Syntaxis" consisting of thirteen books. Books I to IV deal with the "Ptolemaic System". This is a system that holds that the earth is the center of the universe and that the sun, the planets, and all other stars revolve around it. This theory, known also as the "Geocentric System" (The earth is the center of the Solar System, not the Sun), as we saw previously was attacked by Aristarchus as groundless. Book III deals with "Eccentrics and Epicycles". Ptolemy in his effort to prove the veracity of his geocentric system held, that "Eccentrics", that is, great circles whose centers were remote from the earth had "Epicycles", that is paths of planets on their circumferences. Although, at first glance, such a thing sounds plausible thus justifying the notion that the earth is at the center of the universe, in reality, it is groundless. Books VII and VIII contain catalogs of over 1,100 stars that are in the Northern and many in the Southern Hemisphere. It also deals with the precession of the equinoxes discovered by Hipparchus. The remaining five books deal with the five planets of our Solar System, (the other four, were not known in antiquity as they require telescopes in order to be seen), discussing in detail their motions, latitudes, orbits, inclinations, magnitudes, etc.

All the above, plus his "Geocentric Theory", became the "Bible" of astronomers for the second Century AD up to the sixteenth.

In the Sixth Century AD, Alexandria was conquered by the Arabs. In due course, Ptolemy's "Syntaxis" was translated into Arabic and received the title "Almagist". From the Twelfth Century onwards it was translated into Latin and all other European Languages.

Another testament to the Greeks' immense astronomical knowledge is the "Antikythera Mechanism". The mechanism salvaged from the shipwreck in the early 1900s, dates from 150-100 BC. The artifact consists of over 30 precisely crafted gears and relayed exact astronomical information based on the input of the date. Once a user selected a date, past, present or future the hands of the front of the mechanism pinpointed the location of the moon and sun, and the lunar phase. This device was far beyond its time as the level of intricacy was not seen again until the clocks of the 18th century. Ancient Greek astronomy has been the basis for modern advancements.

20
WIZARDS OF NUMBERS AND GEOMETRICAL THEOREMS

Two fields requiring sharp reasoning are mathematics and geometry. As the Greek mind triumphed in all other intellectual fields, so it did in the above two. And, it did so because it placed them on a purely scientific basis.

Before the ancient Greeks used numbers, the Babylonians and the Egyptians were already using them. As their use of numbers, however, was an empirical one, they never advanced beyond the point of making rudimentary computations.

Ancient Greek mathematics and geometry, which laid the foundation of our Western mathematics and geometrical tradition, began in the sixth century B.C., more specifically, with the pioneering work of Thales and the Pythagoreans.

Thales, an astronomer, mathematician and geometer, was the first man who tried to prove mathematical and geometrical statements through a series of arguments, thus inventing the most significant contribution to the field, "deductive mathematics". That is, reaching a conclusion by mental deduction. Two and-a-half centuries later, Euclid would carry this deductive reasoning to its present form. Other well-known geometrical theorems that were discovered by this great pioneer are: "The diameter of the circle divides it into two equal parts", "Vertical angles are equal", "The base angles of an isosceles triangle are equal", and others. He also made very accurate measurements of an Egyptian pyramid's height by comparing the length of its shadow to the shadow of a stick whose size he knew.

The philosophical and mathematical school of Pythagoras, based in the Greek colony of Crotona in southern Italy, likewise dominated fifth century Greek mathematics and geometry. We are all familiar with Pythagoras' "Logarithmic tables" and his solving the famous proposition, "The square of the hypotenuse of a right triangle is equal to the sum of the squares of the two other sides". Pythagoras also divided numbers into "even", "odd" and "irrational". They also contributed many other advances in mathematics.

A notable successor of Pythagoras was Archytas. He was a brilliant geometer, and, among other difficult problems he tried to solve, was one of three "Unsolved" problems of ancient Greek geometry, the "Duplication of the Cube". His trials to solve it with a compass and a straight edge proved futile. In the end, he solved it by means of an ingenious three-dimensional construction, using some artifices of his own that did not quite agree with the traditional methods. He is also credited with the invention of the pulley.

Hippocrates of Chios was another notable geometer, having gained fame for his quadratures of certain lines; a process which he always hoped would help him solve the second "Unsolved" problem of ancient Greek geometry, "The squaring of the circle".

Theaetetus, a native of Athens and a student of Plato, devoted much of his life after his graduation from Plato's Academy to studying the so-called "Irrational" numbers, whose study he was able to systematize. He also studied meticulously Plato's "five regular solids", and was the first to demonstrate that there were only those five and no others.

The fourth century opens with the work of Eudoxus, a native of the Greek colony of Cyzicus, Asia Minor, who was a brilliant astronomer and geometer. He enrolled in Plato's Academy, and, being poor, lived in a modest house located in the Port of Piraeus. This arrangement would necessitate his walking some five miles in the morning to go to the Academy and five miles in the evening to return home. After his graduation, he founded his own school in his hometown, and eventually settled in Athens. He discovered proofs on many geometrical problems, but, while as an astronomer, he observed the orbits of the planets, he was the first to notice that these were not absolutely circular, but somewhat "elliptical". He had made an important discovery.

Euclid, known the world over as "The Father of Geometry", is the most famous fourth century geometer. Following his graduation from Plato's Academy, he moved to Alexandria, which by now, thanks to the patronage of its kings the Ptolemies, was fast becoming the scientific center of the ancient world. The royal dynasty of the Ptolemies had founded two world-famous academic centers: the "Library", largest library in the ancient world, and the "Museum", as the university was called at that time.

It was here that Euclid came to teach and work out some new geometrical theorems, and also write his famous "Elements"- a collection of thirteen books that included all the hitherto geometrical and mathematical theories. His "Elements" begin with Thales' discoveries, and then continues with those of all other Greek geometers. It is a monumental work in that it includes all the theorems of plane and solid geometry. Two of Euclid's books are entitled "Optics" and "Catoptrica". Optics deals with the problems of vision, and, with the use of vision, to determine sizes and objects. Catoptrica (Theory of Mirrors) shows how light rays behave when reflected from plane, concave, and convex mirrors. Ever since the manufacturing of lenses began, Catoptrica has contributed significantly to the development of searchlights.

For 2,300 years, the "Elements", with slight modifications, has been the standard plane and solid geometry book throughout the world. Moreover, after the invention of printing, there have been over one thousand printed editions of it.

The third century B.C. was also the century of many eminent mathematicians and geometers. The first was Apollonius, a native of Perga,

Asia Minor. Apollonius devoted a great part of his life studying the "Conic Sections". He wrote about all his findings in eight books, of which only seven survived intact. In these books, which have been classics on this subject, he treats the properties of three curves "ellipse", "parabola" and "hyperbola," which are produced when cutting through a cone at particular angles.

Archimedes, who was born in the Greek colony of Syracuse in southern Italy, is indisputably the greatest mathematician of the third century B.C., the greatest mathematician of antiquity, and one of the three greatest mathematicians of all time. The other two would be Isaac Newton and F. Gauss.

Archimedes' genius was not interested only in pure mathematics. His interest in mechanics led him to invent the "Compound Pulley"and the "Endless Screw", a device that would drain a flooded area, or a ship, or a home. He was also a top-rated physicist, discovering the laws of "Statics" and "Hydrostatics".

As was stated above, his main interest was in pure mathematics, in the exact measurement of the circle, the sphere, the cone, conoids, spheroids, and the cylinder. He wrote three classic treatises, "Sphere and Cylinder", "Conoid and Spheroids" and the "Quadrature of the Parabola". In certain areas of the above, he had advanced so far, that he anticipated the principle of "Integral Calculus".

A recent event that clearly bespeaks of Archimedes' high esteem is the sale of a medieval Palimpsest (a parchment which has been used twice, the earlier writing having been erased); it contained beneath a prayerbooks' text seven mathematical treatises. It sold at an auction for $2M. The buyer deposited it in the library of Walters Art Gallery of Baltimore, MD for imaging and scholarly study. Three imaging processes have been used, and it is expected that the entire mathematical text will be available to mathematicians soon. They will concentrate on the last treatises – "The Floating Bodies", "Method of Mathematical Theorems" and the "Stomachion."

Nichomachus, a native of Gerasa, Palestine, was another outstanding mathematician. He wrote a compendium entitled "Mathematical Collection", which gained such popularity, that until the middle of the nineteenth century, it served as a basic guide for all schoolbooks on arithmetic all over the world. This book also earned its author the euphemism, "Father of Arithmetic".

During the middle of the third century AD, there appeared a Greek mathematical genius named Diophantus. He was born in Alexandria, Egypt, and beyond this fact we know nothing else about his life. We were fortunate, however, that his novel contribution to mathematics, namely algebra, survived.

Diophantus described his new mathematics in his now famous "Arithmetica", a work originally consisting of thirteen books. Unfortunately, only the first six survived. The surviving books contain algebraic problems involving "determinate", that is, only one possible answer, and "indeterminate", that is, many answers possible. The algebraic equations he invented are of the first and second degree.

His surviving books were passed on to the Arabs when the latter conquered Alexandria in the sixth century AD, and later reached Europe where they were translated into Latin. In the sixteenth century, Diophantus' "Arithmetica", was the only source of inspiration to mathematicians to further advance algebra.

Finally, the last eminent ancient Greek mathematician was Papus, a native of Alexandria. In his eight books, which he entitled "Synagogue" (Collection), he expounds on many geometrical and arithmetical problems, showing, among others, his success in trisecting the right angle, the "Third Unsolved Problem" of ancient Greek geometry. He also discovered the method of measuring the surface and volume of the sphere.

These, very, very briefly, were the most outstanding Greek mathematical thinkers of the ancient world. A rudimentary way of computing was transformed, by them, into a full-fledged science, a science that ever since, has served man in countless ways. By making geometry a science, enriching it with hundreds of terms such as theorem, postulate, proof, plane, solid, monohedral, etc., they made it a most indispensable tool to many other sciences.

21
ALEXANDER THE GREAT

In history, five men have been recognized as and awarded by the world with the title of "Great". They are Constantine the Great-Emperor of Rome and founder of the City of Constantinople, Frederick the Great-King of Prussia, Peter the Great-King of Russia, and Napoleon the Great who was an officer during the French Revolution in 1789, and then became an emperor conquering many countries.

There is one more, and this "Great" man appeared in history six centuries before Constantine the Great, who was mentioned earlier. He is known throughout the world as Alexander the Great, and by the time he was thirty-three years old, he had conquered most of the known world.

Alexander was the son of King Phillip and Queen Olympias. Phillip was the King of Macedonia, which was a region of northern Greece. Even when he was a child, Alexander looked very promising. He was brave, athletic, full of enthusiasm, and energy, and very thoughtful and cautious. When his father noticed these wonderful qualities in the mind and character of his son, he brought to his palace the famous philosopher Aristotle to tutor his son.

Aristotle, at that time, was the most famous thinker in all of Greece. He had been a student of Plato at the latter's "Academy" in Athens, and there, he had learned about politics, science, medicine, geology, the weather, astronomy, mathematics and music. With such a man as a teacher, young Alexander was indeed fortunate. He absorbed all he could from his very learned teacher, and so, by the time he would become king, he would be well-prepared.

During the time young Alexander was growing up, his father was busy organizing the army. In the end, he had the best-trained army plus an excellent cavalry. His plan was to unite all the small Greek states into one, and then, make war against the largest country in the world.

During the second half of the fourth century B.C., King Phillip's dream to see a united Greece came true. In the city of Corinth, the Greek states agreed to unite under Phillip. And so, for the first time in their history, the Greek people and their small states were united. Now, King Phillip started preparing for the second dream.

But that would not happen. Two years after he had united the Greek states, he was assassinated, thus leaving the throne to his young son, Alexander. Alexander, only twenty years old but very mature and well learned, thanks to his teacher Aristotle, and a very well trained soldier, now became King of Macedonia.

Like his father, young Alexander very much desired to make war against Persia for three reasons. First, he wanted to revenge the Persians who, one hundred and fifty years before, had made war against Greece and had destroyed Athens; second, he wished to set free the many Greeks cities of Asia Minor that were under Persian rule; and third, he desired to spread the Greek culture throughout the countries and people that made up the Persian Empire.

With an army that numbered only thirty thousand soldiers and five thousand cavalry divided into six battalions under the very able general's Parmenion, Cleitus, Craterus, Perdycas, Meleager, and Amyntos, Alexander, only twenty-two years old, set out to fight the greatest army in the world. In the spring of 334 B.C., he left Pella, the capital of his kingdom, and, with his army moved eastward, crossed the Straits of Hellespont and entered Asia Minor.

In two great battles, one held at the Granicus River, and the other near the city of Issus, the small but very brave army of Alexander defeated and routed a Persian Army, at least four times larger. These two victories made Alexander the master of Asia Minor, Syria, Lebanon, Palestine, and Egypt.   In Egypt, Alexander founded a new city, which he named Alexandria. In years to come, Alexandria would become the second largest city of the ancient world as its population would reach half a million. Today, Alexandria is still one of the largest cities in the world.

From Egypt, Alexander and his army marched northeast to Gaugamela, where Darius and his army were waiting to do battle. Again, Alexander and his soldiers fought against an army at least seven times larger, and, again they won. Darius was killed as he and his army fled in panic leaving Alexander as the undisputed master of the central Persian Empire that today is represented by the countries of Iraq, Afghanistan, Iran, Uzbekistan, Tadzhikistan, Turkmenistan, and Pakistan.

A most difficult feat that Alexander and his men achieved while in the country we now call Afghanistan was the crossing of the Khawak Pass that is eleven thousand six hundred and fifty feet high. Despite the snow covering the pass and its length, which was forty-seven miles, Alexander, his men and their animals managed to pass it in seventeen days. Then began a long march through the Hindu Kush region where the mountains rise to the height of over twenty-five thousand feet. Until now, no other army had marched through such high ground. Alexander the Great and his men had done the impossible!

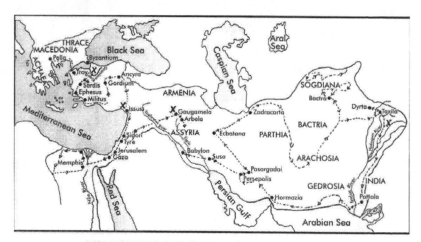

ALEXANDER THE GREAT'S EMPIRE AND HIS CAMPAIGNS 336-323 B.C.

After reaching the furthest point of his march that was in a region called Sogdiana (now called Tadzhikistan), Alexander founded his most northeastern "Alexandria", which he named "Alexandria Eschate", meaning the furthermost Alexandria. From here, some of his scouts went further to the east thus entering the most southwestern tip of the Sinkiang Province of China.

From here, he marched southeast, and after crossing the well-known "Khyber Pass", where mountains rise to the height of almost seventeen thousand feet, he and his men entered India. Today, the region he entered is known as the "Punjab".

Alexander and his army crossed the Indus River, and, when they reached another tributary river of the Indus named Hydaspis (now called Jhelum), King Porus and his army were already there and prepared to fight Alexander. This would be Alexander's fourth major battle. If he won, he would become master of this vast region.

Against Alexander and his army, King Porus had lined up a much larger army, several hundred scythe-bearing chariots and over two hundred elephants. Alexander, after maneuvering his army in different directions to confuse Porus, finally attacked. For eight hours, the two armies fought gallantly. Although Porus had over two hundred elephants, the men of Alexander with their usual courage, threw their spears and used all weapons expertly thereby destroying the enemy. In the end, Porus lost the battle which cost him several thousand dead.

To celebrate his victory, Alexander founded two more cities, "Nicaea" (Victory) and "Bucephala", in honor of his horse Bucephalus. Alexander wanted to go further into India but his army, tired from the long campaign, would not follow him. In disappointment, he began the very long march back to Babylon. When he and his army reached Babylon, after trudging for two months along the coastal region by the Indian Ocean and the Persian Gulf, the people and the city's officials greeted him with great excitement and enthusiasm.

After two months of residence in Babylon, Alexander died on June 10, 323 BC. He was not yet thirty-three years old.

In all of history, no other man has conquered so many countries in only ten years. He defeated a far greater imperial army with only thirty thousand soldiers and five thousand cavalrymen. He had marched and conquered lands that stretched a distance of more than two and a half thousand miles, either on foot or on horseback! The campaign marches of Alexander the Great amount to a total of twenty-two thousand miles. That is equivalent of five-sixths of the circumference of the earth, or four round trip crossings of the breadth of the U.S. That is back and forth and from coast to coast of the U.S. And, he was the first European, the first western man, to go so far into the continent of Asia.

It is not an exaggeration to say that of history's five designated "Greats", he was "The Greatest".

When Alexander the Great died, his vast empire was divided among his generals who in history are known as the "Diadochi", meaning successors. More specifically, Lysimachus took over the region of Thrace, Cassander the region including parts of Macedonia and central Greece, Antigonus the region that included Asia Minor, Syria, Lebanon, and Palestine, Ptolemy the region that included Egypt and Libya, and Seleucus the largest region that extended from Syria to India and included Iraq, Iran, Pakistan, and part of India.

The successors created dynasties which ruled the regions for at least three centuries. They sought as best as they could to apply Alexander the Great's dream of "Hellenization" of their subjects becoming successful mostly in the countries of the Middle East. They built at least thirty new cities in which large numbers of Greek population moved to from Greece. The greatest builder was Seleucus I. In one year alone, he built many cities with a population of at least 200,000 and "Seleucia" in Iraq numbering 600,000, surpassing in this effort even the Roman Emperor Augustus.

On the other hand, the Ptolemies, who ruled Egypt, created one of the most splendid dynasties of the ancient world. Although they did not found very large cities in their domain as the other successors of Alexander the Great did, their fostering of the sciences and learning greatly contributed to the advancement of human knowledge. Queen Cleopatra, the last representative of this long royal dynasty best exemplifies their mentality and aspirations. Not only was she very knowledgeable in Greek Literature, poetry, and unbelievably, in medicine and pharmacy, she was also a most witty, charming, gracious, and captivating woman.

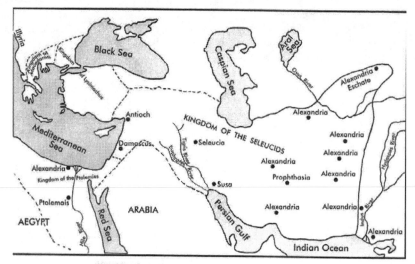

DIVISION OF ALEXANDER'S EMPIRE BY HIS SUCCESSORS.

22
THE INFLUENCE OF GREEK CULTURE
ON THE CONQUERED COUNTRIES

In the previous chapter, Alexander the Great is described as a conqueror. In this chapter, he will be described as a civilizer. How, that is, he influenced the countries that he conquered culturally. How the Greek way of life, Greek customs, Greek manners, Greek ideals, Greek science, art, and literature impacted on the lives of the millions of people he had conquered.

A noble ideal that Aristotle, Alexander's teacher put deep into his young student's mind, was: "How wonderful the world would be if all the people of the earth thought alike. And since Greek thinking (ideas etc.) was the best, if all the peoples of the earth had made it their own, they would definitely live in harmony and progress."

The above idea so impressed young Alexander that he decided to make it a reality. And so, when at the age of twenty-two he became king, and thereafter began a series of campaigns against the Persian Empire, his venerable teacher's idea of a world living in "Homonoia" (united in mind), in thinking, became the goal of his life.

Ancient historians tell us that he founded some seventy cities in the various countries that he conquered. All cities followed the style of the notable city-planner, Hippodamus, that is, they were made of square blocks each including many houses, while the streets intersected each other. Also, all of them had public buildings such as theaters, libraries, schools, temples, gymnasiums, and a marketplace at the center.

All these new cities, that were founded and lay between the Mediterranean Sea and India, and were built in the style of Hippodamus, naturally differed considerably from the cities built by the previous natives . Not only their design appeared neat against the maze-like one of the native cities, they also had many extras that represented the Greek way of life, such as libraries, philosophical schools, theaters, etc.

Libraries, for example, that up to now could only be found in royal palaces and in temples, and which usually had very few books, now could be found in every city of the Empire and contained hundreds of books. Theaters, that in the past were unheard of, now could be seen in every city and town so that the natives and the Greeks, who had come from Greece to live here, could see and enjoy the Greek plays. There were also gymnasiums for young, native people to participate in Greek sports such as boxing, wrestling, running, etc. And there were schools where young people could study math, geometry, astronomy, literature, medicine, botany and other such kinds of instruction. And, the language in which all the above arts and sciences were given, was the Greek Language that by now had become not only a second language, but also, the "Lingua Franca", that is, the international language of all these different nationals.

Greeks from Greece came by the thousands to live in the new cities. Since these immigrant people knew only Greek, the natives who also came to live in the same city began to learn the Greek Language.

Of the seventy cities that were founded by Alexander the Great, only a dozen of them bore the name Alexandria. Most of these cities are still inhabited today. Unfortunately, however, only one of these Alexandrias is called today by the Greek name Alexandria. It is the one that is in Egypt. The others are called by the native version of their name such as "Scandaria", "Kandakar", "Khojend", and other like names.

The influence of Greek culture in all its aspects of art, science, athletics, drama, etc., was mostly in the western countries of Alexander's empire. They were Asia Minor, Syria, Lebanon, Palestine, and Egypt. In these countries, Greek art, architecture and many other aspects of learning were pursued and the Greek Language was spoken widely. In fact, in Egypt, the Greek Language was spoken from the third century B.C., to the end of the fifth century AD with the Greek alphabet being widely used for the writing of the native Egyptian Language. Many sacred books of the "Coptic" Christians, for example, have been written in Greek.

In Asia Minor, Syria, Lebanon, and Palestine, the Greek culture was likewise very influential and the Greek Language widely spoken. In the cities of Ephesus, Pergamum, Smyrna, Philadelphia, and Tarsus of Asia Minor, the Greek Language was the main language of the people who lived in them, and their culture was primarily the Greek one. Ephesus was the fifth largest city of the ancient world and its three hundred thousand population thought, spoke and lived in Greek.

The City of Antioch in Syria, whose population was four hundred thousand, was another center of Greek culture. Of its four hundred thousands population, two hundred and fifty-thousands were Greeks from Athens and the region of Attica. Hence, it was called the "Syrian Athens". Other major Syrian cities had also been strongly influenced by Greek culture.

In Palestine, where at the close of the first century B.C., Jesus was born, the Greek culture was very influential. Nearly all Jews knew the Greek Language and the Greek cities were everywhere, especially in the regions of "Samaria", and the "Decapolis". The Greek mathematician, Nichomahos, whose textbook entitled "Arithmetics", was, in a modified form, the standard one used everywhere as late as two centuries ago, was born at Gerasa.

But, the country where Greek learning in all its aspects was most pursued was Egypt. It had dozens of cities and towns, many of which had been founded by Greeks, and whose population was to a large extent Greek. But the most prominent Greek city in this country, surnamed by the Greek historian Herodotus, was Alexandria, "The Gift of the Nile", which was founded by Alexander the Great.

The famous architect and city planner, Deinocrates, had designed this queen city of Egypt. It had many broad avenues crossing each other at right angles and interrupted often by squares and parks. "Canopus Street" was the main thoroughfare, one hundred feet wide and running through the entire span of the city from east to west. Deinocrates, foreseeing that the city's population would grow very rapidly, introduced a new type of house. It was multi-sectioned and thus many families could live in it. Years later, many other cities, especially Rome, would adopt this type of home. We may recognize this type of structure as being an apartment house. Of Alexandria's half a million population, only the Greeks, who were more than a third, were considered citizens. It follows then that all officials and authorities of the city would be Greeks.

The landmark of Alexandria was its lighthouse - the first of its kind in the history of man and the tallest ever. (A detailed description of the lighthouse is given in the chapter "Five Wonders").

Alexandria could also rightly boast of its famous university and its library, the largest in the ancient world. Historians suspect that half a million books were in that library. Translations of important books from other countries were also available. Instruction at the university was in Greek, and the library's books were also written in Greek. In this library, were also copies of the Old Testament Bible that had been translated from the Hebrew Language into the Greek by seventy rabbis by order of King Ptolemy. Famous Greek thinkers who studied and taught in this city were Euclid, the most famous geometer of antiquity, surnamed the "Father of Geometry"; Galen, one of the most famous physicians of antiquity; Ptolemy, the most famous geographer of ancient times, the astronomer Aristarhos, who first claimed that the earth and the other planets moved around the sun; Eratosthenes, who devised the means of measuring the circumference of the earth; Heron, who built the first steam engine; and Diophantos, who introduced first and second degree equations.

During the three hundred years of Greek rule in Egypt, some fifty medium sized and large temples were built by the Ptolomaic kings. Some have survived in an excellent state of preservation and others are in a semi ruinous or ruinous condition. Besides building temples, most of which were located in Upper Egypt (geographically, southern Egypt), the Ptolemies also added "Pylons" (monumental facades consisting of a pair of flanking towers with sloping walls and flanking the entrance portal) to those temples built by previous Egyptian pharaohs which lacked such imposing facades. "Propylons" (free standing gateways before the entrance of Egyptian temples), completed construction of unfinished ones, repaired and renovated old ones, and embellished with statuary and/or paintings characteristic of Egyptian religious art the exterior and interior walls of those temples which lacked them.

The Ptolemaic kings did not change the traditional Egyptian temple art and architecture, which, for more than 2,500 years had remained rigid in its stylistic expressions. Suspecting that if they had introduced any changes by infusing characteristic aspects of Greek art and architecture, these might offend the sensibilities of the Egyptian priesthood and of the native population, Greek influences were kept at a minimum. The only temple that was built in Greek architectural style was the "Serapium" in Alexandria. It was a colossal temple, the largest in that city, and had, in its interior, a colossal statue of Serapis, which resembled the statues of the god Aesculapius.

Still, however, some aspects of Greek architecture found their way into Egyptian temple construction. An example would be the use of prefabricated, individual stones placed "isodomically'," that is, in regular courses of equal height, thus contributing to an orderly appearance of the entire wall surfaces as in Greek temple architecture. Also, a modified acanthus leaf was introduced as a decorative feature in the capitals of the columns. Until now, the Egyptians used papyrus, lily or lotus leaves as decorative motifs of columnar capitals while the reliefs and hieroglyphics that were to decorate the walls and the columns were done according to sketches and drawings previously drawn. Finally, Greek engineers used their own tools and methods for the quarrying, transportation and lifting of stones and other architectural components.

Of all the temples that were built in Egypt by the Egyptian pharaohs and Ptolemaic kings, the few that have survived intact to this day were built by Ptolemaic kings. They include, the Temple of Horus - best preserved temple in all of Egypt, built by Ptolemy XII at Edfu. Its walls are filled with reliefs and hieroglyphics all of which are in excellent condition. The Temple of goddess Hathor, built by Ptolemy VIII at Dendera, has also been preserved in excellent condition. Hathor was the goddess of music, dance, joy, and of motherhood. Its walls and columns are lavishly decorated with figures and hieroglyphics making the temple a veritable showcase of Egyptian art. The ceiling of one of its halls has a unique feature - astronomical and astrological reliefs.

Other well-preserved temples are the temple of the god Anty, built by Ptolemy VI at Antaeopolis; the temple of goddess Isis, built by Ptolemy II on the Elephantine Island, an island in the River Nile and near the well-known Aswan Dam; the temple of Isis built by Ptolemy VI on Dabod and transferred in its entirety in 1972 to the "Parque de Rosales" in Madrid, Spain; and the Temple of Haroeris and Sobek built by the same king at Komombo.

Besides building beautiful temples, the Ptolemaic kings also founded many new cities. A leading founder of cities was Ptolemy II, surnamed "Philadelphus". He founded seven new cities on the coast of the Red Sea to promote trade with India. The new cities' names are: "Myos Hormos", "Philoteris", "Leucon Limen", (white port) "Berenike" (Bernice), "Trogodytike", "Ptolemaios", and "Adulis". In the district of Fayum, he also founded thirty to forty settlements for the Macedonian veterans of his army.

In the same district, he also founded the city of "Theadelfia".

The twelve Ptolemies that succeeded him founded many new cities which bear such names as "Leontopolis" (lion city), "Heracliopolis" (city of Hercules), "Hermopolis" (city of Hermes), "Lycopolis" (wolf city), "Diospolis" (city of Zeus), and many others.

In far away Iraq, at least twenty Greek cities were founded. They were Dura Europos, Apamea, Neapolis, Orchoe, Methone, Apollonia, Demetrias and others. Most of these were located near the Tigris and Euphrates Rivers, which traverse Iraq and empty into the Persian Gulf. Largest city was Seleucia, with a population that at its peak, had reached half a million. It was located near Baghdad, the present capital of Iraq.

Finally, far away India was another country that, for nearly three centuries, felt the presence of Greek rule. As mentioned in the previous chapter, Alexander the Great had conquered only the region of Punjab, which is India's northwestern-most city. After his death, three of the many Greek rulers that administered this region, were Euthydemus, who with his army, conquered the "Tarin Basin", which today is known as "Chinese Turkestan", thus becoming the first European and white man to penetrate and acquire Chinese territory; Demetrius the Invincible, who with his armies, conquered most of northern India extending his domain from the Persian Gulf to the Bay of Bengal; and Menander, his successor, who ruled this very large domain very ably and peacefully, especially when we bear in mind that in India, the Greeks were a small minority as compared to the vast numbers of the native population.

Besides Greek artifacts and a large number of Greek coins struck in India during the Greek rule, recently, archaeologists have brought to light shreds of scrolls bearing Greek writing, stones with Greek inscriptions and traces of foundations of Greek palaces and towns. Another area where Greek influences appear is in the statues of Buddha, which were carved at the time of the Greek rule of India, which show him wearing Greek dress.

Finally, another area where Alexander's achievements influenced the peoples of the Middle East and of India was their literature. Countless poems and legends were written, especially in Persia and in India, to praise the achievements of "Sescander", as Alexander the Great is called by them. Their poems and legends were also illustrated, and what is interesting, is that Alexander appears in these dressed in Persian or Indian royal attire.

Before closing this chapter, it would be a grave omission if we didn't mention a religious book, which having originated in the Middle East and was destined to spread to all the known world, was written, not in the language of the country of its origin, but in the ancient Greek Language - the international language of ancient times. It is our New Testament Bible!

Alexander the Great lived only thirty-three years, but his influence and legacy are still, being felt by millions if not billions of people.

23
HELLENISM AND THE JEWS

As mentioned in the previous chapter, one of the many peoples that was influenced by Hellenism following the conquests of Alexander the Great, were the Jews. At that time, (4th century B.C.) a good many Jews lived in Palestine. Most of them lived in what was known as the "Diaspora", towns and cities of other countries located in southern Europe, the Middle East and in North Africa. But, when all of these countries fell piecemeal under the sway of the famous conqueror, all the Jews (those living in Palestine and those in the diaspora) did not escape the influence of Hellenism.

In both Palestine and in the cities of the diaspora, learning to speak the Greek language as a second language, or as the only one, was an early Hellenizing influence in which the Jews were impacted; hence, the term "Hellenist", denoting a Jew who spoke Greek. Ancient Greek names were also adopted, to be used either as second names or as the only one. To mention three, Joseph became Menelaus, Solomon became Alexander, and Joshua became Jason.

Learning to speak the Greek language in Palestine (now spoken by Greek immigrants who lived in the newly founded cities along the Mediterranean coast, in northern Galilee, in Samaria, and to the east in Decapolis) was not the only thing the Hellenists sought to acquire. As they lived and daily interacted with the Greek population that lived in the same cities, they also began to adopt Greek customs, a Greek way of life and to cultivate close friendship with their Greek fellow-citizens. Moreover, overlooking the centuries-old separation from the pagan nations which leaders like Ezra and Nehemiah had established, they were now aiming at possible assimilation.

Even high priests of Judaism favored cultural fusion with the Greeks; such as Onias, Jason, Menelaus, and a line of successors all the way to Alcimus. In fact the high priest Jason went so far as to ask the Greek king of Syria – Antiochus Epiphanes, to depose his brother Onias in order to succeed him. He promised Antiochus that if he would do this, he, Jason, would introduce and propagate Greek art in Palestine. Antiochus fulfilled Jason's request, and soon, Greek art in its entire genre became the vogue in Palestine. Simultaneously, Jason ordered the building of a gymnasium (athletic amphitheater) where wrestling, boxing and other various athletic Greek games were held. Even the priests who served at the Temple of Jerusalem were given permission by Jason to participate in athletic contests.

When Menelaus became high priest, the "Maccabean Revolt" occurred in Palestine. What sparked this revolt was the attempt of Antiochus Epiphanes to impose the Greek pagan religion on the Jews. He had not realized the Jewish intransigence in regard to their Monotheism (belief in one God).

The Jewish resurgents, led by the Maccabee brothers; Simon, Judas, Eleazar, and Jonathan, after fighting a series of winning battles against Antiochus' generals (who led a Syrian Army), won the final victory in May of 142 B.C. This resulted in Palestine's independence. Simon Maccabee was given the ranks of High Priest, Ethnarch (ruler of the nation) and Leader. These titles became hereditary to his family that became known as the "Hasmonean".

When the new dynasty established its rule over Palestine, Hasmonaean high priests were now appointed as supreme religious leaders of the nation. Although these high priests strictly forbade any heathen religious practices, a large number of Jews still pursued the Greek customs and ways of life. The establishing of new gymnasia continued to multiply, while Greek athletic games were as enthusiastically pursued by the Jewish youth as before.

The Hasmonaean Dynasty was followed by the "Idumaean". The dynasty's most notable representative was the well known Herod the Great, who surpassing by far the Hellenizing tendencies of the other Idumaean kings, boasted that "He was much more a Greek than a Jew."

Being an adorer of Greek culture in all its aspects, he surrounded himself by Greek sages and poets and built a large hippodrome in Jerusalem and a beautiful theater for the staging of Greek dramas. But his grandest structure was the Temple of Jerusalem. It was a vast esplanade 900 x 1000 feet that was surrounded by porticos whose hundreds of Corinthian columns rendered a most pleasing elegance. More to the north of this vast court stood the Temple, which also featured Corinthian pilasters and columns. Numerous Greek inscriptions reminded the pagan visitors not to trespass from the Temple Court to the sanctuary. Interestingly, the coffers of the Temple wherein the people dropped their "shekels" (coins) were marked by Greek letters. Finally, for visiting Hellenist worshippers to Jerusalem, there were the synagogues of the "Libertines", the "Cyrenaeans", the "Alexandrians", the "Cilicians", and others.

Jewish literature, in all its genres, was also influenced by the Hellenist Jews. As the Hellenist Jews read avidly the hundreds upon hundreds of poetic, dramatic, and prose, works of the Greek writers, they sought to imitate them in their own literary writings.

Eupolemus wrote a chronicle entitled "On the Kings of Judaea", as did Thalos, whose chronicle covers events from the time of the Biblical Creation to the time of Tiberius. Artapanus, an Egyptian Jew, wrote a fictional biography of Moses. He Hellenized his name to "Musaeos" and portrays him as the teacher of Orpheus, conqueror of the Ethiopians, and inventor of the hieroglyphics. Needless to mention, this fictional work was aimed at exalting the Liberator of the Jews in the eyes of gentile readers. Other notable Hellenist writers include Alexander Polyhistor, Aristeas and

Jason of Cyrene. Unfortunately only fragments of the works that we mentioned above have survived.

We also have fragments from the poems of two Hellenists. The first fragment comes from the poem "On Jerusalem" composed by a certain Philo the Presbyter. The poem was written in hexameters. The other fragments come from the poem "Jacob on Shechem". In this poem, the poet unfolds the history of the town of Shechem with interpolations from Greek mythology.

Ezekiel, a Hellenist dramatist, wrote plays in which he imitates the style of the Greek dramatists. Only fragments of one of his plays entitled "Exodus" have survived. The theme of the play is the departure of the Hebrew slaves from Egypt under the leadership of Moses. The text is in Euripidean trimeters.

By far, the most numerous and most Hellenized Jews lived in Alexandria. As the services in the synagogues of that great metropolis and in other cities of Egypt were conducted in the Hebrew language, the service became totally unintelligible to the worshippers. Consequently, a need for a translation of the Bible from Hebrew to Greek became imperative.

Thanks to the munificent patronage of King Ptolemy II Philadelphus (285-246 B.C.), seventy Hellenist rabbis under the direction of Demetrius, (an eminent Jewish historian), translated the "Torah" (law). The Torah is contained in the first five books of the Old Testament Bible, namely Genesis, Exodus, Leviticus, Numbers, Deuteronomy, and which in the church's language are collectively known as the "Pentateuch". Since seventy rabbis participated in the task of the translation, this translation is known as the "Septuagint" (Latin for seventy). This translation is also the official one used by the Greek Orthodox Church. Needless to emphasize, that when this translation was completed, it was received with great joy by the Hellenists of Alexandria, as well as by those in the diaspora.

Years after the translation of the Torah was completed, there appeared Greek versions of other Old Testament books such as Ezra, Esther, Ecclesiastes, and others.

A religious book in whose chapters classical Greek and Hellenistic philosophy seems to echo, is to be found in the Wisdom Books of the Old Testament Bible, namely, Job, Proverbs, Ecclesiastes, and Ecclesiasticus.

Platonic, Stoic, Epicurean, as well as certain Greek poets' and playwrights' reflections on moral, social and theological aspects sporadically echo in their texts.

Four "Deuterocanonical" books entitled "Maccabees" also appeared at this time. Their epic content deals with some of the most glorious pages of ancient Jewish history, the victorious events in the struggle against Antiochus, who tried to impose heathen idolatry on the Jews. The fourth book of Maccabees strongly resembles cynic and stoic philosophical diatribes. In its subject regarding the "Four cardinal virtues", the arguments used are stoic while the forms of disputations are modeled after Plato's dialogue entitled "Gorgias". Although, originally, these four books were written in Hebrew, only the Greek translations have survived. All four books were included in the Septuagint Bible.

Josephus is the best known Alexandrian Hellenist. He wrote the "Jewish Archaeology", a historic account of all the events from the beginning to his own time, and the "Jewish War" in which he describes at length the Jewish revolt against Rome. His books have survived in their entirety.

In philosophy, the Neoplatonist Hellenist thinker Philo, who also hailed from Alexandria, is a notable representative. Philo attempted to show that when Biblical thought is allegorically interpreted, it has close similarity with the teachings of the Greek philosophy. He also held that God is one, self-sufficient, incorporeal, and possesses infinite power and goodness. He contended that man may attain happiness by controlling his desires and by contemplating God. When the fourth century notable Church Father Saint Jerome read the works of Philo, having noticed the strong influence of Platonic thought in them, said: "Either Plato Philonizes or Philo Platonizes." Like Josephus' books, Philo's also have survived in their entirety.

Finally, a considerable number of ancient Greek words were incorporated into the Jewish language. The words made reference to law, the arts, architecture, weapons, tools, weights, furniture, commerce, medicine, pharmacy and any conceivable attitude or thing. Many of these words can be found in the Talmud, which is the authoritative body of legal and moral law based on the Old Testament Bible, and in the "Targums". A sampling of four Greek words that were incorporated in the Jewish language are: "Epikoros", meaning a Jew who is lax about his religious duties; "Bimah", meaning an elevated platform in the synagogue where the rabbi performs the service; "Gematria", meaning the disclosing of the hidden meaning of a Biblical word by reckoning the numerical equivalents of the Hebrew letters; and "Sandak", a word derived from the Greek noun "Synteknos" which meant companion to the child. In the Jewish language it refers to the person who holds the child on his knees during the circumcision ceremony – a kind of Godfather.

Thus, during the centuries in which the Jews of both Palestine and the Diaspora came in very close contact with the Greeks, they stubbornly resisted the acceptance of polytheism (belief in many gods), and remained ever loyal to their monotheism. They eagerly assimilated all other Greek cultural and intellectual pursuits, especially, the Greek ideal of "Paideia", which means study. Education acquired such primary importance that ever since, most Jews have made it their life's goal. The results were inestimable. Greek Philosophy helped them systematize their theology, while Greek literary and scientific scholarship greatly broadened their understanding of the world. Expressing this fact, the late Abba Eban, Israel's Minister of culture, in his book entitled "Heritage" wrote that "The Jews have come to regard study (paideia) as one of the highest goals of human life and the surest path to personal improvement."

On the Feast of Pentecost (traditional year 33 AD), the Church was founded in Jerusalem. Native Jews as well as Hellenists became the church's very first members. These Christians formed the nucleus of the new religion. But, as in later times the apostles set out to preach the Gospel in other countries around the Mediterranean Sea, the number of Christians now coming from converts from Judaism and pagans greatly added to the original number that had been converted in Jerusalem.

Two versions of the Old Testament Bible were used by these very early Christians. The Christians of Palestine, who were converted from native Jews, used the "Palestinian Code" that had been authorized by the rabbis of Palestine; while the Christians who were converted from the Hellenists used the "Alexandrian Code" which was the Septuagint. Besides the Old Testament Bible, early Christians also used the currently circulating Gospels and Epistles written in Greek by the Evangelists and the Apostles. In 325 AD, the Church fathers who participated in the First Ecumenical Councils compiled these to form the New Testament Bible. Interestingly, as of the 2nd century A.D., when overwhelming numbers of Christians were converted from the pagan Greek world, the Greek Bible (Septuagint and New Testament Gospels and Epistles) was in use by the church during the first four centuries.

Two outstanding Hellenist Christians made their mark during the First Century AD. The first was St. Stephen, a gifted and ardent Christian teacher who served the Church of Jerusalem for some months. However, his persistent emphasis that Israel had become unfaithful to its trust, and that the Church which had accepted Jesus as the true Messiah (Savior) was the true Israel, greatly angered the Jewish hierarchy. They summoned him to court and during the trial a mob dragged him out and stoned him to death.

The other famous Hellenist was St. Paul, a native of Tarsus whose dominant culture was Greek. He had good knowledge of the Greek language, a fair knowledge of Greek rhetoric and of many aspects of Greek culture. Thus, armed, he was most effective in preaching the salvation of Jesus to the pagan world.

24
THE BEGINNING OF
THE END OF PAGANISM

In the year 33 AD, a most significant event occurred in the city of Jerusalem (capital of Judaea), whose consequences had a tremendous impact in subsequent history. It was neither a revolution, nor the beginning of a global war, not even the publication of a book whose content would have far reaching effects on most people of the earth, such as the publication of Darwin's "Origin of Species" or Karl Marx's "Communist Manifesto". Actually, it began quietly and, from that initial stage, by the Grace of God, it began spreading rapidly throughout the ancient world and continuing thereafter.

It was towards the end of May or the beginning of June at the latest, that the Jewish Feast of Pentecost was being celebrated. Pentecost was one of the three annual pilgrimage feasts. When these feasts were to be observed, a great number of Jews would come to Jerusalem to witness the special celebrations, particularly in the Temple. The other two feasts were the Passover and the Sukoth (Booths).

Quite unexpectedly, a man by the name of Peter who during the past three years, along with eleven other men had been disciples of Jesus, began preaching in the street that ran by the house where previously the disciples had witnessed the Holy Spirit descending upon them in the form of tongues of fire. This was intended to enlighten and strengthen them in their future mission as apostles of Christ.

Peter's speech about Jesus' redeeming teachings, wondrous miracles, death on the Cross for the salvation of all mankind, and His incredible resurrection three days later, was so dynamic, so moving, that when upon concluding, he called his audience to repent and be baptized in the name of Christ in order to be saved. Three thousand Jews came forward to be baptized. And with this event, the Church, which was to continue the instructive and sanctifying work of Christ to the end of time, had been established on that day.

As Peter and the other eleven apostles continued their preaching in Jerusalem and the neighboring towns, more and more people were abandoning the synagogue and were embracing the Church. At first, they took the Church as another offshoot of Judaism. At that time, Judaism was not a unified religion as it was in the days of Moses, the kings and the Prophets, but had been separated into three religious sects – the "Pharisees" (Separatists), who were the strictest and most conservative of all Jews; the "Saducees," who were the aristocrats and not as strict as the Pharisees; and the "Essenes" (Pietists) who had monastic tendencies, as many of them lived in isolated communes along the shore of the Dead Sea like those of the Qumran.

Those very early followers of Christ were not called Christians but "Nazareans", after Nazareth, the town where Christ had grown. Jews were so impressed by the superb teachings of Christ that they eagerly joined the Church.

But the Church was not to limit itself to converts from Judaism. Since its Divine Founder had died on the Cross as a ransom for the salvation of all mankind, and since during His ministry he had repeatedly stressed his desire to see all of mankind embrace His teachings and be saved, the Apostles, after having founded many Christian communities in Judaea, Samaria, and Galilee, began entering all neighboring countries where the majority of the population was not Jewish but pagan.

Using the same tactics as in Palestine, that is, preaching the Gospel and baptizing those who came forward and expressed their willingness to join the Church, the apostles, after entrusting the newly founded Church to a priest, would depart for other places.

One of the cities where the fledgling Church won many converts was Antioch in Syria. Here the converts named themselves "Christians", that is, followers of Christ. This name eventually brought the segregation of the Church from Judaism, and its determination to henceforth go its own way.

As at this time, Greek people lived by the hundreds of thousands in all the major cities of the Middle East and of north Africa, many of them, dissatisfied with their pagan religion which was based on rituals, non-existing gods and goddesses – figments of poetic and literary fancy, eagerly and enthusiastically were now joining the Church.

The people who lived in Greece also heard the Gospel and received the Baptism, and the apostle, who first introduced the new redeeming religion to this ancient country, was the great apostle, Saint Paul, in the year 51 AD.

The very first city of Greece to which St. Paul arrived by boat from Asia Minor was the city of Neapolis in Northern Greece. Today, this city is known as Cavalla. In Neapolis, St. Paul was well received and, after founding a church, he went to two other nearby cities – Amphipolis and Philippi. Having founded Christian Churches in both those cities, he went to Thessalonica – largest city in Northern Greece, where he stayed for quite a few days. After founding a Church there, he went to Berea to again succeed in establishing a Church. From Berea, he headed south and, after proceeding a distance of at least two hundred and fifty miles, arrived in Athens.

What was Athens like in the year 51 AD? It was neither the city that it had been in the Golden Age five centuries previously, nor was it a commercial center comparable to nearby Corinth. It was, however, still the most revered and famous seat of learning, the intellectual Mecca, the intellectual center of the world.

What kind of people were the Athenians whom St. Paul was hoping to bring into the Church?

In the first place, they were unlike the people the great apostle had addressed in other cities, Athenians loved lectures. They loved to argue, speculate and discuss. If they lived in Medieval Europe, they would be scholastics. Discussing a concept, or moral, social, physical or metaphysical theory pedantically, analyzing all its pros and cons, all its positive and negative aspects, down to the least and last detail, and in the end, pronounce it useful or useless, meaningful or absurd, was to them an "intellectual feast". And how they loved to spend hours on such discussions!

The same attitude was shown toward religion. Like other ideas and concepts, religion was mainly a subject of discussion. They would be content to discuss any religious subject analyzing all its negative and positive aspects, but not practice it.

When the great apostle arrived in Athens, he did not address the Athenians formally in any of their spacious lecture halls. Instead, he roamed the streets to talk informally with the people and thus learn more about their thoughts. During this time, he also discovered that two philosophical schools were now in prominence: the mundane minded, materialistic Epicureans, and the idealistic Stoics.

One day, St. Paul was invited by the Stoics and the Epicureans to speak to them about his religion on Mars Hill that lies opposite the Acropolis. St. Paul accepted the invitation and, facing a large audience, he spoke as follows:

"Men of Athens, I noticed that you are very religious because as I was walking I saw your many altars, and one of them had an inscription on it "To the Unknown God". You have been worshipping him without knowing who he is, and now, I wish to tell you about him.

"It was God who created the universe and the earth and not your gods and goddesses. In fact, this God is so infinite, so immense, so vast, so great that your divinities cannot contain Him; and because He is so great, he does not need anything from you. There is nothing you can offer Him.

"He is the Author of all life, of all living things, and providentially, it is He that cares for their sustenance.

"All people on earth descend from one original couple and, by multiplication, their descendants are everywhere on earth. Moreover, it is God who determines which nations will rise to prominence and which will wane.

"God is not limited in size like the statues of your fictional gods which you make out of stone, wood, or silver and then set them up in temples to worship them. When you do this, you worship stones and wood. God is so infinite, that within Him, the universe, the earth and all of us move and live."

Then Paul concluded his speech by telling his audience that in the future, God would justly judge the world through His Son, after raising all the dead. (Luke ch. 17, 22-31)

There is no doubt that Saint Paul's speech on Mars Hill must have been a great deal lengthier. However, the synopsis that Saint Luke preserved for us in the Book of the Acts, includes all major points that the great apostle revealed to the Athenians, like: There is one God who by virtue of being eternal, infinite, creator of the universe, the earth, and man, and providential, because of all these divine attributes, He and only He, is the true God and not the fictional gods and goddesses the Athenians believed in, and make statues of identifying those statues with the gods and goddesses themselves and even worship them.

Up to this point, St. Paul's speech must have satisfied the intellectual curiosity of his sophisticated audience. But when they heard Paul declaring a resurrection of the dead and a final Judgment, the audience began sneering and departing.

Only the chief justice, Dionysius, a woman by the name of Damaris and few others came forward and were baptized thus forming the nucleus of a Christian Church in a city that for centuries had been the seat of learning.

From other ancient written sources, we learn that Dionysius became Bishop of Athens and later Bishop of Paris, France. But the small church that Paul had founded would not remain static. With the passing of years, it grew, and by the beginning of the fifth century, nearly all the population of Athens had become Christian. Even the city's large and beautiful pagan temples were taken over by the Religion of Christ. To mention three, the incomparable Parthenon became Church of the Most Blessed Virgin Mary, the colossal temple of Olympian Zeus (Jupiter), became the Church of St. John the Divine and the temple of Theseus, by the Agora, and became the Church of St. George.

From Athens, St. Paul headed west to Corinth, which was then the largest city in Greece. Here, he stayed for eighteen months. He labored hard to convert Jews and pagan Greeks to the Religion of Christ.

The response in Corinth was not reluctant as in Athens. The cosmopolitan, and to a certain extent multi-ethnic population of this large city and port, showed great interest in the preaching of Paul. Paul was very successful in Corinth. He succeeded in converting large numbers of Corinthians to Christ. And so, during the middle of the first century, Corinth could rightly boast as having numerically the largest Christian population in Greece.

Before leaving Corinth, St. Paul wrote two epistles (letters) to the Christians of Thessalonica. The letters contained many answers to questions that the newly converted people of that city had regarding many aspects of their new faith. Thus, chronologically speaking, the first two of the total of twenty-seven books that make up our New Testament bible were written in Corinth.

Another apostle of Christ – St. Andrew, the first man to be called by Jesus at the beginning of His ministry, to become a disciple, also came to Greece to preach Jesus and to found the Church. St. Andrew went to Patras – a city and port located in Northwestern Peloponessus, and here he spent the last years of his life preaching Christ and winning many inhabitants to the Christian Religion. When the authorities of the city saw how successful St. Andrew was in bringing people to Christ, and fearing that the pagan religion was in danger, they arrested the Apostle and crucified him on an X shaped cross. Today, on the spot where the Apostle Andrew was crucified, stands the largest Church, not only in Greece, but in all of South Eastern Europe – the magnificent Cathedral of St. Andrew, housing his relics and many pieces of his cross.

During the persecution of the Roman Emperor Domitian against the fledging Church, Saint John the Evangelist, who had spent most of his life in Ephesus – a city of Asia Minor, a city that was the fourth largest city in the then Western world, was exiled to the Greek Island of Patmos. He spent two years in a cave of the island that was used as a prison.

While in this cave, he wrote the book of the "Revelation", which chronologically, is the last book of the New Testament Bible to be written. And so, by the unfolding of events, the writing of our New Testament had its beginning and ending in Greece.

But more of this Holy Book was to be written in Greece. At some time of the first century, that we do not know and perhaps we will never know, Saint Luke the Evangelist also came to Greece to preach about Christ and establish churches. He settled in Achaia, as central Greece was then called, and, at about the year 80 AD, he wrote the Gospel that bears his name and the book of the Acts which contains the history of the early Church from the year of its founding in Jerusalem in 33 AD until the late 60's. And so, one of the four gospels in our possession, and the oldest record that we also have regarding the founding and earliest history of the Church, were also written in Greece.

Saint Paul revisited Greece twice more. During these visits he wrote the following epistles: "Romans", written while in Corinth in 57 AD, "Second Corinthians", written in Macedonia (Northern Greece) in 57 AD, and "First Timothy", also written in Macedonia the same year. (See "St. Paul Preaching in Athens" below.).

Almost two thousand years have passed since the Church was founded in Greece by Sts. Paul, Andrew, John, and Luke. During these twenty, consecutive centuries, the Church never ceased to spiritually guide the people of this ancient land by instructing them the divine, infallible precepts of Christ and sanctifying them through the Sacraments.

25
AN ANCIENT BLUEPRINT FOR OUR FEDERAL GOVERNMENT

When the American Revolutionary War ended, there emerged on the eastern coast of North America, thirteen independent colonies. The English rule that from the founding of the colonies in the 1700's, kept the latter tied to England had ended. Taxes and other unpleasant impositions that the "Mother Country" had imposed on the thirteen colonies and which considerably coerced their lives would from now be a thing of the past.

To justify the cause for the rebellion and to direct the War for American Independence, the thirteen colonies had called two assemblies known as the "First and Second Continental Congresses" which both convened in Philadelphia. It was these congresses that authorized Thomas Jefferson to draw up the "Declaration of Independence", and later, appointed George Washington to take charge of the Revolutionary Army whose fighting would hopefully end English rule in the colonies.

When the protracted war ended, it had accomplished its original objectives. The colonies were free but they lacked a central government to keep them together as a nation. The "Articles of Confederation", an instrument that provided authority to the Continental Congress to raise armies and conduct war, did not provide any clauses for a central government to ensure the thirteen colonies' future existence as a unified nation.

As many serious problems also plagued the newly liberated colonies at the end of the war: such as a debt of forty million dollars to foreign governments; moneyless farmers and businessmen; no funds to pay the soldiers who had fought in the Revolutionary War; and inability of the Continental Congress to finance an army and a navy; the need of a National, Federal Government, became imperative.

In order to decide for the formation of such a Federal Government, without, however, weakening the powers of the individual colonies' governments, fifty-five delegates from the colonies attended the sessions that were held in Philadelphia. They assiduously held sessions for three and-a-half months "behind closed doors," and what resulted from these sessions was "The Constitution", that authorized the formation and workings of Federal Government, the powers of the states' governments, the rights of citizens, etc.

Some of the best-educated American men were present in the sessions. A few would include: James Madison, "Father of the Constitution"; George Washington who presided over the sessions, from Virginia; Alexander Hamilton from New York; William Paterson from New

Jersey; Rufus King from Massachusetts; and Benjamin Franklin along with the distinguished jurist James Wilson from Pennsylvania.

Where did this venerable body of "Fathers" turn for ideas to execute their epoch-making task? Being that all of them were well versed in Greek and Roman History, they turned to the federated system of old Rome with the other cities of Latium. But, it was in Greece that such a government had come to full fruition during the late fifth and fourth century B.C.!

If the early fifth century B.C. produced Democracy in Athens allowing every citizen to participate in the affairs of state, the late fifth and fourth centuries produced a representative National Government in two regions of Greece. The first was the "Achaean League" in southwestern mainland Greece, and the second was the "Aetolian League" in west central mainland Greece. As both leagues had practically the same representative government, we shall briefly consider here the Aetolian League.

The Aetolian League was a federal union of absolutely independent states. It had a federal constitution, which closely resembled that of the Achaean League. The General Assembly, which was convoked every autumn at the city of Thermon, elected officials and formulated the League's general policy. Any free citizen was eligible to participate.

The Council of Deputies from the federated cities undertook the routine of administration and jurisdiction. The "Strategies" (General and Supreme leaders) and the thirty ministers, who correspond to the President and the Cabinet members of our government plus a federal treasurer, and a federal supreme secretary, served no doubt as an ideal prototype to form our Federal Government along these lines.

At the same time, each city of the League had complete autonomy and its own local government, absolute equality with the other federated cities, but all questions of foreign policy such as declaration of war, federal taxes and other such matters, were referred to the "League Council".

And so, a very simple, ancient prototype of a Federal Government became the blueprint for the Federal Government of a modern nation – The United States of America!

Doric

Ionic

Corinthian

The three orders of capitals of Classical Greek Architecture

26
THE CONQUEROR BECOMES CONQUERED

When the Romans conquered all of the Italian Peninsula, they then turned their attention to the east. After conquering the Country of Illyria, which stretches along the coastal region of present day Yugoslavia, they then conquered the Greek Island of Corcyra. The conquest of this island greatly angered King Phillip of Macedonia, who vainly tried to dislodge the Romans from the island.

Later, the Macedonian Army conquered regions of Asia Minor. This made the other Greeks unite against the Macedonians. They even requested the help of the Romans. The latter, capitalizing on this ill-conceived request, sent a sizable army to Greece which, after battling the Macedonian Army, emerged victorious. This victory greatly pleased the other Greeks who now regarded the Romans as "Liberators". Little did they suspect the real motives and goals of this seemingly "friendly ally".

In vain, Perseus, the Macedonian King, sought to unite the Greeks to make war against this actually foreign invader who had now firmly entrenched himself on Greek territory. In fact, when the Romans were informed of what Perseus was trying to do, they attacked, defeated his army and captured him. They then proceeded to conquer the other cities of Greece until they reached Leucopetra near Corinth in Southern Greece. There, in 146 B.C., the defenders of freedom raised the last resistance against a numerically superior foe. Their brave resistance failed to win them victory, an event that resulted to Greece's turning into yet another Roman province.

Momius proceeded to Corinth, destroyed the city, slaughtered many of its male population and carried off to Rome three thousand statues, many paintings and other artistic artifacts of incalculable value. As for the rest of Greece, from now until 330 AD, at which time it would be incorporated into the Byzantine Empire, the country would remain under Roman occupation.

This was not the first time in which the less civilized conqueror came face-to-face with a people of a superior culture. Romans already had come in contact with the Greeks who for centuries had established numerous colonies in Southern Italy and Sicily, and had already become familiar with the latter's superior art, philosophy and technology.

If now, having become masters of the heart of the Greek world, they would benefit far more, oddly from a people they would for three and-a-half centuries occupy. Moreover, as in future centuries they would conquer Western Europe that includes the present day states of Spain, France, England, Holland, Belgium, and southern Germany they would become the carriers of many aspects of the Greek Civilization to these countries.

It was the Roman's eventual realization of the Greeks' uniqueness among all the peoples they had conquered, that irresistibly they began to admire them and consequently almost slavishly imitated every aspect of the latters' superior culture.

Very early, Athens, Olympia and Delphi would be granted the status of "Civitas Libera" (Free City), a status very few cities throughout the Empire enjoyed.

Greek professionals, such as, doctors, engineers, architects, and teachers were in demand in Rome and in the other provinces. Greek physicians not only had won high esteem as being the most knowledgeable in the art of curing, many of them had served as imperial physicians - a most coveted position. The famous Galen is a case in point.

Greek doctors and engineers were very much in demand when the Empire was about to construct some of its grandest buildings in Rome and in the Provinces. And so, a slightly "Romanized" Greek Architecture would dominate the cities that lay between Britain to Dacia (Romania) and from Germany to North Africa.

Greek teachers would also travel throughout the cities of the Empire to be hired as tutors of the Greek Language of Homer and other ancient Greek writers. It added distinction to a Roman to know the Greek Language whose vocal sounds they considered far more pleasant then those of their own Latin language. In fact, patricians and Romans of higher classes regarded it quite apropos while speaking in their native language to suddenly use a few Greek words or sentences and thus impress their fellow conversationalist.

Greek philosophers would also profit tremendously from the Romans' eagerness to enrich themselves with the gems of Platonism, Aristotelianism, Stoicism, and Epicurianism. Those who taught in Athens and Rhodes had young students come to them and matriculate for a few years – young men who later would become leaders and prominent men of their Empire such as Cicero, Scipio Africans, Julius Caesar, Marcus Aurelius and a host of others.

And last but not least, Romans would use Greek sculptors and painters to lavish their homes and public buildings with fine copies of Greek sculpture and paintings. By the hundreds, Greek sculptors came to Rome and the other provincial cities to be hired by the wealthy, to carve their busts or make replicas of famous ancient Greek statues to adorn their homes, their gardens and their fountains. Or, statues could have been ordered from Greece and, after their completion, be shipped to their destinations. Greek painters were also hired by emperors and patricians to adorn the walls of their palaces and residences with beautiful murals, whose figures, like those of the statues, were imbued with superb elegance, grace and proper polychromic coloring.

Ancient Greek drama, in both its tragic and comedic form, became most popular throughout the Empire. Particularly the plays of Euripidis were of the most performed. Romans equally delighted hearing them performed in Latin or Greek.

DENNIS MICHELIS

Just as today Leipzig, Germany, New York, Paris, London and other such cities are "Printing Centers", so was Athens during those centuries of Roman suzerainty. Copies of philosophical, poetic, dramatic, and scientific works were produced in great numbers to be destined for export to Rome and other major cities of the Empire.

Some Roman emperors were of the staunchest admirers of Greek culture and learning. Emperor Hadrian was a typical example. Not only did he know the Greek Language very well, he even enjoyed the company of Greek sages and poets in his palace. When he built a fabulous villa at Tivoli, covering many acres, the complex was a miniature Greece. He recreated a replica of the famous Valle of Tempe, of the Temple of Theseum, a Greek theater, a Greek gymnasium, a stadium, and a round reflecting pool with statues of the "Caryatides" like those of the Erechtheum Temple on the Athens Acropolis.

When he came to Athens, he added a new section to the city almost half the area of the existing one which he called "Novae Atenae" (New Athens), he completed the gigantic Temple of Olympian Zeus, a reservoir, a triumphant arch, and a most impressive library containing 100,000 books.

Julius Caesar likewise loved Athens. He built a new, very large marketplace whose ruins still stand. Agrippa – a relative of Emperor Augustus also built a large theater in Athens.

" Novae Atenae"
The new section of Athens that Emperor Hadrian added to the Old City of Athens

180

From the beginning of the third century B.C., down to the beginning of the first century A.D., Roman Literature in all its aspects, would be strongly influenced by Greek Literature. The process began with Livius Andronicus.

When in 268 B.C., the Romans captured Tarentum – a Greek colony and native city of Andronicus, he and his fellow Greeks were brought as captives to Rome. When their captors learned that many of them were highly educated in many aspects of Greek learning, they made them tutors of the Greek Language and of Greek Literature to their children.

Livius Andronicus, however, would go much further than that. He translated the "Odyssey" into Latin, a translation that for centuries thereafter would serve as a standard textbook in Roman schools, and introduced Greek dramatic performances in public games.

Notable Roman dramatists such as Naevius, Plautus and Ennius who wrote many tragedies and comedies strongly imitated the themes and style of Greek originals.

The notable poet Lucretius, author of the philosophical poem "De Rerum Natura", used Greek metre and his subject is the philosophy of the Greek thinker, Epicurus.

The well-known Virgil, a poet of the "Augustan Age" and a thoroughly Hellenized Roman, in writing his "Bucolics", would strongly imitate the pastoral works of Theocritus, while in his "Georgics", he would draw heavily from other Greek authors.

Finally, Horace, who was also a prominent poet of the Augustan Age, was steeped in Greek lyric poetry. He also imbued his poems with Greek philosophy. In one of his writings, acknowledging the superiority of the Greek civilization, he wrote: "Greece conquered with weapons, nevertheless won over the savage conqueror and brought the arts to uncivilized Latium."

The great influence of Greek learning and of Greek cultural aspect in the thinking and the daily life of the Roman people began alarming certain conservative citizens who wanted Roman culture to remain unchanged. But the majority of the people, including the majority of their thinkers, thought otherwise.

To quote verbatim a Roman chronicler who included in his writings this antagonist, he wrote, "Some say, 'Non possumus ferre Graecum urbem.' (We cannot accept to see Rome turning Greek)," to which the majority would answer, "Doctrina Graeca omni genere superat (Greek learning is superior to ours in everything)."

How ironic! Even though mighty Rome had conquered Greece, turning it into another province, little could she foresee the lasting conquests the Greek spirit and culture would have on her own people.

Emperor Augustus

The strong influence of Hellenistic sculpture
is most evident in this Roman statue.

27
APOLLODORUS

Back at the beginning of the second century AD, that is, almost 1800 years ago, a boy was born in the ancient city of Damascus, the capital of Syria and whom his parents named Apollodorus (Gift of Apollo). His parents and all his ancestors were Greek. They originally had come from Greece and had settled in the Syrian capital. Syria, which borders with Palestine – the country of Jesus, is in the Middle East, and, like all other countries around the Mediterranean Sea was part of the Roman Empire.

When Apollodorus grew up, he studied architecture. When he completed his studies, he designed many homes in Damascus and then decided to move to Rome, the capital of the Roman Empire. There, among a population of nearly one million, Apollodorus was very busy designing homes right from the beginning. Wealthy Romans also came to him to have him design large and beautiful homes.

At this time, the man who ruled the Roman Empire was Trajan. Trajan spent most of his life fighting to conquer more lands and thus make his empire bigger. The most recent land that he had conquered was Dacia (today's Romania) – a land rich and fertile. Since Dacia was fertile, other tribes beyond the frontiers of the empire would frequently try to reconquer it thus forcing the Romans to keep a large army there to defend it.

The River Danube, which was one of the largest, deepest and widest rivers of Europe separated Dacia from the other lands of the Roman Empire. A large bridge, therefore, had to be built to make easy the passage of people and armies to and from Dacia.

Emperor Trajan had heard of Apollodorus as being one of the most capable architects in his domain and decided to have him design and build the bridge. Apollodorus left Rome, went to the River Danube, chose the right spot where he would build the bridge, designed it, and, with the help of the army, built it.

When the mighty stone bridge was completed, it was one of the largest bridges built in ancient times. It was nearly a third of a mile long and was supported on sixteen stone towers each sixty feet high. The bridge was a marvel of engineering and was built in only one year.

The emperor, very pleased with the work of his young architect, rewarded him with the title, "Imperial Architect". Soon he asked him to make designs for a large gymnasium, a college, large public baths, an Odeum (theater for musical performances), and two beautiful triumphal arenas for the cities of Benevento and Ancona. Again and again the emperor was pleased with the beautiful buildings his Greek architect had designed. Apollodorus had become famous.

Now, Trajan would give him one more commission – his greatest. Apollodorus was asked to make designs for a large forum that would be named for the emperor. Apollodorus made scores of designs for so great a complex. Moreover, he made sure that all of these buildings would be connected in such a way as to make up a unified whole. And when it was completed, it was the most beautiful of all the forums in the capital.

Its spacious plaza was flanked by two rows of hundreds of Corinthian columns behind which were walkways with shops. At the opposite end of the entrance to the plaza, was the "Basilica Ulpia" that spanned the width of the plaza. The Basilica was used as a Law Court. Its columns, floor and walls were of marble of different colors and imported to Rome from the countries of Europe, the Middle East and of Northern Africa. It was a most splendid interior. Behind the basilica were two smaller buildings. They were the Greek and Roman Libraries with each containing 22,000 Greek and Roman scrolls.

Between the two libraries, a column of 110 feet rose with a statue of Trajan on top. It was not just another column, but a "Historiated Column", in that its surface depicted, in spiraling form, the wars of Trajan against the Dacians. The "historiated column" was thus an invention of Apollodorus and was to be repeated in many other countries. At the base of this column was the tomb of Trajan. Two and a half thousand human figures were carved on the downward spiraling of this column.

Beyond the column and the two libraries, was the very large Temple of Trajan. This was built in Corinthian Style with the interior containing a large bronze gilded statue of the emperor dressed as the god Jupiter. A grand and opulent complex such as this had not been built in Rome until now. It remained unsurpassable in the future also. Moreover, it set the pace for many such unified forums to be built in other parts of the Empire.

As for Apollodorus, the Greek architect from Damascus who had designed so many impressive buildings, his lasting reward has been his recognition as "A Very Famous Architect".

The historiated column of Emperor Trajan in his
forum designed by architect Apollodorus.

PART II

BYZANTINE TIMES

28
THE BYZANTINE EMPIRE
(MEDIEVAL GREEK WORLD 330-1453 AD)

During the fourth century, and, to be more exact, in the year 324 AD, the Roman Emperor, Constantine the Great, whose Roman Empire included every country that lay around the Mediterranean Sea, was seriously thinking of moving the capital of his empire from Rome to Byzantium.

Byzantium was an ancient Greek colony by the Straits of the Bosporus where southeastern Europe and Asia meet. He believed that if the capital of the empire were moved here, it would better-defend the eastern countries of the empire that recently had been under constant threats by the Goths and the Persians.

Having decided to move the capital, he ordered his best architects and builders to make plans to enlarge the city many times its present size. Constantine hoped to contain all the imperial administration buildings and the hundreds of thousands of people that would come to live there. By the year 330 AD, the new capital had been built. The emperor took up residence in the new and big palace, as did the ministers and nobles of the government in the many mansions of the city, and, along with them, thousands of people as well as military and naval personnel.

Constantine the Great died in 337 AD. Until the end of the Empire, that is, in the next 1,116 years, some eighty-five emperors, belonging to thirteen dynasties, would rule in succession. And so, the empire, that in the future, would come to be known as the "Byzantine Empire" would last longer than any other in western history — more than eleven centuries.

Constantine the Great had many worthy successors. Theodosius was one of them. He ruled the empire from 379 to 395, that is, for sixteen years, and the following are some of his most important policies instituted.

In 380 AD, he made the Christian Religion the official one of the empire. In 391 AD, he forbade the worship of the pagan gods and goddesses, and, in 394 AD, he stopped the Olympic Games. The Olympic Games would again resume in 1896 in Athens, Greece, that is 1,502 years later.

Theodosius was also the last emperor who ruled the entire Roman Empire from Constantinople. Before he died, he divided it into an Eastern and a Western Empire. He gave the eastern half to his son Arcadius, and the Western to his son, Honorius. With the passing of the years, the Goths would take over the western part, forming new countries, while the eastern part would remain intact.

During the sixth century, one of the greatest rulers of all times would rule the Byzantine Empire. His name was Justinian. He began his reign in 527, and ruled until his death in 565 AD, that is for thirty-eight consecutive years. Details about the life and accomplishments of this greatest of all Byzantine emperors are described in the next chapter.

Just as the sixth century was dominated by Justinian, so the seventh century was dominated by Heracleius. Triumphant victories won by the Byzantine Armies marked the beginning of this century. The Persian Army, led by King Chosroes, conquered Palestine, entered Jerusalem and took the Cross of Christ to Ctesiphon, the Persian capital. Emperor Heracleius, at the head of his army, marched all the way to faraway Ctesiphon, utterly defeated the Persian Army, entered Ctesiphon, found the Holy Cross intact in the palace, and brought it back to Jerusalem.

But the latter part of the century brought reverses to the Byzantine Empire. Arabic armies entered Syria, Egypt, Armenia, and North Africa, and wrested away all the territories from Byzantium. Moreover, in Italy, the Lombards wrested most of northern Italy from Byzantine domination, while in the Balkan Peninsula, the Bulgars settled in its eastern-central half and the Serbs and Croats in its western.

In the eighth century, a new royal dynasty took over the "Isaurian". From the beginning of this century and for the next one hundred and twenty years, a religious controversy, known as "Iconomachy", (an effort to do away with icons), dominated the scene. During these years, the Christian people of the Byzantine Empire were divided between those who wanted sacred icons and murals in their churches and called themselves "Iconolatres", and those who did not, the "Iconomachs". In the end, an Ecumenical Council, which was convened at Constantinople, settled the controversy in favor of the iconolatres.

The ninth, tenth, and most of the eleventh centuries were dominated by the able emperors who belonged to the "Macedonian Dynasty". During these centuries, the Empire experienced a significant cultural rebirth and recovery of most of its lost territories. Brilliant, patriotic, and strong-willed emperors, such as Basil I, Nicephorus, John Tzimisces, and Basil II, led the empire to new heights of prestige and glory. Through their military expertise, they were able to recover many hitherto lost territories. In the East, they pushed the Persians back to the Euphrates River, they reconquered Syria and Palestine, and, in the Balkan Peninsula, they made the states of the Bulgars and of the Serbs and Croats into Byzantine provinces. Thus, by the year 1025, when Basil the second died, the empire stretched from Syria to the south, to the Danube River in the north, and from Armenia in the east, to southern Italy in the west. It was during the tenure of the Macedonian Dynasty, and, to be more exact, during the ninth decade of the tenth century, that Greek Orthodox missionaries went to Russia by the hundreds to convert the Russians to the Orthodox Faith and to transmit to them the Byzantine culture.

During the latter part of the eleventh century, a new foe appeared from the east - a barbarous Asiatic horde known as Turks. In 1071, they invaded Asia Minor, and, when the Byzantine Army, headed by Emperor

Romanus met them at Manzikert, the latter was defeated. From this time on, and until 1453, Asia Minor would slowly slip to Turkish domination.

A new dynasty, the "Comneni", would dominate Byzantium from 1081 to 1185. The emperors of this dynasty gave stability to the Empire by holding the Turks at bay in the east and the Normans in the west. But their successors, the dynasty of the "Angeli", were very weak. Exploiting their weaknesses, the armies of the Fourth Crusade conquered Constantinople in 1204.

The crusaders, headed by the Venetian dogue (leader) Dandolo, following their entry into the capital, pillaged the homes, the palaces, mansions, churches, and monasteries for days. They stripped them of all religious art, rare books, jewelry, and every kind of artistic artifact. Today, these pieces of art can be seen in the various museums of Europe.

While Constantinople was occupied by the crusaders, a new dynasty of Byzantine emperors, the "Palaeologi", were reigning from Nicaea, a city in northwestern Turkey, waiting for the opportune moment to return to Constantinople. That moment came, when in 1261, Emperor Michael Palaeologus, having been informed that there were no crusaders in the city, for they had left to wage battle in a faraway city, entered the capital with his army and was crowned king. Thus, he inaugurated the last dynasty to rule the Empire until May 29, 1453, when a Turkish Army, after many days of siege, conquered the capital, bringing an end to an empire that had lasted for 1,121 years.

THE BYZANTINE EMPIRE
AT ITS HEIGHT
A.D. 565

29
BYZANTIUM'S
MOST FAMOUS EMPEROR

From 330 AD, the year Constantinople was founded, until 1453, the year Constantinople fell to the Turks, some eighty-seven emperors ruled the Byzantine (medieval Greek) Empire. Justinian I was unquestionably the most famous of all Byzantine emperors.

Flavius Anicius, as Justinian was originally named, was born in the town of Tauresium located near modern day Naissus.

He was the only son of Sabatius, who was a farmer. His mother was the sister of the Justin commander of the imperial guards of Emperor Anastasius whom he succeeded at his death in 518 AD. While still a very young man, Justinian came to Constantinople to receive an excellent education. After his graduation, his uncle adopted him, changed his name to Justinian and was commissioned in the palace guards. But military life was not his "cup of tea". After serving for a short time in the palace guards, he was appointed adviser to his imperial uncle on all matters of domestic and foreign policy.

For almost nine years, Justinian served as a very able adviser to his uncle. In fact, it was at this time that he chanced to meet Theodora, a woman fifteen years his junior, very attractive, very firm and prudent. In 525 AD, he married her, and, on April 4, 527, Justinian and Theodora were crowned emperor and empress of Byzantium. When four months later Justin died, Justinian, now aged forty-five ascended the throne becoming the most powerful ruler in the entire Western World.

A grandiose dream dominated the mind of the new emperor. He wished to restore the fallen Roman Empire to its past territorial and cultural glory. But in order to achieve this, he would have to wrest the vast western territories of Europe from the Vandals and the Goths who now occupied them.

Justinian had the knack of selecting the ablest men, who, would not only remain faithful to him through thick and thin, but who would also do anything to help him achieve this grandiose dream. They were John of Cappadocia who became the chief administrator of his realm, the generals - Belissarius and Narses, the most famous architects of his realm - Anthemius of Tralles and Isidorus of Miletus, and last but not least, the most learned jurist of his realm - Tribonian.

The first years of his reign were occupied by wars against the Persians, whose still mighty nation lay east of the Byzantine Empire. But, by the year 532, Justinian signed a treaty with the Persian King Chosroes I - a treaty that enabled Justinian to withdraw most of his armies back to his capital for use in any military eventuality elsewhere. Somehow, this next eventuality was not long coming, and, as it turned out, it seriously challenged his imperial authority.

In January, 532, a great riot broke out at the Hippodrome of the capital. Heavy taxation and corruption among many high officials were the two main reasons that caused the furiously indignant citizens of the capital to turn against the empire's governing body. To be more exact, the fury of the people had "zeroed in" on two individuals who were advisors and close collaborators of the emperor - John of Cappadocia and Tribonian.

The riot soon spread to all parts of the city resulting in the destruction of most public buildings and incendiary assaults on numberless private homes. In no time, the rioters were in control of nearly all the districts of the capital excluding the one where the palace was, because it was ably defended by the imperial guards.

Justinian, greatly intimidated by this ever-growing menace and fearing for his life, was now seriously thinking of abdicating his throne and deserting the capital. Never in his entire life had he ever felt so discouraged, so desperate, so lost. But auspicious circumstances were soon to turn the tables. They didn't come from his trusted men around him - his advisors, his magistrates, or his guards, but from his beloved consort.

While at this most critical and low point, the ever-firm, cool and optimistic Theodora came to him, and, with the following counsel, greatly animated his spirits, freeing him totally of the discouragement he was experiencing. She said to him:

"If flight were the only means of safety, yet I should disdain to fly. Death is the condition of our birth, but they who have reigned should never survive the loss of dignity and dominion. I implore Heaven that I may never be seen, not a day, without, my diadem and purple; that I may no longer behold the light when I cease to be saluted with the name of the queen. If you resolve, O Caesar to fly, you have treasures; behold the sea, you have ships; but tremble lest the desire of life should expose you to wretched exile and ignominious death. For my own part, I adhere to the maxim of antiquity, that the throne is a glorious sepulcher."

These words so stirred the heart of the emperor that he immediately ordered his imperial guards to strike against the rioters who were still destroying and pillaging the capital. They were ordered to achieve nothing short of complete suppression of the revolt no matter what the cost. The result was a mass bloodbath.

Thirty thousand rioters were put to the sword, and thus, the riot of "Nika", as it was called, was suppressed. The suppression made such an impact on the people, that during the long remainder of his reign, Justinian never faced a similar crisis.

When peace and order were fully restored to the semi-ruined capital, Justinian thought that the time had come to initiate action to materialize his grandiose dream. Thereupon, he ordered Belissarius to conduct a campaign against the Vandals who presently occupied North

Africa. In 533, the able general landed his troops in North Africa and, after two decisive battles that were fought against the Vandals who were in possession of North Africa, the barbarian vandals laid down their arms and thus all this vast territory came under Byzantine domination. The Vandal King Gelimeros surrendered to Belissarius who now, having completed the conquest of North Africa, went on and conquered Southeastern Spain, the Ballearic Islands and the islands of Sardinia and Corsica.

Following an almost two year rest, Belissarius began the second and very important phase of his whole campaign that aimed at the restoration of the Roman Empire - the conquest of Sicily and Italy, presently occupied by the Ostrogoths. In 535, he landed his troops in Syracuse, Sicily and, after conquering Palermo and Messina, he landed in Italy proper. Using brilliant strategies, he advanced north conquering Naples, Capua, Rome, Rimini, Ravenna, and Milan. It took him six years to complete the conquest of Italy (535-541), and strangely, even though Belissarius had defeated the Ostrogoths, the latter, after some time, having risen against their Byzantine masters, were able to set up a certain Totilla as the king of Italy. In order to suppress this insurrection, Justinian sent fresh troops to Italy under the able general Narses, who, having entered Italy from the North pushed southward totally defeating Totilla and his armies. From that point, Italy would be another province of the Byzantine Empire.

With this last campaign, Justinian's dream had become a reality. The Mediterranean Sea had become a Byzantine lake. The Byzantine navy would henceforth be master of both the Eastern and the Western Mediterranean while the Byzantine armies, along with administrative officials, would hold and administer all the vast territories around the Mediterranean Sea. The old Roman Empire had been resuscitated.

Like many other great leaders before and after him, Justinian was a great builder. He rebuilt all the public buildings that had been destroyed by the "Nika" rioters and ordered the redesigning of the entire city. He also provided for the construction of many underground cisterns for the storage of water. He commissioned the building of twenty-five churches in the capital, one of which was his famous Cathedral of Saint Sophia - largest Christian church at the time of its construction. Likewise, in many cities of his empire, he built new aqueducts; while in various regions he built fortresses, bridges and fortifications as needed. In provincial cities, he built new cathedrals such as the "Nea" Church in Jerusalem, the Church of St. John the Divine in Ephesus, and the Churches of St. Vitale and St. Apollinare in Classe in Ravenna. High on the slopes of Mt. Sinai where God gave the Ten Commandments to Moses, he built the famous Monastery of St. Catherine. His grand building program also included the rebuilding of cities partly or wholly destroyed by armies or earthquakes as well as at least twenty-five entirely new cities that bore the name "Justiniana". Last but not least, in order to specially honor the place of his birth, he built the city of "Justiniana Prima" near Naissus.

From all the above it becomes evident that Justinian was one of the greatest builders in history. One may safely say that only a handful of rulers can match the extent of his building programs.

Just as Justinian was a great builder, so was he a great lawgiver. Wishing to codify the laws of his "universal empire", he authorized the most learned jurist, Tribonian, to codify all the existing laws, old and recent.

On February 13, 528, a commission of ten judges, ex-judges, and jurists, under the direction of the most eminent jurist of the Empire, Tribonian, undertook the tedious and copious task of codifying the laws. They were to eliminate all existing contradictions, thus rendering a codification free of antagonistic laws. By 529, the Commission presented the emperor a new and comprehensive code known as the "Code of Justinian".

Twenty months after the publication of the above code, Tribonian, assisted by seventeen jurists, was again hard at work to codify another. This commission was to collect and study two thousand books containing a tremendous amount of commentary on the laws. It took the commission three years to study, to coordinate the vast commentary and then publish it. It bore the title "Digesta", and consisted of twenty books. The same commission proceeded likewise to publish four additional books that served as a manual of laws for students of law who studied at the legal schools of Constantinople, Beirut and Rome. The title of this compilation is "Institutes".

The final codification, which Tribonian and his commission published in the year 534, bore the name of "Novellae". It included the most recent laws decreed by Emperor Justinian.

It took in all five years for this monumental compilation to take place, and what a significant contribution it made to mankind! As the civilian and ecclesiastical legislation of Justinian served as the foundation of nearly all Western European nations and presently of most non-European nations, one might safely say that this codification was one of the most significant milestones in the history of jurisprudence.

Some of the most shining aspects of this codification include; the doing away with laws that were against the emancipation of slaves, and the severe curtailment of the right of the father over the lives and property of his children. It simplified the laws of adoption; divorce became more difficult. It made ordinances protecting married women and debtors as well as laws on controlling rates of interest. Maiming was substituted for the death penalty and made imprisonment a chastisement.

In later centuries, the codification of Justinian's laws would be known by the title, "Corpus Juris Civilis". Referring to their everlasting value and great significance, a contemporary American jurist wrote: "When a renaissance of interest in the Roman Law began to draw Europe out of the Dark Ages and to afford a base for the development of modern jurisprudence, it was Justinian's law books which were studied; and his codes formed the foundation stones for the eventual structure of European and a great deal of English and American law."

During his long reign, Justinian, believing, that in his capacity as Byzantine emperor, was also God's regent on earth, he felt that one of his main tasks would be the promotion of uniformity of Christian Belief. Hence, in 529, he ordered the closing of the Platonic Academy of Athens, which taught pagan philosophy. He turned against the heretical Monophysites, that is, Christians who believed that Christ did not have a human and a divine nature, but only one - the divine, and he also turned against the Jews.

With the respect to the Jews, he forbade them to recite during their worship service, the "Shema", that is, the Old Testament Biblical passage: "Hear O' Israel, the Lord is your God, the Lord is the One" as going against the Christian dogma of the Holy Trinity, the "Shimone Ezre", that is, the Nineteen Benedictions that are a fundamental part of the Jewish worship service, and the "Deuterosis", that is, the homily which the rabbi traditionally delivers after the reading of an excerpt from the Bible. Thus, by ordering the curtailment of the above most essential parts of the Jewish worship service, Justinian deprived it of its most important aspects.

The expensive projects that Justinian undertook to accomplish in many regions of his empire could be financed only through the taxation of the people. Ruthlessly, the tax collectors of John of Cappadocia would collect the taxes, a process that soon created the hatred of both the rich landowners and the city dwellers against the emperor. Yet, by eliminating corruption among the tax collectors and high officials, he always managed to collect the awesome amounts that he needed to run the state bureaucracies and to sponsor his buildings projects. He also imported silkworms from China, thus creating the silk industry, which remained the state monopoly.

During his long reign, there also appeared an epidemic - a bubonic plague, whose high death toll caused considerable depopulation of his empire. More than three hundred thousand died in the capital, while many times that number died in the countryside.

This, very, very briefly was the life of the greatest Medieval Greek emperor, who ruled his vast realm for thirty-eight consecutive years. His many activities and accomplishments reveal that he had incredible energy. His dream of recreating the Roman Empire and his unwavering pursuit to see it through, reveal a rare and most admirable determination in reaching one's goal. Although he possessed weaknesses, his perseverance to see his projects and goals materialize causes us to wonder at his dedication to the endeavor to which he had committed himself. He tolerated the criticisms against him, and always loved Theodora sincerely and most dearly. After her death, he remained loyal to all her wishes. In short, Justinian loved grandeur, and grandeur he achieved.

30
JUSTINIAN'S GEM

Throughout history certain national leaders have also been great builders. Egypt's pharaohs built the stupendous pyramids, classical Greece's Pericles built the Parthenon, Rome's Augustus boasted that "he inherited Rome a city of brick and left it a city of marble." Roman Emperor Constantine who founded Constantinople, France's Louis the Fourteenth who built the Versailles and Russia's Peter the Great who built St. Petersburg were great builders.

Justinian, Byzantine Greece's most famous emperor, was likewise a great builder. He built many monuments, forts and all kinds of public works throughout his empire and some of the largest churches, such as the Church of St. John the Divine at Ephesus, the Church of St. Catherine on Mount Sinai, and the Nea Church in Jerusalem – one of the largest and most beautiful churches of that time, many churches in Constantinople like the Church of the Holy Apostles, of St. Irene and others. Now, he was contemplating to build the largest church in the entire Christian world – the Cathedral of St. Sophia.

As the new cathedral was to by far exceed any existing church, he summoned to the capital two of the ablest architects of his domain – Anthemius of Tralles and Isidorus of Militus. They would build a basilica topped by a huge dome.

Until now the Romans had built many domical structures of which the most famous was Rome's "Pantheon" – a pagan temple dedicated to all known gods. The dome always rested upon a circular wall. Thus far, no solution had been found to rest a dome on a rectangular or square structure. Thus, to build a rectangular church topped by a dome presented Anthemius and his nephew Isidorus a most difficult, a most challenging problem.

Besides being a most highly talented architect, Anthemius was also an expert geometer and this additional expertise proved most helpful to bringing about the final solution. As resting a dome on a rectangular structure was definitely impossible, Anthemius rightly reasoned that it should rest on some other architectural element – an element that had to be invented.

After much study and thought, he at last found the solution. Since the rectangular shape of the church demanded that its dome rest on four massive piers that would form a square, and since a circular dome cannot stand on four piers, the connective architectural elements that needed to be invented ought to be of such shape so as for each to be able to assume one fourth of the dome's thrust and transfer it to the massive square piers. Having arrived at this conclusion, the shape of the architectural element that had to be invented was already in his mind – it was a concave, spherical triangle now called "pendentive".

In its upper part, the pendentive would extend to a length that would be equal to one-fourth of the base of the dome. Thus, it would receive one-fourth of the dome's weight, and, as it tapered down to a square equal to the top of the pier, it would effectively transfer the weight to the pier. As the other three pendentives would function the same way, the weight, the thrust of the dome would safely rest on four square piers.

With the awesome problem solved in the year 532 AD, Justinian ordered his architects to commence construction. Some ten thousand skilled and unskilled workers – bricklayers, marble carvers and other kinds of craftsmen from every part of the Byzantine Empire were assembled in the capital to work on the awesome project.

Building materials also came from different provinces of the empire. White marble came from the Island of Marmara, yellow marble from North Africa, verd-antique from Thessaly (a region of central Greece), ancient red porphyry from Egypt, and columns from the Temple of the Sun from Baalbeck, Syria.

The cathedral had three aisles with upper galleries to accommodate more worshippers. The length of the cathedral from the back wall of the sanctuary to the exonarthex (outer vestibule) was 335 feet; its width was 225 feet and its height, from the floor of the nave to the highest point of the dome, 185 feet and the diameter of the dome 105 feet.

Exquisite polychromic, mosaic murals, depicting scenes from the life of Christ, His blessed Mother and figures of saints set against a golden or deep blue field, adorned many parts of the interior walls. Huge marble slabs replete with subtle veining and polished to shine brightly, covered the interior walls up to the galleries' level. Mosaic decorations covered all arches and vaults. The many columns, most of which were of verd-green color, had white delicately carved capitals with the monograms of Justinian and his wife on them. The white marble spandrels above the capitals that formed arcaded colonnades were also delicately carved, thus rendering a most delightful sight to the beholder.

A great number of arched large and small windows allow much sunlight to stream in and light up the entire interior. At the base of the dome, hourly windows allow additional light to enter, which not only illuminates the nave, but the dome as well. This is where the mural of Christ the Almighty was located. Thus, the people who stood at the nave 185 feet below could clearly see the superb mosaic bust of Christ that dominated the center of the dome.

Describing the impression one receives as he enters the vast cathedral, Andre Grabar, professor of Paleo-Christian and Byzantine Art at the College de France, in his book entitled "The Golden Age of Justinian" wrote: "When one enters inside he soon perceives that everything conspires to produce the impression of an immense space ideally organized. From the main door of the nave, looking along the axis of the church towards the apse, the beholder can appreciate the noble sweep and majestic proportions of the vast interior, with its supporting columns and walls covered with colored marbles. His gaze is drawn towards the mighty vaults overhead which – apparently so cambrous when seen from the outside – seem to float in air, released from the pull of gravity, the moment one has entered the church.

"The effect derives from the exquisite proportioning of all the structural elements and the skill with which the massive bulk of the four great piers and their lateral buttresses is concealed from the eye. Finally, the illuminated zone set up at the base of the dome, and many windows with which it is pierced, create an impression of soaring lightness that makes us forget that this exceptionally wide vault, representing a tremendous weight, is up born only by means of the great piers and arches on which it rests.

"No praise is too high for the skill with which the architects of St. Sophia exploited all the possibilities of sunlight. Each hour of the day has its own pattern of light; entering by different windows, the rays are focused on this or that point, or crisscrossing at different levels, glance along the walls and flow across the pavements. The play of light is continually changing, and its shifting patterns enhance the strangely unreal effect of this gigantic 'fabric of a vision?' "

Such is St. Sophia's special touches, special effects on those who enter it and gaze at its marvelous interior culminating to its magnificent dome that lightly soars above like the sky outside. What grandeur prevailed in its interior when Patriarchal liturgies were held, or in other special cases such as royal coronations, weddings and

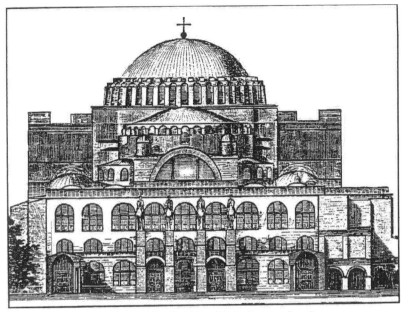

The Cathedral of Saint Sophia in Constantinople.

baptisms, thanksgiving doxologies over victories won against enemies and other such special occasions!

Presently, Justianian's Gem is at least fifteen centuries old. Amazingly, structurally it is still in excellent condition, and although it is located only thirteen miles away from one of the most active fault lines on earth, which over the centuries has caused repeated catastrophic earthquakes, St. Sophia has managed to emerge unscathed. Even the 1999 most violent earthquake that registered 7.5 in the Richter scale, causing the collapse of countless concrete structures and great loss of human life, in no way did it damage the ancient religious edifice. Not a single crack has been noticed in its walls or its dome!

Why is this marvelous religious edifice an exception? The answer is in the building's lightness and flexibility. Although its dome, for example, appears massive, actually it is very light.

Two factors contribute to the dome's lightness, First, it is made of very light materials, and secondly, its base, instead of being solid as in all other domes, it has forty windows. The presence of so many windows at the dome's base greatly reduces the weight of the dome. Thus, while previously built domes, by being solid at their bases exercised an enormous weight on the supporting substructures causing cracks on the walls and in some cases the collapsing of the building, St. Sophia's dome never caused such a danger.

Another basic factor that greatly contributed to St. Sophia's firmness was its mortar that was used as a solidifying medium. Its three ingredients - crushed bricks, lime and sand, made it tremendously cohesive, and, hence, enduringly strong. No wonder, that today, it is just as strong as it was fifteen centuries ago when it was first applied to the other structural components. These and other novel applications that were initiated by its most innovative architects, have kept the world-famous sacred edifice intact.

Justinian desired to build a masterpiece for the glory of God and the sanctification of his people. By carefully selecting the proper architects, the best building materials, and skilled and unskilled workers, his wish was answered. His masterpiece is still admired today – fourteen centuries later.

He spent three hundred and sixty million golden drachmas for its construction and hagiographical decoration. It was more than worth it.

31
THE VASILEVOUSA

Its euphemistic name was "Visilevousa", which meant "the Queen City", and a queen city she was from the fourth century AD to the fifteenth, when she was captured by the Turks.

From the year three hundred and twenty-six AD when it was founded by Emperor Constantine the Great, until its fall in the year one thousand four hundred and fifty-three AD, Constantinople – the actual name of the capital, remained the administrative and commercial hub of the Byzantine Empire, and indisputably, the leading city of the Western World. No other city could match it in population, in its architectural and artistic splendor, in its notoriety for scholarship, its industrial verve, its commercial bustling, and for nine centuries, its invincibility. As a tenth century poet aptly put it, it is "the illustrious and venerable city that dominates the world, radiant with a multitude of marvels; the splendor of tall buildings and superb churches, the long galleries and porticoes, the soaring columns."

The reason Emperor Constantine decided to build a new capital for the Roman Empire was mainly due to the danger the empire was facing on its eastern borders from barbarian incursions. Rome, the old capital of the empire, was too far from the vital eastern provinces of the empire that were now harassed by the ever-increasing barbarian attacks. So, Constantine logically decided to move his capital eastward, closer to the threatened borders, and thus be able to respond faster and more effectively to the attacks. The strategic site that he chose for his new capital was a triangular peninsula at the point of which was the City of Byzantium. Byzantium had been founded a thousand years earlier by Byzas, a citizen of Megara – a city near Athens, who had left, with many fellow colonists their native town, hoping for a better life.

Strangely, the location which Emperor Constantine chose to build his new capital contained seven hills. Thus, just as Rome – the old capital sprawled, in the same way, the new Capital would also sprawl on seven hills. The shape of the city was to be triangular, following the configuration of the peninsula. Thus, the city was bound on the south side by the Sea of Marmara, on the northeast by the Sea of Propontis and the Gulf of the Golden Horn. The landward side faced the Thracian Plain.

Once the Imperial Founder determined his new capital's size, Greek and Roman architects and builders began designing the plans. Construction began in the year 326 AD, and on May 11, 330 AD the city was formally inaugurated as the new capital of the empire.

The emperor named it "New Rome", but that name did not survive for long. Its inhabitants began calling it "Constantinopolis" (city of Constantine) and this name was the one by which it became known in history – Constantinople. For its future protection, Emperor Constantine ordered that mighty walls be built on all three sides. Fifty years later, during the reign of Emperor Theodosius, as the city had extended beyond the walls of the landward side; Theodosius ordered that new walls be built for the protection of the city. The new wall had a moat before it that was sixty feet wide and twenty-two feet deep. Behind the moat, rose three successive walls the one higher than the other. The second and third walls were some twenty-seven feet high. The third wall also had octagonal towers some seventy feet high. Their outward projection from the third wall would entrap the attackers, who now would have a rain of arrows and missiles coming at them from three sides. On the seaward side, the walls were single. This fortification was so strong that the city remained impregnable for 800 years.

The new capital was a marvel! It had wide avenues and streets, and the main ones had arcades on both sides. The almost interminable arcades provided shade to the pedestrians as well as protection from rain. There were also many beautiful squares, government buildings built in the classical Greco Roman style, a huge hippodrome, large public baths, many park shops and markets of all kinds, marvelous churches, and a splendid royal palace.

Patricians and nobles came from Rome and Italy to settle in the new capital to continue the administrative affairs of the empire. Greeks came from Greece and from countries of the Middle East, as did other ethnic minorities. Thus, from the very beginning, Constantinople's population was quite cosmopolitan.

By the fifth century and in less than a hundred years, its population had reached a million persons and remained at that level until the beginning of the thirteenth century – the time when the capital was taken over by the soldiers of the Fourth Crusade. From that time, the population began to steadily decrease to a level of about a hundred thousand during the capital's conquest by the Turks in 1453.

As in Rome, so in Constantinople the imperial palace was the largest and most imposing complex. Situated on the slopes that descended toward the eastern seaward point of the triangular city, and consisting of many terraced buildings, collectively, they furnished a most impressive overall view when seen from ships far out at sea.

As every succeeding emperor kept adding new apartments to the original palace of Constantine, by the eleventh century, the complex had become the largest palatial residence in the world. When Byzantine and foreign dignitaries visited, they were amazed at its spacious marble parlor whose walls were covered with glittering mosaic murals depicting hypaethral, hunting, martial and all kinds of religious and secular themes, the magnificent throne room, featuring among other decorative masterpieces, such mechanical marvels as golden lions that roared and golden birds that sang, its numerous reception halls, its baths, libraries, chapels, gardens, fountains and, of course, barracks housing hundreds of imperial guards.

Such, in size and magnificence, was the Byzantine imperial palace, virtually a city within the capital, the very heart that administered the first Christian empire of the world.

Close, and to the northeast of the palace, was the imposing senate building. Directly to the north and across the Augusteum Square, was the Christian world's largest and most magnificent church – the Cathedral of Saint Sophia. Since its construction in the sixth century AD and for a whole millennium thereafter, it remained the largest Christian church in the world. Its awesome inspiring interior was embellished by exquisite mosaic murals, marble floors and walls and guilded chandeliers. It was the Patriarchal Cathedral and the place of royal coronations, weddings, baptisms, as well as for those of the nobility.

West of the palace and close to it ran the 1,300 foot long Hippodrome, with a seating capacity of 40,000 spectators. Here the people enjoyed watching horse races, chariot races, and all sorts of athletic contests.

In the midst of the above mentioned most significant buildings of the capital, was the most important square – the Augusteum. Flanked by such magnificent buildings, one might liken it to Paris' "Place dela Concorde", or to Moscow's "Red Square", or to Venice's "Piazza di San Marco". It was in this square that the people could view the most solemn religious and secular ceremonies, and each year, on Holy Friday, a "Passion Play" reenacting the trial, crucifixion and death of Christ – a precursor of the more recent Passion Play held every ten years at Oberammergau, Germany.

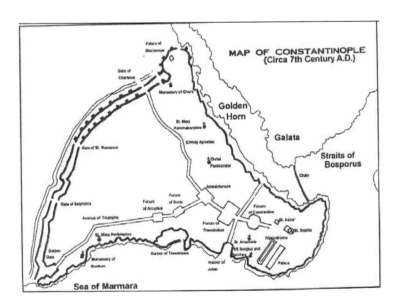

The Augusteum Square is also the starting point of one of the two most important boulevards of the capital – The "Mese" (central street). This well-paved boulevard, flanked on both sides by seemingly endless colonnades, supporting overhead covers providing shade and protection from rain, was the "par excellence" commercial artery of the capital. Every conceivable kind of shop, selling almost anything a person might need lined the entire almost six mile length of this bustling boulevard.

Mese wound westward through many blocks of the capital and passed through the "Forum of Constantine" which was one of the most elegant spots of the city. The Forum was oval in shape and was surrounded by beautiful arcades. These sheltered numerous ancient Greek statues that had survived destruction. Surrounding the forum were the mansions of the many nobles of the city. At the center of the forum, a porphyry column, topped by a golden large cross, rendered additional solemn beauty to this forum. It also served as the place where emperors celebrated victories.

As the Mese continued west, it passed through the "Square of Theodosius", whose statue was at the top of a column located in the middle of the square and resembling somewhat the column of Trajan in Rome, that stood in the forum that bore his name, and which had been designed by the Greek architect, Apollodorus.

From this square, the Mese continued west. It passed through another square – the "Amastrianum", for an additional three miles, terminating at the wall – Gate of Charisius.

Throughout the Middle Ages, no other city in Europe, the Middle East or North Africa could boast of having such a commercial artery, an artery that in a sense could be likened to Paris' Champs Elysees, or New York's Fifth Avenue. All kinds of shops, stocked with domestic products or foreign imports, could be found here, such as colored yard goods and exquisite jewelry made by local goldsmiths and silversmiths who then were the best in the world. Calligraphically, hand-written, illuminated manuscripts, beautifully crafted furniture, beautifully painted china, household utensils, iron goods, weapons, crystal and glass goods, and carts were available in the shops of Mese. This was the most celebrated boulevard of the Medieval World.

This is not to say that Mese had a monopoly on shops. Many other streets of the capital had shops that sold a great variety of things.

The other main artery of Constantinople was the "Street of the Triumphs". Whenever the Byzantine Army returned from a campaign, it paraded through the streets, whose starting point was the "Golden Gate" of the Wall of Theodosius and ended at the Square of Theodosius. As the victorious regiments paraded through this famous street, the throngs from the sidewalks would boisterously cheer them and shower them with flower petals.

A maze of secondary streets wound through every sector of the capital, and unlike our modern cities, where the upper, middle and lower classes live in more or less separate zones, in Constantinople, the tenements or hovels of the poor could be seen, often sharing the same wall with the mansion of the patrician. Interestingly, according to the Building Code of the capital, no secondary street could be less than twelve feet wide.

Besides grocery stores that were located in every part of the capital, there were also open markets where besides vegetables and fruits, live animals were sold. As for the fish markets, those were located on the quays along the Gulf of the Golden Horn.

A description of the variety of people one could see walking along the quay of the harbor of the Golden Horn would be as follows. "The harbor, both along the Golden Horn and on the shores of the Propontis, swarmed from morning till night with a cosmopolitan crowd, as if the whole world had arranged to meet here. Hook-nosed Asiatics with pointed beards and black hair falling to the shoulder, turbaned traders from Babylon, Syria, Egypt, or Persia, shaven, dirty Bulgars, wearing an iron chain round their waists instead of a belt, Russians, with long drooping mustaches, green eyed, snub-nosed, and dressed all in furs, Khazars and Pechenegs, men from Spain and Lombardy, merchants from Pisa and Amalfi, Genoa and Venice, who had their own quarter – with its quays, warehouses and churches on the Golden Horn, all races, languages and religions met and mingled here. Storehouses were crammed with precious merchandise from all over the world. Bargaining was tremendously lively, and marveling visitors noted that merchants from all over the world came to Constantinople by land and sea."

Entertainment of great variety was offered in the capital. Most spectacular entertainment, however, was available at the Hippodrome where forty thousand spectators could simultaneously watch horse races, chariot races, fights with wild beasts, and theatrical plays, some written in ancient times and others more recently. In the later centuries of the empire, Western European-type tournaments were introduced in the Hippodrome. The shows lasted for hours, and, for the poor, admission required no fee.

Byzantine people from every corner of the empire would come to Constantinople either for business or for leisure. For, in what other city would they find a market where their goods would be sold so easily? And in what other Byzantine or non-Byzantine city would their eyes feast so insatiably beholding the most beautiful buildings – palaces, mansions, churches, monasteries, convents, and, for the curious, to eyewitness how various industries and skilled artisans produced their products.

Like Athens and Alexandria of bygone eras, whose unrivaled schools of higher learning had made those cities the most renowned intellectual centers of the world, Constantinople was now their worthy successor. What the capital's educated elite sought to preserve and build upon were the two fundamental concepts of Orthodox Theology and the classical Greek philosophical, scientific and artistic heritage.

The most famous institution of higher learning in the capital was the University of Constantinople, called the "Pandidacterion." It was founded in the last quarter of the fourth century AD by Emperor Theodosius II, underwent a major reorganization under Caesar Bardas in the ninth century, and continued to educate whole generations of young Byzantine students in all literary, scientific, legal and artistic fields until the fifteenth century. Top-notch professors of philosophy, law, literature, mathematics, medicine, astronomy and of every known field, for almost ten centuries, taught the knowledge of the past, along with current advances in their respective fields. Other such schools of higher learning were also in the capital, making the city "the Intellectual Mecca" during most of the Middle Ages. Along with its institutions of higher learning, Constantinople could justly pride itself as possessing the richest libraries of the then Western World.

A plethora of churches and all kinds of ecclesiastical institutions could also be seen in every sector of the capital. Besides the Cathedral of Saint Sophia – largest and most magnificent church in the world, second in importance was the Church of the Holy Apostles, easily recognized by its five large domes. A replica of this beautiful church is the Church of Saint Mark in Venice. Besides being a house of worship with an interior full of sacred murals made of brilliantly shining mosaics, the church was also a mausoleum of ten generations of Byzantine Emperors whose bodies were reposing in porphyry and marble sarcophagi. Thus, we might safely say that this church was a precursor of London's Westminster Abbey – a veritable mausoleum of many British kings, and of Paris' Church of Saint Dennis – mausoleum of many French kings and queens.

Unfortunately, this famous church, no longer exits. It was razed to the ground by the Moslem Turks shortly after they captured the capital. The reason for destroying this church was because it was the burial place of Byzantine Emperors, many of whom had, in the past, successfully repelled the Turkish Armies when the latter were attempting to invade and take over Byzantine provinces.

Other famous churches in the capital were those of Saint Irene, located close to Saint Sophia's Cathedral, of St. Theodore, of Saint Mary Panachrantos (All-Pure), of the Divine Savior of Chora and many others. Many of these churches had orphanages, hospitals, hostels, and schools, which were maintained and supervised. A saying has it that "In Constantinople, there were as many churches as there are days of the year."

Dispersed in every sector of the capital were many monasteries and convents. Each monastery and convent had its own library with hundreds of hand-written, illuminated manuscripts dealing with every aspect of Orthodox Theology. The Monastery of Studion was the most famous. Most of its monks were expert theologians, and some of them became illustrious Patriarchs of the Orthodox Church.

Byzantine Capital

32
BYZANTINE LITERATURE

Byzantine literature is an unbroken continuation of the literature of classical Greece. Its beginning is during the reign of Constantine the Great (306-337) and its end in the year 1453, the year Constantinople was conquered by the Ottoman Turks. Thus, for over a thousand years, the Byzantine Empire, having become the heiress of classical Greece, continued not only to cultivate the literary heritage she inherited, but even outshone every other dominion of Western Europe. To be more exact, Byzantine literary activity was the only one in the Western World from the fifth to the eleventh centuries.

During this literary productive millennium, all genres of literature were cultivated. This prodigious literary output included theological, philosophical, historical, and poetic (both religious and secular) works, chronicles, romances, and even animal fables. As the language of the empire was the Greek "Koine," the common language of the writers of late classical Greece, the works of Greek writers were looked upon as models to be taught and even to be emulated. Moreover, under the influence of the great Cappadocian Fathers, Saints Basil, Gregory, and Chrysostom, who were not only steeped in the Greek classics, but were great admirers of them as well.

Having recognized the classics' great value, they urged their study and when taught, it would have to be within the Christian framework. Thus, more than any other Country of the West, it was the Byzantine world that preserved the heritage of classical and Hellenistic Greek antiquity. This was later transmitted to the West during the Renaissance.

Theology It was the great Greek Church Fathers, all of whom were born and lived within the territories of the Byzantine Empire, whose prodigious theological writings, particularly from the fourth to the eighth centuries laid the foundation of Christian theology.

As the Byzantine Empire was the first to recognize the religion of Christ as its official one, there were many heresies that successively plagued the Church. They had to be met head on and disproved. The Church Fathers, who lived within the boundaries of the empire, successfully counteracted them in their writings as well as in the Seven Ecumenical Councils, which convened within the empire. And so, the most fundamental dogmas and other aspects of the religion of Christ, dogmas such as those concerning God, the Trinity, the Creation, man, his "Fall", Christology (divinity of Christ), Soteriology (salvation), the Church, Sacraments, life hereafter as well as worship, monasticism and other such fundamental aspects, were all expounded and systematized during those centuries.

It was in Egypt, a then Byzantine province, that monasticism had its beginnings. St. Anthony was the first man to leave the town where he lived and withdrew to the desert to attain full spirituality. Since that time, monasteries and convents are to be seen in every Orthodox and Catholic country.

Saints Athanasius, Basil, Gregory, Gregory of Nyssa, Chrysostom, Cyril of Alexandria, Cyril of Jerusalem, and dozens of others, contributed an immense amount of theological literature, touching upon every aspect of religion. Toward the end of the sixth century, Leontius of Byzantium introduced Aristotelian definitions into theology, thus becoming the "First Scholastic" theologian.

The eighth century was dominated by the "Iconoclastic" movement, a movement which sought to remove all iconography from the interior of all churches. The theologian who challenged this movement and eventually quelled it was St. John of Damascus. Besides speaking and writing polemics against the iconoclastics, he also composed hymns and wrote a book entitled "The Fountain of Knowledge". This book represents the first comprehensive exposition of Christian dogmas.

During the ninth century, there were many contributors to Byzantine literature. Outstanding among them were Emperor Leo VI "The Wise", who wrote many engaging homilies and religious hymns, Theodore of Studium, whose writings contain useful reflection on monastic life, and St. Photius, patriarch of Constantinople, who wrote excellent theological treatises. (See next chapter for more details on St. Photius.)

Euthemius Zigabenus whose most important work was the "Dogmatic Panoply", which won him equal stature to St. John of Damascus. Zigabenus is the most significant representative of the eleventh century.

The fifteenth century is ably represented by Emperor Manuel II Palaeologus, who wrote the "Apologia", a polemic work against Islam.

Hagiography is a religious literature which concerns itself with acts of martyrs and the lives of saints. As such, this type of literature focuses mainly on the personalities of martyrs and saints. Symeon Metaphrastes is the par-excellence representative of this kind of religious literature. His "Acts of Martyrs", a work of many volumes, is a classic of this kind of literature.

Religious Poetry St. Gregory of Nazianzus is the pioneer of this religious literary genre. He wrote superb hymns. Best known are his "Maidens Song" and his "Evening Hymn". His use of ancient Greek language, however, made most of his poetic works unintelligible to most people.

It was St. Romanos the "Melodos", who, in the first half of the sixth century made hymnology attain its highest perfection. He composed one thousand hymns of which only eighty survived. All of his hymns are replete with magnificent pictures, descriptive language, a deep feeling, and a zestful faith.

In the seventh century, there appeared a new form of hymnology - the "Canons". These are hymns built from eight or nine lyrics. Andrew, Archbishop of Crete is the inventor of this new clan of hymnology. His chief work - the "Great Canon" comprises two hundred-fifty strophes. The most celebrated writers of canons are John of Damascus, and Cosmas of Jerusalem. They lived during the eighth century. Toward the end of the same century, Theodore, the famous abbot of the Monastery of Studium at Constantinople, also wrote many canons, making himself yet another worthy representative of this type of religious hymnology.

Indisputably, the greatest and most popular canon of all Byzantine hymnology is the Akathistos Hymn. In his book entitled "Theotokos", the Roman Catholic author, Fr. Michael O'Carroll, referring to the rare poetic qualities of this hymn (which, from its opening verse to its last is an exultant praise of the Virgin Mary) wrote: "Few will challenge the judgment that this is the most beautiful, most profound, the most ancient Marian hymn of all Christian literature." Some claim that the author of this hymn was Sergius, Patriarch of Constantinople. Other sources claim that it is Georgius Pissidis. Be that as it may, this superb hymn exalts the virtues and high station of the Mother of God, besides being the most beloved hymn of all Orthodox Hymnology; it has also become a source of inspiration for many Marian hymns of the Catholic Church.

In the nineteenth century, the nun Cassia, also known as Cassiane, a poetess of very high repute, wrote many religious hymns. One of her hymns sung during the Matins of Holy Tuesday, is one of the most popular hymns of the Orthodox Church.

History, which is the discipline that records past and present events, was another field that Byzantine writers pursued. Some of them recorded the events that occurred in their times, and others, recorded events that were steered by the men at the helm of the empire – the emperors. In gathering the necessary incidents they were very meticulous and methodic. After compiling a whole narrative, the writers would also add their own criticism as to why these events evolved as they did.

Many Byzantine historians used their predecessors as models. They were fond of the way ancient Greek historians presented their facts. Furthermore, just as the ancient Greek historians, the Byzantine historians presented the events exactly as they happened without adding any critiques or thoughts of their own, as in the case of Herodotus, the "Father of history". Other Byzantine historians, wishing to emulate Thucydides, who always liked to speculate for or against the way events evolved, emulated his example.

Reading the records of Byzantine historians, we find that Procupius and Agathias covered meticulously the many events that occurred during the reign of the Emperor Justinian, thus furnishing us with an ample and detailed record of what happened during the first half of the sixth century. Leo Diaconus wrote an excellent history about the bloody wars of the Byzantines against the Bulgarians. The scholarly emperor Constantine VII, Porphyrogenitus, who authored many books on different subjects, also wrote histories.

The history of the empire during the times of the Crusades was recorded by Nicephorus Bryennius. Princess Anna Comnena, who lived in the fourteenth century, wrote a history of the reign of her father, Alexius Comnenus. She entitled her work "Alexias".

Lastly, the death struggle between the Byzantine defenders of the capital and the Ottoman besiegers was recorded by three historians – Laonicus Chalcocndyles, Ducas and Georgius Frantzes.

Chronicles are brief histories of the world beginning with the creation and ending at the time of the author's writing. The chroniclers were mostly monks. Byzantine chroniclers who distinguished themselves in this genre were: John Malalas, who wrote a chronicle beginning with Adam and ending with the time of his writing, Georgius Syncellus, Georgius Cedzenus and Glycas. The "Universal Chronicles" of these last two chroniclers gained much popularity.

Philosophy Byzantine philosophy does not have the giants of thought and originality that classical Greek antiquity had. Byzantine philosophers endeavored to expound on the philosophical thought of Greek antiquity with special emphasis on Aristotle. It was to the initiative of Michael Psellus, that in the eleventh century, Plato was introduced into the curriculum of the

University of Constantinople. Psellus had such admiration for Plato that he considered him "the greatest of philosophers and a forerunner of Christianity". Ancient learning and philosophy were not the only passions of Constantine Psellus. His knowledge extended to many fields. Hence, he wrote treatises on theological, philosophical, legal, mathematical, physical, agricultural, and astronomical topics. He even wrote poems. In his "Etudes sur L'histoire Byzantine" (on Byzantine history), Rimbaud speaks of him: "He was the most important Byzantine philosopher and the first great humanist."

Poetry   Byzantine secular poetry begins with the poems of George Pisidis (seventh century) in which he extols the military exploits of Emperor Heraclius. Theodosius, a deacon (tenth century), employing extravagant language, praises highly the victories of the brave Nicephorus Phocas.

Voluminous poems written in the twelfth century were in style and theme imitations of ancient Greek romances. These became very popular. Three poets stand out at this time. They are Theodore Prodromus, a man of manifold literary activity. He wrote in duodecacyllable (twelve-syllable) meter the story of "Rhodamne and Dosicles". Nicetas Eugenianos also composed in duodecacyllable meter the poem "Drusilla and Charicles." Lastly, there was Constantine Manasses with his love poem "Aristander and Callithea".

Vernacular Greek Literature   is literature in which the Byzantine authors gave poetry center stage while prose had fewer representative works. Of this literary genre, there have survived a large number of Rhodian love songs, epic poems relating to legends about Troy and Alexander, romances written in verse such as "Callimachus and Chrysorrhoe", "Belthandrus and Chrysantza", long poems about the taking of Athens, and the well-known "Digenis Akritas" – a man who represents the brave sentinels of the fortifications in the eastern borders of the empire.

Finally, there were lexicographers of which Suidas' encyclopedic lexicon was the most outstanding. The writings were on geography and the sciences, and even animal fables.

In retrospect, during the Middle Ages, no other nation produced such a plethora of writings on every literary genre as those written during the lifespan of the Byzantine Empire.

33
FIVE GREAT CHURCH FATHERS

By the end of the sixth century AD, the multiethnic population of the Byzantine Empire, which stretched from the Mediterranean coastal regions of Spain to Iran, had become Christian. There were five Patriarchs, namely, those of Constantinople, Rome, Antioch, Jerusalem, and Alexandria, guiding the Christian population as well as hundreds of archbishops, metropolitans, bishops, and priests.

Monasticism, that first appeared in Egypt in the late third century, had by now spread everywhere with countless monasteries and convents to be seen in the countryside and in urban areas. The persecutions, against the Church from the time of Nero (67 AD) until the reign of Diocletian (302 AD) had claimed the lives of thousands of Christians, ceased officially by 313 AD. In that year, Emperor Constantine the Great issued the "Decree of Milan", whereby legal status was granted to the Church. Thus, as of that year, the Church enjoyed peace, and with it came rapid expansion.

But the Church now faced new enemies - the heresies, that is, beliefs that sharply deviated from the traditional beliefs faithfully followed since the time of Christ and of His Holy Apostles. As these false beliefs were spreading, causing problems and divisions within the Church, the latter had to suppress them. And, the way to do it was by convoking an ecumenical council to which the heretical leaders were invited. Issues were debated, issues were refuted, and thus their fallacies were exposed.

The first such heresy that seriously challenged the Church was the one preached by a Libyan priest named Arius. He held that Christ was not divine, not God, and therefore, not the second Person of the Holy Trinity. Arius claimed that Christ was a plain man, who at the age of thirty received much enlightenment from God as well as miraculous powers.

As the "Arian heresy" was rapidly expanding and causing all sorts of frictions and divisions, Emperor Constantine the Great, wishing to restore peace and unity within the Empire, summoned the First Ecumenical Council in the City of Nicea not far from Constantinople. The council was held in 325 AD, and was attended by 318 church fathers. Among the leading representatives was Alexander - the Patriarch of Alexandria, Egypt. He was accompanied by his secretary - the deacon Athanasius. Nobody expected that this obscure deacon would, in the course of the Council's sessions, astonish all attendants by becoming the staunchest defender of the Divinity of Christ.

St. Athanasius (295 - 373 AD),   one of the greatest Church Fathers, was born in Alexandria. As a young man, he studied philosophy in the highly acclaimed institutes of his native city as well as biblical studies. He became proficient in both.

In 319 AD, he was ordained a deacon, and as such, he accompanied Patriarch Alexander to Nicea. Being profoundly knowledgeable in the Holy Scriptures and in philosophy, day after day he dauntlessly confronted the Arianist heretical opponents in long and heated debates, always being able to refute their shallow arguments, thus proving the grave errancy of their unfounded beliefs. As a result of Athanasius' successful debates, the Church's traditional belief in the Divinity of Christ was preserved while the Arian heresy would, from this point on, head to its gradual eclipse.

Athanasius returned to Alexandria as "Pillar of the Faith" and "Champion of the Council". Naturally, ahead of him, lay a great future. When Patriarch Alexander died, Athanasius was unanimously elected as his successor.

One would expect his patriarchal tenure to be peaceful. It wasn't. As Arian heretics were still in existence their intrigues with the imperial court succeeded in having him exiled five times. He spent his second exile in Rome as guest of the Patriarch Julius. In fact, when Julius learned that Athanasius' other title was "Pope", Julius asked if he could also use that title. Without hesitation Athanasius granted his request, and so, since that time, the spiritual leaders of Rome were called Popes.

South of Egypt lay the country of Ethiopia. Wishing to convert it to Christianity, Athanasius sent missionaries under the leadership of Frumentius. Soon, the people from king to commoners were converted to Christ, and so, from that remote time to this day, Ethiopia is a Christian country.

Despite his stormy patriarchal tenure, Athanasius still found time to write treatises and letters, stating in all of them, the Church's correct belief. The two very brief excerpts below are from his treatise, "The Incarnation of the Word".

"He became man enough so that we might be made God; and He manifested Himself in the flesh, so that we might grasp the idea of the unseen Father; and He endured the insolence of men, so that we might receive the inheritance of immortality.

"Accordingly, the Son of God became Son of Man, so that the sons of man, that is, of Adam, might become sons of God. The Word begotten of the Father from on high, inexpressibly, inexplicably, incomprehensively and eternally, is He that is born in time here below, of the Virgin Mary, the Mother of God - so that those who are in the first place born here below might have a second birth from on high, that is, of God. He, then, has on earth only a Mother, while we have in heaven only a Father. And for this reason He calls Himself Son of Man so that we men might call God our Father in heaven. 'Our Father,' He says 'Who art in heaven' (Matt. 6:9)."

Athanasius' last years were peaceful. He died in Alexandria, and presently his body reposes in the Church of Saint Zacharias in Venice, Italy. A Latin inscription on his tomb reads: "Sanctus Athanasius magnus doctor

Ecclesial, Alexandriniensis", (Saint Athanasius great teacher of the Church from Alexandria).

St. Basil the Great

Basil's name means "royal", but never in his life did he conduct himself in a royal manner. Doing his duty humbly was his daily rule. Basil (330 – 379 AD), was born in Caesarea, which was a town in the district of Cappadocia, Turkey. Cappadocia has one of the roughest terrains on earth, and rough as the terrain was, so were its people - rough, crude, biting, scheming. Basil, however, did not share these traits. His Christian mother, Emmelia, molded him into one of the gentlest souls that ever lived.

He studied, for eight years at the Universities of Constantinople and Athens, philosophy, literature, the natural sciences, medicine and astronomy. Similarly, having also become proficient in the knowledge of Holy Scriptures, he decided to devote his life as a cleric. He was ordained a priest and later, Bishop of Caesarea, his native city.

Being the chief shepherd of his diocese, he made himself an ideal example of Christian virtuous living, and, fully conscious that high Episcopal office entailed the defense of Christian dogmas, of the Christian beliefs, then harassed by heresies, he fought them with all the might of his word and pen.

His religious writing was also profuse. His topics included almost everything from dogma to morals, and from ecclesiastical rules to worship. His Divine Liturgy, conducted in Orthodox churches ten times during the year, is replete with masterful invocational and supplicatory prayers.

The following brief excerpts from his treatises clearly show the extraordinary fertility of his theological thought.

In his homily on Psalm 114, speaking of the Heavenly rewards he wrote: "Turn to your rest; for the Lord has been kind to you. Eternal rest awaits those who have struggled through the present life observant of the laws, not as payment owed for their works, but bestowed as a gift on the munificent God on those who have hoped in Him."

In a homily on the dogma of the Holy Trinity, he thus explains the relations of God the Father and God the Son: "One God and Father, One God and the Son, and not two gods, since the Son has identity with the Father. I do not perceive one Godhead in the Father and another in the Son; not one nature in one and another in the other. You may make the individuality of the Persons clear by numbering the Father and the Son separately, but confess one essence in both, so as not to divide them into a multiplicity of gods."

Few Christian theologians have attempted to grope so deeply into the mysteries of such Christian beliefs as The Holy Trinity, The Relation of its Divine Persons, Incarnation, Redemption and other such transient dogmas. St. Basil's groping remains one of the deepest.

A work of this famous Hierarch has remained classic is his monastic rules. Even though written so long ago, the rules expounded therein are still the guiding fundamental rules of monastic life.

A philanthropic establishment that greatly reveals the genuinely compassionate heart of this truly saintly man was his "Basilias" - a veritable "city" which he founded to serve as an old age home, as an orphanage, and as a haven for the indigent. Shelter, education for young orphans, medical care, and food were daily available to all who found refuge in it.

When on January 1, 379 this great Church leader died, the words "Father into thy hands I commend my spirit," that Jesus uttered from the Cross, were also Basil's last.

Saint Gregory the Theologian

Saint Gregory (330 - 389 AD), the son of Bishop Gregory and Nona, a very pious Christian mother, was born in Arianzos, Turkey. Like Caesarea, the native city of St. Basil, Arianzos was also in the region of Cappadocia. Gregory was a contemporary of Basil, and, when the two studied at Athens, they became very close friends.

In his temperament, he was mild and gentle. In the many letters that have survived, we read warm words toward those they are addressed while their subject matter reveals the writer's cool logic.

By 362 AD, at the demand of the congregation of the City of Nazianzus where his father was a bishop, Gregory was ordained a priest, and years later when his father died, he was ordained Bishop of Nazianzos. In 379 AD, at the request of the people of Constantinople and as a result of a new heresy that now was threatening the ancient and genuine Faith of the Church, the heresy of "Pneumatomachoi", the word means against the Holy Spirit, in other words, the adherents of that heresy did not believe that the Holy Spirit was God, Patriarch Gregory was the first president of that historic Council.

Later, Gregory returned to Nazianzus, and, when he became too old, he retired in his father's family estate at Arianzus where he died in 389 AD.

Like his friend St. Basil, St. Gregory, from the day he was ordained to the priesthood, until he died twenty-seven years later, wholly dedicated himself to the service of the Church. He was daily in touch with the hundreds of his spiritual children, doing his utmost to answer their spiritual needs.

When reading carefully his writings, particularly his "Orations", contemporary theologians unanimously agree that what characterizes their themes are loftiness of composition and acuity in the theological insights that to this day remain mostly unparalleled. Hence, the most deserving title the ancient church gave to this highly distinguished Greek Father "The Divine", that is "The Theologian", was most deserved.

The excerpt below from one of his orations confirms the above highly honored title.

"What a profound paradox our divine Redeemer really was. He was born, but he already existed with God the Father in Heaven eternally. He issued from a woman, but she was a virgin. He was wrapped in swaddling bands, but he removed the swaddling clothes of the grave when he arose again. He was laid in a manger, but he was glorified by angels and proclaimed by a star and worshiped by the wise men.

"He was baptized as man, but remitted sins as God. He was tempted as man, but he conquered as God. He hungered, but fed thousands. He thirsted, but he cried: 'If any man thirst let him come to me and drink.' He was weary, but he is the peace of them that are sorrowful and heavy laden."

A sketch showing a mosaic mural of Christ

"He prays, but he hears prayers. He weeps, but he puts an end to tears. He asks where Lazarus was laid, for he was man; and he raised Lazarus, for he is God. As a sheep he is led to the slaughter, but he is the shepherd of Israel and now of the whole world. He is bruised and wounded, but he heals every disease and every infirmity. He dies, but he gives life and by his death destroys death. He is bruised, but he rises again."

What a wealth of contrasts! What an unusual way of putting the antitheses in Jesus' personality, his divine infinity as against his human limitedness, his divine timelessness as against his temporary human existence. St. Gregory was indeed a master, a master orator and theologian.

St. John Chrysostom, Patriarch of Constantinople Unquestionably, the greatest orator of Christian antiquity was Saint John Chrysostom. His eloquence was so phenomenal, that since that time, few preachers have been able to equal him. Because of this rare charisma, since the sixth century, the euphemism "Chrysostom", Greek for "Gold Mouth", was affixed to him.

John Chrysostom (345 - 407 AD), the son of Secundus, a superior officer, and Anthusa, was born in Antioch, Syria. At that time, his native city had a population of four hundred thousand making it the third largest city in the Western World. Of this number, two hundred and fifty thousand were Greeks. Because of its large Greek population and its being an academic center, the city was called "The Syrian Athens".

John never knew his father since he died shortly after John's birth. Consequently, John was raised by his twenty year old mother. While a young man, he studied philosophy and law in the academic schools of Antioch under the famous jurist, Libanius, and for some time after his graduation, he pursued the legal profession. Eventually, his attraction to the Christian Religion induced him to quit the legal profession and enroll at the theological school of Antioch, which was located within the Monastery of Saint Eurprepius. At the age of twenty-five, he was baptized, and, for nine years thereafter, lived as a hermit in a nearby desert. In 380 AD, he returned to Antioch and was ordained a deacon, he was ordained into the priesthood five years later.

John served as priest in Antioch for eleven years. Besides his priestly duties, he also assumed the Herculean and most responsible task of caring for the three thousand indigents - widows, infirm, poor, strangers, prisoners, and orphans. By inspiring through his homilies the wealthy Antiocheans to contribute generously toward the care of so many poor souls, John was able to run smoothly one of the greatest philanthropic, ecclesiastical organizations in the early medieval world.

An innate charisma that also contributed to John's fame during the ten years that he served as priest in Antioch was his mellifluous eloquence that characterized his preaching. Examples from Biblical and secular literature, historical facts, and examples of nature plus an ample use of Biblical and secular passages always colored his homilies. Interwoven

217

skillfully into an organic and well-integrated whole made his homilies most appealing and, in a sense, unique. It has been said, that on Sundays people walked for miles to come to Antioch to hear the young priest preach. In his preaching, he was indeed incomparable.

When in 379 AD Patriarch Nectarius of Constantinople died, John was invited to the capital to succeed him. On February 26 he was consecrated Bishop and he was installed Patriarch of Constantinople.

As Patriarch, John continued with the same intense fervor his diverse tasks. His homilies continued to be gems of Christian oratory, while all other tasks were carried on with efficiency.

St. John Chrysostom's success caused other hierarchs to become envious of him, to such a point that through intrigues, succeeded to have him deposed and then exiled to Cucusos, Armenia, where he eventually died.

No other ancient Greek Church Father has left us such a voluminous collection of ecclesiastical writings as St. John Chrysostom. His letters to clergy and lay persons, his practical and moral treatises, and, especially, his very large number of homilies on Old and New Testament subjects and other religious aspects, make up a veritable library.

A most celebrated theological work of his is his treatise entitled "On the Priesthood". It is the best ever written on this Sacrament and the excerpt below, clearly speaks of its unexcelled content.

"The office of the priesthood is performed on earth, but it ranks among the heavenly things. And with good reason; for this ministry was set up not by an angel, or an archangel, or by any created power, but by the Paraclete himself....He commanded that men who are still in the flesh should imitate the actions of angels. Therefore the priest ought to be as pure as if he stood among those Powers in heaven itself....When you see the Lord offered there in sacrifice, and the priest standing and praying, and all being redeemed by the precious blood, do you feel that you are still standing among men, on earth? Do you not rather feel transported straightway into heaven?....You will easily realize to what dignity the Grace of the Holy Spirit has raised priests, if you consider how great a matter it is for a man yet clothed in flesh and blood to approach that pure and blessed nature. For it is by priests that these things are accomplished, and others of no less importance, that concern our redemption and salvation. For men, who inhabit the earth and spend their lives there, have been entrusted with responsibility for heavenly things. They have received a power, which God did not give to angels or archangels. For it was not said to them: 'Whatever you find on earth will be bound in heaven....Earthly rulers have the power to find; but they only bind the body. This bond extends to the soul itself, and passes on through the heavens: for what priests do on earth God confirms on high, the Lord ratifies the decisions of his servants....What greater authority could there be?' The Father has entrusted all judgment to the Son, and here I see the Son giving it all into the hands of his priests."

Saint Photius, Patriarch of Constantinople was the most erudite, the most polymath, the most encyclopedic, and the most scholarly ecclesiastic of the ninth century AD. In the wealth of his diversified knowledge, he was a reincarnation of the fourth century Aristotle, and a precursor of the twentieth century's Albert Schweitzer who had doctorates in theology, philosophy, medicine, and music. No other learned man in the Western world could stand up to him, for his diversified learning by far exceeded that of his contemporaries. He was the brightest intellectual beacon of his day.

Photius, the scion, was of wealthy and aristocratic parents. Sergius, his father was a superior officer of the royal guards, and Irene, his pious mother, also hailed from an upper class family.

When Photius was attending the University of Constantinople, which, at that time, was the foremost institute of learning in the western world, he studied philosophy, theology, law, literature, medicine, and botany. He excelled in all these academic disciplines, making him a "living encyclopedia".

Upon completing his studies, Photius opted for a career in civil service. In no time, he climbed to the highest post, that of being the Emperor's chief advisor. What a fast meteoric rise in a very short time! He had risen to one of the top positions of the imperial government where his word and opinion influenced national policy.

But, he was not to remain in this glittering post for life. Although he held the Empire's most coveted post, Photius also had a strong love for the Church. Consequently, when Patriarch Tarasius died, and the other prelates turned to him to become his successor, he without hesitation relinquished his high post and accepted the prelates' offer. Following ordination in all three Holy Orders, he was elevated to the Patriarchal throne on December 25, 858.

Photius' Patriarchal tenure was not a peaceful one. Actually, it was a stormy one. When we consider, however, that storm and not calm causes a man to show the best of his physical, mental, and psychical qualities, Photius, by overcoming them, placed his name in the Church's history.

A clash that Patriarch Photius braved for years was with the popes of Rome. Recently, the latter, aspiring to be recognized as supreme spiritual leaders of all Christendom, began meddling in the patriarchal affairs of the four eastern Patriarchates.

Patriarch Photius would have none of that. Since he was a profoundly learned theologian, versed in the Holy Scriptures, Synodal decisions and in the opinion of Church fathers, he retaliated against the popes' unfounded assertions with all the might of his pen. It was a long struggle, but in the end, rewarding.

Despite his embroilment in such a protracted struggle, this situation in no way hindered him from attending to the other ecclesiastical affairs. Thus, when the Slavs of Eastern Europe, and, to be more exact, those of Moravia and Hungary looked to the Patriarchal Sea of Constantinople to send missionaries to convert them to Christianity, Photius sent many missionaries, headed by two brothers from Thessalonica, Saint Cyril and Methodius. Their mission was most successful. Besides converting them to Christ, they also transmitted many aspects of the Byzantine civilization to them.

The most energetic and indefatigable patriarch also found time to write many books in which he revealed his theological, literary, legal, and scientific profundity. His most important literary work was the "Myriobiblon", also called "Bibliothec". It is an invaluable collection of the extracts and abridgements of two hundred and eighty volumes of classical writers whose original works have been lost. Had not Photius written this voluminous work, today, many ancient authors and their literary works would not be known. We owe immense gratitude to this venerable Patriarch for such a providential work.

A large number of homilies, which he delivered on church feasts such as Christmas, Easter, Epiphany, and others, as well as homilies on moral subjects and heresies' refutations, are also extant in their entirety.

His treatise entitled "On the Holy Spirit", is a theological classic. Using patristic views from ancient and medieval Church Fathers and philosophical syllogisms, he masterfully defends the Scriptural and traditional belief of the Church that the Holy Spirit proceeds only from the father, and not also from the Son, as some of Rome's theologians were recently promulgating.

Of equal interest is his treatise, "On Papal Primacy", in which evidence from the Holy Scripture and Holy Tradition are masterfully woven to prove the fallacy of such papal assertions.

Finally, Patriarch Photius wrote beautiful hymns, and hundreds of letters whose moral, dogmatic, exegetical, and admonitory content not only are perennially valuable, but also show the depth of the author's vast learning.

He died peacefully on February sixth of the year 893 in a monastery outside Constantinople, and was buried at the Church of St. John the Baptist located inside the convent of St. Jeremiah.

Since his death, many critiques were written on his personality, character, and achievements. The one below best describes him:

"Nature bestowed on Photius all its gifts - noble birth, a sharp mind, capable of absorbing all knowledge of his time, a will malleable as gold but also as hard as steel, indefatigable industry, ambition, ability on how to capitalize on circumstances. He can alternate from orator to poet, from a historian to a superb critic, from a theologian to a pure scientist. And, all these mental attitudes were expressed modestly and with poise. No wonder he had such an influence on people of every stride, mentality and temper."

The above critique did not come from a friend but from a foe. It is the foe's admiration; however, that represents the truth.

34
BYZANTINE PHILANTHROPY

Byzantium, the first Christian Empire within whose vast boundaries Christian theology, worship, morality, monasticism, and every other religious practice exercised a great influence on the lives of its millions of inhabitants, philanthropy also flourished. Amazingly, from the time of the empire's founding in 330 AD, to its demise in 1453, Church and State - supported philanthropic institutions could be found not only in the capital but in every provincial city. Thus, before welfare institutions appeared in the Christian states of Western Europe, the Byzantine Empire had already, on a grand scale, set the pace from the beginning of the fourth century.

During the first two centuries of the Empire's existence, that is, from the early fourth to the sixth centuries, philanthropy was the responsibility of the Church. But since the time of Justinian, the state began to involve itself in the dispensation of philanthropy by aiding the Church financially, and in some areas founding state institutions for this purpose. Moreover, as the Byzantine Empire included in its boundaries some provinces which are now known as Western states, such as Italy, southern Spain and most islands in the Mediterranean Sea, the newly and diversified philanthropic activity was introduced in those western areas as well. In the following centuries they would spread to other western countries.

The diversity of these philanthropic institutions, where the needs of the poor were answered without cost, included: "Brephotrophia", that is, institutions for the care of the poor infants; "Orphanotrophia", which is orphanages; "Gerocomia", where indigent old people were provided with shelter and food; "Xenodochia", that is, hostelries for the poor who came from another town and had no money with which to provide themselves shelter; and "Nosocomia", where the poor would receive free medical care. Interestingly, the physicians in many of the nosocomia were not civilians but priests who had received the same medical training as the lay doctors. Clustered around cathedrals, or other large churches in the provincial cities of the empire, these institutions efficiently answered the needs of the poor and the unfortunate.

When the above Byzantine philanthropic organizational structure was eventually adopted by all Western European states, the Byzantine terminology designating the various institutions was also adopted. The only change that was made was that the Greek terms were Latinized. Thus, an old age home was known as "Gerocomium", a hospital was called "Nosocomium", etc. It wasn't until the 17th century that this terminology was replaced by words derived from the spoken languages of the respective countries.

Indisputably, one of the distinctive marks of a civilized society is its care of the poor, orphans, the homeless and the indigent sick. It is a humanitarian endeavor and a noble one at that, for it shows the sensitivity of that society's well-to-do citizens to alleviate the misery of the unfortunate ones in their midst. The care which both the church and the Byzantine State provided to countless indigent citizens during the millennium of the Empire's existence was a pioneer record hitherto unprecedented in human history and a great legacy for future western states to emulate.

35
BYZANTINE ART

During the period of the Byzantine Empire which lasted from 330 AD, the year Constantinople became the capital of the Byzantine Empire until 1453 AD - the year the Ottoman Turks conquered Constantinople, classical Greek art and architecture were succeeded by the "Byzantine art and architecture" both of which were somewhat different from those developed in the classical era.

Architecture

By the fourth century AD, the Christian Religion had spread to all major cities of the countries around the Mediterranean Sea. This caused many temples to fall into disuse and eventually became "Quarries" of ready cut and polished marble to be used in private homes or in churches.

In contrast to pagan peoples whose religious ceremonies were held outside the temple, and therefore they did not need to gather inside to pray, for Christians, the church became the very place where the Divine Liturgy and other services would be conducted.

The earliest Christian Churches that were built during the fourth and fifth centuries AD were of the Greco-Roman Basilica type. They were rectangular in shape having an apse at one end and a vertical façade at the other end where the entrance was. Their ceiling was either "barreled" or flat. Two arched columniations to the right and left of the interior ran from the rear to the front of the nave. Churches that were very large usually had four arched columniations in their naves.

A new style of church architecture appeared by the sixth century AD in Constantinople, the capital of the Byzantine Empire. It was the "Byzantine Style". The churches that were built in this new style were usually square in shape and topped by a dome. Symbolically, the dome represented the heavens where God is, and the lower part of the church, which is square, represented the earth, where people live and worship.

When the Byzantine Emperor Justinian decided to build the Cathedral of St. Sophia in Constantinople, which became the largest Christian Church in the world for 1,000 years, a very difficult problem was presented to its two brilliant architects - Anthemios and Isidoros, "How can a round dome be placed on a square building?" Up until now, the only way to have a dome over a building was to have either a circular wall under the dome to receive equally its tremendous thrust, its tremendous weight, or to have many columns to receive the thrust instead of a round wall.

Anthemios and Isidoros, who besides being excellent architects, were also expert geometers and able to do away with both aforementioned traditional supports. They invented "The Pendentives" which were four concave triangular structures which, when attached to the base of the dome, each received one fourth of the dome's thrust passing it afterwards in four massive piers. And so, from now on, a dome could be built over a square building.

Other significant architectural developments that appeared during the latter centuries of the Byzantine Period were the "High Drum" and the "Cruciform Shape" of many Orthodox Churches. The high drum was a circular wall that was built between the dome and the pendentives, thus elevating considerably the dome. In many churches the drum was pierced with windows and allowed much light to stream through and make the mural of Christ Almighty painted on the interior surface of the dome, very visible. The cruciform shape of the churches built at this period followed the Greek Cross whose four sides were equal.

Many churches built during the Byzantine Period have survived in very good condition to this day. Of the rectangular Basilica type are the Churches of St. Demetrios and Acheiropoeitos in Thessalonica, Greece, the Church of the Nativity in Bethlehem, Israel, the Church of St. Catherine on Mt. Sinai in Egypt, the Churches of S. Vitale, S. Apollinare and S. Apollinare in Classe in Ravenna, Italy, and the Churches of St. Anastasia, St. Giorgio in Velabro, St. Paul Beyond the Walls, St. Mary Major and St. Laurence in Rome, Italy.

Churches of the square type, or of the hexagonal, octagonal or cruciform type with dome that were built during the Byzantine Period and have survived in very good condition to this day include, the Cathedral of St. Sophia, St. Irene and S.S. Sergius and Bacchus of Constantinople, the Churches of St. Sophia and of the Holy Apostles at Thessalonica, Greece, the small Churches of Capnicarea, Sts. Theodore, and of Daphne at Athens, Greece, the Church of St. Luke in Boeotia, Greece, the Church of Nea Moni, in Chios, Greece. The Church of St. Mark's in Venice, Italy, the Churches at Torcello, Palermo, Monreale and Cefalu in southern Italy, the Church of St. Stephen in Rome, Italy, and the Church of St. Sophia in Kiev, Russia.

Today, churches built in Byzantine Style can be seen in all the countries of Europe whose people are Orthodox and in others such as France. The Church of "Sacre Coeur" (Sacred Heart) built on the Hill of Montmantre, Paris, the Cathedral of St. Therse in Orleans - third largest church in the world and the Church of Perigneux are the most conspicuous churches built in Byzantine Style. In England the chapel of the "Tower of London" is of Byzantine Style, in the U.S. the sanctuary of the Cathedral of St. John the Divine in New York City and the impressive dome of the administration building of the University of Princeton are of such a style.

Iconography

From the fourth century AD when Byzantine basilicas and other types of Byzantine churches succeeded them, their interiors were always filled with iconography, that is, with sacred images and murals depicting Christ, the Holy Virgin, the Saints, Martyrs and great Church Fathers, as well as with scenes from the life of Christ.

Byzantine iconography has had three "Golden Ages": The first occurred during the "Age of Justinian", that is, during the sixth century AD when the Cathedral of St. Sophia was built, whose interior was embellished with exquisite mosaics; the second occurred during the ninth, tenth and first half of the eleventh century when the "Macedonian Dynasty" ruled the Empire; and the third occurred during the "Palaeologan Dynasty", that is during the thirteenth, fourteenth and fifteenth centuries.

As in the case of Byzantine Architecture, where only Byzantine churches have survived, and not secular buildings, such as the imperial palaces of which only a few ruins remain, so is the case of Byzantine Painting. Only a few secular paintings that were made in mosaic or in fresco have survived. The vast majority of Byzantine Painting has survived in the iconography of the churches.

Although Byzantine Art succeeded ancient Greek Art, it did not follow the trends of the latter. Whereas ancient Greek Art was naturalistic, that is it sought in both religious and secular sculpture and painting to find idealistic forms in man and in nature, Byzantine Art, being mainly religious, sought to portray and remind, through its iconography, the spiritual, the supernatural, the transcendent. Also, while classical Greek Art used both paintings and sculpture to portray its secular and religious themes, Byzantine Art concentrated mostly on painting.

Interestingly, when Byzantine Iconography began depicting its religious themes in the interior walls of the churches, it did not do this with paint but in mosaic. The ancient Greeks and Romans used mosaics, but only on the floors of their homes. They depicted human form, animals, plants, marine and aviary life. The colors of the tesserae (tiny marble stones) were very bright and of many hue varieties rendering to the floor a most beautiful appearance. But, when in the fourth century AD the Christians began building churches, they used mosaics in the sacred murals that graced the interior walls of their churches.

With the passing of the centuries, however, iconographers began using paints. They used paints to make church murals and to make small icons on wooden panels.

Unlike classical Greek painters, and later, European painters, who enjoyed much freedom in the choice of their themes and colors, Byzantine iconographers, when engaged to paint the interior of churches were compelled to abide by certain artistic rules that the Church had imposed. For example, in the case of painting the Holy Virgin or the saints, the painter strove to express as best as he could, the meekness, humility and holiness that distinguished these persons. Icons depicting saints, necessitated that their faces ought not to be those of men who resembled them. Orthodox Iconography also prescribed which colors ought to be used for garments or other things that were to be painted. To mention three: Christ's garments had to be purple and blue; the Holy Virgin's, deep red-wine and dark colors; and, for St. John the Baptist, green.

The Church Fathers, martyrs and saints, whether painted in their entirety on the interior walls of churches or as busts on small wooden panels, it was required the background must always be painted gold. Gold, symbolizes heaven, where the saint is now and for all eternity. Saints must never be depicted as fat, well-fed and with ruddy faces, but always ascetic and somewhat elongated. Such rules, although they restrained the iconographer's freedom, considerably helped him to achieve in the saintly figures he was painting, the expression of Christian spirituality that is the hallmark of Orthodox Iconography.

The rules of Byzantine Iconography also provided what ought to be painted in the various sections of the Church's interior. For example, in the dome, which symbolizes the universe, the mural of Christ as God Almighty must always dominate it. On the circular drum below the dome, would be angels. On the four pendentives, would be the four evangelists. On the apse above the altar, would be the Virgin Mary with the child Christ on her lap. In the semicircular wall below the apse, would be the Last Supper and the composers of the Divine Liturgy. On the Iconostasis, would be Christ, His Holy Mother, St. John the Baptist and others. On the interior walls of the nave (Church proper where the people sit), would be the figures of the Fathers and Martyrs, on the lower part, murals depicting scenes from the life of Christ and His Holy Mother. Thus, through such a logical iconographic arrangement, the interior of the church becomes an open Bible, pointing out Christ's and the Church's redeeming task.

Byzantine Art also expressed itself in many other creative areas. Byzantine textiles whether fabrics, embroideries, or silks were of the finest of the medieval world. Exquisite jewelry, whether gold-plated, silver-plated or plain, whether encrusted with gems or not, all exhibited superb craftsmanship, fine detail, and originality of design. Ivory was another material that expert Byzantine carvers used for making religious and secular statues, carved icons, carved book covers, reliquaries (boxes for the keeping of saints' relics) beautifully carved with religious scenes, and beautifully carved pyxes (small containers) for the keeping of various things. Engraving on metals was another fine art of the Byzantine Period. Doors made of copper or bronze, and bearing religious or secular motifs in relief, were made in Constantinople in great quantities to meet local demands and for export.

Today, American and European museums are proud to count in their collections these exquisite products of the Byzantine Minor Arts.

The same thing can be said about the Byzantine secular and especially the ecclesiastical handwritten illuminated manuscripts that have survived by the thousands and are exhibited, particularly the latter, in the various national libraries or Cathedral "Treasuries". The text is written in beautiful Byzantine curvilinear letters, and on most pages, if not all of them, complementary artistic themes occupy the margins or a good portion of the page. The figures are stylized and are always in color.

Aside from the large collections of Byzantine manuscripts in the four Patriarchal Libraries, and of those in the monastery libraries of Greece, the National Libraries of various countries also own large collections of such manuscripts. A few would include France's National Library - 600, Austria's National Library - 450, and the Vatican Library - 2,632. Private libraries such as the Palatini - 432, Ottoboniani - 473, Barberiniani - 595, Pope Alexander VIII - 165, and Queen Christina of Sweden - 190.

36
BYZANTINE SCIENCE

The Byzantines did not distinguish themselves to the extent that their ancestors, the Greeks did. The latter's spectacular advances in so many scientific fields had no follow-up during this medieval period. The Byzantines used the scientific progress of the ancient Greeks to their benefit, adding little advancements to the already existing scientific corpus of their predecessors. The following are some significant advances, which they made in certain fields.

Medicine and Pharmacy

A most famous Byzantine doctor was Oreivasius, who hailed from the city of Pergamum, Asia Minor. He studied medicine in Alexandria and in Athens. He spent his life in Constantinople, and served as imperial doctor to three Byzantine emperors.

Oreivasius was the first doctor to use antiseptic drugs, invented drugs against vertigo, invented ways to treat abscesses, phlebitis, teeth, and was an expert dietician advising what must be eaten in childhood, middle age, and in old age. He wrote a book against obesity, and a medical encyclopedia consisting of seventy-two books.

Another famous Byzantine doctor was Paul of Aegina. He was born on the Island of Aegina near Athens and studied medicine in Alexandria. He became famous as a physician, surgeon and especially as a gynecologist. He wrote a book on women's diseases and a medical encyclopedia.

Aetius was yet another famous Byzantine physician. He was born in Amida, a town by the River Tigris in Iraq. He studied medicine at Alexandria and spent his life in Constantinople becoming doctor to Emperor Justinian. He wrote sixteen medical books describing various diseases and their treatment and, in one of those books, he described every aspect of the disease diphtheria in great detail.

The most famous pharmacist in Byzantine Times was Nicholas Myrepsos. He was born in Alexandria during the thirteen century. He was called "Myrepsos" because he owned an industry that made myrrh and aromas. He lived in Constantinople, Alexandria and Rome. He served as doctor to Emperor John Ducas of Constantinople.

He wrote the most complete, up to that time, book on pharmacology, which consisted of forty-eight chapters and contained 2,656 medical prescriptions. His book was the standard of pharmacology until the seventeenth century, that is, for four hundred years. Its Greek title was "Dynameron". In its Latin translation, the book bears the title "Codex Medicamentarius".

Astronomy

In Byzantine Times, the most notable astronomer was Synecius - Bishop of the Greek city of Cyrene that was located on the Mediterranean coast of Libya. Bishop Synecius owned one of the largest astrolabs ever built. The astrolab indicated the position of one thousand stars, which was an incredibly large number of indications to be carried by one instrument. Bishop Synecius was also an excellent theologian and philosopher.

Nicholas Cabasilas, the Archbishop of Thessalonica, was another famous theologian and astronomer. He lived during the fourteenth century and wrote many scholarly comments on the third book of the "Almagest" of Ptolemy.

Chemistry

During Byzantine Times, Callimachus was the most celebrated chemist. At the end of the fifth century, he invented the "Greek Fire", which was a thick liquid, which when hurled against a target, would ignite on contact and set fire to the target, be it a ship, or any other target. The Greek Fire, once ignited, could not be extinguished. It would continue burning until it had consumed all of its flammable ingredients.

When the Greek Fire was invented, it was decided that it would be used by the navy. Special ships called "Fireships" were built to facilitate the hurling of this fire to great distances. The ships were equipped with two catapults, one at the bow and the other at the stern. Fireships soon became the terror of the enemy.

The ingredients of the Greek Fire were a highly-guarded secret by the Byzantine Government. No employee who worked at the place where this liquid was prepared was allowed to leave the capital. He would be a resident of the capital for life. He was frequently watched lest, through contact with a foreign agent, he might reveal the secret. The very strict measures proved successful. The secret never passed into foreign hands.

Exploration

Cosmas Indicopleustis – "He who sailed the Indian Ocean", was the best known Byzantine traveler and explorer of the Red Sea and the Indian Ocean. He visited the countries of Abyssinia (Ethiopia), Western India and the very large Island of Taprobane (Ceylon), located some 130 miles southeast of India.

Cosmas hailed from Alexandria, and while still a very young man, developed an irresistible desire to visit foreign lands, especially India and Ceylon. He fulfilled his desire by not only visiting these large countries, but taking extensive notes regarding their natural features and the way their people behaved and lived. When he ended his travels, he became a monk in the Monastery of Saint Catherine, which was located on Mt. Sinai, and there, he wrote a book, which he entitled, "Christian Topography".

John Focas was another notable Byzantine explorer who lived in the fifteenth century. While still young, he entered the service of the King of Spain, hispanicizing his name to Juan de Fuca - a name by which he is since known. Being an expert mariner, he was given a ship to explore the northwestern coast of the United States. Eventually, Focas reached the region and was the first European to discover and enter the big straits between the Island of Vancouver and the State of Washington. Since that time, the straits bear his name and are thus known as the Straits of Juan de Fuca. This is the only place in the western world that was explored by a Greek explorer and bears his name.

Juan de Fuca

37
BYZANTINE MISSIONS
TO THE SLAVIC WORLD

One of the triumphs of Byzantium was the propagation of its Orthodox Faith and culture to the Slavic world.

During the sixth century AD, Europe experienced the invasion of yet another Indo-European group, the Slavs. Although Slavic hordes had come and settled in Europe as far back as the first century AD, the number of these original settlers was small. They were known to the Romans by the name of "Venedae", and to the Germanic tribes as "Wends". They settled in Eastern Europe and farming became their main preoccupation. But, the Slavic invaders of the sixth century came in very large numbers, therefore the peoples of today's eastern and southeastern European nations are their descendants.

Cultural anthropologists categorize the newcomers in three major groups. They are: the "Western Slavs" whose descendants are today's Poles, Czechs and Slovaks, the "Eastern Slavs" whose descendants are today's Russians, and "Southeastern Slavs" who settled in the Balkan Penninsula, and whose descendents today are the Serbs, Croats, Slovenes, and Bulgars.

All of the invaders were pagan, illiterate and tribal in their social makeup. They all spoke the Slavic language, which like the other early European languages (Greek, Roman, Gaelic, and Germanic) belonged to the Indo-European language group.

The newcomers were very fortunate in choosing to settle near the most advanced state of the medieval Western World, namely the Byzantine Empire. As in the future, the Byzantine Empire would conquer them not territorially, but religiously and culturally. This double influence would immensely benefit them, for it would raise them from a tribal state to a well-organized civilized one.

In his book entitled "Byzance: Grandeur et Decadence" (Byzantium: Greatness and Decline), the distinguished French Byzantine scholar thus expresses the inestimable benevolent influence of Byzantium upon the Slavs: "The strong hands of Byzantium kneaded these barbarian tribes and shaped them into nations. From these Slavic, Bulgarian, Magyar, and Varangian hordes, Byzantium made the Christian states of Serbia, Croatia, Bulgaria, Hungary, and Russia. Byzantium gave them the elements of survival – the elements of future greatness. It was Byzantine missionaries who, by propagating Orthodoxy, led these wild peoples to Christianity, and who through religion, gradually taught them the things that make up an organized, civilized state. To the nations that Byzantium converted, it introduced the concept of government, the principles of law, a more civilized way of life, and an intellectual and artistic culture. Most important of all, Byzantium gave the Slavs their alphabet and their literary language."

Moravia, a region that, during the ninth century consisted of parts of Slovakia, southern Poland, Bohemia and parts of eastern Germany, was the first Slavic region to which Byzantium sent missionaries to convert its natives to Orthodoxy and transmit to them its Byzantine culture. Heading this historic missionary venture were the brothers Cyril and Methodius.

Cyril and Methodius were born in Thessalonica, Greece in 827 AD and 825 AD respectively. Being scions of a distinguished family, both received an excellent education at the University of Constantinople. Moreover, as pockets of Slavs lived inside and outside Thessalonica, they also learned the Slavonic language.

In 862, an emissary was sent by Rastislav, Prince of Moravia, to the Byzantine emperor Michael III. The envoy expressed to the emperor and to Patriarch Photius the desire of their ruler to receive Byzantine missionaries to convert the pagan people to Christianity. The emperor and the Patriarch willingly agreed to respond to Rastislav's request, sending a delegation headed by Cyril and Methodius.

The choice of the two brothers as leaders of this mission was precisely what such an undertaking needed. The brothers, besides being brilliant in planning and directing such a serious operation, were also very knowledgeable of the Slavonic language and customs. In fact, in order to secure the success of their mission, they immediately undertook the translation of the Orthodox Church's lectionary (the book that contains all of the Sunday and weekday Gospel readings of the year), the Divine Liturgy and all other services. In this way, the services would be celebrated in the natives' Slavonic language.

But, as mentioned previously, there was no Slavonic alphabet in existence when the request for missions was made. Thereupon, Cyril sought hard to invent one. Being fully acquainted with the Slavonic language's sounds, it didn't take him long to generate an alphabet whose forty-three letters covered completely the phonetic range of all the Slavonic linguistic sounds. His alphabet, henceforward to be known as "Cyrillic," consisted of mostly borrowed Greek letters, a few Latin and Hebrew ones. This alphabet, moreover, would become the alphabet of all Slavic nations, that is, of Moravia, Bulgaria, Russia, Serbia and of others. And so, armed with an alphabet and scores of translations of the divine services into the Slavonic language, and accompanied by many priests, the two brothers set out to Moravia.

For twenty consecutive years they carried on their blessed work, converting thousands of natives to Christ and to the Church. A seminary was even established to train native young men to be the future priests of the newly founded church.

The success of the Byzantine missionaries did not go unnoticed by the Latin missionaries, who, before the arrival of the Byzantine ones were already in Moravia seeking to convert the natives to the Latin rites.

As tensions between the two groups kept mounting, Pope Nicholas I invited Cyril and Methodius to Rome to discuss the situation. But, by the time the two brothers arrived in Rome, Pope Nicholas had died and Hadrian II had taken the throne. Hadrian received the brothers cordially, blessed their mission, and told them to return to Moravia to continue their missions. Unfortunately, while in Rome, Cyril died and was buried in the Church of St. Clemente. Methodius was ordained by the Pope Archbishop of Panonia, and then returned to Moravia.

But now the Latin priests were being encouraged by Swatopluk – the new king of Moravia who favored them over the Byzantine missionaries, thereby creating tensions. This antagonism, however, in no way intimidated Archbishop Methodius, and his missionaries continued their successful missions. On April 6, 885, when Archbishop Methodius died, his Byzantine missionaries who were facing increasing oppostion from both the King and the Latin priests, left Moravia and went south to Bulgaria where other Byzantine missionaries were already converting the natives to Christ and to the Church. There, working hand-in-hand with them, the conversion of the Bulgarian people came to completion much earlier.

What happened to the converted people of Moravia after the departure of the Byzantine missionaries? Soon, the parishes came under the jurisdiction of Rome whose Latin liturgies were totally unintelligible to the faithful. In view of the above, are we to assume that Cyril and Methodius' mission had failed? Not really, because the Byzantine missionaries and their illustrious leaders had succeeded to convert countless pagan Slavs to Christ and to the Church. Secondly, the invention of the Cyrillic alphabet and the scores of translations that were made for the benefit of the Moravian Slavs would be used in the future by other Byzantine missionaries for the benefit of millions of pagan Slavs that lived in the other Slavic countries, and whose language was the Slavonic.

Assessing the work of Cyril and Methodius, Dimitri Obolensky, professor emeritus of Russian and Balkan history at Oxford University, in his book entitled, "Byzantium and the Slavs", wrote: "The debt which the Slavs owe to Cyril and Methodius is great indeed. A mission, whose original purpose was to preach Christianity in the idiom of the Moravians, led to the rise of a whole Slavonic culture. A liturgy, in a language rich, supple and intelligible; the Christian scriptures, translated into the same vernacular tongue; access to the treasury of Greek patristic literature and Byzantine secular learning: truly a new world was opened to the Slavs by the work of Cyril and Methodius. The two brothers were aware of the importance of their mission...."

What an inestimable contribution the two Thessalonean brothers offered to the Slavic world!

Bulgaria   The year 864 AD is a milestone in Bulgaria's history. In that year, Boris, czar of Bulgaria received Baptism thereby becoming his kingdom's first Christian ruler.

What induced this pagan ruler to request Baptism and thus embrace the Orthodox Faith? According to one story, whenever the czar would look at a mural in his palace which depicted Christ's Last Judgment, he would be taken by such fear, that, in order to escape the ceaseless, eternal torments of hell, decided to receive the Baptism. According to the other story, which is more believable, Boris became Christian because he had no other choice. As his domain lay between Moravia, which now was converting to the Orthodox Faith, and the Byzantine Empire, he decided that it was an appropriate time to receive his Baptism.

Following the example of their king, the people would run in throngs to the Byzantine missionaries, who now had streamed into Byzantium in great numbers, converting the people to Orthodoxy.

Byzantine Missions to the Slavic Peoples

It was when King Symeon succeeded his father Boris that Orthodoxy and Byzantine culture made great inroads in Bulgaria. Symeon, having spent many years in Constantinople as a young prince, was enthralled by the splendor of the Byzantine capital.

His dream did come true. When he became king, he invited Byzantine architects, artists and iconographers from Constantinople to build and decorate his new impressive palace along with large and beautiful Byzantine churches and cathedrals. He also had Orthodox theological books and secular Byzantine literature translated into Bulgarian.

Byzantine cultural influence reached its climax when Symeon's son, Peter, ascended the throne. He had married a Byzantine princess, thus establishing very close ties with the Byzantine Court. More missionaries, architects, artists, and technicians came to Bulgaria under his reign, transforming Bulgaria into an Orthodox and well-organized state.

Russia   In the opening lines of this chapter it was stated that the eastern branch of the Slavic peoples settled in the vast plains of Eastern Europe. Today's Russians are their descendants.

Contacts between the Byzantine State and those Slavic settlers, especially those who had settled north of the Black Sea, began early. With the passing of years, Byzantine influence began to penetrate southern Russia as far as Kiev. Capitalizing on this influence, the Byzantine emperor, Basil I, began dreaming of converting the Russian people to the Orthodox faith, and to realize this dream, he created a diocese.

In 957, the Grand Princess Olga went to Constantinople to be baptized in the Orthodox Church. But not many Russian nobles emulated her example. It was forty years later, when her grandson, Vladimir received the Orthodox baptism, that Orthodox Christianity began making inroads into Russia.

According to a medieval chronicle entitled "The Chronicle of Nestor", we are informed that Vladimir, before choosing Orthodox Christianity, sent envoys to examine the religions of the other nations neighboring his domain. When the envoys returned, this was their report: referring to Moslems who lived along the Volga River they said: "There is no gladness among them; only sorrow and a great stench; their religion is not a good one." Referring to the temples of the Germans they saw "no beauty", but when they visited Constantinople and attended the performance of the Divine Liturgy in the Cathedral of Saint Sophia – Christendom's largest and most magnificent church, they said: "We no longer knew whether we were in heaven or on earth, nor such beauty, and we know not how to tell of it." It would be safe to assume that this report plus the offer of the Byzantine emperor, Basil II, to give his sister Anna in marriage to Vladimir were the two factors that made him receive the Orthodox Baptism. His baptism and wedding to Princess Anna took place in Kherson, a city located in the Crimean Peninsula. Then, the royal couple returned to Kiev and ordered the nobles and commoners of his capital to be baptized in the Orthodox Faith.

In the years that followed, the pagan city of Kiev was transformed into an Orthodox Christian capital. Beautiful Byzantine style churches were built in every section of the city, as was a Byzantine style palace, plus government buildings and schools for the teaching of secular and religious subjects. Churches, schools and municipal buildings were also built in all other cities of Vladimir's domain as the Orthodox religion and the Byzantine culture became the dominant features of christianized Russia. And all of this transformation was effected by countless Byzantine priests, architects and technicians who went to Russia to give it its new face. The priests, using the Cyrillic alphabet, translated the religious and secular Byzantine literature which, by being copied by the thousands, would spread to every provincial town and city. It took sixty years for this transformation to take place, but in the end, the result was that Russia had become a "second Byzantium".

This transformation continued with the same pace under Vladimir's son, Jaroslav. Like his father, he too kept inviting priests, technicians, architects and professionals to continue a building program on the scale as his father. Monastic life was introduced at this time by monks from Mt. Athos of Greece, who layed down the monastic rules of Athonite monasticism.

Byzantine priests taught Russian priests and cantors how to chant, Byzantine craftsmen struck the first Russian coins, while the Byzantine imperial etiquette through all of its pageants and ceremonial pomp would from this day forward be emulated by the Russian monarchs.

From all of the above, it becomes evident, that in Russia, Byzantium left its greatest religious and cultural stamp.

Serbia   During the seventh century AD, the mountainous, northwestern region of the Balkan Peninsula was invaded by Slavs, who are the ancestors of today's Serbs, and of the inhabitants of the newly independent state of FYROM (former Yugoslavian Republic of Macedonia). As this large region is divided mainly by the Dinaric Alps, the Serbs became a hardy, strong, and brave people.

By the middle of the ninth century, the Serbs welcomed Byzantine missionaries, who, after years of missionary labors, were able to convert the natives into Orthodox faith and to transmit to them many basic aspects of the Byzantine culture.   It was during the twelfth century and the centuries thereafter, however, when the country was led by the dynasty of Stephen Nemanja, that the Serbians absorbed, with almost a passion, nearly all aspects of Byzantine culture. Most members of the dynasty had married Byzantine princesses and so, for centuries, a very close tie existed between the Byzantine and Serbian state. Moreover, Byzantine royal titles were adopted by the Serbian Court.

In Serbia as in Russia, Byzantine priests, architects and all sorts of skilled craftsmen came to transmit the religious, technical and intellectual writings of Byzantium. Using the Cyrillic alphabet, priests translated them into the Slavonic language spoken in Serbia, including the lectionary and all liturgical books of the Church. They also translated the legal code of Byzantium and any Byzantine literary genre. Byzantine architects and iconographers designed and decorated with beautiful iconography countless cathedrals and churches throughout the region.   Also monasteries and convents, modeled after the Byzantine ones, were founded in every area of this mountainous country.

And so, tribal people, in a matter of years were transformed into an Orthodox and cultural nation.

Rumania   In ancient times, this country was known as Dacia and was inhabited by a people whose main preoccupation was to farm their fertile land.

In the second century AD, the Roman emperor Trajan conquered Dacia encouraging thousands of Roman families to settle in that fertile land. But during the reign of Hadrian, those Roman families returned to Italy, leaving the country speaking a Romance Language – the "Romanian Language". (The other Romance languages are: Italian, French, Spanish, Portuguese, and Romanche, spoken by many inhabitants of Switzerland.)

By the fourteenth century, Byzantine missionaries were busy in Rumania spreading the Orthodox Faith and the Byzantine culture. The results were as they were in the other cases. They succeeded to convert all of the inhabitants into Orthodoxy, while Byzantine culture was also firmly implanted in the country. Byzantine Law became the country's law, and education, literature, social customs, Byzantine architecture, and art were effectively absorbed.

Charles Diehl, in his book "Byzantium: Greatness and Decline," has the following interesting information: "In the sixteenth century, and even the seventeenth, Greek influence prevailed throughout the Danubian provinces. Princes took Greek brides, married their daughters to Greeks, spoke Greek, surrounded themselves with Greek officials, and installed Greek prelates in their churches. Greek books were translated into the Romanian language and the Greek language was taught in schools. Although this influence never reached the lower social strata, and often met with fierce hostility, it was powerful at court and in society. Indeed in the seventeenth century, the Wallachian Court presented a most striking proof of the great Hellenistic revival that followed the fall of Byzantium."

Summing up the content of this chapter, we can safely say that the conversion of the Slavs was one of Byzantium's most praiseworthy and successful undertakings.

38
THE FALL

An old saying goes: "There is a beginning and an end to everything." How true is this saying, because it applies to nature, to man, and to all the expressions of man. There is a beginning and an end to stellar systems, to suns and stars, to human life, to all animal and plant life, to all elements of nature, to nations, empires, cities, cultures, civilizations, and human institutions.

In the history of Greece, this saying was demonstrated to be true many times. As we have already seen, it applied to its Minoan Age, its Mycenaean Age, the Classical, the Hellenistic, and now, it would apply to one of its longest – the Byzantine.

Many factors contributed to the weakening of the Byzantine Empire, which, by the fifteenth century, would come to an end. During the previous century, it had lost valuable territories in Asia Minor and the Balkan Peninsula as a result of military conquests achieved by the Turkish Sultans Murad I and Murad II. Its commerce had been seriously challenged by Venice, but most of its weakening was the result of Constantinople's conquest by the crusaders of the Fourth Crusade. In 1204, they captured the city, pillaged it for days and established a Venetian rule that lasted until 1260. They also dismembered Greece forming small territories, which were ruled by French, Italian and Spanish noblemen. Although by 1260 when Constantinople was freed of its foreign occupants, and a Byzantine State was revived again, it was a "ghost state".

In the year 1451, twenty-one year old Mohammed II became Sultan. He was young, daring, and courageous and had many other character qualifications. His great dream, rather his passion, was to conquer Constantinople and its surrounding territory and thus eliminate forever this last remnant of the Byzantine Empire. When on certain nights he could not sleep, he would repeatedly whisper the words of Mohammed, the religious founder of Islam – "The greatest military leader will be the one who will conquer Constantinople." He made this obsession the priority of his reign and thus, from the day he ascended the throne, he began preparing his army in order to realize this goal.

Meanwhile, the wealthy inhabitants of Constantinople recognized that the end of their city's freedom and of the "Empire" was fast approaching and began packing their belongings preparatory to departing to cities of Europe.

And so, merchants, officials, magistrates, professionals, and professors boarded the merchant ships with their families and began the migration to Venice, Naples, Genoa, Florence and some as far as Paris. There they would settle to spend the remainder of their lives. In the eleven centuries long history of Constantinople, never before had such a mass exodus taken place.

In the beginning of April 1453, Mohammed surrounded the city with two hundred and fifty thousand soldiers and a large number of cannons. In fact, his possession of one huge cannon, whose stone shells were capable of ripping open large areas on the walls of the city, rendered him significantly superior to the defenders. In defense of the capital was a force of only seven thousand. Thus the ratio of the opponent forces was one versus thirty.

One week prior to the sultan giving the order to begin the storming of the capital, he sent emissaries to Emperor Constantine to surrender the city, assuring him that he would let him free to go to southern Greece and spend the remainder of his life as an independent ruler.

The emperor, after consulting with his council, and like another Leonidas proudly answered: "Neither do I have any authority to hand you over the City, nor any of its citizenry for we have all decided to die defending it."

The above stern and proud answer much angered the sultan who ordered his army to prepare for the assault. Moreover, in order to raise the "Elan" of his combatants he promised his troops that following their entry into the city, they would be free to pillage it for three days. As for those who would be killed in the battles, they were told that their souls would go straight to Paradise to be always with Mohammed the Prophet, enjoying the spiritual goods that Allah (God) would avail them eternally and in abundance.

Inside the besieged capital, the emperor was also busy preparing the defenders. On the eve of May 29 – the day of the assault, the people flocked to the Cathedral of Saint Sophia and to all the other churches to attend the last Divine Liturgy and to receive Holy Communion. The emperor and those of the officials who had not departed to settle in other countries went to receive Holy Communion at Saint Sophia's Cathedral.

When the moving Liturgy ended, the emperor mounted his horse and visited all the defenders who stood behind the ramparts ready to repel the attackers. He exhorted them to fight with all their strength "for the Faith and for the Country".

In the early morning of May 29, 1453, thousands of Turkish hordes attacked the walls of the city in an effort to scale them. At the same time, their cannon fired continuously against specified areas of the walls hoping to make an opening so that the army could enter the city. Despite however, this continuous bombardment and the four assaults that the massive Turkish Army made, the high walls of the city successfully withstood the enemy's persistent efforts.

When the emperor saw the successful repulsion of the enemy, he cried to his brave defenders: "Fellow soldiers, the victory will be ours." Unfortunately, however, these victories were the very last ones the outmanned and outgunned Byzantine defenders would attain. The city's capitulation was only a matter of time.

During a renewed attack, John Justinianis – the leader of the Byzantine Army, was fatally wounded. This unfortunate development in those critical moments caused much confusion among the Byzantine defenders. Meantime, quite unexpectedly Turkish contingents appeared inside the city, having gained entrance through a wall gate that mysteriously was left open. Soon many Turkish intruders surrounded the emperor who was fighting like a lion. Before receiving a fatal blow on his head, he cried: "The City is falling and I am still alive. Isn't there any Christian to cut off my head?"

It was such a heroic fashion in which the life of the last Byzantine emperor ended. His life did not end while sitting comfortable in his royal throne, but fighting heroically defending his city. Not sitting on his throne and holding his royal scepter, but with a sword in his hand defending his people. He did not die while surrounded by courtiers enthusiastically acclaiming him, but he died fighting desperately against angered barbarians who groaned like wild beasts. Finally, he did not die when triumphant trumpeting vibrated the air, but in the midst of a deafening sword clanking.

With the enemy's troops now inside the city, Turkish barbarism was to manifest itself in its ugliest, bestial fashion. Describing the inhuman fashion by which the armies of the barbarian conqueror treated the people of the capital, Critobulus, a contemporary historian and an eyewitness of this tragedy, wrote: "No tragedy could equal it in horror…for three days and three nights, Mohammed delivered the city over the rapine, and there was more destruction than plunder. Forty thousand perished during the sack of the city." Franzes, another eyewitness historian, wrote:

> *"The greatest misfortune of all was to see the Temple of Agia Sofia defiled. Priceless manuscripts and icons were burned, while the Turks placed cooking pots over the flames. All the churches were plundered in like manner. The Orthodox Churches furnished the conqueror with plentiful harvest. The city was made desolation; the Turks left nothing of value except the buildings. Constantinople was as silent as a tomb with its inhabitants gone, women destined to servitude, its nobles massacred, and temples of God desecrated…"*

The Venetian humanist and patrician Lauro Quirini thus bewailed the destruction of Constantinople: "Her citizens have been slain before their fathers' eyes, her noble maidens, gentle boys, gracious matrons, holy nuns, have been seized, isolated, cut to pieces. Her grand and gorgeous temples, wonderful to behold, have been shockingly defiled, her sacred objects of devotion fully polluted…for as the city was nobler than the rest, so is her fate more fearful…over one hundred and twenty thousand books have been destroyed…the literature which once illuminated the whole world, is perishing."

Such was the tragic end of the city that, for one thousand one hundred and twenty-three years, had been the capital of medieval Hellenism. From now on, however, it would no longer be the "Vasilevousa" – (the Queen City) of Hellenism, but a city the barbarian conqueror would transform into a typical Asiatic one. Its beautiful Christian Churches would be converted to Muslim mosques, its gorgeous palaces into seraglios, while its commercial centers would become Turkish Bazaars. Worst of all, in the next four centuries, the Greek people would live as slaves.

Yet despite the fall of Constantinople, which also sealed the end of the Byzantine Empire, its culture, its civilization, its spirit, its arts and other contributions would not only survive, but to this day continue to influence the life and social structure of many millions of people.

To briefly cite some very important facts:

When Napoleon, the Great ordered the famous French jurist, Eugene Cabasserais, to structure a new penal code, Cabasserais used the Byzantine "Corpus Juris Civilis" as a prototype. Eventually, the "Napoleonic Code" that was set forth by Cabasserais and his assistants became the prototype of the civil code of most nations. The American State of Louisiana has the Napoleonic Code as the basis for his legal structure.

Most of the basic Christian doctrines now believed by the Orthodox, the Catholic and the conservative Protestant churches were formulated by Ecumenical Councils that convened in cities within the boundaries of the Byzantine Empire and by the great Church Fathers who lived in the same areas.

If Russia and most of the Balkan countries adhere to the Orthodox Church, they owe this to Byzantine missionaries who many centuries ago preached the Orthodox Faith to the people of those countries.

Byzantine ecclesiastical art and architecture are still pursued in all Orthodox countries of the world. This is also evident to a lesser degree in many countries of the West such as Italy, France, and others. When after the Second World War a new cathedral was built in the City of Orleans, France, a cathedral whose enormous size makes it the third largest church in the world, it was built in Byzantine Style.

During the Middle Ages, in no other country was the classical Greek literature and science preserved as in the Byzantine Empire. Thus, if today, we know so much about ancient Greece's cultural, artistic, scientific, and literary achievements that laid the foundation of our Western Civilization, we owe it to the highly enlightened scholars and monks who ceaselessly and meticulously copied and thus preserved for posterity these inestimable writings of antiquity.

The enlightened Byzantine Greeks who fled Constantinople prior to its fall to the Turks, and went to Western Europe especially in Italy, were also great contributors to the "bursting out" of that marvelous artistic and intellectual movement known as the "Renaissance". This was a movement that, after so many centuries of stagnation, touched its entire attention to the achievements of ancient Greek thought and culture for inspiration so necessary to move ahead.

Last but not least, it was the Byzantine Greeks who used the Greek Language as a means of verbal communication, thereby preserving it for future generations.

And so, even though the Byzantine Empire ceased to exist as a political and territorial entity, its cultural, literary and other achievements continue to dominate the lives of millions of people.

39
THE LONGEST DARKNESS

The capture of Constantinople by the Turks in 1453, and of the remaining Greek territories by 1460, initiated to the Greek world one of the darkest periods of its four thousand year history. The subjugation was to last for four consecutive centuries, affecting in the negative, the lives of at least twelve generations.

Thus, while during the fifteenth century the movement of the Renaissance – an intellectual and artistic movement was bursting forth in Florence, Italy, the Renaissance, which aimed at reviving the ancient Greek intellectual and artistic spirit as its intellectual and artistic representatives drew heavily from the wisdom that was in the philosophical, political, scientific, and artistic repositories of ancient Greece, and giving the Western World a tremendous cultural leap forward, the Greek world was sinking into cultural darkness and stagnation.

Prior to the conquest of the Byzantine capital and shortly afterwards, nearly all Byzantine thinkers fled to Western Europe. Many of them would settle permanently in Italy as well as in other countries of Western Europe.

Thirty-eight thinkers chose to settle permanently in Venice. Eventually, their erudition made such an impression on the native academics and the common citizenry, that the names of all thirty-eight intellectual refugees were included in the famous "Libro d' Auro" (Golden Book), as the Republic's record of its elite citizenry was called.

The mass exodus, the mass effluence of so many Byzantine thinkers, naturally deprived the Hellenic world of its most vital, its most needed pillars of learning. In its four thousand year history, never before was Greece bled of so many of its learned men. Moreover, the Barbarian conqueror's decision to shut down all schools and many of the churches of Greece further intensified the problem. His purpose? To put it briefly, by shutting down the schools, he was hoping to ultimately extinguish in the youth its Greek identity, and by shutting down churches to ultimately convert people to Islam.

Faced by such harsh and oppressive measures the people of Greece began to think seriously of how they would cope with this blow successfully.

With God's providence a solution was found. The priests and the monks who were quite knowledgeable, not only in the Orthodox Religion but in many aspects of Greek learning, would, from now on, undertake to carry on this challenging and most responsible task. Since the schools had been shut down, and since the teaching of Greek education and culture had been forbidden, classes would be held in the cellars of churches or monasteries and would always be held during the night.

And so, from the conquest of Greece in the fifteenth century, until the seventeenth century, at which time these harsh measures were lifted, the Greek youth would leave the house late at night and go to a designated church or nearby monastery to be taught the Greek Language and other basic subjects. On the way to "school" and back home, they would need to be very careful not to be spotted by Turkish soldiers who might thus follow them in order to learn where instruction was being given. Needless to mention, that if they were discovered, Turkish reprisals would be very harsh on the inhabitants of the town.

Once they had arrived safely to the church or monastery cellar, a priest or a monk would welcome them and then he would ask them to sit on flat stones that had been placed in a semicircle on the dirt floor of the cellar. Light from a single candle was the only source of illumination available in the sultry and damp "classrooms".

The session always started and ended with a prayer, recited by all students, while the subjects taught included reading, writing, history, geography, and culture of Greece, as well as the Orthodox Religion. Since there were no books and tablets available, everything had to be committed to memory to be remembered well thereafter.

Amazingly, these primitive instructional methods somehow thwarted the scheme of the conqueror. At least, eight generations of children, by being taught the rudiments of education and religion, proudly held fast to their Greek identity and the Orthodox Religion. Thanks to those poor, humble but patient and persistent priests and monks, the Greek identity and the Orthodox Religion remained alive. The debt of the Greek Nation to those obscure teachers will forever remain inestimable.

As mentioned above, by the late seventeenth century, the barbarian conqueror, realizing that his scheme had failed, decided to relax the harsh measures that had been imposed more than two centuries prior. In most towns, schools re-opened, and teachers, who had been trained in teachers' academies located in Constantinople, Smyrna, Jassy, Romania, Bucharest, Romania, Chios, Giannena, Thessalonica, Metsovon, Pelion, and Demetsana, were now staffing the schools.

A new breed of brilliant men - some clerics and other laity, many of them graduates of universities of Western Europe, taught in the teachers' academies. To mention a few, the many worthy of note would be Elias Meniates, Eugene Bulgaris, Nicephoros Theotokis, Anthimos Gazis, Neophytus Vamvas, Constantine Economus and a host of others. Their devotion to the sacred cause to which they had committed themselves was such that their enthusiasm never waned.

The teachers they trained were what the nation needed. As for books, these were printed in Western Europe and were steadily supplied to the schools of Greece, thanks to the generous donations of wealthy Greeks who lived abroad. The long night of Greek education was over.

Education was not the only aspect of life that suffered. The barbarian oppressor struck hard at many other aspects of civic life.

Almost from the beginning of the occupation, the Muslim rulers made it clear, that henceforth, a sharp distinction would exist between the conqueror and the conquered. Thus, right from the start, the unfortunate Greek people were subjected to all sorts of rules, which regulated the color of their garments, the size and styles of their houses, and the kind of profession or vocation they were to pursue. If a Turk wanted to lodge in the house of a Greek, the latter had to provide him with meals and have him housed in the best room.

Whenever a Turk passed on the street, the Greek must show respect by standing up to greet the Turk. Greeks could not ride horses, keep weapons or swords, nor strike a Muslim in self-defense. If a Greek dared to raise his hand and strike a Turk, the penalty would be the loss of the offending hand. It was forbidden to kill a Turk in self-defense. If he struck a Turk, the offender would be put to death or have imposed such heavy fines that, in order to be able to pay them, he might have to sell his property. Again, if he were to accidentally strike a descendant of Mohammed the prophet who wore green turbans to distinguish himself from other ordinary Muslims, the penalty would be death.

If a Greek was murdered by a Turk or a Christian wife was violated, in either case, the offended person could not appeal to the court for justice. If a Turk had converted a woman to Islam, such an act was considered meritorious. Thus, there was no equality even in a court of justice between the conqueror and the conquered.

Another very harsh measure the barbarian conquerors imposed on the conquered was the forced conscription of young Greek boys in order to serve for life in the army or in the navy. From the Greek Islands the Turks recruited young men to serve in their fleet. From mainland Greece, they would recruit young boys to be soldiers in the Turkish Army for life.

The conscription of young Greek boys to serve in the Turkish Army was far more numerous than that for the navy. Every four years, recruiting officers visited the Greek villages ordering the village priest to gather all the boys between the ages of six and nine, from whom the recruiting officer selected one in five. Needless to say, the ones selected were the healthiest and the most intelligent.

The conscripts were then transported to Constantinople, given red jackets and caps and formed into companies. Next, they would be circumcised, since they were ordered to embrace the Mohammedan (Muslim) Religion. They would then receive extensive instruction in all aspects of the new religion, and at the same time, they were subjected to rigorous military training that was always suitable to their age and stamina.

When they reached the age of eighteen, they were full-fledged "Jannissaries", that is, the elite, crack troops of the sultan. They were so thoroughly brainwashed, so devoted to the sultan that they were always ready to march into the fiercest battle where death could come from every direction. Sacrificing their lives for victory was an honor to them. For serving in the Turkish Army under such a strict and demanding military code, they were paid the highest salary, and, always enjoyed many privileges not available to the other regular military troops. If, for some reason, they contracted a disease that incapacitated them from being battle worthy, they could withdraw from the army ranks spending the remainder of their lives as civilians supported by the state. It is ironic that the sultan's elite troops which fought the most important battles that expanded Turkey's dominations were not Turks, but Greeks. Recruiting the Jannissary troops came to an end in the seventeenth century.

From 1453, when Constantinople was captured by the Turks, until Greece became independent four centuries later, the Patriarch of Constantinople was the "Ethnarch" (leader of nation) of all the Greeks. He was also their chief representative to the sultan. Moreover, he was responsible to no authority except the "Divan" (sultan and his ministers.)

Others, who were responsible to the Turkish authorities on the local level, were a group of elders in every village. They were the administrative authorities of the villages, responsible to levy taxes on every Greek inhabitant according to his earnings, and be sure that these would be handed over to the Turkish provincial authorities. They were also responsible in overseeing the repairs of roads, bridges, public wells and other public facilities. Thus, the Turkish authorities never meddled with local community affairs. Their only concern was to receive the predetermined amount of taxes and to be sure that the public facilities were not neglected by the elders.

By the seventeenth century, the Turks began recruiting well-educated Greeks for their diplomatic services. Because the Koran forbids Muslins from learning foreign languages, the Turks had to recruit well-educated Greeks who also knew one or more foreign languages, and thus be able to undertake diplomatic tasks and especially diplomatic negotiations. And so, Greeks represented Turkey in peace treaties or other diplomatic negotiations held in European capitals or in Constantinople. Two notable such diplomats were P. Nicousios and Alexander Mavrocordatos.

From the beginning of the eighteenth century, educated Greeks from the Phanar District of Constantinople were appointed as chief administrators of European domains which had been conquered by Turkey. These Greek chief administrators also had the privilege of forming armies to keep order in their respective domains, enact laws, and engage in diplomatic negotiations with other European leaders.

In conclusion, although the four centuries of Turkish occupation was harsh, cruel and oppressive, it failed totally to make the Greeks forget their Greek identity and their Orthodox Religion. On the contrary, not only did they resist it successfully for whole generations, it even helped them to unite themselves so cohesively that, when the time was ripe for rebellion, united they rose and they won.

40
GREAT CONTRIBUTORS
TO THE RENAISSANCE

About the middle of the fifteenth century, a sudden outburst of creativity in literature, poetry, in the arts and in architecture occurred in Italy. Not since the Golden Age of Greece, the fifth century BC, had such a flowering of intellectual and artistic creativity been seen. It seemed like a reawakening after a long lethargy, an explosion of intellectual energy after centuries of mental inertia.

In Western history, this phenomenal revival is known as the "Renaissance" - a word that denoted "rebirth". It first appeared in Italy, and to be more specific, in Florence, euphemistically called "L' Atene d' Italia" (the Athens of Italy). From there it spread to Rome, Venice, Milan, and, afterwards, to all other western countries, such as France, Spain, Germany, Austria, Holland, and England.

"Humanism", a philosophy that centers on man was, to a great extent, behind this rare Cultural Revolution. After the long period of the Middle Ages, characterized by a mentality influenced largely by theology and the Church, people began to turn to a predominately mundane mentality as expressed through the pleasures of literature, poetry, philosophy, painting, drama, and classical sculpture and architecture.

Poets like Petrarch, surnamed "The first modern man", along with Boccacio, Ariosto, Tasso, and the humanist Greek scholar Marsilio Ficino, led the "New Age". In sculpture and painting, Pisano, Michelangelo and Raphael were of the first to rediscover the ideal beauty of the classical models. And, in architecture, Palladio, Bramante, and Sansovino were of the first revivalists of Greco-Roman architecture.

Initially, humanists had great respect for all Latin literary genres. But, when in the course of their intensive studies they discovered the Hellenic substratum, the Greek background that under- laid all Latin literary genres, a tremendous interest to study the gems of Greek literature in the original Greek Language began spreading like fever among students of all western academies and universities. Since Greek literature and the Greek Language were now placed side-by-side with Latin, Greek scholars, Greek manuscripts, and Greek printed classics were now in great demand.

As at this time, the Byzantine Empire was breathing its last, and Constantinople, its capital, was with every passing day, coming closer to its demise, Byzantine scholars of ancient Greek and Byzantine literature began fleeing from the capital and other cities in large numbers, embarking for Italy where their scholarly expertise would be greatly needed.

Unfortunately, the Byzantine State, and Greece in particular, did not participate in this monumental artistic and intellectual revival. Their conquest by a nomadic, Asiatic and backward people, the Turks, totally deprived them from sharing its marvelous yields. Yet, even though Greece and the now equally reduced-in-size Byzantine State did not enjoy any yields, they were leading contributors to this epochal movement. The galaxy of the illustrious Byzantine scholars that had come and settled in Italy and other European countries, contributed immensely to the success of this "Rebirth".

An early arrival to Italy was the Byzantine scholar, Manuel Chrysoloras. He settled in Florence, and, besides teaching ancient Greek philosophy at its Academy, he would hold philosophical discussions in literary circles consisting of Florentine scholars, like Salutati, Strozzi, Bruni, Aretino, who later became the leader of Italian humanism, Guarino and others. Guarino described him as "not only a teacher, but a father."

George Trapezountios who hailed from Crete was another renowned Byzantine scholar who came to Italy to teach Greek philosophy and literature. He settled in Rome and eventually became the secretary of Pope Eugenius IV. At the request of the enlightened Pope, he translated the works of many Greek philosophers and works of such Greek Church Fathers as St. John Chrysostom, St. Gregory and others. After many years of residence in Rome, he moved to Florence, where he assumed the chair of Greek philosophy at the Academia.

John Argyropoulos was the scion of a distinguished Byzantine family. Not long after his arrival, the distinguished scholar became the dean of the Academia. Like Chrysoloras - his predecessor, he enjoyed much respect from his students as well as from the members of an academic circle known as "Chorus Academiae Florentinae". Some of this circle's members included Lorenzo Medico, the most famous Florentine, who later became known as "Lorenzo il Magnifico" (Lorenzo the Magnificent), Carlo di Silvestri and others. Lorenzo the Magnificent had such an admiration for this most erudite teacher that a lifetime friendship developed between the two men. Very often on Sunday, Lorenzo would invite his teacher and the other members of the "Chorus" to his opulent "Palazzo", where the distinguished teacher would lead in long discussions on Plato and Aristotle. Distinguished non-Italian students of Argyropoulos included, the British Duke of Worcester, the Spanish Bishop of Miletus, the famous Hungarian poet, Jan Panonnius, Count Eberhardt of Wurtenmburg, and the famous German Hellenist, Johann Reuchlein.

Andronicus Callistus succeeded Argyropoulos when the latter moved to Padua and retired. Callistus, a master of Aristotelian philosophy, always preferred to teach Aristotle at the expense of Plato. His partiality resulted in alienating many of his students who preferred to hear about Plato. In reality, Callistus had failed to discern that Florence was by far more "Platonic" than "Aristotelian". As he continued to emphasize Aristotle, he lost most of his students, who joined the class of the Platonist, Marsilio Ficcino. In the end, he lost his position as dean to the Platonist, Ficcino.

In 1473, Demetrios Chalcocondyles arrived in Florence. He soon came to the attention of Lorenzo Magnifico, who appointed him professor of ancient Greek philosophy and literature at the "Florence Studio". Like Argyropoulos, the newcomer scholar gained the respect and admiration of many distinguished Florentines. His admirers included Picco de la Mirandola, the notable poet Polizziano, Ugolino Verino, and John Medico, who later became Pope Leo I. Chalcocondyles, received the greatest praise of his life from Marcilio Ficcino when he said: "That he would never publish any of his Platonic translations unless they had first been reviewed by Chalcocondyles."

George Trapezountios, an Aristotelian scholar and "An enemy of Plato", was another top-notch scholar who came to Rome to lecture on Aristotle. He became secretary of Pope Nicholas V, who, being a great admirer and an ardent enthusiast of the Greek classics, commissioned Trapezountios to translate as many of them as he could. Upon completing the Pope's request, he moved to Venice where more high positions awaited him. Having made the acquaintance of Venice's Doge, L. Malipiezzo, the latter, impressed by scholar's erudition, appointed him professor of Greek philosophy in the college of the "Ducal Chancellery". The doge, admiring the professor's academic brilliance, asked him to translate Plato's "Laws". The professor produced such a masterful Latin translation that the doge and the city's academics heaped upon him the highest honors.

Of the many dozens of Byzantine scholars who left the Byzantine State, and went to Italy and other countries to teach, the most illustrious was Bessarion.

John Bessarion (c. 1395-1472) was born in Trepizond, a city located on the Black Sea coast of Northern Turkey. He was educated at the University of Constantinople where he studied philosophy under the famous Platonist philosopher Pletho Gemistus. Following his graduation, he entered a monastery, and it was at this time that he was given the name of Bessarion. In 1437, he was elevated to the rank of Archbishop of his Archdiocese of Nicaea.

Right from the start of his clerical vocation, Bessarion was highly admired, not only for his theological profundity, but for his profundity in the ancient classics as well. He had mastered both the Greek and the Latin classical literature as no other of his time. He was the Orthodox Church's most learned hierarch.

When attempts were made by both the Orthodox and the Catholic Churches to abridge the Schism that had separated the two churches in 1504, delegations from both sides met in two councils convened in Ferrara (1438) and in Florence (1438). Archbishop Bessarion attended both Councils representing the Orthodox Church. In the council of Florence, he accompanied Joseph, Patriarch of Constantinople, and Palaeologus, the Byzantine Emperor. Both the Patriarch and the Emperor were seeking a union of the two churches, hoping that in this way that armies of western

European nations would come to the aid of the Byzantines against the Turks. The latter would attack in the future to conquer the capital.

Unfortunately, at the Council of Florence, Bessarion utterly disappointed the Orthodox delegation. Instead of becoming a firm supporter of the Orthodox theological positions, he leaned toward the Catholic ones. In the end, he defected to the Catholic side, gained easily the favor of Pope Eugenius IV, who not long after made him a cardinal.

Although Bessarion's apostasy was a serious loss to the Orthodox Church, it was a tremendous gain especially to Greek Culture's immense impact in the West, which was now experiencing the "fresh winds" of the Renaissance Movement.

Cardinal Bessarion's great skills in carrying on negotiations made him the Pope's most successful "legate" (ambassador) to different European courts. He also served as ambassador to the King of France, Louis XI, for five years. Other European kings also used him as ambassador to conduct successful negotiations.

Besides accomplishing his multifarious duties as cardinal, Bessarion also worked indefatigably for the propagation of the Greek classical literature in Rome and in Italy. His great collection of ancient Greek and Latin manuscripts was incomparable. He donated a large number of Greek manuscripts to the Library of Saint Mark in Venice that made up the nucleus of that famous library. Other beneficiaries of his invaluable manuscript collection were the Vatican Library and the Library of Grotta Feratta, a famous monastery near Rome.

In his palace, located next to the Church of the Holy Apostles in Rome, and in his private villa near the "Thermae (springs) of Caracalla", the most celebrated literati of his time gathered every evening to debate philosophical and theological subjects with the most illustrious clerical scholar of their time. The circle included Francesco Filelfo, who greatly admired the cardinal, the Papal biographer, Bartolomeo Platina, the humanist, Lorenzo Valla who later became Pope Francesco dela Rovere, and other humanists.

Greek intellectuals who had come to Rome from Greece and Constantinople also came to the house of the celebrated cardinal. The group included Theodore Gazes from Thessalonica who had translated Homer into Latin and had written commentaries on Plato and Aristotle, and who later became professor of Greek literature and language at the College of Sapienza, in Rome, Janos and Constantine Lascaris and many others. Bessarion presided over the lengthy philosophical and theological discussions, which usually lasted until late at night.

Before his death, Bessarion translated the "Metaphysics" of Aristotle and Xenophon's "Memorabilia". Following his death, he was buried in Rome, while his private villa became property of the Vatican, which has maintained it as a museum.

No other Greek scholar contributed so much to the Renaissance's appreciation of the Greek classical literatures and philosophy as Bessarion. His impact on the Renaissance is incalculable. In the opinion of many experts, he is considered one of the five greatest contributors to the Renaissance.

Janus (John) Lascaris (1445-1535) was another Greek scholar of high repute. He was born in Constantinople, and, after its fall, at the age of eight, together with his parents, fled to Crete. While an adolescent, he enrolled at the University of Padua. After his graduation, he went to Florence, where, having won the favor of Lorenzo de' Medici, became a resident at his court. At the request of Lorenzo, he went to Greece and Turkey where he purchased two hundred rare Greek manuscripts that were totally unknown to Western scholars. The manuscripts became the property of the famous "Lorenziana", Florence's public library, and the first public library of modern times, which had been founded by the Medici Family.

When the Medici were expelled from Florence, Lascaris moved to Paris, having been invited by King Charles VIII of France to teach the Greek classics to the French intellectuals and the young noblemen. When Louis XII succeeded King Charles, he made Lascaris his ambassador, sending him to European royal courts to negotiate. Amazingly, Lascaris proved most successful in all his diplomatic missions.

When John Medico of Florence became Pope Leo X, he invited Lascaris to Rome to become dean of the Greek College which the Pope had founded in Rome. Lascaris accepted the invitation, and, besides directing the college, he also found time to translate into Latin many untranslated Greek classics. He wrote commentaries on Pausanias, Aristotle and the poet Pindar, translated Polybius into Latin, published an anthology of Greek epigrams and a commentary on Greek Orthodox Canonical Law. In 1518, Lascaris, at the invitation of Francis I, King of France, came to Paris, where, in collaboration with Budaeus, worked for the formation of the Library of Fountainebleau. King Francis, recognizing Lascaris' erudition, wanted him to stay in France. But Lascaris returned to Rome at the summons of Pope Paul III in 1535, only to die a few months thereafter.

His brother, Constantine Lascaris (d. 1500), also came to Italy. Not long after his arrival, the powerful and very influential Duke of Milan - Francesco Sforza, appointed him tutor of Greek to his daughters. It was during this time that Constantine published his "Grammatica Graeca", the first complete Greek Grammar, which was also the first book to be printed in Greek in its entirety. Other places in Italy where Constantine taught were Rome, Naples and Messina, Sicily, where he died.

Another Cretan scholar who came to Rome during the 15th century was the Cretan priest, George Alexandrou, who became Pope Alexander VI's (Borgia) priest, co-celebrating mass with the above-mentioned Pontiff at St. Peter's Basilica, and reading the Gospel, always in Greek, and the Cretan Zachary Kallerghis.

He was a grandson of the Kallerghises, who, a few decades after the invention of the printing press, had established in Venice their own, printing the Greek classics by the thousands. Their printing house was one of the first to be established in Venice.

Zachary Kallerghis had come to Rome to print for Pope Leo I, who was a philosopher and generous pope who always patronized the printing of the Greek classics and encouraged their study by the young students. Among other Greek classics Kallergis printed, at the request of the Pope, Pindar's poems and the "Idylls of Theocritus".

Many other Greek scholars taught at the academies of Mantua, Mirandola, Pessaro, Urbino, Ferrara, Naples, Milan, Padua, and Bologna.

Thus, refugee intellectuals from Constantinople and Greece played a key role in the Renaissance's turning its attention and embracing classical Greek learning in all its aspects, be it philosophy, historiography, politics, art, or architecture. They rekindled the interest of generations of students and thinkers since the fifteenth century to study the ancient Greek Language so that they could better understand the countless ideals included in the ancient Greek writings. The incalculable value of Greek learning had been again rediscovered, to be employed ever since as a tool and foundation for all Western thinkers in their developing of new philosophies, political theories and like intellectual pursuits.

Moreover, as the Renaissance began spreading to the other countries of Europe, ancient Greek learning, art, architecture, and now, ancient Greek science likewise became objects of intense study to be used as springboards for further development, a development that in our time achieved phenomenal progress.

As was stated at the beginning of the chapter, Renaissance means rebirth, and what was reborn was attention to the eternal Hellenic Ideals that guided the forward march of the Western World.

Bessarion

Chalcocondyles

Chrysoloras

41
MEHMET SINAN

In a past chapter, we learned about a famous Greek architect, who in the second Century AD became the court architect of the Roman Emperor, Trajan. This chapter is about another Greek architect, who in the sixteenth century also became a famous court architect. His name was Mehmet Sinan.

In 1491, only a year before Columbus discovered America, a baby boy was born to the Greek family of Chrisodoulou who lived in the town of Carmania, Turkey. His parents, who were pious Orthodox Christians, had the baby baptized in the local church. Unfortunately, we have no record of the name that was given to the baby at the baptism.

At that time, the Turkish authorities would frequently do a barbarous act to the Greek people who lived in Turkey as well as in other land of the Turkish Empire. They would go to the Greek homes and would take away the male children of the family. They would then place them in special camps, change their Greek names to Turkish ones, and would force them to deny their Christian Religion and become Moslems. When the boys would grow up, they would join the Turkish Army. And that's exactly what happened to the Christodoulou boy. They changed his name to Mehmet Sinan and made him deny Christ and become a Moslem.

Mehmet Sinan was a very bright boy and his superiors soon recognized this. Since he excelled in math and science, they decided to transfer him to a school of engineering to become an army engineer. Once studies had been completed, he was placed in the army where his superior officers soon became aware of his excellent engineering skills.

One day, as Sinan was building a bridge, the Sultan (king) of Turkey, Suleiman the "Magnificent" passed by, and, noticing the methodic way by which the engineer was doing his work, ordered him to immediately leave his work and follow him to the capital which was Istanbul (Constantinople). When they arrived at the palace, he was given a whole apartment in which to live and work as the court architect. Not long after, fourteen other architects, who were all Greeks, would come to the palace and assist the master architect in his drawings.

Suleiman the Magnificent, besides conquering the countries of the Middle East and other lands in Eastern Europe, and even besieging Vienna – the capital of Austria, was also a man of culture and a great builder. He loved to add new buildings in his capital and in the other cities of his great empire. And to whom would he entrust the designing of so many buildings? To Sinan, his royal architect!

Sinan was forty-seven years old when he became a royal architect. He would serve his royal master for the next fifty years until his death at the age of ninety-seven. During the fifty years that he served as royal architect, he designed detailed plans for eighty-seven large mosques, fifty smaller mosques (a mosque is a Moslem house of prayer), thirty-two palaces, twenty-two public baths, nineteen mausoleums, six aqueducts, and two bridges.

Besides the above impressive record of designs, Suleiman asked his architect to design plans for three minarets that were to be built on three corners of the Cathedral of St. Sophia which now had been converted into a mosque, and already had a minaret on one of its four corners. Sinan, mindful that St. Sophia was once the cathedral of Orthodox Christians for more than 1,000 years, designed three very beautiful minarets.

When Suleiman conquered Palestine, wishing to beautify its capital, Jerusalem, he asked his architect to design plans for: "New City Walls" that would enclose the entire city, and which today, are seen and admired by all tourists who visit the Holy City, "The Damascus Gate", which since its construction is the most beautiful of all the other gates, an "Esplanade" in front of the Wall which Jews regard as the holiest spot on earth, and a "Mosaic Facing of The exterior of The Dome of The Rock." To the Moslem world, the Dome of the Rock is the third most sacred shrine, next to those of Mecca and Medina. It had been built during the seventh century AD, that is, one thousand years earlier, by Omar, the Caliph of Jerusalem, with superb mosaic decorations on its interior walls but not on its exterior ones. Sinan drew very beautiful designs made of interlacing geometrical patterns of different colors which, when they were done in mosaic on the exterior walls, made the shrine one of the most beautiful in the world.

Sinan's masterpiece, however, was the "Suleimaniya", that is, the Mosque of Suleiman the Magnificent. It was to be built on the summit of the highest hill of Istanbul (Constantinople) thus making it most visible.

Where did Sinan turn for inspiration to make superb designs for a mosque that would be the greatest in the capital? Where else, but to St. Sophia – the masterpiece of Byzantine architecture! His choice more than rewarded him. When completed, his mosque was regarded ever since as "the finest and most sumptuous" of the imperial Mosques of Constantinople. Today, it is considered to be the most important building of that city.

For the construction of the mosque, 5,300 laborers and craftsmen were employed. Marble facing of many colors covered the walls and the floor making the entire interior glitter. The mosque is square in plan, crowned by a central dome flanked by four half domes, and capped at all corners by smaller domes. The main dome has a diameter of ninety feet and rises 154 feet above the floor. In the courtyard of the mosque are the tombs of Suleiman the Magnificent and of Sinan.

And so, the greatest Sultan of the Ottoman Period of Turkish History from the eleventh to the twentieth centuries and the greatest architect of the same period of Turkish History rest for all eternity in the courtyard of a mosque that is the greatest architectural masterpiece of the same period.

The Selimiye Mosque at Edirne
One of Mehmet Sinan's masterpieces.

42
THE MASTER ARTIST

Spain's most famous artists are five - El Greco, Velasquez, Murillo, Goya, and Picasso. Of these the first was Greek while the other four were Spaniards.

El Greco was born Kyriacos Theotocopoulos in the City of Canea, one of the major cities of the green, fertile and sun-drenched Island of Crete. He was born in 1542, the younger son of George Theotocopoulos.

From early adolescence Kyriacos began to show a great interest in painting - a predilection his father was not slow to notice. In fact, he encouraged his son to remain faithful to such an aspiration. Soon Kyriacos became a pupil to the monastic painter Michael Damaskinos who taught him how to paint icons in the Byzantine Style. Today, at the Cathedral of St. Menas in the City of Herakleion, one can see a beautiful Byzantine icon which the very young student had painted during his apprenticeship with the experienced monastic iconographer. Thus, in his native town, Kyriacos mastered the first artistic style - the Byzantine, which later he was to blend with those which he would acquire in the West, that is, in Venice, Rome and Spain.

At this time, Greece was under Turkish occupation - a condition under which the Greek people suffered all kinds of deprivations. An exception of this status quo was the Ionian Islands that lie to the west of the Greek mainland, some isolated spots on the Greek mainland and some Aegean Islands, including the largest Greek island - Crete. As the above-mentioned exceptions were under Venetian rule, their occupation was a mild one.

By 1560, Kyriacos, now aged twenty-two, left his native Canea and went to Venice never to return to his birthplace. He settled in the large Greek enclave of Venice whose center was the Greek Orthodox Church of "San Giorgio dei Greci" (Saint George of the Greeks). In Venice, he apprenticed at the studio of the famous Venetian artist, Titian, who taught him the technique of brilliant landscaping as a background for human figures or other principal objects. During this time, he became acquainted with Bassano and Tintoretto. From Tintoretto, he would familiarize himself with the dramatic style of his subjects as well as his background landscapes. As these three artists belonged to the "Mannerist " School, mannerism was the second artistic style that Kyriacos, by now called "El Greco", (The Greek), had appropriated.

During his stay in Venice, El Greco painted quite a few paintings of high quality. They have all become permanent collections of various museums of Europe and of the U.S., a fact confirming the high artistic skill the still very young artist had attained.

By 1570, El Greco moved to Rome where he would stay at the palace of Cardinal Alessandro Farnese. In fact, this is how he acquired residence in this most sumptuous palace. A letter sent to the Cardinal by manuscript illuminator Giulio Clovio and dated November 16, 1570 read: "A young Candiote (native of Canea) pupil of Titian has arrived in Rome, a really excellent painter in my opinion. Among other things he has done a portrait of himself which has astonished all the painters in Rome. I should like to recommend him to the patronage of your Eminence, his only practical necessity being a room in the Palazzo Farnese for a short time, until he can find more suitable lodging. I should be grateful if your Eminence would accede to this and write to Count Ludovico, your steward, instructing him to provide this man with some room in the upper part of the palace. In this your Eminence and I should be much obliged to your Eminence, kissing your hands in all reverence, I remain, Your Eminence's most humble servant."

Cardinal Farnese did provide El Greco with lodging at his palace, and there, during the three years of his stay, the young artist made paintings of considerable artistry, three of which have become very well known to art lovers. They are: "Boy Lighting a Candle", "Christ healing the Blind Man", and "The Cleansing of the Temple", now in the National Gallery of Washington, D.C.

During this time, El Greco became acquainted with many high ranking clergy attached to the Vatican, and who, admiring his artistic creations, invited him to Spain. Without much hesitation, the young artist was off to Toledo, Spain in 1573.

In Spain, El Greco's first major commission was a triptych in the Church of Santo Domingo el Antiguo in the City of Toledo. Besides the paintings, El Greco also designed the architectural and sculptural elements of the altar piece. In the center of the triptych, which is now in the Chicago Art Institute, he painted "The Assumption of the Virgin". The painting is full of intensity, overwhelming the viewer. On either side of the central triptych are the imposing figures of Saint John the Baptist and Saint John the

El Greco. The Holy Family
Cleveland Museum of Art

Evangelist. On the side altars of the church, he painted "The Adoration of the Shepherds" and the "Resurrection". Another impressive painting was "The Holy Trinity" showing the dead Christ in the arms of God the Father.

El Greco stunned the people of Toledo. Never before had they seen such superb artistry. As art experts claim by analyzing these works: "Byzantine idealism, Venetian colors, composition taken partly from Titian and partly from Tintoretto, the heroic style of Michelangelo modifying the latter, and a manneristic elongation of the proportions, all these different characteristics are superbly synthesized to create El Greco's first artistic creations in his new adopted country- a country in which he would spend the remainder of his life."

Having done his best at the Church of Santo Domingo, El Greco was now hoping to get commissions from King Phillip II for the Escorial. In 1850, his expectations did materialize when the King asked him to create an altar piece for the Church of Saint Maurice in the Monastery of Escorial. The painting was to show the martyrdom of Saint Maurice and his Theban Legionnaires who were executed during the persecution of Emperor Maximian because they refused to pay homage to the pagan gods. El Greco, instead of showing Saint Maurice and his legionnaires being executed, as other artists before him and after him have depicted martyrdom scenes, he introduced an innovation. He masterfully depicted the indifference of those about to be executed toward the excruciating process by which their lives would end, showing their faces serene, turned heavenward, and with eyes full of ecstasy - a characteristic that would become cliché in future paintings. Although this innovation did not please King Phillip, who instead expected a "bloody scene", art critics of all ages have been greatly admiring and praising the artist's innovative masterpiece.

El Greco's next important work became the finest he ever painted, finest in conception, arrangement of its many components, use of color and other outstanding qualities. It is called "Burial of Count Orgaz", for the Church of San Tome (Saint Thomas), and to this day, it still hangs in the original place in the Church of San Tome.

The theme of the painting reenacts a miracle that occurred during the burial of the count. Don Gonzalo Ruiz, Governor of Orgaz, had, during his life, been a fervent devotee of Saint Augustine and Saint Stephen. When his body was about to be buried in the Church of San Tome, a miracle occurred. Saint Augustine and Saint Stephen came down from heaven and laid him to rest to the astonishment of the clergy and the people attending the burial.

It is this miracle that is masterfully depicted in the lower half of the painting. We see at the center of the foreground Sts. Augustine and Stephen laying to rest the Count of Orgaz. Clergy and lay attendants are depicted in wonder. The lay attendants are shown in a long row of heads on a horizontal line across the picture. The upper arched section of the painting depicts heaven. Flanking the entrance to the celestial region, are the Virgin and St. John, receiving the count's soul, which is carried by an angel who holds it in the form of a child wrapped in transparent clothes. Above the Virgin and St John, Christ appears seated, while to His right is a group of righteous, and to

His left are seated figures of David, Noah, and Moses, while above them is Saint Peter.

Thus, in one painting, heaven and earth are masterfully depicted and united. The lower half, full of human figures painted in the wind and with dark colors, making them appear solid material. In the upper part which depicts heaven, the figures are painted in lighter colors which make them look ethereal, almost devoid of solidity. The clouds, on the other hand, are painted in mostly light and a little dark colors with opalescent tones rendering them tufty.

Many other commissions followed, like altar pieces and paintings depicting scenes from the life of Christ for the Church of Donna Maria de Aragon in Madrid. They are full of dramatic expressions and with exaggerations and distortions that the artist was inclined to repeat in many of his paintings, figures are elongated, limbs appear twisted, while strange streaks of light flash across. Another famous painting of his is "The Assumption" in the Church of San Vincente in Toledo. In it, the Virgin is shown rising through the air among clouds of angels.

El Greco also painted many pictures depicting the apostles, the evangelists, saints, martyrs, cardinals, monastics, mystics as well as secular people - kings, counts, princes, dukes, governors, and military men. He also painted ladies and cities like Toledo against a dark background with white streaks. From antiquity, he painted the Theme of Laocoon whose human figures are very elongated, looking almost ascetic.

He painted 115 paintings, fifteen sketches, and 150 drawings. In his spare time, he liked to read the works of Homer, Plutarch, Aristotle, Torquato Tasso, Petrarch, Ariosto and books on architecture.

He died at the age of seventy-five and was interred like a noble in the Church of Santo Domingo el Antiguo on April 7, 1614. He was survived by his son, Jorge Emmanuel, who also became a competent artist.

Reflecting on the unique characteristics that are present in the paintings of this artist - one of the greatest in the world, a contemporary art critic wrote: "His Coronations of the Virgin, his Assumptions, his resurrections show us that he is the only painter who has really spread celestial visions before our mortal eyes; he painted them as he saw them. And in the great canvas which is his masterpiece, the Burial of Count Orgaz, he achieved, as no one before him had done, and probably no one after him will do, an understanding and interrelation, which seem quite natural, between the supernatural and the material."

El Greco

43
A MOST WELCOME EXODUS

By the first half of the eighteenth century, the strict restrictions of the movements of the ethnic minorities within the Ottoman (Turkish) Empire were considerably relaxed. Thus, if Greeks, for example, wished to immigrate to other regions of the Empire, or even to independent countries, they could do so. As a result, a large number of Greeks living in Greece proper, or in the regions of the Empire, began to immigrate either to other areas within the Empire, or to other countries of Europe and of the Middle East.

The regions and countries to which they moved in hope of obtaining a fresh start and greater prosperity, were Serbia, Bulgaria, Romania, Hungary, Poland, Russia, Austria, Italy, the Islands of Corsica and Malta, France, Holland, Portugal, England, and Egypt.

Owing to their traditional entrepreneurial spirit and hard work, the Greek immigrants soon became prosperous. Especially those who settled in Russia, Austria, Romania, and Egypt, amassed great wealth, thus becoming benefactors to the host country where they had settled, as well as to Greece, during the latter's war for its independence, and in subsequent restoration.

As mentioned in chapter thirty-four, refugee scholars and upper class merchants and aristocrats had left Constantinople before 1453, and settled in Venice and other nearby cities in order to escape the harsh Turkish occupation. In the seventeenth and eighteenth centuries, more Greeks from the Venetian-held Islands of Crete and the Ionian Islands came and settled in Venice.

Of the many Greek communities that were founded in Italy, those of Venice, Livorno (Leghorn) Naples and Ancona, were the most prosperous.

In Venice, the Greeks distinguished themselves as scholars and merchants. By the middle of the seventeenth century, they built the beautiful Church of St. George on the banks of the "Canale dei Graeci" (Canal of the Greeks), and adjacent to the Church, the "Flaginian Institute" – a hearth where generations of distinguished Greek teachers promulgated Greek studies. Today, the school bears the name "Hellenic Institute of Byzantine Iconography". Students, mainly from European, Catholic countries, attend classes here to learn various techniques of Byzantine Iconography.

The printing of Greek books, first initiated by the Cretan Kallerghis during the Renaissance, was continued later by such printing establishments as those of Glykidis, Saros and Theodosiou. Their printed material was so abundant, that Greek books were now available not only to Greeks of the Diaspora, but to those of occupied Greece as well.

Pisa, an ancient Greek colony founded by the "Pisates," the Greeks who lived in the region of Elis (Southwestern Greece), and for centuries known to the world for its "Leaning Tower", also had a flourishing Greek community. In fact, many of its members taught for generations at its notable university.

Moldavia and Wallachia, the two large and fertile provinces of Romania, also became settling grounds for Greek immigrants. With the passing of time, the immigrants became rich farmers and leading merchants.

During the seventeenth and the eighteenth centuries, Rumania, like the other Balkan countries, was under Turkish occupation. Its Turkish governors, however, were not native Turks, but Greeks who had been born in the district of Phanar in Constantinople. They were very learned men, very skilled in diplomacy and administrative ability. Best known among them were Nicholas and Constantine Mavrocordatos who were governors of Wallachia, and the Gikas brothers, Matthew and Gregory, Michael Soustos and Alexander Ypsilantis, who were governors of Moldavia.

Egypt was another country where a large number of immigrant Greeks from Greece and other regions of the Ottoman Empire had settled. Alexandria, Egypt's largest port, became those immigrants' favorite settling ground. In fact, following the successful War for Greek Independence, more immigrants came and settled in this ancient land. By the twentieth century, their descendents amounted to 100,000 thereby forming the largest community in Egypt.

The Greek community of Cairo, although not as numerous as that of Alexandria, also boasted its professional class. In fact, as in Alexandria, Greek architects had designed many of its public buildings, and even recent mosques, including the famous "Alabaster Mosque" in the citadel of the capital.

Russia, today's territorially largest country, also welcomed Greek immigrants. To be more exact, it was the last quarter of the eighteenth century that many Greeks settled in Nizni, Norgorod and in Moscow. Their numbers, however, were limited.

It was during the reign of Catherine the Great that Greeks settled in Russia by the thousands. After the Russo-Turkish War, which resulted in Russia's gaining all the territories that Turkey had occupied in the northern coastal areas of the Black Sea, Catherine the Great, at the suggestion of one of her advisors, Prince Alexius Orloff, issued on March 28, 1775, a decree whereby the Russian Government extended the privilege of citizenship to as many Greeks as wished to immigrate to Russia. The immigrants would be granted free land, would pay no taxes during the first thirty years and would have self-administration. As these offers were most attractive, thousands of Greeks from Peloponnessos and the Aegean Islands immigrated to the region known as Azof, and whole cities, such as Mariopolis, Stavropolis, Constantinople, Ignatia and dozens of others, were founded by the immigrants. Eventually the export of caviar, a very expensive delicacy, was dominated by the Greeks, becoming their monopoly.

The newly-acquired land from the Turks needed a port. By special decree, issued by the then reigning czar, on May 27, 1794, a new city was founded, the well known Odessa, whose first inhabitants were Greek immigrants. Although Russians also came to live in the new city, the Greeks of Odessa continued for generations to form the upper class as shipping, banking, and trading remained in their hands.

During the War for Greek Independence, the prosperous Greeks of Odessa financed a great part of that heroic struggle, while many young, Odessan Greeks volunteered to go to Greece and fight for independence.

Since the first quarter of the eighteenth century, Greeks came to settle in Austria and especially in Vienna. They came mostly from northern Greece, specifically, from Epirus, Thessaly, Thrace, and the Aegean Islands.

In Vienna, the overwhelming majority of the Greeks lived in six districts near the center of the capital. In fact, the districts of Fleishmarkt, Hoermarkt and Hafnersteig were replete with Greek settlers. Today, "Greichengasse" (Greek Street), near the heart of this cosmopolitan capital, is a reminder of once being the street lined with Greek mercantile enterprises.

The wealthy Greeks of Vienna, not only donated generously toward many very important cultural projects of their adopted country, but also donated huge sums toward the cause of the War for Greece's Independence. Greek-owned printing houses published Greek books in huge quantities, many of which would end up in Turkish-occupied Greece, to be read by the peoples and school children.

In the year of 1790, the Poulios Brothers began printing the first Greek newspaper. It was a weekly publication entitled "Ephemeris", meaning "News of the Day". In today's Greek Language, the title of that first Greek paper has come to mean "newspaper". Also, the first printed Greek magazines, namely, the "Calliope" and the "Logios Hermes" (Intellectual Mercury), were printed in Vienna.

Thanks to the generous donations of Viennese Greeks, two large and beautiful churches were also built in the Austrian Capital. They are the Church of Saint George and the Cathedral of the Holy Trinity. The cathedral was designed by Vienna's distinguished architect, Theofil Hansen, who also designed the impressive Austrian Parliament, and, in Athens, Greece, the elegant building of the "Academy", the National Observatory and Greece's Parliament. The Cathedral of the Holy Trinity in Vienna, has beautiful, sacred murals, exquisite furnishings, and is regarded as one of the capital's landmarks.

Of the many Greeks who became "Maecenas", that is, fabulously wealthy, Barons George Sinas and Stergios Dumbas top the list. George Sinas' diversified mercantile enterprises are described in the chapter "Three Great Greek Benefactors". Stergio Dumbas will be treated in this chapter.

Stergio Dumbas (1794-1870) was born in the small Macedonian town of Beltsi and came to Vienna as a very young man. At first, he worked as a servant, and eventually, thanks to his ingenuity, became one of the most successful merchants in all of Austria. He amassed a tremendous fortune and used the greater part of his wealth to finance several Viennese civic projects as well as the National University of Greece.

Nicholas Dumbas' – only son and sole heir of his father's fabulous wealth, continued the philanthropic and humanitarian work. He was one of the founders and the contributor of most of the cost of construction of Vienna's famous "Musikverein" (Music Hall), an elegant neoclassical building designed by Theofil Hansen and located in the heart of the city. It is the home of the world-famous "Vienna Philharmonic", and home of the "Musikfreunde" (Association of Friends of Music). He was also a member of the "Wiener Maennergesang-Vezein" (Vienna Men's Chorus), and for many years its president.

Nicholas Dumbas, a man who loved culture with all his heart, was also a close friend of some of Vienna's and the world's greatest composers such as Franz Schubert, Johannes Brahms, Richard Wagner, and Johann Strauss from whom he even received autographed compositions. He also patronized many artists among them was the notable Gustav Klemp.

For all these benefactions that Nicholas Dumbas made to his native city, the grateful capital named the avenue on which the Musikverein is located, "Dumbastrasse" (Dumba Street). His fabulous mansion, known as "Dumbas Palais", located on Park Ring, is one of Vienna's most famous residences, while the impressive residences of the other Greek Maecenases –

Baron Sinas' Gekas' and others still grace the "Ringstrasse" – Vienna's most famous thoroughfare.

The Greek Orthodox Cathedral of
Holy Trinity in Vienna, Austria

44
A GREAT PATRIOT

In his second book entitled "De Finibus", the famous Roman Orator, Cicero quoting Plato, wrote: "Man was not born for self alone, but for country and for kindred." Adamantios Coraes lived up to this maxim as very few men have done in all of human history.

Coraes was born of Chian parents in 1748 in the City of Smyrna, Turkey. His father was a prosperous merchant and his mother was the daughter of a teacher. He owed his future love of education to his mother.

Being a gifted child not only was he an excellent student at school, he also could learn foreign languages easily. By the time he had grown, he had mastered not one or two foreign languages, but incredibly, ten! Among the ten languages he knew, he sought to master the ancient Greek Language as best he could.

When the gifted young lad was eighteen, his father, who wanted him to be the heir to his business, sent him to Amsterdam, Holland to work in the branch of his firm located in that city. The father hoped that here his son would have a good opportunity to master every aspect of business administration. Young Adamantios, besides fulfilling the purpose for which his father had sent him to Amsterdam, also came in contact with many intellectuals of Amsterdam from whose erudite company he benefited a great deal.

After six years of residence in Amsterdam, Coraes returned to his native Smyrna. A shocking surprise awaited him there. His beautiful native city was almost gone. A wild fire had spread throughout the city and had burned everything in its way. Smyrna was not presently a viable city. It would take many years for Smyrna to be rebuilt and resume its past bustling life and trade.

His father's business had also collapsed. Young Coraes, realizing that there was no future for him in Smyrna, packed his belongings, bid farewell to his parents and set out for Montpellier, France. He had decided to study medicine and the city's thirteenth century university was the proper place to pursue the study of this discipline. The university's school of medicine was one of the oldest in Europe.

Upon completing six years of study, Coraes graduated with honors. Graduating with honors made him eligible for membership in the French Academy of Sciences – a membership that gained more prestige for the young doctor.

Adamantios Coraes, who henceforward will be known in France by the French version of his name – Diamant Coray, never ceased to be an enthusiastic Greek patriot. He continued to love the country of his parents with a passion that is rare in most people and this love made him assume a new direction in the way he would spend the remainder of his life.

He reasoned that since his country was occupied by a backward and barbarous nation – a nation that for four centuries had kept whole generations almost illiterate, he decided to devote his life to help the youth of the present generation become educated. He was absolutely convinced that education would eventually spur them to rise up against the oppressors and thus regain their freedom.

Having come to this decision he determined to, from then on, pursue this goal and it alone. He would not practice medicine so that he could devote all his time to the study of the Greek classics particularly those that dealt with political ideas such as democracy, freedom, loyalty to country, just laws, justice and the like. He would annotate them, have them published and then have them sent to Greece to be studied by the youth.

By the year 1788, Coraes was forty years old. He moved to Paris and settled in a very modest dwelling. In the unassuming abode, he would spend the remainder of his life – forty-five odd years to realize his dream.

In 1789, the world-known French Revolution occurred. Its purpose was to abolish royalty, the aristocracy, and all the privileges held by this group at the expense of the common people's well being.

Coraes, who lived in Paris – the very core where all these dramatic and earth-shaking events were taking place, lost no chance to become an eyewitness of all these epochal happenings. He repeatedly sought to mingle with the risen masses and their leaders in order to learn all about their ideals pertaining to the radical restructuring of the French Society on democratic principles rather than the old absolutistic ones. This social change deeply impressed and greatly enlightened the keen Greek observer. All these political developments that helped shape the new France provided an inestimable enlightenment to Coraes, and enlightenment that he believed might prove very useful in the future rebirth of Greece.

After studying meticulously the works of Plato, Aristotle, Xenophon, Homer and many others, he wrote extensive introductions, comments and many useful annotations. He had them published using funds provided by wealthy Greeks who lived in Paris, and had them sent to Greece to be read by youth. He also wrote many pamphlets that dealt with basic and useful topics, and while he was doing all this, he also sought to purify the Modern Greek Language of certain "Barbarisms" by substituting those with ancient words. He succeeded in instituting changes in the language of literature, art and science but not in the common, everyday usage of the language.

The Greeks revolted on March 25, 1821 in order to regain their independence. Coraes wanted to participate in the titanic struggle of his people but he was too old. He was seventy-three years old.

He did not stand by as a mere observer, however. During the eight years of that heroic struggle, from his humble dwelling, he wrote one thousand letters to monarchs, prime ministers, princes, lords, barons, bankers, industrialists, military leaders and to other men and women of influence eliciting their sympathy and material help in support of the Greek cause. He also corresponded with Thomas Jefferson and Napoleon. He would also review the appeals of Greek revolutionary leaders and federations before these were sent to persons or organizations.

No other man, indeed, worked so hard, so persistently, and for so long as this preeminent Greek patriot who lived in Paris. He worked tirelessly at his desk until the late night hours and many a time until the very early morning hours, hoping to see his country free again and its youth properly educated.

In the course of forty-four years of residence in Paris, Coraes made many friends, friends who greatly admired him for his wide knowledge, genuine patriotism and marvelous consistency of character. That such a thing was true became evident at his funeral. When on April 6, 1833, Coraes died at the age of eighty-five, all the Greeks that lived in Paris, along with thousands of Parisians, attended his funeral, accompanying the deceased all the way to Pere La Chese – the Paris cemetery.

Forty-four years later, the Greek Government requested that the relics of Coraes be brought to Greece for burial at the Athens Cemetery. The relics were brought to Athens in a very elegant urn, and, in the presence of countless people and government officials, were interred with honors at the Athens Cemetery.

Coraes never stepped foot on Greek soil. He spent his eighty-five years away from Greece never having the opportunity to see the beauty of its countryside, its lofty mountains, its warm, hospitable people and the historic sites where immortal Greek minds shaped the destiny of their country and of the world.

And yet, despite the fact that Coraes never saw the country he so loved, he knew far more about it through his lifetime studies. Moreover, the books that he wrote or annotated for the benefit of the Greek youth so that they could learn more about their country's glorious ancient and medieval past, is another indication of how much this man knew about the country he had never seen.

In order to honor properly and show its immense gratitude to this great patriot, the Greek Government ordered that a marble statue be prepared and placed before the University of Athens. Seen by students and passersby of future generations, they would be reminded immediately of his inestimable and unselfish services and contributions to the Land of his Fathers.

The quote again from Cicero – his "De Re Publica", how fitting to Coraes, the maxim. "To good men there is no limit of devotion to their country." Coraes was an ideal embodiment of this maxim throughout his long and distinguished life.

Adamantios Coraes

PART III

RECENT TIMES

45
THE WAR FOR
GREEK INDEPENDENCE IN 1821

By the year 1821, the Greek people thought that the time was ripe to revolt. Already, there were thousands of armed Greek fighters in the mountains prepared to fight against the hated enemy whose armies were in every city of Greece. Also, at sea, there were hundreds of Greek merchant ships, which had been equipped with cannons to defend themselves against piracy, could now be used as naval vessels.

On March 25, 1821, the Feast of Annunciation, the leaders from many regions of Greece gathered at the Monastery of St. Laura in Peloponnesos. Here, after the Divine Liturgy, Germanos, the Bishop of the City of Patra, raised a holy standard before all the people who had gathered in the monastery, and asked all to take the oath promising that they would fight for the freedom of the country. Until the end of the war, their war-cry was "Freedom or Death".

It was in such a way that the long war for the independence of Greece began. In no time, it had spread to all the regions of Greece. The armed Greek fighters, known as "Armatoles" and "Cleftes", would constantly attack the Turks in towns, cities, mountains, ravines, narrow passes, valleys, virtually everywhere. At sea, the same thing happened. The small Greek ships would attack the much larger warships of the enemy and sink them.

In vain, the Turks sent large armies to Greece to subdue the revolution. Although their armies were well-equipped and far superior in numbers, in the end, they failed.

The war continued for eight years, and, during most of this period, the Greeks fought alone. No other nation sent troops to help them in the fight. It was towards the end of the war that England, France and Russia sent their fleets, headed by Admirals Codrington, Derigny and Heyden respectively, to Navarino, which was a bay very near the southwestern most tip of mainland Greece. When the admiral of the Turkish fleet, which was already at the bay, saw the combined fleets approaching, he ordered his forces to fire upon them. In the deadly engagement that followed, the Turkish Fleet was totally annihilated. In history, this significant naval battle, which took place on October 20, 1827, is known as the Sea Battle of Navarino. This naval engagement that resulted in such total disaster to the Turkish Fleet also signaled to Turkey the beginning of the end of its repeated, futile efforts to suppress the Greek Revolution.

In January 1830, in London, England, and in the presence of many representatives of prominent European countries, Turkey was compelled to sign an agreement thereby recognizing the independence of Greece.

The newly liberated state, which took the ancient name "Hellas" and its people "Hellenes", was first governed by John Capodistrias. He was a man of great diplomatic ability and statesmanship. He had acquired the above-mentioned experiences by serving as "Minister of Foreign Affairs" in the Russian Czar's government for many years. Being, however, an ardent Greek at heart, he did not hesitate to abandon this so prestigious post and came to his very small country to assume its leadership.

From the day he set foot on Greek soil, he quickly noted the vast devastation brought on by the eight-year war. He also noticed that his country was far behind the other European countries and immediately sought to reorganize it. Soon, compulsory education was instituted, teachers and agricultural academies and technical schools were founded in many provincial towns, printing houses and banks were also founded, money was issued, new harbors were constructed and old ones were renovated, roads were paved and an army and navy were founded.

It is unfortunate that this statesman, whose tenure was a blessing, since he did so much to reorganize his small, poor and ruined country, ended his most beneficial tenure at the hands of an assassin. This person was an office seeker who had been denied a request for public employment.

John Capodistrias

46
A SAVAGE GENOCIDE

In the Eastern Aegean Sea and close to the Turkish coast is the Island of Chios – fifth largest island of Greece. The northern part of Chios is rocky and mountainous terminating at the highest peak of Mt. Pelenaeon some five thousand feet above sea level. The southern part of the island is mostly valley covered by mastic trees, olive trees, a variety of fruit trees and vineyards.

People have lived on this island for more than three millennia. They have distinguished themselves as merchants owning their own ships on which they carried the rich yields of their island to ports of both the eastern and western Mediterranean in order to sell them. As a result of their entrepreneurial drive, they have always enjoyed great prosperity. Today, they own the largest Greek merchant fleet, and their ships of all types ply the seven seas of the globe.

Besides Homer, whom Chians for almost twenty-eight centuries prefer to claim as a native of their island, although six other Greek cities claim him, the island is the home of two other famous writers. They are the fifth century B.C. playwright Ion, who wrote many excellent dramas, and the fourth century B.C. philosopher Theopompus, who was a keen observer of human nature and the causes of events. He believed that statesmen and leaders of people were not upright people, but as a rule, "the scum of society".

To Glafkos, another seventh century B.C. native of this island, we owe the invention of iron welding. Although none of his iron products have survived, ancient, written records reveal that his products were masterpieces.

In Byzantine Times, Chios continued to enjoy the prosperity that it did in antiquity. Its high quality wine was carried to every port, while in Constantinople – the Byzantine capital, this wine was served at the palace at royal dinners for centuries.

From the eleventh century to the year 1566 AD, Chios was under Venetian and then under Genoese occupation. During the last two hundred years, the Giustiniani Family was for many generations the ruling family, which alone exploited the mastic trade.

In 1474 and at the age of twenty-three, the Genoese explorer, Christopher Columbus, visited Chios and resided there until 1476. This is not the first time that the world famous explorer came in contact with Greeks. There were already many of them living in Genoa for generations, plus those who had settled there recently having fled from Constantinople prior to the latter's capture by the Turks in 1453.

While the rest of Greece by 1460 had been conquered by the Turks, Chios and a few other small territorial enclaves in some islands and on the mainland continued to enjoy the mild rule of the Venetians and the Genoese. But in 1566, Chios, too, was occupied and came under the rule of the Turks.

The Turkish takeover of the island did not result in the imposition of the same harsh measures and rules on the Chians that it did on the Greeks who lived on the mainland and on the other islands. Self-government, which had been allowed by the Genoese, continued under the Turks. Trade of Chian products continued with the west while the Turks took the mastic production. Trade and prosperity were so expansive that the taxes paid annually to the Turks were of the highest in Greece.

For all its good fortune, Chios was not to enjoy its prosperity and privileges forever. During the Greek Revolution, cruel fate had decided that this island too must pay a heavy price.

When the Greek revolt began in March of 1821 and spread rapidly thereafter to all parts of mainland Greece and to many islands, the Chians did not join the cause. There were two reasons for this: First, the privileges the Turks had granted them had made them prosperous and happy; and secondly, their island was very close to the Turkish coast. They figured that if they had revolted, the Turkish reprisals would be swift and heavy. So, for almost a year they remained neutral

On March 11, 1822, however, existing conditions and special relationships would end. A rebel leader named Lycurgos Logothetis from the nearby Island of Samos landed on Chios with two thousand men and called on the Chians to join in the revolt. Against their will the Chians armed themselves and, together with the Samians, began attacking the Turkish garrison and the Turkish civilians who lived on the island. In panic, the Turkish garrison and the civilians barricaded themselves in the citadel of the capital.

When news of the Chians uprising reached Constantinople, the sultan became so enraged that he ordered his troops to gather all the Chian civilians who lived in the capital and to put them to death. This was the first atrocious reprisal against the Chians for having joined the revolt. A "Holocaust" was to follow.

On March 30, 1822, a Turkish Armada, consisting of six warships-of-the-line, ten frigates and eighteen smaller warships under the command of Admiral Pasha Karalis, appeared near the harbor. Logothetis, seeing such a response, calculated that his two thousand ill-equipped rebels were no match for the fully-armed Turkish soldiers. He ordered his troops to board the ships, and they hastily withdrew from the island leaving the Chians to the mercy of the barbarians.

When the Turks landed, they quickly put down the weak resistance the few armed Chians had offered and for the next fifteen days began a methodical destruction of the houses of the capital and of the towns by setting fire to them. They then put to the sword all the male population of the island.

According to statistics, of the one hundred thousand Chians who lived on the island, at least 24,000 males were put to the sword, 47,000 women and children were rounded up and sold in the slave markets of Turkey and in other middle-eastern countries. Only 25,000 managed to escape to other islands and 3,000 remained on the devastated island.

Such an inhuman, savage, brutal, and beastly mass carnage, such a horrendous slaughter, such a mass crime had never been committed against any Greek civilians. Turkish barbarism against an unarmed civilian population had reached its apex. The brutal nature of it was severe.

When this horrific and unprecedented crime was reported by newspapers to the peoples of Europe, it moved them to the core. It caused such a shock and abhorrence in their hearts that most of them openly condemned the Turkish barbarism and began to sympathize with the Greek cause. Soon the sympathy spread among prominent writers and poets who used their intellectual creativity to express sympathy for the Greeks and direct stern condemnation toward the Asian perpetrators. At the same time, prominent artists in France, Germany, England, and Italy began painting pictures depicting the massacre of Chios and other episodes of the revolt.

Three months after this abominable event, and to be exact, on the night of June 6-7, Admiral Constantine Canaris determined to revenge this genocide. During the night, he entered the harbor of Chios on his fire ship and managed to remain undetected by the Turks. He attached his fire ship to the side of the Turkish flagship that was in the harbor. On that night, as written sources have it, some two thousand Turks were on the ship celebrating the Ramadan – holiest feast of the Muslim Religion.

Quickly, Canaris lighted the wick, jumped into a small boat and had his men row away as fast as they could. A few minutes later, a massive explosion ripped away a large section of the side of the flagship while flames quickly engulfed the ship. Its tall masts caught fire, its burning sails and rigging fell to the deck and the spreading fire killed the Turks by the hundreds. Soon the ship had become a burning inferno, burning the panicked and terrified crew alive. Since the flames had engulfed the ship on all sides, those on board found escape impossible.

When Admiral Karalis attempted to escape, a piece of burning wood fell on him wounding him fatally. An hour later he lay dead on the shore.

The revenge affected by the brave Greek admiral provided some satisfaction, but the price paid by the freedom-seeking Chians was huge. It provided no solace and comfort to the brave citizenry of Chios.

The Massacre of Chios by Eugene Delacroix

Museum of Louvre – Paris, France

47
EUROPEAN PHILHELLENISM

As mentioned previously, when on March 25, 1821 the Greek people unable to bear any longer the four hundred year Ottoman oppression that had stripped them of their liberty, civil rights, education, and human dignity, rose up in arms.

Neither the European government nor the American would grant military aid to the risen Greeks. Single-handedly the hitherto oppressed Greek rebels would fight against a vastly superior army – superior in numbers, training and weapons. But as they had sworn to march against the hated oppressor, there was no turning back.

What was the reaction of the European peoples toward the Greek insurgent who like the Spartans of old, fought with superhuman bravery? The answer is most favorable. Reading in their daily newspapers about the heroic struggle of a small nation trying to regain its freedom, and the shocking bloodbaths, the inhuman massacres the enraged Turks were carrying out against innocent Greeks living in Constantinople and other cities of Turkey as well as against the populations of the Islands of Chios, Psara and other Greek Islands, a strong wave of sympathy and a great desire to aid those intrepid fighters seized them all.

In continental Europe, the first ones to express their philhellenic sentiments were, of course, the intellectuals. Being steeped in the Greek Classics and Greek History, they saw in the present heroic struggle a repeat of Marathon, of Thermopylae, of Salamis, and of Plataea. They saw a dauntless David braving a mighty Goliath, a numerically small-enslaved people trying alone to break the shackles of slavery and they were amazed.

A nation on which the Greek uprising made a significant impact right from the beginning was Germany. So great was the impact of this event on the German people that their response was more immediate and widespread than that of any other European people.

There was a reason for such an immediate response. In no other country of Europe was there so much interest, so much enthusiasm for the Greek classical tradition as the one cultivated in the German universities and pursued widely by students. This tradition, moreover, did not start in the nineteenth century but in the beginning of the eighteenth.

Johann Winckelmann was the first Greek scholar to initiate such a movement – a movement that had many followers in the subsequent decades – men such as Gotthold Lessing, Johann Herder, Goethe, Johann von Schiller, Johann Christian Holderlin, and Christian Heine. Their works, fully inspired by the unexcelled beauty of ancient Greek poetry and literature, along with a systematic study of the Greek classics themselves taught at the universities, afforded the students of the eighteenth and nineteenth centuries an opportunity to pursue Greek learning and Greek culture as in no other country. It logically follows that when news of the uprising of the descendants of that ancient elite race had taken place, sympathy for their cause for freedom and coming to their aid was a must.

First to circulate proclamations and pamphlets to arouse interest and generate real concern for active assistance to the embattled Greeks were the university professors. Consider, for example the following words of Wilhelm Krug of the University of Leipzig, Saxony:

"Would that the Greeks might rise from their political torpor, and with youthful vigor and glorious prospects re-enter the rank of European nations. This is the fervent wish of one who regards the event not only as a European but as a man and a Christian...The Greeks have a powerful demand both on our gratitude and compassion. Though more than two thousand years have elapsed since Greece flowered, the Greeks of the present day are yet descendants of those whose immortal works still delight and form our minds; the descendants of those whose wisdom and science have become the common property of the world."

A notice which reads as follows was delivered to all the homes in the City of Hamburg: "Proclamation to the Youth of Germany! The fight for Religion, Life and Freedom call us to arms! Humanity and Duty challenge us to hurry to the aid of our brothers, the noble Greeks, to risk our blood, our lives for the Sacred Cause! The reign of the Moslems in Europe in nearing its end; Europe's most beautiful country must be freed, freed from the monsters! Let us throw our strength into the struggle! Seize your weapons honorable youth of Germany let us form a Greek-German Legion and soon bring support to our brothers! Officers with experience of service are ready to lead us! – God will be with us, for it is a sacred cause – the cause of Humanity – it is the fight for Religion, Life and Freedom, the fight against monsters!"

So called "Greek Committees" had also been founded in most cities and towns of Germany to collect moneys, food, pharmaceuticals, clothing and any other item the Greek combatants would need in their hard and protracted struggle. As the German people responded generously throughout the duration of the war the mission of the Greek Committees was most successful.

Newspapers in every city and town printed daily the progress of the Greek struggle, praising editorially the bravery of the Greeks and deliberately derogating their Asiatic opponents. On the other hand, clergymen in the churches delivered euphemistic homilies in favor of the Greek fighters and prayed for their deliverance. Ludwig Van Beethoven – the nineteenth century's most eminent composer and freedom lover set to music Kotzebue's "Ruins of Athens" – a work alluding to Athena's abandoning the Parthenon to found a new temple of the Muses in Europe, while Willhelm Muller – a distinguished poet wrote three volumes of poems entitled "Sons of the Greeks". Thousands of copies were sold.

Three hundred and forty students and citizens volunteered to go to Greece and fight for the freedom of the country, which they held in high respect. Although when they found themselves in a country devastated by war, a country in poverty and ruin, none of them became disheartened wishing to return to his native homeland. They all remained in Greece to the end of the war exposing themselves to all kinds of deprivations, rigors and risks, remaining faithful to their decision to fulfill the noble purpose for which they had come to Greece.

England was another European country where cultivation of the Greek classics in the universities caused philhellenic feelings among the British people to favor the Greek uprising. However, the man who more than any other stirred in the hearts of the British sympathy for the Greek cause was George Gordon Byron better known as Lord Byron.

Lord Byron was a scion of a wealthy Scotch-English family, a knower of the classical Greek and Latin Languages which he had studies at Harrow and Trinity College, Cambridge. He was a poet of the highest repute and was very familiar with the land of Greece and its people.

In September of 1809, he landed at the Greek port of Preveza. From there he traveled north to Albania to visit Ali Pasha at Tepeleni. From there, he headed south to Athens arriving in December.

Lord Byron
Painting in the National Historical Museum of Athens

From the date he set foot on Greek soil, the heart of this romantic was filled with pain. Seeing that a once glorious country lay in ruins, and its people, descendants of a race that in the past had achieved so much were now deprived of their freedom, he was moved deeply. The tragic fate that had befallen that land and its people, instead of utterly disappointing him, to the contrary, it generated in him an optimism that the Country would be free again. Graphically he expressed these impressions and sentiments in the following verses:

> *"Fair Greece! Sad relic of departed worth!*
> *Immortal, though no more; though fallen, great!*
> *Who now shall lead thy scattered children forth,*
> *And long accustom'd bondage uncreate?*
> *Not such thy sons who whilom did await,*
> *The hopeless warriors of a willing doom.*
> *In bleak Thermopylae's sepulchral strait-*
> *Oh! Who that gallant spirit shall resume,*
> *Leap from Eurota's banks, and call thee from the tomb?"*
> *(Childe Harold's Pilgrimage, Canto II)*

During his first visit to Greece and his lodging in Athens at the home of Theresa Macris, Byron learned Modern Greek and even ventured to write some poems in that language. He also traveled to Cape Sunion where he scratched his name on one of the columns of the Temple of Poseidon and felt rare moments of inner bliss while looking at the sun-drenched Aegean Islands floating in the tranquil blue waters, to historic Marathon and to Patra. Then he traveled to Asia Minor to visit the ancient City of Ephesus, and thence, he headed north to visit the region of Troad. While there, despite his congenital paralysis, he swam across the Hellespont Straits.

It was during his stay in Athens that Byron penned much of his masterful poem, "Childe Harold", notes on the "Siege of Corinth", and "The Curse of Minerva", a skit whereby he vehemently condemns Lord Elgin for having removed the frieze from the Parthenon. Late in 1810, he returned to London. A few years later while working on another masterful poem entitled "Don Juan", he included some verses about the Greek Islands and the Land of Greece – verses that more than any others express the romantic Poet's love for Greece.

> *"The isles of Greece, the isles of Greece!*
> *Where burning Sappho loved and sung,*
> *Where grew the arts of war and peace,*
> *Where Delos rose and Phoebus sprung!*
> *Eternal summer gilds them yet,*
> *But all, except their sun, is set.*
>
> *The mountains look on Marathon –*
> *And Marathon looks on the sea;*

And musing there an hour alone.
I dreamed that Greece might still be free;
For standing on the Persian's grave,
I could not deem myself a slave.

These verses were published in London between the years 1810 and 1821 – the year of the outbreak of the Greek Revolution. The verses revealed a warm and sincere philhellenic sentiment that Greece might rise to freedom again and caused a deep sympathetic sentiment in the hearts of the British people. Needless to say, since his poems were reprinted many times in order to be read by English speaking people scattered throughout the British Empire, brought considerable wealth to Byron – a wealth, however, he was to use in the future to help the war effort of the risen Greeks.

In 1823 while in Genoa, Italy, he received a letter informing him that the Greeks who were now in the third year of their struggle for independence, had elected him a member of the "Greek Commission". This was an organization that consisted of Philhellenes who supported the cause of Greece's freedom.

Byron left Genoa and came to Argostoli – capital of the Greek Island of Cephalonia. He was informed of dissensions among the Greek war leaders who had gathered at Messolonghi. Byron went to Messolonghi and after talking to them he succeeded in reconciling them. He donated substantial sums for the repairs of the city's walls and undertook to lead a regiment whose future target would be the siege of Nafpactos, presently in Turkish hands.

He greatly rejoiced when he was informed that the Greek Government had appointed him General Governor of all the liberated regions of Greece. He was destined, however, never to enjoy this most deserving high honor, as he was not blessed to see his dream – a free Greece, materialize. His perennially weak constitution began to worsen as continuous fever, chills, dizziness, and rheumatic pains eventually caused his death on April 19, 1824. He was only thirty-six. His embalmed body was sent to England, while his heart was buried in Messolonghi.

Byron's philhellenic poetry and active participation in the cause of freedom caused many of his compatriots to join the Greek struggle. The Greek Committees of London and of other cities collected great sums of money, clothing, food and war material while many of the influential British nobility, the higher ranks of the army and navy, bankers, industrialists, members of Parliament, of the House of Lords, and the literary and the scientific communities not only donated generously to the Greek Committees, they also became members of them.

Although the British Government remained neutral during most of the struggle, towards the end it allowed its Fleet to join the French and the Russian Fleets and move against the Turkish Fleet in the Battle of Navarino. Also, another move by the British Government that was favorable to the

Greek cause was Prime Minister Andrew Canning's recognition of the Greek rebels as belligerents. In the end, if their struggle was victorious, national independence would be endorsed. Finally, two English officers of the highest rank joined the Greek cause. They were Admiral Thomas Cochrane and Sir Richard Church, who as supreme commander of the Greek rebels during the last years of the war, also directed an unsuccessful siege of the Acropolis at Athens.

France, whose intellectuals always looked to Greece for inspiration in every literary genre, was another major European Power that became very sympathetic to the Greek cause. Their love of freedom, generated since their successful revolution against the "Ancient Regime," – the old aristocratic and royalist regime that was oppressive to the common people, made them extremely sensitive toward the risen Greeks who now had resorted to arms to regain what they had been deprived of for four consecutive centuries.

And so, when the struggle for independence began, Greek Committees in Paris and every city and town were founded to collect moneys and other needed items for the Greek combatants. It is interesting to know that the Greek Committee of Paris known as "Societe Philanthropique en faveur des Grecs" (Philanthropic Society in favor of the Greeks), was unquestionably the most energetic of all Committees not only of those of France, but of those in all other countries of Europe as well.

In three years since its founding, it had collected six times the amount the London Greek Committee had collected. Leading members of the Committee were the dukes – de Choiseul, de Broglie, de Dalberg, de Fitzjames, the comtes d' Harcourt and de Laborde, the banker Lafitte, the publisher Didot and, last but not least, the renown in America – Marquis de Lafayette.

Hundreds of different books and pamphlets written in prose or poetry and extolling the heroic struggles of the Greeks were now sold by the thousands all over France. The best seller was the "History of the Regeneration of Greece". Other manifestations of French Philhellenism to aid the cause of the revolution include musical performances of the lyrical tragedy "The Siege of Corinth", with music by Rossini, the tragedy "Leonidas" by Pichald and a specially composed "Greek Cantata" by the famous French composer Hector Berlioz.

Famous French contemporary artists also joined the Greek cause. The one who painted the most – thirty paintings depicting different war themes - was Eugene Delacroix. Most notable of these were "The Massacre of Chios", bought by the king to be in the permanent collection of the Louvre and his "Greece Expiring on the Ruins of Messolonghi". Among the many other French artists who painted similar themes, the paintings of Schefer and Colin are of the more dramatic.

In 1825, a pamphlet, written by the Father of the French Romanticism – the eminent Vicomte Chateaubriand and bearing the title "Note sur la Grece" (Note on Greece), made its appearance in all bookstores.

One of its paragraphs reads: "Will our century, watch hordes of savages extinguish civilization at its rebirth on the tomb of a people who civilized the world? Will Christendom calmly allow the Turks to strangle Christians? And will the Legitimate Monarchs of Europe shamelessly permit their sacred name to be given to a tyranny which could have reddened the Tiber?"

Chateaubriand's above caustic remarks against the Turks were not imaginary. Ten years before the outbreak of the revolution he had traveled through Greece and had seen the sufferings of its people. This is why he used such stern language to arouse the sympathy of his compatriots. Another masterwork by the same author that greatly contributed to the cause of Greece was his itinerary, "From Paris to Jerusalem". In this book, after praising the greatness of Greece in the most eloquent manner, he then proceeded to describe the present utmost deprivations and degradations of its people imposed by the barbarian conqueror.

Victor Hugo who like Chateaubriand was a romantic writer and poet – the author of such immortal works as "Les Miserables", "Torquemade", "The Easterners" and dozens of others, was also a great Philhellene. His poem "The Greek Boy", in which he describes a Chian teenager's feelings of desperation while beholding his devastated home island after the Turks had massacred a great number of its population and had sold the remainder as slaves, greatly moved the hearts of his compatriots. Later his ode: "The Heads of the Seraglio" in which he imagines the heads of Greeks of Constantinople and of other combatants from Greece exposed in the streets of Constantinople was another work that deeply moved the French people.

As in the case of England, the French Government remained neutral in the struggle of Greece. Toward the end of the struggle, however, her fleet, together with the British and the Russian fleets completely destroyed the Turkish fleet at the Bay of Navarino.

This chapter is only a brief sketch of the Philhellenic movement in Europe. Nearly all European nations sent money, aid and volunteers to help the Greeks in their cause. To mention a few: from Italy came Count Santor re di Santa Rosa, an enlightened Piedmontese from Northern Italy. He took part in many battles. In May of 1825, he was killed by the Turks. From Switzerland came the highly esteemed banker, Eynard. He never went to Greece but organized numerous Greek Committees in his native country and personally traveled throughout Western Europe to collect money for the Greek cause, and sent whole shiploads of all kinds of provisions to the people of Greece. Scores of others from Poland, Hungary, Sweden, Denmark, Holland, Belgium, and Spain also sent money and aid through their Greek Committees and many of them volunteered to fight alongside the Greeks.

Victor Hugo

48
AMERICAN PHILHELLENES

It didn't take long for news of the Greek revolt against the Turkish oppressor to reach the United States of America five thousand miles away to the west. As "news travels fast," in a few days Americans living even in the remotest villages read in their newspapers that the small country of Greece had risen up against its Asian barbarian oppressors.

Reaction to the news was not any different in America than it was in Europe. Just as the European governments kept strict neutrality of refusing to send military and naval aid, lest such a move would seriously damage their lucrative trade with the Ottoman Empire, so did the American government. And, just as in the European countries it was the people who helped the Greek cause by sending monetary and material aid the same happened in America. It was its people who from the beginning of the uprising sought to help the Greek revolt.

The leaders of the Greek uprising had great hopes for a positive response coming from America. Bearing in mind that it was only four decades previously that Americans had won their independence from England by fighting alone a hard and protracted war, the Greeks were sure that Americans would quickly understand and significantly sympathize with their cause. Furthermore, they were convinced that American aid would be considerable.

And so, not long after the war began, an appeal for help was sent from Calamata – a major city in southern Greece, to the United States. At the suggestion of Adamantios Coraes who lived in Paris, the appeal was sent to Edward Everett who was a professor of classics at Harvard University, Cambridge. It read in part:

"To the citizens of the United States: Having formed the resolution to live or die for freedom we are drawn toward you by a just sympathetic cause since it is in your land that Liberty has fixed her abode, and by you that she is prized as by our fathers....We esteem you nearer than the nations on our frontiers....Free and prosperous yourselves you are desirous that all men should share the same blessings; that all should enjoy those rights to which all are by nature equally entitled. It is you who first proclaimed these rights....The fellow citizens of Penn, of Washington and of Franklin will not refuse their aid to descendants of Phocion and Thrasybulus or Aratus and Philopoemen."

When the above appeal reached Everett, he, without wasting any time, made sure that copies would reach many prominent and influential Americans in every field of endeavor so that interest in the Greek cause and aid may soon materialize. Before, however, we relate how the American people expressed their Philhellenic interest to the Greek uprising, a brief account of the worthy lives of three top American Philhellenes must be given.

When we speak of American Philhellenism, three names are prominent. They are the names of Edward Everett, Daniel Webster and Samuel Gridley Howe.

Edward Everett, a very young man hailing from Dorchester, Massachusetts graduated with honors from Harvard University at the age of only sixteen. His acquaintance with the poetry of Byron especially "Childe Harold" and Chateaubriand's accounts of his travels in Greece had so impressed him that he desired to visit that country. Moreover, his classical studies had so strong an impact on his thought, that long before the Greek Revolution he had begun to publicly declare that Greece should be liberated.

Following his graduation from Harvard, he went to Europe. He studied in France, in England and at the University of Gotingen in Germany where he earned a PhD, the first American to do so. After his graduation, he met with Byron in London with whom he discussed the hard conditions in Greece, and with Adamantios Coraes in Paris.

Coraes was a Greek intellectual who had dedicated his life in order to bring Europeans to the cause of Greece. Everett was so impressed by Coraes that a lifelong association began between the two men.

In 1818, Everett visited Greece where he became an eyewitness of the lamentable conditions in which people lived. It was this pathetic reality that convinced him that Americans should help the suffering, helpless country to free itself from the barbarous yoke of their Asiatic tyrant.

Everett returned to Boston in late 1819 and resumed his seat as Professor of Classics at Harvard University and began publishing the prestigious journal the "North American Review". Meanwhile, he continued corresponding with prominent men whom he had met in Greece, and, when the Greek Revolution began, the letters he received from its leaders which described the progress of the revolution were used to inform prominent Americans in the hope of eliciting their help for the Greek cause.

Subsequently, Everett was elected congressman, Governor of Massachusetts, U.S. Minister to Great Britain, President of Harvard University, Secretary of State under the Fillmore Administration, and then senator. What an impressive rise to the most influential positions! With the exception of Daniel Webster, no other American raised his voice so loudly, so clearly, so eloquently and so persuasively for the struggle of Greece as Everett had. During the eight years of the war, he worked tirelessly, indefatigably speaking for the success of the Greek cause. And, when the war ended, how happy he was to see that the people he so fervently supported were free again.

Daniel Webster, hailing from Boston, Massachusetts was a close friend of Everett and another great American Philhellene. His repeated, brilliant orations at the U.S. Senate for the cause of Greek Independence influenced many American congressmen, senators and other prominent citizens to favor the Greek cause. His enthusiasm for the Greek cause never waned, always wishing to see the country that had offered so much to the world to be free again.

The third most prominent American Philhellene who, "body and soul" dedicated himself to the Greek cause, was Samuel Gridley Howe. A Bostonian by birth, he attended Brown University and Harvard Medical School. Not long after he was admitted to practice, he abandoned his medical profession and went to Greece to fight and to offer his medical services to the wounded Greek rebels.

Howe is considered by the Greeks to have been the greatest American Philhellene. His participation in the Greek Army as a fighter, doctor and surgeon, plus his fundraising activities and never-ending appeals to his American compatriots for clothing, food, pharmaceuticals and other badly needed items, could only be done by a sincere idealist. No other American Philhellene carried on such a crusade for Greece.

After serving for four years in the rebels' ranks and braving all kinds of weather conditions, continuously tramping over mountainous rough terrain and narrow goat paths on precipitous slopes, sleeping in caves with only his coat as his blanket, eating little food and carrying his rifle and medical case, Howe returned to America. He visited New York, Chicago and Philadelphia where he delivered spirited lectures to thousands of Americans about the hard struggle of the Greek rebels and the indescribable deprivations of the

Samuel Gridley Howe

old people, the women and children. He exhorted them to contribute generous monetary donations, food, clothing, pharmaceuticals and whatever else they could spare. He also encouraged them to adopt Greek orphans whose parents had been killed during the war.

Having raised thousands of dollars and huge quantities of food such as flour, dry meat and other such foodstuffs, he had them loaded on ships and carried to Greece. When he returned to Greece, he personally supervised the distribution of food and of the other items thus preventing any mishandling of the precious cargo.

Describing a relief mission which he personally carried on in a mountainous area, this is what he wrote in his diary: "We began the ascent, and after a tedious climbing of two hours we came to a little plain where we found about six hundred persons, but not a single house, only huts, if they even merit that name. Here was a sight. Six hundred persons, mostly widows and orphans, driven from their homes, hunted in the mountains like wild beasts, and living upon herbs, grass and what they could pick up from the rocks. Many women came to be haggard and wan, their skin blistered by the sun, their feet torn by rocks, and their limbs half exposed to view by the raggedness of their clothes, and they swore upon their faith that for many weeks they had not tasted bread.

"I gave them orders for about ten hundred weight of flour, and each one, seizing the billet, ran toward the sea, blessing God that he had created men like Americans to succor them in their distress…."

When the ships that had carried the relief cargo to Greece were emptied, they sailed back bringing orphans who had lost their parents during the revolutionary battles. Upon their arrival in America, they were adopted by Americans and many of these children achieved in their lives very distinguishing careers. They became senators, congressmen, colonels, admirals, ambassadors, businessmen, and professionals.

Despite his extremely busy schedule, Howe wrote a "Historical Sketch of the Greek Revolution". It sold a great number of copies and all proceeds from the sales went to the war effort.

On hearing of the disastrous defeat of the Turkish Fleet in the Bay of Navarino located in southwestern Greece, Howe, feeling exhilarated, wrote in his diary: "This day has been to me one of the happiest of my existence, and to all Greece one of joy and exultation. For it brought the confirmation of the news of the destruction of the Turkish Fleet of Navarino, and forever puts at rest the question of the re-conquest of Greece by Turkey…"

Before his return to America, Howe provided the expenses necessary for a new quay in the harbor of the Island of Aegina and for the founding of a new village near Hexamilia in the region of Corinth. Refugees from Athens, Chios and Kydonies came and settled here and were very grateful to Howe who provided them with a home for the remainder of their lives. He also built a hospital on the Island of Poros large enough for two hundred beds. Many fighters who had been wounded in land and sea battles were treated free-of-charge in this hospital.

Upon returning to the U.S., Samuel Howe settled in Boston. Here, he founded the "Perkins Institute for the Deaf and Blind". Helen Keller's teacher was a graduate of this Institute. He also invented a method of educating and communicating with the mentally disabled.

When in 1829 Howe returned to the U.S., he was only thirty years old. Amazingly, while only thirty years old, he had accomplished more things than others do in a lifetime. He married Julia Ward who later authored the now famous "Battle Hymn of the Republic".

In 1867 when the Greek Island of Crete still under Turkish occupation revolted in an effort to gain its independence, Howe now seventy, together with his wife, returned to Greece to again administer aid to the victims of the war. He was indisputably one of the greatest Philhellenes, a philanthropist to whom Greece will forever owe an inestimable debt.

When news of the outbreak of the Greek Revolution reached America, the Press became pro-Greek and sought to arouse interest in the Greek struggle. Daily stories praised the Greek victories and vehemently denounced Turkish atrocities in graphic detail and with horror. Stories expressed shock at the massacre of Chios and the destruction of Kasos and Psara. Leading newspapers such as "The Albany Argus", the "Richmond Enquirer" and many others passionately denounced the brutal Turkish atrocities.

From the East Coast to the West Coast, American newspapers praised Greek revolutionary leaders like Kolokotronis, Miaoulis and Canaris. They depicted them as true heirs of the ancient Greeks, fighting, as their ancestors once did, at Marathon, Thermopylae and Salamis for civilization and freedom against hordes of barbarians. Most every publication called for freedom-loving persons everywhere to provide aid. Slowly, the American people began to respond.

The first city to send aid to Greece was Charleston, South Carolina. They sent huge quantities of dry meat. Soon other American cities began to participate in the humanitarian effort. At a mass meeting of citizens in Albany, NY, a speaker emphasized, "The Greek revolt was comparable to the uprising of the American colonists against England, and, as such, should have the sympathy of Americans."

During the years 1823 and 1824, pro-Greek committees began mushrooming in almost every major city of the US. Most important were the Boston, Philadelphia and New York Committees composed of merchants, bankers, businessmen, professors, lawyers, politicians, army officers, and clergymen. Through circulars, which they were sending to other cities and towns, they urged the recipients to send their generous donations.

Fundraising was also conducted through theatrical performances, concerts and benefit balls. American cities received Greek names such as Athens, Sparta, Corinth, Ithaca, Ypsilanti (a Greek hero), and Coraes (the Greek intellectual in Paris).

At a benefit concert held in Cincinnati, preceded by a speech delivered by General William Henry Harrison, the future president of the US, after describing the Greek revolt and Greece's cultural and intellectual contributions, told the audience, "We must send our free will offering. The

Star Spangled Banner must wave in the Aegean....It will be to her the harbinger of victory and success; to her enemy...the signal of defeat and ruin."

49

WHEN THE GREEKS
CAME TO AMERICA

When Columbus discovered America, the only people he found here were the Indians. But as years and centuries passed, people from different countries came to settle here. They came from Spain, Portugal, England, Ireland, Holland, Germany, Poland, Italy, Africa, and Asia. All these people were the ancestors of today's Americans.

People from Greece also came to live in the United States. As the country of Greece was small and mountainous, many Greek people decided to leave their country and come to America in hope of having a better life for themselves and their families. But before we talk about the large immigration of Greek people to America, let us see who came here first. Who was the first Greek man to set foot in America?

Well, the first Greek to ever set foot in America was John Griego (Griego, Spanish for Greek). He was a sailor and he belonged to the crew of the ship of Christopher Columbus, the man who discovered America in 1492. Thus a Greek was among the first men who came here from the Old World to the New One.

The first Greek who came to settle in America, according to Spanish records, was a man by the name of Theodore. He spent the rest of his life here, most likely in a region of Alabama, and we do not know how he earned his living.

In 1680, with the help of a wealthy Scottish physician named Turnbull, a large number of Greek people who lived in Smyrna, Turkey, came and settled near the City of St. Augustine, Florida. They built a new town for themselves near St. Augustine, which they named New Smyrna. The school, which they used to teach their children Greek, is now the oldest standing school in the U.S.

In 1844, Basil Constantin arrived in New York City from Greece and settled there. In the following years, many other Greeks came from Greece and settled there, and by 1857, the first Greek Coffee Shop, named "Peloponnesos", opened in New York City.

In 1870, many Greek merchants who imported and exported cotton came and settled in New Orleans, Louisiana and, in the city, founded the first Greek Orthodox Church in the New World.

On March 25, 1873, the Greek flag was hoisted at New York's City Hall for the first time in honor of Greek Independence Day, and on March 25, 1895 the first Greek Independence Day parade took place in New York.

In 1894, Solon Vlastos published the first issue of his Greek newspaper entitled "Atlantis". As we can see, by now the Greeks had multiplied and also had their own Greek Language newspaper.

Many more Greek people continued to come to the United States in the 1890's and the first two decades of the twentieth century. When in 1917 America entered the First World War on the side of the English and the French who were fighting against the Germans since 1914, some 60,000 Greeks enlisted in the American Army. The "Great Pappous" of some of us probably served in the Army during the War.

Not all the Greek people who came to America settled in New York. Many of them went to other large cities such as Chicago, Philadelphia, Boston, Detroit, St. Louis, Atlanta, and San Francisco. Many worked hard, saved their money by working in factories and opened their own restaurants, grocery stores, candy stores or other small businesses. Others polished shoes in the streets and others continued to work in the factories. But the ones who worked in the hardest jobs were those who laid rails for railroads and those who worked in the mines. In both of these jobs, the early Greek immigrants suffered much.

In the decades of 1920 and 1930, some 50,000 Greek people came to America. When in 1941 the United States entered World War II, thousands of young Greek-Americans who had been born in America and who now were in their twenties and thirties, volunteered or were drafted to serve in the armed services to fight against the Axis Powers which were Germany, Italy and Japan. Thousands of Greek-Americans, served in the Army, Navy, Marines, and as Airmen.

When the War ended, new waves of Greek immigrants came to America. In the decades from 1950 on, they came in much larger numbers than ever before. In the decade of 1980, some 42,000 Greek People came to live here.

Wherever the Greek people settled, and, by now, they were settled in cities and towns from Maine to California and from Oregon to Florida, they worked hard to take care of their families, to buy a home, a car, and start their own business if they so desired. As for their children that were born here, upon finishing high school they would encourage them to go to college or to a university to study law, medicine, engineering, chemistry, economics, and education. And so, while many Greek-Americans chose to continue the business of their fathers, others went on to college to become professionals.

Finally, other vital things, which the Greek immigrants founded in their communities, were the beautiful churches and cathedrals that can be seen in many cities and towns of the United States. Moreover, for the education of the priests who serve those churches, Archbishop Athenagoras in 1936 founded, in Pomfret, Connecticut, a theological school, which, in 1946, was relocated to Brookline, Massachusetts – a suburb of Boston. Today, it has expanded into a college and theological school and young Greek-American men as well as students from other African and Asian countries come to this school to study theology that is so necessary in order for them to become priests. In addition, the Greek People in America, besides supporting their churches and the Theological School, supported many Greek Parochial Schools, orphanages, old age homes and other such institutions, not only in the United States, but in other countries of the world as well.

50
GREAT BENEFACTORS

Since ancient times, many wealthy people have been great benefactors to their native countries. Realizing the great need their countries had for universities, colleges, libraries, theaters, stadia, museums, orphanages, and other such public institutions, they gladly gave a part of their fortunes for the founding and construction of such institutions.

In ancient Athens, for example, the beautiful stoas of Attalus and Eumenes were the generous donations of those two Pergamene kings, who while they were princes, had studied in the philosophical schools of Athens.

When by 1829 Greece had won its independence, in 1834 the small town of Athens was chosen to become the capital of the new country. Athens, then, had a population of only five thousand inhabitants, and its small and old houses ringed the historic Hill of the Acropolis.

Soon, however, great numbers of people from other newly liberated parts of Greece began coming to the new capital to live. They came to build new houses, to start businesses, to teach in schools, and find employment in the government. In a few years, Athens' population had become tenfold and the increase did not seem to ever stop.

New government buildings were in great need as the existing ones were very old, small, and unable to avail the normally required space to those who worked there. Although the government was aware of this pressing problem, the national treasury could not provide the required sums.

The solution was not too late in coming as dozens and dozens of very wealthy Greeks, who lived in London, Paris, Vienna, St. Petersburg, Odessa, Alexandria, and Constantinople, realizing the grave needs of their native country decided to fund them. Their fabulous donations, given whole-heartedly, not only helped to build government buildings but orphanages, schools, universities, museums, a national library, theaters, hospitals, churches and other philanthropic institutions.

As neoclassical Greek architecture was in vogue during the nineteenth century, all these public buildings were designed in the above-mentioned style. To this day, they are still admired for their elegant and graceful aesthetic appeal despite the fact that many of them are at least well over one hundred and fifty years old.

George Averoff, hailing from the town of Metsovo, located in northwestern Greece, was a truly great benefactor. He was born in August 1818 and died in 1899. His parents and ancestors were well-to-do people in his native city and had made many donations to improve their town. From them, Averof had inherited the virtue of charity, a virtue he was to manifest a thousand times over.

In 1840, at the age of twenty-two, George went to Egypt to work at the mercantile firm of his uncle, Nicholas Sturnaras. As soon as he mastered the business of trading and had earned enough money, he started his own import-export firm that dealt with yard goods, cotton, foodstuffs and ivory – a trade that, in a few years, had helped amass a fabulous fortune.

He was now able to do what his parents and his ancestors had done long ago. But he was to surpass them by leaps and bounds.

His first benefaction was toward the Greek community of Alexandria. He also provided additional funds for the building of a hospital and two high schools.

To Metsovo – his native town, he donated one and a half million golden drachmas to be used for public works, and a substantial portion for the completion of the National Polytechnic Institute of Greece whose construction was begun with funds provided by two compatriots of his. He also paid for the cost of the statues of two great revolutionary martyrs – the poet Regas Fereos and the Patriarch Gregory V, which were placed in front of the University of Athens.

When in 1859 the newly elected International Olympic Committee decided that the first modern Olympic Games be held in Athens, Averof immediately donated the amount of one million drachmas for the remarbalizing of the ancient stadium of Athens which only a few years prior had been excavated. He also gave monies to fund a new military school complex.

In his will, he stated that a bequest in the amount of two and a-half million drachmas be made to the treasury of the Greek naval fleet for the building of a warship that would be named after him. An additional bequest in the amount of one-and-a-half million drachmas was made to the community of Alexandria, and an additional one million drachmas for the completion of the stadium. Two additional endowments of five hundred thousand drachmas each directed toward the National Conservatory of Athens and the National Polytechnic. Another five hundred thousand drachmas bequest was made available for the funding of an agricultural college in the City of Larissa.

In grateful recognition of this long chain of impressive benefactions, the Greek Government decreed that a marble statue of Averof be set up before the Stadium.

George Sinas was born in the town of Nyssa of northwestern Greece. He was another outstanding benefactor.

While still a young boy, he went to Vienna, Austria where his father had already established himself as a very successful merchant. George was more entrepreneurial than his father and, when he took over the business, made it successful many times over. He exploited an economic crisis that occurred in that country by buying hundreds of acres of prime land and making a tremendous fortune when he sold it later.

When he thought that the time had come to begin giving away his huge fortune for philanthropic purposes, his very first benefaction was directed toward the restoration of the Austrian economy. He founded the

National Austrian Bank and became its first director. He also founded many savings banks, an insurance agency for fire and the Vienna Polytechnic Institute.

He was the first to introduce the practice of tobacco cultivation to Austria and paid the entire cost of the now famous suspension bridge of Budapest, Hungary. For all these benefactions, the Austrian Government awarded him the nation's most honorable title, the title of Baron.

Baron Sinas never forgot the country from which he came. When his native country had gained independence, he gave a grant for the founding of a national observatory at Athens. He also paid the cost of all four telescopes and for other astronomical instruments that were installed in the observatory. He also endowed many philanthropic and educational institutions and donated a very large sum to the National Bank of Greece.

For all these benefactions to his native country, King Otho of Greece awarded him the Cross of the Brigadiers. He also received honorary distinctions from the Emperor of Austria, Joseph the first, and from Emperor Alexander the First of Russia.

Baron Sinas had a son named Simon. The son was born in Vienna and as he matured, his father taught him to manage his big firm. Being a bright young man, he learned quickly. When he assumed leadership of his father's business, he was determined to make it bigger and more profitable.

In 1859, Simon Sinas, continuing his father's philanthropic tradition, decided to pay the entire cost of the construction of the Academy of Athens, which to this day, is one of the most elegant buildings in the Greek capital. He hired Theofil Hansen – a distinguished Viennese architect to design the beautiful edifice, a Viennese artist to paint a series of impressive murals in the Academy's auditorium, which relate the story of Prometheus, and Greek sculptors to carve statues of Apollo, Athena, and of ancient Greek thinkers in order to enhance the exterior décor of the Academy.

Finally, he endowed the National Observatory, which his father had founded, paid the balance of the cost for the completion of the Cathedral of Athens and provided many scholarships to Greek students who wished to attend the University of Vienna and other Viennese colleges in order to study science and mathematics.

In grateful recognition, the Greek Government decreed that one of the main streets of Athens be named in his honor, and appointed him Greek Ambassador to Vienna. The Emperor of Austria also honored Simon Sinas for his many benefactions toward Viennese institutions.

Andrew Sygros was another prominent benefactor to the capital of Greece. He was born of Chian parents in Constantinople, Turkey. He went to school on the Island of Andros, and attended a junior business college at the Island of Syros. Eventually, Sygros started a business in Constantinople and with shrewd and skillful management, earned a fortune.

In 1876, he immigrated to Athens where he funded a bank that soon became one of the most prominent in Greece's capital. Having become very successful as a banker and as a businessman, and seeing his country in dire need of funds to acquire the proper edifices for its administrative services, he decided to use a very large part of his wealth to answer the above and some other of its needs.

His first benefactions were specifically for the construction of two museums – those of Delphi and of Olympia. Then he founded the construction of the large and imposing "Municipal Theatre" of Athens and of an orphanage in Thessalonica. He also funded the cost for the construction of a rehabilitation prison in Thessalonica and of the hospital for the treatment of patients suffering from contagious diseases, and for the construction of a new wing at the Evangelismos Hospital at Athens.

When funds for the completion of the Corinth Canal were depleted, Sygros gladly provided the balance. His last benefaction went to the funding of a wide avenue that connects Athens with the Phaleron Coastline. The avenue was named after him. He died in Athens in 1892, ever-thankful to God for being a successful entrepreneur and a prominent benefactor to his country.

The Academy of Athens
A Gift of Baron Sinas

51
CONSTANTINO BRUMIDI

One of the most impressive buildings in our nation's capital is the US Capitol. Its overwhelming rotunda, the two very large chambers where congressmen and senators assemble in order to propose and enact new laws, the long walkways, and, last but not least, the beautiful murals, paintings and decorations that fill its rotunda and its interior walls, make this structure a most admirable landmark.

Who made all those beautiful paintings that show presidents, congressmen, senators, and many scenes from our nation's history? It took many artists to do all those paintings and decorations but the most important of these were made by an artist whose name was Constantino Brumidi.

More than 225 years ago when Greece was not a free country but was under Turkish occupation, there lived in the small town of Chiliatia in the province of Arcadia, a young man by the name of Stavros Brumidis. Stavros could not bear to live in a country that was not free. So, he left Greece and went to live in Rome, the capital of Italy. There were many Greek people living in Rome and so Stavros did not feel a complete stranger in his new country. One day, he met a young girl by the name of Anna Bianchini; the two fell in love, and later, were married.

In 1805, a baby boy was born to them and they named him Constantino. It was the name of Stavros' father. Years later two more children were born to them – Maria and Joseph.

As a young boy, Constantino loved to draw. When his father took notice of his son's talent, he enrolled him in Rome's "Academy of Fine Arts", and later, in the "Academy of San Lucca". Young Constantino was trained to paint frescos. Let us briefly explain what a fresco is. When an artist paints a fresco, he uses watercolors on freshly laid plaster. As the plaster hardens in six to eight hours, the white lime and crystalline sand rise to the surface giving the watercolors that have been applied to it a sparkling quality.

When Brumidi finished his training, the Pope of Rome, Gregory the Sixteenth hired him. When Pope Gregory died and was succeeded by Pope Pius the Ninth, he too hired Brumidi to restore many paintings that had been painted by Raphael 250 years earlier. He did an excellent job, and for this, he was rewarded with a gold medal. He was now an established, first rate artist.

When civil war broke out in Rome, Brumidi served as a captain in the National Guards. On a certain day, because he refused an order to have his troops fire at a crowd, he was thrown into prison for fourteen months. Thanks to the Pope's intervention, he was set free on condition that he leave the country for good.

Brumidi, now aged forty-seven, boarded a ship, and on September 19, 1853 arrived in New York. A year later, upon learning that the new Capitol Building was near completion, he went to Washington, DC, hoping to be hired as a painter to do frescos on the walls and on the dome.

Captain Montgomery Meigs, the army engineer in charge of the Capitol's construction, rejected Brumidi's application. But as the latter insisted on being hired, Meigs relented, and let him paint the "Agricultural Committee's Room". When Brumidi finished his frescos, Meigs and several congressmen were so impressed by the beauty of the classical style of his art, they asked him to spend the rest of his life painting the rooms of the Capitol. He was given a free hand and a great commission. Brumidi, full of new energy, vigor, and never exhausting imaginative concepts, devoted himself with all his mind, heart and soul to the painting of our nation's legislative hearth. He painted beautiful frescos on the walls and ceilings of six Capitol Committee Rooms, many long corridors on the ground floor of the Senate wing, and designed the four bronze stairways in both the Senate and the House wings.

The tireless artist painted literally hundreds and hundreds of small and large paintings in the Capitol. His paintings abound in the basement, in the large and small rooms of the main floor of the building and, of course, on the dome. They show brilliantly and vividly many different important scenes from America's history, thus reminding the visitor of our nation's glorious past. In the Military Affairs Committee Room, for example, Brumidi has painted four large wall paintings showing some of the most critical moments of America's War for Independence. They are "The Boston Massacre", "The Battle of Lexington", "Washington at Valley Forge", and the "Storming of Stony Point".

But the grandeur of Brumidi's artistic expertise is on the majestic dome of the Capitol. In the upper area of the dome, which has a diameter of sixty-five feet and rises 185 above the floor, the intrepid Brumidi painted the

The "Apotheosis" of George Washington in the Rotunda of the
United States Capitol, Washington, D.C.

"Glorification of George Washington". The first President of the US is shown flanked by two women, which represent Liberty at his right and Victory at his left. Included in this majestic painting are thirteen maidens holding a ribbon, on which is the motto "E Pluribus Unum". The maidens represent the first thirteen states of the Union. In the lower section of the dome, are more human figures representing different ideals and historic persons.

When in October of 1879 Brumidi was painting "Penn's Treaty with the Indians" on the dome, he slipped and fell eighty feet. He never recovered from this fall, and on February 19, 1880, he died.

Brumidi, who painted in the Capitol through the terms of six Presidents – Franklin Pierce, James Buchanan, Abraham Lincoln, Andrew Johnson, Ulysses Grant, and Rutherford Hayes, is no longer with us. But his superb paintings are still with us. They are in one of our nation's most revered buildings, embellishing its interior with superb classical beauty and imprinting in our minds some of our nation's noblest moments.

52
A RECENT OUTSTANDING VISIONARY AND ACTUATOR STATESMAN

When in 1832 Greece was officially recognized as an independent European country, hardly half of its present territorial size had become independent. To be more specific, it consisted of the southernmost region of mainland Greece known as Peloponnesus, the Central one and the Cyclades Islands. The remainder, more than half consisting of the regions of Thesaly, Epirus, Macedonia, Thrace, and the large Island of Crete, was still under Turkish control.

It was a sad, an unhappy and difficult situation, because if any of the Turkish-controlled regions wished to rebel for the purpose of uniting with independent Greece, the Greek government would face the problem of whether to go to war with Turkey in order to help them. This problem occurred when the inhabitants of Crete rebelled against their Turkish governors in 1860 and in 1890.

If the Greek government had come to the help of the rebelling Greeks by officially declaring war against Turkey, other complications would follow. Many nations of Western Europe, particularly Great Britain, would come to the aid of Turkey because they considered the latter as a barrier against Russian expansion and influence in the Eastern Mediterranean Sea. In fact, when the people of Crete rebelled against the Turkish governor, the British fleet immediately steamed to Greek waters threatening both independent Greece and the Island of Crete.

Other problems that independent Greece faced during these difficult times were a poor economy, overpopulation, plus having foreign monarchs as rulers that were unpopular. A very able statesman, therefore, was gravely needed whose skillful policies would free the still Turkish-controlled Greece, and relieve the country of its main problems. And the man who accomplished this was the country's greatest twentieth century statesman – Eleftherios Venizelos.

Venizelos was born on August 23, 1864 in the small town of Mournies, located near the City of Canea on the Island of Crete. His father – a merchant, having participated in the rebellion of 1806, had been expelled from Crete by the Turkish authorities and had taken up residence in Athens where he also acquired Greek citizenship. During this time, his young son also acquired Greek citizenship. Years later, however, they were allowed to return to Crete.

Although his father wanted his son to succeed him as a merchant, the son would have none of that. Instead, he went to Athens, enrolled at the National University's School of Law, from which he graduated with honors. Then, in 1887, he returned to Crete to practice law. Soon, however, he entered politics – initially the politics of his island, a field that later would eventually lead him to the politics of Greece.

In the Cretan Rebellion of 1896-1897 against Turkey, Venizelos was one of the leaders of the uprising. However, the intervention of the British, French and Italians in favor of Turkey, did not help the Cretan uprising succeed its purpose. When the British, French and Italian admirals landed in Crete to negotiate a settlement between the insurgents and the Turks, Venizelos was the Cretans' chief representative. Thereafter, Venizelos continued his involvement with the politics of his island eventually becoming chief of the Cretan Government.

As chief of Crete's government, he had the opportunity to meet with two eminent prime ministers – Great Britain's Joseph Chamberlain who was very impressed with Venizelos' sharp diplomatic mind, and France's George Clemanceau, who, upon returning to France after a visit to Crete and parley with the Cretan chief, wrote: "The whole of Europe will be speaking of him in a few years."

The Cretan Rebellion of 1896-1897 was a most important point in the life of Venizelos, for its ensuing events would catapult him to a political career in independent Greece. In fact, this is how it happened. When rebellion broke out in Crete, the Greek Government also declared war against Turkey. Although Turkey won the war, Turkish control in Crete collapsed, resulting in Venizelos' emergence as the island's leader. In 1908 under Venizelos' leadership, the Cretan assembly declared the island united with Greece. But the government of independent Greece was unwilling to accept annexation. This hesitation rendered the Greek Government very unpopular in the eyes of many army officers whose great dissatisfaction led them eventually to stage a coup against it. The coup was successful, and in 1909, Venizelos was invited to come to Athens and take over as the country's Prime Minister. Venizelos arrived in Athens, and by 1910 after some constitutional revisions, he became Greece's Prime Minister.

In his effort to improve the country's internal conditions, he initiated sweeping reforms. Thus, between 1910 and 1920, he succeeded in creating for the first time, a state of law. More specifically, he placed all the courts of law under a Ministry of Justice, and the principle of tenure of judges was established. The civil service was reorganized, and in the constitution of 1911, he made sure that stronger guarantees of individual liberties were promulgated. He turned his attention to agriculture and established many technical and agricultural schools in various districts of the country. But it was the country's armed forces that the new Prime Minister sought to reorganize, actually to modernize to such an extent as to be no longer second to Turkey's. Foreseeing that in the future there would be wars on the European continent and wars between Greece and Turkey, he made the Greek Army second to none, a first class fighting organization.

His reorganization of the army soon paid off with spectacular successes in the Balkan Wars which took place in 1912 and 1913. In 1912,

Greece allied itself with Serbia and Bulgaria against Turkey, a war that ended with the defeat of Turkey. In 1913, Greece allied itself with Serbia and Rumania against Bulgaria. The war ended with the defeat of Bulgaria. As a result of these two wars, Greece gained, the regions of Thessaly, Epirus, Macedonia and Venizelo's homeland – the large Island of Crete. Thus, these two victorious wars doubled the size of Greece and the Greek population of these newly acquired regions was at last freed from Turkish rule. Actually, these new territorial acquisition along with their populations, increased the territory of Greece from 25,014 to 41,933 square miles, and her population from 2,666,000 to 4,363,000.

Fourteen months after the end of the Second Balkan War, the First World War broke out on August 1914. Right from the start, Greece's King Constantine and Venizelos found their policies diametrically opposed. King Constantine, being the brother-in-law of Emperor Wilhelm II had naturally close ties with Germany, and, as such, he wanted to keep Greece neutral. Perhaps suspecting that England's and France's combined sea powers would threaten Greece if she had joined the "Central Powers" (Germany and Austria), he wanted Greece to have no sides in this war.

Venizelos, on the other hand, foreseeing that England and France would emerge victorious, believed that if Greece would join them right from the beginning of the war, in the end, she might gain worthy benefits. Also, with Turkey and Bulgaria going on the side of Germany and Austria, he was hoping, that if England and France would win the war, a sizable territory around the city of Smyrna that lay in the western coast of Turkey, a city, furthermore, with a very large Greek population, as well as some kind of control over the city of Constantinople might be given to Greece. But, when offered to join England and France in 1914 against the Central Powers, both countries declined the offer, for they did not want the war to spread in the Balkans also.

When in 1915 Bulgaria joined Germany and Austria against Serbia, Venizelos permitted British and French troops to land in Greece and head north to help the Serbs. But, as the allied troops were landing in Greece, King Constantine forced Venizelos from office. Venizelos fled to northern Greece where he formed a provisional government opposed to the king.

In 1917, the Allies (British, French and Italians) forced Constantine to abdicate and recalled Venizelos to return to Athens as Prime Minister of Greece. Venizelos did return and entered the war against the Central Powers. By 1918, Venizelos had mobilized 250,000 Greeks, and by September, together with the British, the French and the Serbian armies, the Greek Army began an offensive against Bulgaria. In one month, Bulgaria capitulated and Turkey made an armistice. The Greek Army together with the other three armies entered triumphantly into Constantinople while the Greek fleet along with allied ones lay anchor in the harbor of Constantinople.

When the First World War ended in 1918 with victory on the side of the Allies, Venizelos went to Versailles, France where the Peace Conference was held in the famous palace. There, his superb diplomatic ability and eloquence made a deep impression on the conferees present; resulting to Greece's gaining additional territories. The victorious powers pressed Bulgaria to cede the territory of Western Thrace, a transfer that was officially sealed by the Treaty of Neully (November 27, 1919) and pressed Turkey to cede Eastern Thrace, without Constantinople to Greece – a deal which was finalized at the Treaty of Sevres (August 10, 1920). Also, the same Treaty finalized the transfer of the Aegean Islands along the Turkish coast, like Samos, Chios, and Mytilene as well as the City of Smyrna along with a large district around it which would be formally annexed to Greece after a plebiscite. As for Venizelos he had never been so elated. These latest territorial accessions had further contributed to the expansion of the Greek Nation.

Unfortunately, while the Greek Prime Minister was basking in glory and was enjoying the fruits of his diplomatic labors, as he had reached the pinnacle of his brilliant diplomatic career, suddenly he was informed that he had been deprived of his presidential authority. The presidential election of 1920 was decided on domestic issues and the heavy taxation he had imposed on his people to support his war policies. These contributed to his defeat.

Although the successor of Venizelos and King Constantine, who now had returned to Greece, tried to pursue Venizelos' policies, the return of King Constantine was not welcomed by the Allies. They clearly stipulated that he was their enemy, and, therefore, they would change their policies towards Greece. Thus, when the Greek Army initiated an offensive against the Turks in order to gain more territory around Smyrna, an offensive, which heading eastward would eventually advance to a point only forty miles west of Ankara – the Turks' capital, the Greek Army found itself fighting alone in deep enemy territory. Moreover, having overextended its supply lines, the Greek Army was now finding it difficult to hold firmly the newly gained territory.

Meanwhile, the Allies, who from the beginning of the Greek offensive had kept strict neutrality, now began to help the new Turkish leader – Mustapha Kemal who had succeeded in deposing the Sultan (King of the Turks) and who now was ready to counterattack the advancing Greek Army hoping to drive it all the way back to Smyrna. With arms, guns and ammunition supplied to him by France, Italy and Communist Russia, Mustapha Kemal Ataturk, in August 1922, made a big counteroffensive against the Greek Army, which had reached Afion Karahissar. The Greek Army was unable to hold its line and retreated. That retreat continued all the way back to Smyrna. At the same time, Turkish civilians, encouraged by success of the Turkish Army, began falling upon the Greek civilian inhabitants of Turkey setting fire to Greek homes, committing rape and slaughter.

By September 9th, the Turkish Army entered Smyrna setting fire to the Greek and Armenian sectors of the city, killing many Greek civilians, including the metropolitan of Smyrna – Chrysostom. Throngs of thousands of Greek civilians had gathered on the long waterfront of the harbor to board the ships and thus escape to Greece, leaving behind their homes, their shops, their commercial enterprises, their professional offices, their farms, and most of their belongings. In Greek History both the retreat of the Greek Army and the evacuation of Greek civilians from Smyrna and surrounding regions, would be known as "The Catastrophe (disaster) of 1922".

On July 24, 1923, a peace treaty was signed by Greece and Turkey after negotiations at the Lausanne Conference. It was agreed that Greece would return to Turkey Eastern Thrace and the Island of Imbros and Tenedos. It was also agreed that an exchange of populations take place – 400,000 Turks in Greece for 1,200,000 Greeks in Turkey, while 100,000 Turks would remain to reside in the region of Western Thrace of Greece and 100,000 Greeks would remain as residents of Constantinople. Needless to say that the City of Smyrna and the surrounding region that formerly belonged to Greece had become part of Turkey as soon as Kernal Ataturk had entered with his army.

In Greece, the defeat of the Greek Army caused two colonels – Plastiras and Gonatas to lead an army revolt and seize power. They deposed King Constantine on September 27, 1922, and sent, for trial, five political leaders and the commander-in-chief of the army. All six were sentenced to death and executed on November 28, 1922. The deposed king was taken to Palermo, Italy where he died on January 11, 1923.

During the following twelve years, unstable governments kept succeeding one another. It was during this time that Venizelos was reelected Prime Minister twice again. It was in 1924 and in 1928-1932. During these terms, Venizelos sought with great vigor to accomplish many things. It was in foreign policy, however, where he again showed his tremendous expertise. He sought to improve relations with Greece's Balkan neighbors and with Italy, and was quite successful in securing a rapprochement with Turkey. And so, relations with Turkey, that had been very strenuous since 1921, greatly improved. In 1935, modern Greece's political giant was again forced to exile in France. He died in Paris in 1936. His body was returned to his beloved Island Crete and was buried at Acrotiri.

Few statesmen have benefited their country as Venizelos did his own. He was the architect of his island's independence from Turkey, and thereafter, its union with Greece, he displayed an unusual understanding of global politics, was a shrewd diplomat and a man with a keen foresight. Summarizing his personality and statesmanship, C.M. Woodhous wrote: "Venizelos was the dominant figure of Southeast Europe…a genius in diplomacy, a humane and far-seeing statesman, and an unchallenged leader of his fellow-countrymen."

53
THE ASSIDUOUS AREOLOGIST

Of the nine planets that make up our solar system, none has excited the human imagination more during the last one hundred and fifty years than Mars. Its unique color, its nearness to the earth, its dust-storms, its polar caps, its earth like terrain, and its twenty-four hour and forty minutes rotation around its axis, plus Schiaparelli's erroneous discovery of its surface being filled with "canals" most likely made by intelligent creatures, all these spawned all kinds of outlandish literary, artistic, cinematographic, and lately, television fantasies.

Many books written at different periods in Europe and in America have Martian themes and fantastic illustrations. Paintings have also rendered fantastic conceptions of Martian creatures and cinematic productions have Martians invading our planet, while television even featured a series, "My favorite Martian".

While literature, art, the cinema, and television produced a plethora of Martian themes, astronomers always remained skeptical about life on Mars, let alone discovering reasoning creatures there. What they actually did was to turn their telescopes on the "intriguing" neighbor, and thus learned more about its morphology and conditions favorable for the sustenance of life.

Since the time of Giovanni Schiaparelli – the Italian astronomer, who in 1877, first interpreted the long furrows of the Martian surfaces as "canals" made by reasoning creatures, astronomers like E. Bernard, P. Lowell and W. Pickering devoted a considerable part of their astronomical observations examining the planet's surface. To the above distinguished triad, we must also add the name of Eugene Antoniadi, who, having at his disposal one of the finest telescopes of his time, devoted most of his life studying the planet hoping to unravel the truth about its various and peculiar features.

Thus, "Areology" (as the scientific study of the Planet Mars is now called in Astronomy) and not phantasy became the lifelong research of this distinguished Greek astronomer.

Eugene Antoniadi was born in 1870 to Greek parents who lived in Constantinople. During his childhood and early adolescence, the majesty of the stellar heavens always attracted his attention and wonder. So intense was the interest of the young lad in the stars, that we may rightly call him "Astrophile" (Lover of stars).

By the time he was eighteen, and having at his disposal very modest instruments, he began to systematically observe the heavens. His observations and the records he kept, despite his youth and lack of scientific training resembled those of a trained astronomer. Being of so high quality and scientific accuracy, eventually they were included in the astronomical reviews of the distinguished French astronomer Camille Flammarion that bore the title "L'astronomie". Amazingly, the young Greek observer of the stars was already showing signs of future greatness.

Eugene also had another fine gift – a gift that would greatly help him in his future astronomical field. He was artistically inclined. He could make accurate drawings of what he saw. In the future, his astronomical drawings would far surpass those of many of his colleagues.

By 1893, Eugene Antoniadi, twenty-three years of age and having studied astronomy at the University of Constantinople, moved to France, a country where he would spend the remainder of his life. In that year, at the request of Camille Flammarion, he came to Jurisy, which was near Paris, and there, Flammarion placed at his disposal his private telescope – a forty-two centimeter equatorial telescope in order to observe the planet Mars which was the young astronomer's prime concern.

Flammarion, besides being an eminent astronomer, was also an ardent popularizer of astronomy. He published his famous "L'astronomie Populaire" (Popular Astronomy), and was also the founder of the "Societe Astronomique de France" (Astronomical Society of France). Antoniadi could not have asked for a better patron.

For sixteen years, the young Greek astronomer would observe faithfully the behavior of stars, but especially that of the planet Mars that had become his almost all-consuming concern. Methodically, he would record his observations and findings, which were then published in the "Review" – an astronomical monthly founded and published by Flammarion. Thus, France and the world kept learning of his works and findings.

With the passing of time, the British became concerned with the work of Antoniadi, and impressed by his methodic research on the planet, appointed him director of the section on Mars of the British Astronomical Association.

In 1909, H. Deslandres, Director of the Observatory of Meudon, authorized him to make use of the large telescope of the observatory. And so, what the young astronomer had for years dreamed of, having at his disposal a large telescope that would enable him to see clearly and in somewhat detail the planet surface had now become a reality.

With tremendous elation and enthusiasm, Antoniadi, concentrated on observing his "red spot" in the sky, which in 1909, was close to the earth. This enabled Antoniadi to see surface details of Mars which he had never seen before.

What the Greek astronomer had discovered was that the so called network of canals, whose discovery Schiaparelli had announced thirty-two years earlier, and which many had wrongfully thought were man made, were nothing more than an effect produced by very minute details. In fact, to be more exact, he concluded that seventy percent of the "canals" were irregular dark bands, twenty-one percent were irregular ones of gray diffuse spots, and nine percent were isolated and complex nuclei.

Thus, the myth of man-made canals on the surface of Mars that had been promulgated by Schiaparelli and many others after him was given a decisive blow. No longer will people believe that Mars was inhabited by humans who possessing high technology allowing them to ring the entire surface of that planet with a dense network of canals that spanned thousands of miles. What seemed so in the past, therefore, was nothing but an illusion, just irregular furrows and spots that look continuous from far away.

Honors and recognition now came to the Greek astronomer from countries near and far. His discoveries, which took him many years, were now accepted by all astronomers. Antoniadi, not only had put an end to a fallacy, he had also provided the science of astronomy with the most accurate and detailed maps of the entire surface of Mars. Furthermore, he had also named many features of the Martian surface with Greek names, such as Hellas, Arcadia, Tempe, Xanthe, Icaria, Mt. Olympus; highest Mountain known to man over 85,000 feet high. In short, Antoniadi had advanced "Areology" (the study of Mars) immensely.

During the last years of his life, Antoniadi, besides continuing his astronomical work, became interested in the history of Greek and Egyptian astronomy. The results of his studies were published. In 1907, he also published important studies on the Basilica of Saint Sophia in Constantinople.

In 1928, the French government awarded him the Cross of Chevalier of the Legion of Honor.

He died in Meudon, France on February 10, 1944 and was buried with great honors, accorded to him by the astronomical and the scientific community of his adopted country.

Urania, the Greek muse of astronomy, must have been very happy. One of her protégés had really honored the celestial studies in the 20th century. He had added significantly to the work that his ancient, illustrious ancestors had begun two-and-a-half thousand years earlier.

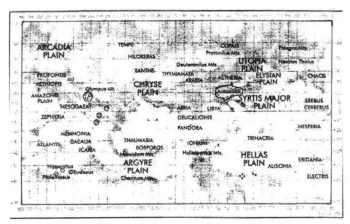

A detailed map of Planet Mars made by Antoniadi.

54

A CALCULUS GENIUS

Modern mathematics, more specifically calculus, began in the early part of the seventeenth century. This was the time when famous mathematicians such as Pierre Fermat, Rene Descartes and Blaise Pascal appeared. To the above, we must add two more, who, unlike the already mentioned, invented a new and higher form of mathematics – calculus. The first was Isaac Newton, a British mathematician, astronomer and physicist. The second was Gottfried Willhelm Leibniz, German philosopher and mathematician. They invented calculus independently.

Many mathematicians since the seventeenth century contributed to the development of this higher form of mathematics, which, to put it in very simple language, is a method of computation or calculation by using special symbolic notation. They were Bernoullis, Lagrange, Poincare, and Riemann, all mathematicians of high stature.

To these men who advanced this new kind of mathematics that helped man to achieve significant breakthroughs in science and in space, one must also add the name of Constantin Caratheodory.

Caratheodory was born of Greek parents in Berlin, Germany on September 13, 1873. His grandfather had been a professor at the Academy of Medicine in Constantinople. His father was a diplomat in the service of the Turkish Government, serving as Ambassador of Turkey in the Turkish Embassies of St. Petersburg, Russia, Berlin, Germany, and later, in Brussels, Belgium.

From early childhood, Constantin exhibited signs of future proficiency in mathematics. While attending secondary schools, he repeatedly won prizes in mathematical contests. When his father was serving as ambassador in Belgium, he entered the Ecole Militarie de Belgique (Military Academy of Belgium) and attended there for four years graduating as an army engineer.

Following his graduation, he was hired by the British Government to work as assistant engineer at the construction of the Asyut Dam in Egypt. When construction of the dam ended, Caratheodory went to Berlin to study mathematics at its prestigious university.

For two years, young Constantin thoroughly enjoyed the lectures of Professor Hermann Amandus Schwarz, who was an authority in calculus. Then, having completed the study, and accompanied by his close friend, Echard Schmidt, he went to Gottingen to continue mathematical studies at the city's famous university. Here, Constantin furthered his knowledge of calculus as he attended the lectures of Herman Minkowski. Two years later, Constantin's brilliant scholastic record earned him a doctorate, which he was awarded in 1904. A year later, he was offered a professorship of mathematics in the very university in which he had earned his doctorate. In the next sixteen years, besides teaching calculus at the University of Gottingen, he would also teach at the Universities of Bonn, Hannover, Breslau, and Berlin - his native city.

Up until now, Constantin had not visited Greece - the country of his ancestry. What knowledge he had gained of Greece and its literary and scientific contributions to the world he had acquired in the secondary schools that he had attended, and especially at the universities. At this point of his life, however, an unexpected opportunity was presented to him, and it came from a source he least expected.

In 1920, at the invitation of the Greek government, he went to Smyrna, Turkey to direct the completion of its university. But he was not to enjoy the fruits of his labors for long. In 1922, the Turkish troops, after having recaptured a large region around Smyrna hitherto occupied by Greece, now entered the city and set fire to the large Greek section. As the Greek population of the city was twice as large as the Turkish, most of the city was in flames. Caratheodory, despite the chaos that reigned in the city, and aided by many courageous Greek students, was able to rescue the books of the library and have them transported safely to Greece.

In the next two years, he taught mathematics and calculus at the University of Athens and, among other valuable services that he offered, he strongly urged the Greek Government to found another university in Thessalonica - the country's second largest city. His stern and patriotic advice fell upon receptive ears, and, a few years later, the "Aristotelian University of Thessalonica" was founded. Today, its modern and beautiful campus offers quality higher education to thousands of students in all academic disciplines.

In 1924, Caratheodory, at the invitation of the University of Munich, Germany, departed from Athens to henceforward head the school of mathematics of this most prestigious German university. Here, he taught for twenty-six consecutive years until his death in 1950.

Upon assuming professorship at the University of Munich, Caratheodory, besides lecturing, also became the editor of the university's mathematical publication entitled "Mathematische Annalen" (Mathematical Annals). In addition, he was a member of scientific societies and academies in many countries, including membership in the Papal Academy of the Vatican.

Caratheodory's work was mainly theoretical in both fields of mathematics and geometry. In fact, in his research and publications, he sought to achieve two things - the completion of mathematical and calculus theorems that had been proposed by mathematicians long before him, and the addition of new concepts in the field of calculus.

In the field of "Calculus of Variations", Caratheodory was able to devise a comprehensive theory of "Discontinuous Solutions" (curves with corners). He also achieved significant progress in solving the so-called problem of Lagrange. He also delved into applying the calculus of variations to geometrical optics. The book he wrote on this theme is an enduring classic.

In the field of calculus, known as "Theory of Functions", Caratheodory's achievements are numerous. The most important are answering the problems related to Picard's Theorem, answering problems arising from Schwarz's Lemma, advancing the theory of the functions of many variables, and greatly simplifying the proof of a central theorem of conformal representation.

In the field of the "Theory of Real Functions" and in the "Theory of the Measure of Point Sets and of the Integral," begun years previously by Borel and Lebesgue, Caratheodory solved them brilliantly.

Finally, in applied mathematics, Caratheodory wrote papers on mechanics, thermodynamics and on Einstein's Special Theory on Relativity.

On February 2, 1950, the now famous mathematician and calculus authority died. He was survived by his wife Efrosyne, and his son and daughter.

His was a life of continuous, positive, productive contributions in what is today considered the most advanced and difficult field of mathematics. Thousands of students attended his lectures. Among them was Albert Einstein, who especially esteemed his profoundly knowledgeable mentor.

Caratheodory left a veritable mathematical library consisting of

dozens of volumes, replete with mathematical articles, particularly his own contributions to calculus.

Recognizing his contributions and high stature attained in the field of mathematics, science author H. Boerner, wrote: "He was the most notable Greek mathematician of recent times, and the only one who does not suffer by comparison with the famous names of Greek antiquity."

In order to properly honor the great twentieth century mathematician, the Aristotelian University of Thessalonica, whose founding he pioneered, has named its administration building after him, and fittingly, erected a sculptured bust of his likeness on campus.

55

THE VICTOR OVER
CERVICAL CANCER

According to statistics, cancer occurs more frequently in a woman's uterus than in any other structure of her body. To be more specific, the very part of the uterus that is usually affected is the cervix, which is the neck of the uterus.

Although cervical cancer may occur in the thirties and even in the twenties, it is quite common from the forties to the sixties. During these two decades, the menopause takes place resulting in the diminishing of the ovarian endocrines. Like many other types of cancer, if cervical cancer is diagnosed early, it can be cured. If not, it becomes fatal.

Thus, early diagnosis of cervical cancer is the way to prevent it from reaching the stage of being fatal, and the man who eventually was able to invent an effective method of early diagnosis was Dr. George Papanicolaou.

George Papanicolaou was born in the provincial town of Kimi, Greece on May 13, 1883. His father, Nicholas Papanicolaou, was a medical practitioner in the above-mentioned town. When George grew, he decided to follow his father's profession by enrolling in the University of Athens' Medical School.

Following his graduation in 1904, he went on to Germany to continue his studies in the Universities of Jena, Freiberg and Munich. In all three, he pursued advanced biological studies, earning a doctorate in that field in 1910.

Upon returning to his native Greece, Papanicolaou married Mary Mavroyeni, the daughter of a high-ranking military officer. She became his lifelong associate.

At this time the young scientist decided not to follow a medical practice but rather to pursue an academic career. He left Greece, with Paris, France being his destination. On the way, he stopped in Monaco to visit the famous Oceanographic Institute. With top credentials in biology and cytology (Science of the cell), he was offered a post in the institute to work as a physiologist. He accepted the offer, and after spending a year studying the physiological process of the institute's aquatic species, he returned to Greece upon the death of his mother.

After serving for two years as a second lieutenant in the medical corps of the Greek Army during the Balkan Wars in 1913, he decided to leave his native country, this time, immigrating to the United States.

Possessing two doctorates was a tremendous advantage. He could well be a successful medical practitioner during the rest of his life, or, since he had decided not to pursue that practice, his doctorate in biology and cytology could immediately qualify him to be a researcher in any biological institute of his new country.

Not long after his arrival, he was appointed assistant in the pathology department of New York Hospital, and in 1914, he became assistant in anatomy at Cornell Medical College. In this post, he would devote forty-seven years of research until his retirement in 1961.

Most of his research during these more than four and a half decades centered in the physiology of reproduction and in "Exfoliative Cytology". In fact, as an appreciation of his brilliant work, the two institutes in which he carried on his experiments named the two laboratories after him.

In 1951, he was designated professor emeritus of clinical anatomy at Cornell, and in November of 1961, he moved to Florida to become director of the Miami Cancer Institute. Following his death three month later, the institute was renamed: "Papanicolaou Cancer Research Institute".

In 1917, Dr. Charles R. Stockard – chairman of the Cornell Medical School Department of Anatomy, invited Dr. Papanicolaou to join him in his work in experimental genetics. This invitation was what set the brilliant researcher on the path that would eventually lead him to achieve his benevolent discoveries.

Right from the start, Dr. Papanicolaou focused on the role which the chromosomes played in the determination of sex. In fact, it was while he was engaged in this kind of research that he noticed recurring cytological (cellular) changes in a fifteen to sixteen day cycle in the vaginal discharge of guinea pigs. He then correlated these cytologist changes with the cycles of the uterus and the ova, and his method became standard for measuring the sexual cycles in many different animal species.

In 1923, Papanicolaou focused his research on human beings. More specifically he tried to discover whether comparable vaginal changes occurred in women in connection with their menstrual cycle. He observed that a woman with cervical cancer showed abnormal cells whose nuclei were enlarged, very deformed and hyper chromatic. Later, in describing this brilliant discovery he said that it was "one of the most thrilling experiences of his scientific career."

Clinicians, however, were not eager to accept his findings. Thereupon, Dr. Papanicolaou, assisted by gynecologist – Dr. Herbert Traut, who greatly admired Papanicolaou's findings, began carrying on hundreds of experiments on people. After many years of persistent work, recording every experiment they had carried out, in 1943, Dr. Papanicolaou published the massive evidence he had accumulated. And his brilliant work that bore the title "Diagnosis of Uterine Cancer by the Vaginal Smear" which included 179 cases of uterine cancer detected very early by the smear, plus other types of cancer also detected by the smear, has become a milestone in the history of the fight against this dreadful disease.

The work was immediately accepted by clinicians. In the words of a then oncologist: "What this work mainly achieved was to make the smear a viable and most trustworthy medium of cancer diagnosis, for doctors could now detect superficial lesions in their incipient pre-invasive phase before the appearance of any symptoms."

And so, after years of painstaking and persistent research, Dr. Papanicolaou had achieved the main goal of his life. His smear, which eventually became known as the "Pap Test", soon achieved worldwide application as a routine screening technique. The results were unbelievable! In a short time, cervical cancer that in the 1940's was the number one killer of women was greatly reduced. Commenting on this tremendous reversal that Papanicolaou's discovery had effected, the executive director of Cervical Cancer Health stated: "Rarely has medical science seen such success."

The application of Dr. Papanicolaou's smear has not been limited to cervical cancer. Soon its use was applied in all other types of cancer such as breast cancer, stomach cancer, and pharyngeal cancer and on dozens of other types. Finally, it can also be applied to the prediction of cancer radio-sensitivity, the evaluation of the effectiveness of radiotherapy, and the detection of recurrence after treatment.

It has been estimated that thirty-five million women annually from all over the world use the "Pap Test" to make sure that they either have no cancer at all, or, if any, it is in its incipient stage and thus can be cured with the prescribed therapy.

In 1954, the eminent, assiduous doctor published another history-making publication – his "Atlas of Exfoliative Cytology". Since its publication, it has become a standard textbook in the field of malignancy in the shed cells.

Many honors and awards were heaped upon the brilliant doctor for his most benevolent discoveries for the benefit of mankind. They came from the American Medical Association as well as from the medical associations of all nations of the world. He more than deserved them for his discoveries, when applied, saved millions of human lives the world over.

Summing up his inestimable contribution, a contemporary medical authority wrote: "Papanicolaou's work ranks with the discoveries of Roentgen and Marie Curie in reducing the burden of cancer."

56
THE STRATEGIST OF "DEEP BATTLES"

Empress Catherine the Great of Russia was one of the rare women of the eighteenth century. She was ambitious, intelligent, witty, very sociable, extroverted and with considerable administrative talent. She frequently corresponded with the French philosopher Voltaire who was a prominent representative of the "Encyclopaedistic Movement", and, despite the demands of her daily duties, she would find time to write poems and even plays.

Catherine, a German princess, the daughter of Christian Augustus, Prince of Anhalt and his wife Johanna Elizabeth of Holstein, was born in Stettin, Germany and was baptized Sophia Augusta Frederica. Before marrying Prince Peter III who was the grandson of Peter the Great, she was received into the Orthodox Faith and was given the name of Catherine Alexeyeuna (Alexandrea). Her marriage to Prince Peter, who, after the death of his father, became Emperor of Russia, was not a happy one. He was a frequent blunderer, insulting to men of his court and even to foreign monarchs, and often threatened his intelligent and prudent wife that he would divorce her. But this did not happen, for quite unexpectedly, a "pronunciamiento" proclaimed by the regiments of the guards, removed the inept monarch from his throne thereby placing Catherine upon it as Empress of Russia.

Catherine soon proved to be a very able administrator. She maintained excellent relations with the nobility, and, since she was an admirer of the Encyclopaedistic Movement, her policies were always those of benevolent despotism. She pursued a brilliant foreign policy, and, as a result of a war with Turkey, her country gained the Crimean Penninsula and other sizable regions around the Black Sea.

A foreign element that Catherine encouraged to immigrate to Russia was the Greeks. As a result, over the years, thousands of Greeks who lived in the territories of the Ottoman Empire made their way into Russia, where, thanks to their industry and inherent drive for success, made a better life for themselves and their descendants, and contributed to society.

This was not the first time that Greeks came and settled in Russia. Since the fall of Constantinople in 1453, large numbers of Greeks immigrated to Russia. Many Greeks had even settled in Kiev- Russia's first capital as far back as the tenth century when Russia was converted to the Orthodox Faith.

Many of the Greeks who came to Russia after the conquest of Constantinople by the Turks assumed academic posts, while others rose to high ranks in the army, the navy and in the diplomatic service. A case in point was Nicholas Spatharios, who was at the head of a Russian delegation that negotiated the Treaty of Nerchinsk with the Chinese in 1693.

In those bygone eras, Greeks who lived in foreign lands always tended to live in pockets of large cities so that they might maintain their language, ethnicity, culture, and religion. Thus, at this time, one would find thousands of Greeks living in Kiev, Kharkov and Nezhin. In fact, as during the reign of Peter the Great, since a new and large immigration of Greeks took place, large Russian cities such as Mariopolis, Stavropolis, Nicopolis, Sebastopol, Odessa and many others had populations that were overwhelmingly Greek.

Catherine the Great, aware of the large number of Greeks living in southern Russia and in the Crimean Peninsula, proceeded to do something that no other monarch had done up to that time. She founded a military academy in the Crimea for the training of army and navy Greek officers. With the passing of years, hundreds of Greek Army and naval officers had graduated from this academy. One of them, the well known John Capodistrias, rose to the rank of Russia's foreign minister under Czar Alexander I. Later in his life, when Greece won its independence, Capodistrias became Greece's first governor.

Among the Greeks who lived in Russia during the last three decades of the nineteenth century was Kyriakovich (Cyriacos) Triantafillov. His grandfather's last name was Triantafillou. Some time after settling in Russia, he Russianized it to Triantafillov. Kyriakovich and his wife lived in Magaradzlieeking managing an existence from a small farm.

On March 26, 1894, a baby boy was born to this poor family. At his baptism, he received the name of Vladimir. When he grew, Vladimir joined the army, having decided to make it his career. At this time, Russia was still under the rule of the czars. Then, when in 1914, the First World War broke out, Triantafillov served valiantly and honorably rising to the rank of staff captain.

In 1917, Lenin and the Bolsheviks seized power and made peace with the Central Powers (Germany and Austria) with whom Russia was at war until now. They also abolished the royalty, the Boyars (old aristocracy), and introduced Marx's communism as the country's political system. Triandafillov joined the army of the new regime and fought during the Civil War that followed the Bolshevik takeover. During the Civil War, he first fought in the region of the Ural Mountains, and then was transferred to the southern and southwest fronts. In both these fronts, he fought as a brigade commander. It was at this time that the young brigade commander attracted the attention of the commander of the southwest front, M. Frunze, who was impressed by Triantafillov's tactics, and strongly recommended the latter's acceptance to the Military Academy after the Civil War.

In 1924, Triantafillov, having completed four years of advanced military studies, graduated with honors. He was appointed to deputy chief of staff and a chair was established for him in the Academy. It was during these years that the young and brilliant professor of military science, besides teaching, also found time to write many books on military theories of which his "The Nature of the Operations of Modern Armies" is his most comprehensive.

In formulating his novel military theories, Triantafillov based some of them on his personal experiences and adapted to the modern developments in weapons and warfare. He carefully considered the physical status and capabilities of current weapons and tried to imagine their developmental trends that might occur in the future.

He noticed, for example, that infantry weapons (rifles, machineguns, etc.) Were getting lighter, that their range was getting longer, and that their rate of fire kept increasing. He also took into consideration that the explosive power of artillery shells kept increasing, and wisely observed that, while the mobility of tanks and mechanized infantry would increase in the future, for a commensurate mobility of the artillery, no considerations had been made. Likewise, concerning the tanks' role in battle, he was one of the finest military theorists to recognize that the tank, besides being very effective in offensive operations, could be equally so in bringing great harassment to retreating enemy troops.

He was correct in observing that, when mechanized infantry, tanks and other weapons were operating in vast expanses of terrain, new systems of command and control ought to be employed. He wisely chose the radio as the best means of transmitting communications between supreme commanders and unit commanders. Finally, foreseeing that in a future war, again millions of combatants would be committed to the battlefields - an event that actually happened during the Second World War, he again correctly asserted that these could fight according to the new rules that would suit the future, fast moving mechanized units. Last but not least, he speculated, such a new kind of warfare would also require new logistics of supplies.

The airplane, which made its appearance during the First World War initially as a reconnaissance medium, and then as a fighter and bomber, was recognized by Triantafillov as potentially a most effective new weapon in future warfare. Bombers could destroy the enemy's supplies many miles behind the lines, could bomb troops in the field of engagements and could be used to transport fresh airborne troops.

In describing very briefly the offensive strategy, Triantafillov outlined it as follows:

"Initially, in order for an attacking army to succeed in making a breach in the enemy's defensive line, the attacking army would need to employ two echelons - the attack echelon, consisting of mechanized infantry and reinforced with artillery and tanks, and an envelopment echelon consisting of highly mobile motorized units whose aim would be to make a breach in the defense to operational depth.

The breach must have a frontage of at least five miles. Once the breach has been made, the envelopment echelon would go into action advancing deeply to take over the enemy's second defense line before he would have the time to commit his reserves.

The penetration must continue to the depth of forty-five to seventy miles, where usually the enemy's main supply depots and army headquarters would be located.

Light bombers had to bombard the enemy line before the attack echelon would begin the offensive, and continue bombing the enemy when the envelopment echelon was fighting. Long range bombers had to isolate the break in sector completely from the enemy's strategic depth and indirect movement of his strategic reserves.

Finally, airborne forces should be brought to the area where the enemy's main supply dumps and army headquarter were situated, so that, in collaboration with the envelopment echelon, to attack them and destroy them."

Triantafillov, whose "brainchild" is the above-mentioned deep offensive operation theory, did not live to put it into practice. On June 12, 1931, only a year after he had published his so novel and valuable theory, while traveling by plane with Kalinovskii, commander of motorized forces, was killed as the plane crashed. Thus, one of the most modern battle theorists was dead at the age of thirty-seven. Had he lived, no doubt, when the Second World War began, Triantafillov's fast rise in the highest ranks of the Russian Army might have found him as its supreme commander.

In 1943 and 1944, when the Russian Armies were fighting hard against the retreating German Armies, Marshal Zhukov often applied Triantafillov's deep penetration tactics. Each time the results produced the expulsion of the Nazi invaders from vast areas of his country.

57
A DISTINGUISHED CONDUCTOR

No one expected the offspring of a family that, for many generations had been producing priests for the Orthodox Church, to become a conductor. Dimitri Mitropoulos' parents, whose forbearers had been priests for generations, expected also that their son would become a priest.

But this wasn't to be. Dimitri, although as a young child was contemplating to spend his life serving the Orthodox Church when he matured, decided to attend the National Conservatory of Athens to devote his life to music. Music had captivated him.

Dimitri Mitropoulos was born in Athens in 1896. He spent a happy childhood and adolescence in the home of his God-fearing and devout parents whose sole desire was to see him enter the Holy Orders. But young Dimitri, who by now had developed a tremendous love and intense interest for music, instead of entering the seminary, entered the "National Odeum" as the Athens Conservatory was then called. With great enthusiasm, he studied piano under the stern tutelage of Wassenhoven and harmony under Marsick.

Young Mitropoulos' matriculation at the National Odeum soon bore fruit. In 1918, when Dimitri was only twenty-two years old, he gave a piano recital in which he won a gold medal. Two years later, young Dimitri achieved another triumph. Maetternlick's operatic libretto "Soeur Beatrice" (Sister Beatrice), for which he composed beautiful music, was successfully performed in the theater of the conservatory. The critics' comments were very favorable toward the musical score, but, what was actually a tremendous bonus to the young composer, were the laudatory comments made by one of France's outstanding composers - Saint Saens. Foresensing a great future in composition, he urged Mitropoulos to concentrate on that musical field in Paris. Mitropoulos, however, chose instead to study in Brussels under the notable Gilson.

After a year of studying composition, Dimitri went to Berlin to enroll in the "Berlin Hochshule Fur Music" to study piano under the famous master Fericio Busoni. At the same time, he was appointed assistant conductor to the Berlin State opera – a position he held with great success showing once more that a brilliant musical future lay ahead for him.

In 1924, the young musician returned to his birthplace – Athens, in order to teach composition and to conduct the orchestra of the National Odeum. His great success in both these very important musical fields spread his fame throughout Europe, resulting in an invitation in 1930, to conduct concerts with such leading orchestras as those of Paris, Liverpool, Berlin, and Brussels. He was so successful in these prime appearances that, in 1932, he was again invited to lead in concert the orchestras of Rome, Naples, Florence, London, and Paris. All these appearances brought him additional fame, especially in some of the piano concertos in which he was both conductor and pianist. He was now a well-established conductor ranking among the top in Europe – a position he had achieved at a rather young age. He was only thirty-six years of age.

Mitropoulos' fame as a distinguished conductor and pianist had by now reached the New World. Unhesitant, he seized the opportunity when he was invited by Koussevitzki – the conductor of the famous Boston Symphony Orchestra, and came to America in 1936 to begin the second chapter of a successful musical career.

His American debut took place at the Boston Symphony Hall. Bostonians and others from all over New England and New York filled the hall to capacity in order to witness the first appearance of the newly arrived famous Greek conductor. As expected, Dimitri was masterful. His performance received a thunderous response from the audience and most favorable critiques from musical analysts who had come to Boston from many leading American cities.

A new meteoric career in America was now beginning for the young immigrant Greek conductor. In 1937, he was invited to become the conductor of the Minneapolis Symphony Orchestra succeeding its notable conductor Eugene Ormandy.

From the start, Mitropoulos sought to improve the quality of its players. He also embarked on a program of expansion by including, in the repertory, works of new composers such as those by Schoenberg and others. Until now, other American orchestras had hardly attempted to venture into such new challenges. Mitropoulos would frequently include them in his concerts thus introducing his audience to new sounds, somewhat different from the baroque, classical, and romantic pieces by such European composers as Bach, Mozart, Beethoven, and Brahms to which they were accustomed to hearing.

For twelve consecutive years, Mitropoulos was the conductor of the Minneapolis Symphony Orchestra. Standards had considerably improved, making it one of the best in the United States. In 1940, he received the medal of the American Mahler Society for promoting the music of this contemporary Austrian composer. He also turned his attention to another form of musical performances – the "Operatic Concerts" performing such rare operas as "Elektra", "Arlecchico" and others.

While he served as a conductor of the Minneapolis Symphony Orchestra, he frequently came to New York to conduct the New York Philharmonic, and the Orchestra of the Metropolitan Opera of New York. He would also travel to Europe, to conduct on important occasions, various symphony orchestras as for example, at the annual Salzburg Festival.

Mitropoulos never forgot the county of his birth and of his parents. In 1955, he brought the New York Symphony to Athens to perform at its summer festival. In 1958, he came to the same festival with the Vienna Orchestra.

Despite his busy schedule, Mitropoulos found time to compose music. Besides his "Sister Beatrice" – a work of his youth, he composed a symphonic poem, "La mise au tombeau de Christ" (Mass of the tomb of Christ), a cencerto grosso, a piano sonata, a song cycle "Hedonica", incidental music for plays, piano chamber music, and orchestrations of organ works of Bach.

Mitropoulos achieved great fame. Believing that excellent orchestral sound can be produced only by high quality players, he insisted that his players always try to do their best. He always conducted the orchestra with passion, which he considered to be a prerequisite to perfection. He never used a baton, and, as he knew by heart the music he was conducting, never had the book of the musical score, before him to use.

Very difficult musical pieces never intimidated him, nor did he ever shirk from performing them. He would patiently rehearse them over and over showing his players how to overcome the difficult spots until a very satisfactory performance was achieved.

When in 1982, Leonard Bernstein – the conductor of the New York Philharmonic presented a series of Beethoven's nine symphonies on television, which he had taped while conducting the Vienna Symphony Orchestra, he concluded the series with Beethoven's "Trio" – a very difficult piece very rarely performed. In introducing it, he remarked: "The last time I heard this Trio performed was thirty years ago in Berlin with Dimitri Mitropoulos conducting. What a masterful performance that was. It was performed flawlessly, effortlessly, and expertly. Mitropoulos – a master conductor with whom nothing was difficult - had made it sound very easy."

Mitropoulos died of a heart attack at the age of sixty-four while rehearsing Mahler's Third Symphony with the orchestra of La Scala in Milan, Italy.

In order to honor the memory of this most famous Greek conductor, an International Conductors' Competition was established in New York in 1961.

58
THE GREATEST OF TYCOONS

He was a small man in stature, but he was a giant in his dreams, his ambitions and in all his business dealings. He wasn't handsome but ladies of royalty as well as aristocracy found him most charming, and enjoyed his company tremendously. He never attended a college or a university, and yet, top notables of the twentieth century like Sir Winston Churchill, heads of states, writers, scientists, and leading industrialists found his company most interesting. He never studied business, finance or other such relevant fields associated with his entrepreneurial adventures, and yet, his inborn business talent helped him succeed in most of the deals he transacted and which amounted to millions of dollars. He was aggressive and ruthless in the office, but in his opulent mansion, the hotels, or the palaces where he very often appeared as a guest or as a host, he was affable, courteous, and most amiable. His name? Aristotle Onassis.

Aristotle Onassis, the son of Socrates and Penelope Onassis, was born in Smyrna, Turkey on January 20, 1906. His father, a prosperous tobacco merchant, was also strict. His mother, who married his father at the age of seventeen, was a religious woman. The Onassises also had a daughter - Artemis.

When Aristotle was six, his beloved mother died of kidney failure. Eventually, Socrates remarried and fortunately for Artemis and Aristotle, their stepmother was a kind woman. From her previous marriage, she had two daughters and so Socrates now had four children.

Following the conclusion of the First World War, in which Greece joined the Allies (England, France, the U.S., and Italy), and Turkey joined the central powers (Germany, and Austria-Hungary), the victorious Allies encouraged the Greek reoccupation of Smyrna and of a large territory around it. In fact, at that time, although Smyrna was a Turkish city, its population consisted of 165,000 Greeks and 80,000 Turks.

In July 1922, the Greek Army conducted an offensive for the purpose of conquering more Turkish land. They were able to advance deep into Turkey until they halted forty miles west of Ankara, the capital of Turkey. But by August of the same year, the Turkish Army, led now by Mustafa Kemal, began a counteroffensive forcing the Greek Army to retreat all the way back to Smyrna.

The large Greek population of Smyrna, foreseeing the ill fate that was certain to befall them if they chose to stay in Smyrna, in great haste began evacuating the city by boarding the ships that were in the harbor to take them to the Greek Islands or to mainland Greece. Among them were Socrates' wife, his mother and three daughters. The ship took them to the Island of Lesbos, and then, to Piraeus, Greece. Socrates and Aristotle remained in Smyrna. When the Turkish Army entered the city, setting fire to all the Greek sections, Aristotle and Socrates were arrested and put in prison, but not long after, they were set free and went to Athens to reunite with the rest of the family.

Aristotle now aged sixteen did not wish to stay in Greece. He had a strong urge to immigrate to a far away country - a country where he would start a new life and realize his dreams. Possessed by such an irresistible desire, he said farewell to his parents and sisters, boarded the Italian Liner "Tomaso di Savoia" and left for Argentina. By September 21, 1923, he arrived at Buenos Aires.

With the help of some Greeks, the seventeen year old immigrant found a job working as a telephone operator. In his spare time, he read the financial pages of the London and New York Stock Exchanges and did not hesitate to invest some of his earnings in the aforementioned exchanges from which he received a seven hundred dollar return. By now, possessed by an urge for social climbing, an urge that would persist throughout his life, he bought new clothes and began to frequent the night clubs. He also acquired cultural tastes, beginning to frequent the opera house. In time, he became soprano Claudia Muzio's lover - an association that introduced Aristotle to many influential Argentinians - businessmen, bankers, industrialists, and others.

While still working as a telephone operator, Aristotle came up with a bright idea. He thought of introducing Turkish tobacco to Argentina. He believed that Turkish tobacco could especially appeal to the women of Argentina because it was of higher quality than the commonly used Cuban. Although, at the start, the sales were limited, later, with males requesting cigarettes with Turkish tobacco, Aristotle began a successful manufacturing and sale of cigarettes, which he named "Oscans" and "Primeros". The venture brought thousands of dollars in profit and that represented his first real success.

His early success reached the government of Greece, which, recognizing his many talents and abilities, appointed him Greek Consul in Buenos Aires. This appointment greatly benefited the young entrepreneur especially in the realm of shipping. He became quite proficient in solving problems of ships while in port and, furthermore, he gained much knowledge about sea transportation, its problems and all sorts of adverse situations peculiar to freighters.

Having gained this new experience, Onassis began to now turn his attention to shipping. Having accumulated enough capital, he began to seriously think of buying ships. He believed, that a modest start, if handled rightly, would eventually propel him to success, which meant the owning of many ships. And so, having convinced himself that in shipping he would succeed, he began examining the opportunities of buying ships.

The opportunity came when Canada began offering for sale freighters weighing up to ten thousand tons for scrap metal prices. After examining the ships, Onassis expressed his desire to buy six ships at $20,000 each. Although the company was initially reluctant to sell him the number of ships he had requested, the company agreed to fulfill his request. Onassis bought all six and in the forthcoming decades, his firm would develop into the largest privately and individually owned merchant fleet in the world.

Following this purchase which yielded to the ship owner substantial earnings, Onassis directed his interest to oil tankers. Up until now, oil tankers were of nine thousand tons; Onassis desired to have much larger ones. After searching many ship yards that would accept orders to build larger oil tankers, he at last located one in Norway. He ordered two fifteen thousand tonners, naming them "Aristo" and "Aristophanes" respectively. When launched before the outbreak of the Second World War, they were the largest oil tankers ever built. Then when the war began, the Norwegian Government, having declared strict neutrality, seized both ships. They were released to Onassis after the war ended. A third sister ship was built after the war which Onassis named "Buenos Aires".

When the Second World War ended, the United States Naval Commission decided to sell the "Liberty" ships that were built during the war. He bought sixteen of them at the price of $550,000. With this purchase, Onassis had come a long way. He had acquired a sizable merchant fleet, and, as it appeared, it would be only a matter of time before this man would eventually become one of the most notable tycoons.

By the 1960's, shipbuilding companies in Europe and Japan, thanks to some technological developments, such as high-tensile-strength steel, improved corrosion control systems and very big and powerful engines, made the construction of 170,000 and 210,000 ton oil tankers possible. The size of such ships would enable them to carry a large amount of oil from producing countries. Moreover, such huge oil carriers would be able to avoid "hot spots," that is war zones which usually prohibit the passage of ships.

Onassis, realizing at once the advantage these new supertankers had over the older, small ones, besides ordering 50,000 and 60,000 tonners, he also ordered the construction of 170,000 and 200,000 tonners in Japan. With three new orders, he proudly announced that his merchant fleet would soon amount to four million tons. With this amount to tonnage, he became one of the leading shipowners of the world.

In the 1950's, Onassis bought a Canadian frigate - the "Stormont" at the price of $34,000. It had been built in 1943 in order to escort convoys in the Atlantic. The frigate weighed 1,450 tons. With the most expert advice of a German professor of architecture, Caesar Pinnau, the frigate was redesigned into the renown yacht, the "Christina", one of the most modern and opulent yachts in the world. It was a floating palace. The conversion cost Onassis over $4,000,000.

The highest quality of marble, wood and tile were used for its interior renovation and decoration. Rare, priceless paintings hang on the walls of its library, dining room, living room and in other rooms. On the deck, the bottom of its swimming pool showed the Bull of Minos in mosaic.

Since Onassis used his yacht to entertain international celebrities as well as a base for important shipping operations, the ship was equipped with the most efficient electronic communications system, perhaps rivaling that of Air Force One. Last but not least, the ship was perennially stocked with the finest and rarest edibles from every corner of the world. To be wined and dined on the "Christina" was, for the international jet set, who were fortunate to be Onassis' guests, one of the rarest experiences of their lives.

Among the hundreds of the elite guests entertained on the "Christina" were Sir Winston Churchill, the former Prime Minister of Great Britain, and a frequent guest, Prince Rainier and Princess Grace, the Kennedy's, other heads of states, Maria Callas and her husband Giovanni Meneghini, and some of the best known actors of Hollywood such as Elizabeth Taylor, Richard Burton, Cary Grant, Greta Garbo, Veronica Lake, Anthony Quinn, and dozens of others. Arabian sheiks and princes, who controlled oil, were also frequent guests. Hard to believe that an individual who started his career as a telephone operator in Buenos Aires would someday be the host of the world's elite.

In 1949, Onassis entered a new venture, that of whaling. In Kiel, Germany, he assembled his whaling fleet. It consisted of a factory ship - the "Olympic Challenger", and seventeen British and Canadian Corvettes that had been converted into hunter-killer catching ships. The fleet was manned by 519 German seamen, plus fifteen Norwegian expert gunners at the head of whom he placed the notorious Norwegian Nazi collaborator, Lars Andersen, who was the best harpoonist alive. With such a fleet and expert human complement, Onassis was out for another most lucrative venture of his ever-expanding business operations.

Right from the start, the new venture was most successful. In 1950, and in one day of the hunting season, his ships caught and slaughtered 124 whales. Moreover, in 1950 alone, his whaling expedition had earned him $4.2 million dollars. In the following years, as his fleet often ignored international rules of whale hunting, this often illegal hunting would not go on forever.

As the number of whales in the Arctic Zone had been greatly reduced and many of them had gone to the coastal waters of Peru, Onassis ordered his fleet to move there. Peru's limits were 405 miles from the coast. When the Peruvian Navy opened fire, five ships surrendered. The other ten found refuge in Panama, while the ones that surrendered were forced to steam to the port of Peru where their four hundred crew were put in prison.

At a trial, the "Olympic Whaling" was fined $2,800,000 with payment due in five days. Lloyd's of London and not Onassis paid the fine, thanks to a foresighted clause that had been included in the insurance agreements proposed by Onassis. After this incident, Onassis sold his whaling fleet to the Japanese at the price of $8,200,000, and so, his whaling venture which had earned him millions of dollars, had come to an end.

Having achieved tremendous success in shipping, Onassis was now turning his attention to the air. The opportunity was presented by Greece's Prime Minister Constantine Caramanlis in 1957. He asked Onassis to start an introductory, reputable airline. In the discussions that followed behind closed door, Onassis was able to obtain numerous concessions and attractive compensations from the Greek Government. Onassis agreed to augment the already existing domestic airline, consisting of thirteen small passenger planes, by buying additional, new and much bigger planes such as two "Comet" English built jets and three Boeing 707's. Moreover, with the help of the Frenchman, Tom Fabre, who had directed very successfully many French Airlines, he was able to organize the now "Olympic Airways" to a satisfactory level.

In his marriage, Onassis did not fare as well as he did in his business. Tina Livanos, the younger daughter of tycoon Stavros Livanos, was the first girl Aristotle thought seriously of marrying. He met her in 1945 at Oyster Bay, Long island where both Livanos and Onassis had seaside residences. She had blonde hair, light brown eyes, and a delicate face. She was seventeen; Aristotle was forty. Although her father hoped that Onassis would ask to marry his older daughter, Eugenie, in the end, he agreed to let him marry Tina.

The marriage took place at the Greek Orthodox Cathedral of Holy Trinity in New York City. A most lavish reception followed, and then, the couple went on a two month honeymoon. On their return, the couple settled at Oyster Bay, and in 1948, Tina gave birth to a son whom they named Alexander, and in 1950, to a daughter whom they named Christina.

By 1960, Tina filed for divorce on grounds of infidelity. Even after his marriage to Tina, Onassis continued to entertain on his yacht or in his European villas many women such as the most famous diva - Maria Callas.

In the summer of 1963, upon learning that the Island of Skorpios was for sale at the price of $110,000, Onassis bought the island. He ordered countless cypress, walnut and almond trees to be planted throughout the island transforming it into a true paradise on earth.

On October 17, 1968 much to the surprise of the world and of Alexander and Christina, Aristotle married Jackie Kennedy widow of United States President, John F. Kennedy. They were married in the chapel of "Panayitsa" (Little Virgin) with the international elite attending.

Aristotle knew Jackie long before they were married. She had cruised with him several times on board the "Christina" and a mutual bond had developed between the two. At the time of their marriage she was thirty-nine and he was sixty-two.

In 1973, a fatal accident caused deep pain to Aristotle Onassis. His son Alexander, only twenty-five and a pilot, upon taking off from Athens airport, and only seconds airborne, the plane's engine failed and the plane crashed to the ground killing Alexander. After his son's death, Onassis never recovered emotionally. Somehow sensing that he might soon die, he began to disclose his complex financial assets to his daughter Christina.

After his son's death, Onassis petitioned to build a refinery in New Hampshire. Approval was not granted as the inhabitants of the proposed region, at a town meeting, unanimously turned down his request.

Two years later, Onassis still inconsolable over his son's death and having lost Olympic Airways to the Greek Government, died at the American Hospital at Neuilly near Paris, France. The cause of his death was bronchial pneumonia. He was buried next to his son in the chapel of Panayitsa.

Before he died, Onassis was a billionaire owning over one hundred ships, many of which were over 150,000 tons each. He had control of seventy firms, and among others, owned a Swiss Bank. He owned many mansions in America and Europe. He bought insurance for everything he owned in order to cover any eventuality. He was the Twentieth Century's "King of Tycoons".

59
MODERN GREEK LITERATURE

Modern Greek Literature continues the onward march of its predecessors - the Ancient and the Byzantine. It thus forms an unbroken continuity that makes it the oldest continuous literature in the Western World. This chapter will include the most notable contributors.

Following the fall of Constantinople, Greek literary productivity flourished on the island of Crete. Best known writers of this time are Vincenzo Cornaros who composed the romantic poem "Erotokritos", and Nicholas Drimitinos who composed the very charming and lengthy poem "The Fair Shepherdess".

During the 17th and the 18th centuries, Greek literature deals not only with secular themes but theological as well. Notable representatives of this time are the prelates Nicephoros Theotokis and Eugenios Vulgaris and the poet Constantine Rhigas, who composed many patriotic poems.

The outbreak of the Greek Revolution of 1821 greatly stirred poetic productivity. In fact, it is at this time that the beginnings of the real modern Greek poetry and prose occurred. The Ionian Islands, which ring the western coast of mainland Greece, were the very place where the new literary productivity had its beginnings.

Dionysios (Dennis) Solomos (1798 -1857), born in the Ionian Island of Zakynthos, is not only the pioneer but the most outstanding representative of the Ionian School. He studied law at the University of Padua in Italy, but turned to poetry after his graduation. He wrote his first poems in Italian, but on his return to Greece in 1918, he would hence write them in Greek. He wrote all his poems in the "Demotic" (Vernacular, spoken) Greek infusing them with a deep romantic feeling.

The outbreak of the Greek Revolution, whose aim was independence from Turkey, deeply impressed the young poet. The siege of Mesolonghi (1825-1826) so moved him that, inspired by the indescribable heroism of its inhabitants, he wrote his best-known poem - "The Ode to Liberty." It consists of 158 lyrical verses, which vividly and expressively describe the sufferings of the Greeks under Turkish occupation, their longings for freedom, their heroic struggles to win independence, and their hopes for a bright future. In 1828, the composer Nicholas Mantzaros set the poem to music and in 1864, seven years after the poet's death, by an act of the Greek Parliament, the poem became the Greek National Anthem. Solomos wrote many other superb poems, all of which are characterized by flowing lyricism, love of freedom and idealism. Of his prose works, "The Woman of Zakynthos" is a strikingly modern satire describing the ugliness of contemporary society. Today, Solomos is regarded as one of the greatest Greek poets and Greece's National Poet.

A group of young writers got together in 1880 founded the so-called "New School of Athens". Early notables of this school include Emmanuel Roads (1835-1904), who wrote a historical-satirical romance entitled "Pope Joan", and the brothers Alexander and Panayotis Soutsos. The latter two had studied in Paris, and, having been imbued by French Romanticism, on returning to Greece, carried the theme of love of country in their writings "In extremis".

Indisputably, the outstanding literary figure of this school was Costis Palamas (1859-1943). He studied law at the University of Athens and later served as its General Secretary.

His voluminous output covers every conceivable literary genre - proof of his many-faceted intellect. He wrote poetry, novels, critiques, studies, chronicles, and countless articles in newspapers and magazines. He drew his inspiration from the long history of Greece, from contemporary intellectualism, and from the sentimentalism of his time. His best known works are "The Grave", a most moving lyrical elegy replete with deep emotions over the death of his son Alkis, "The King's Flute", in which he extols great Byzantine eras, "The Immutable Life", inspired by French Intellectualism, and a work that established him as a famous poet internationally, and "Longings for the Lagoon", teeming with vivid reminiscences of his childhood.

Today, at the inaugural and closing ceremonies of the Olympic Games held every four years, Palamas' "Olympic Anthem", sung by a chorus of the host country, is heard around the world.

John Psycharis (1854-1929), whose parents and forebears hailed from the island of Chios, was born in Odessa, Russia. He spent his childhood in Marseilles, France, studied in Germany and France, and taught for many years in the school of Modern Oriental Languages of the University of Paris. He established a very close friendship with Ernest Renan and eventually married his daughter. Of the marriage, two sons were born, both of whom were killed during the First World War. In their memory, Psycharis donated, to the Library of Luxemburg, 25,000 books dealing with mental subjects.

He was a prolific writer, and the following are his best known novels: "Julia", which when translated into French received high praising critiques; "The Dream of Gianniri", a masterful synthesis of the Greek psyche; "Life and Love in Solitude"; "The Sick Maid", a novel that advocates many social demands; and "Two Brothers".

John Psycharis fought against the advocates of the "Pure" language with all the might of his mouth and pen. He wrote the novel "My Journey" by which he encourages young novelists to write in the vernacular. He also wrote poems in French which he published under the title "Petites Poemes", and a poetic collection in Italian entitled "Fioretti per Francesca". To the above, one must also add his countless glossological studies which were published in French magazines.

Angelo Sikelianos (1884-1951), a native of the Ionian Island of Lefkas and an adorer of the ancient Greek spirit, spent most of his creative years in trying to synthesize the ancient Greek myths with the teachings of the Church. He wrote a great number of lyrical poems which show his great imagination. Today, he is regarded as one of the top Modern Greek poets. Excellent poems of his include such titles as "Mother of God", "The Easter of the Greeks" and "A Prologue to Life". He also wrote the poetic tragedies, "The Dithyramb of Roses", "Daedalus in Crete", "Sibylla", "Christ in Rome" and others. All these poetic tragedies contain some of the most powerful dramatic elements that can be found in Modern Greek literature.

To promote peace among the nations of the world, as well as brotherhood, he conceived the idea of founding a center at Delphi for the gathering of representatives from all countries to discuss ways of achieving this ideal goal. Also, together with his wife, Eve, he endeavored to revive ancient Greek drama to also be performed at Delphi. To achieve this noble and worthy goal, he organized in 1927 and in 1930, two very successful intellectual and artistic festivals. In the 1927 festival, he directed Aeschylus' "Prometheus Bound" in Modern Greek translation, and in the 1930 festival, he directed Euripides' "Suppliants" also in Modern Greek translation.

Stratis Myrivilis (1892-1969) is Greece's first modern war novelist. Myrivilis' first war novel, entitled "Life in a Tomb", was published in 1923 a year after the retreat of the Greek armies and of the Greek population from Turkey. His work consisted of war impressions which Sergeant Kostulas sent in the form of letters to his wife from the front. The book was first printed in daily installments in the newspaper "Campana" which was owned by the author. As the newspaper circulated only on the island of Mytilene, the publication did not have much success. Thereupon, the author reworked it and published it in Athens, where it was received with enthusiasm. People were accustomed to war novels. But up to now, all available war novels were translations of originals written by foreign authors. Now, the Greek people had a war book for the first time, written by a Greek author, describing a Greek war, and experiences which Greek soldiers confront.

John Ritsos (1909-1990) was another famous 20th century poet. A sickly man, frequently suffering from tuberculosis, Ritsos nevertheless wrote worthy poems. In his early twenties, he also began to study Marx, and by the age of twenty-seven, he had become a confirmed communist. At the age of twenty-seven, he wrote his first very fine poem entitled "Epitaphios". It is a denunciation of the police of Thessaloniki, who had killed twelve tobacco workers during a strike. What followed the above poem was "The Song of my Sister", which he wrote when his sister was committed to a sanatorium. Two equally great poems that saw publication in the late forties were "Romiosyne" (Greekness) and the "Moonlight Sonata", the latter written after his return to Greece, after having visited the Soviet Union. It also brought him the State Prize in poetry. In the early sixties, his "Epitaphios" and his "Romiosyne" were put to music by Mikis Theodorakis. This brought additional fame to Ritsos.

When a military junta took over the government in 1967, Ritsos was exiled to many islands. The protests staged by many literati around the world, however, caused the government to reconsider and set him free. He returned to Athens and continued to write poetry until his death. In all, he composed thirty-eight poems and collections of poems that made him a most prolific poet. He received many honors in Greece and abroad including two Nobel Prize nominations.

Towering above any other 20th century Greek poet and novelist was Nikos (Nicholas) Kazantzakis (1897-1957) whose achievements in both those genres remained unequalled. He studied at the University of Athens and then went to Paris to study philosophy under Henri Bergson, who introduced him to the philosophy of Friedrich Nietzsche. He also went to Vienna to study Buddhism, and from there, he traveled to Russia to determine how Lenin's communism faired so that he could introduce it to Greece. Disillusioned, he returned to Greece to begin writing his own works.

In 1938, he published his first narrative poem entitled "Odyssey", consisting of 33,333 seventeen syllable lines. He meant it to be a sequel of Homer's that had the same title. Briefly, Odysseus returns to his native Ithaca and is reunited with his wife and his people. What follows his return is a constant struggle to achieve the author's ideal, namely action that aims at a worthy objective, a worthy purpose. If this superb work had been translated into English and published a year before the author's death, the author would definitely have received the Nobel Prize.

"Zorba", published in 1946 and made widely-known through the motion picture "Zorba the Greek", was another outstanding publication. Unlike Homer's hero - Odysseus, who was wandering on the ocean and to many countries, Zorba, firmly entrenched in his home island of Crete, is wandering about theories and ideas.

In his "Kapetan Mihalis" (Captain Michael), the author recounts a war episode he had experienced during his childhood. It is an episode relating to the war between the Cretans and the Turks in 1889 when the struggle was reaching a peak. Besides extolling the patriotism of his fellow Cretans, the author correctly discerns that behind the clash of the Greeks and the Turks, one could see the antagonism of the Islamic Religion against the Christian.

Finally, in his last great novel, "The Last Temptation of Christ", the author juxtaposes the image of Christ, an image he presents as heroic, admirable and inspiring, with his humanity, a humanity presented as weak, not perfect, and recognizing his Divinity very slowly. As a result of having presented such an unorthodox picture of Christ, the Greek Orthodox Church excommunicated him while the film bearing the same title was widely boycotted.

Kazantzakis wrote many other novels as well as detailed descriptions of his many travels to various Countries. Translations of his novels into English and in more than forty other languages made him the best known Greek author in the English-speaking world and one of the greatest of the 20th century.

When the distinguished author died, Albert Camus best expressed Kazantzakis' prominence when informed of his death. He said: "With him, one of our last great artists vanished. I am one of those who feel and will go on feeling the void that he has left." In such a manner did one of his peers express sorrow of Kazantzakis' death as well as dramatize his genius.

Other 20th century notable poets and novelists are: Nicholas Engonopoulos, a poet as well as an accomplished painter; Nikeforos Vrettakos, composer of lyrical poems which earned him a State Prize; Kostas Varnalis, who was awarded the Lenin Peace Prize in 1958; Pantelis Prevelakis, poet and novelist; John Panayotopoulos, poet and novelist earning a State Prize for his novels, and many others who now carry on the long march of Greek Literature into the 21st century.

Nikos Kazantzakis

60
TWO NOBEL PRIZE WINNERS

During the twentieth century, two Greek poets were among those who received the most prestigious award the world over – the Nobel Prize. The two poets were George Seferis and Odysseus Elytis.

George Seferis was born in 1900 in Smyrna (a city and port in Western Turkey). His family moved to Athens in 1914 where his father became a professor of International Law at the University of Athens. When Seferis finished high school, he enrolled at the Law School of the University of Athens and then continued his studies in Paris, France.

Although Seferis moved to Athens, he never forgot his native city of Smyrna, which he continued to consider as his home. In fact, in 1922, when he learned that Smyrna had been burned down by the Turks as a result of a war between Greece and Turkey and that its large Greek community had been displaced, Seferis never stopped to regard this event as a personal loss – a loss that later contributed to the tragic sense of life that dominated his poetry.

Upon completing his studies in Paris in 1924, he went to London to perfect his English as he was aspiring to enter the Greek Diplomatic Service. At this time, he also met two famous English poets with whom he became close friends – T.S. Eliot and Ezra Pound. Their poetic style greatly influenced him.

During the Second World War, he was with the exiled Greek Government in the Middle East. When the war ended, he served in Greek embassies in the Middle East, the Balkans and in Europe, and in 1957 he was appointed Ambassador of Greece to London. During all this time, besides performing his diplomatic duties, he also wrote whole collections of poems.

Eventually, the high quality of his poetic compositions came to the attention of the Swedish Literary Academy, and, in 1963, he was honored with the Nobel Prize – the first Greek man of Letters to receive this highest international recognition. Subsequently, he received honorary doctorates from the University of Oxford, Cambridge, Princeton, and Thessalonica, and, in 1966, he was elected an honorary member of the American Academy of Arts and Sciences.

Seferis' diplomatic career, that forced him to frequently change countries, made him feel like another modern Odysseus – a man who felt a constant alienation and loss, continuously traveling from one place to another as though he was looking for a "Place in the Sun" or a "Paradise Lost".

Despite the above, Seferis did not look at life with total pessimism. He was a realist and so he saw life full of episodes that do cause bitterness and disgust. But these episodes did not convince him that man couldn't find meaning and happiness in life.

In 1971 and at the age of seventy-one, George Seferis died. Summing up his literary achievement, a critic in the "Times Literary Supplement" wrote: "More than any other of his contemporaries or successors, Seferis has extended the frontier of Greek literature and created for it a poetry which is attuned to the poetic idiom of the contemporary western world. He has introduced new harmonies and discords into poetic diction and utilized the use of figurative language, and in doing all this he has employed the demotic tongue and vindicated his lifelong conviction that the poetry of his country can and must be written in the language of everyday speech."

When Seferis died, the same journal spoke of him as "the greatest poet of his generation in Europe...If there were never any other children of Homer, and Seferis were the last, it would not be a bad ending."

The other famous Greek poet who like George Seferis, also received the Nobel Prize, was Odysseus Elytis.

Elytis was born on November 2, 1911 in the town and port of Heraclion located in the middle of the beautiful Island of Crete. Describing his childhood in one of his writings he wrote,

"My family came originally from the Island of Lesbos (commonly called Mytilene), but I was born in Heraclion, Crete, where my father, a soap manufacturer, had set up his first factory. Later on, however, we moved to Athens, where I was brought up, went to high school, and, finally, studied law at the University of Athens. Nevertheless, I always spent my summer vacations on the Islands of Hydra, Spetsai, Tinos, Myconos, or Mytilene – and this was later to have a deep influence on my work as a poet. When my interest in poetry was first awakened at the age of seventeen, I found myself in possession of a fund of experience acquired from my life on the islands; my imagination had developed among the rocks and the small island boats – among the rectangular, whitewashed houses, and the windmills. The Aegean had indelibly stamped my consciousness."

In the 1930s, Elytis began to write poetry and he composed some sixteen collections in all – a most worthy and admirable output. Let us briefly consider three of them beginning with the collection entitled "The Aegean Sea".

The "Aegean Sea" was published in 1933. The beautiful impressions he had acquired in his mind while spending his summer months in the sun-drenched islands of the Aegean became the very essence of his poems. The blue Aegean Sea, drenched continuously by the golden beams of the every-bright Greek sun, and the ceaseless playful reflection of the latter like sparkling diamonds on the waves, is masterfully portrayed in the verses. Actually, his poem is an allegory of love, of a love felt by a young man bedazzled by beauty.

Elytis continued to write more poems. But when the Second World War broke out, and, in October of 1940 Italy attacked Greece, Elytis was drafted into the Greek Army to fight as a second lieutenant. He fought for six consecutive months on the Greek-Albanian border exposing him to the dangers of continuing enemy fire. When the war ended, he had endured for three and-a-half years the hardships of his country's occupation by the Nazis and the Fascists.

The horrors of battle and of the occupation gave Elytis a new experience – an experience that would somehow change his outlook on human life, and this new outlook would cause him to write poems with a different perspective.

His war experiences would inspire him to write a long elegy entitled: "A Heroic and Mournful Ballad for the Lost Lieutenant in Albania". It is one of his most lyrical poems, and, like all his poems, an allegory about the struggles against evil, and the heroic resistance the Greek people offered when occupied by the Nazi and the Fascist forces.

Following the liberation of Greece in October 1944, Elytis went to live in Paris and spent four years there studying at the Sorbonne University, forming permanent friendships with many leading poets and painters. From there he traveled to other countries – Italy, Spain, Switzerland, and England – and later on as a guest of their respective governments, he visited the United States and Russia. On his return to Greece, he worked as a director of the Broadcasting Section of Athens Radio and an advisor to the National Theatre.

In 1958, Elytis would publish his finest and most lyrical poem entitled "To Axion Esti". It is a long poem with interjected prose sections and it took him fourteen years to write it. It is divided into three units. The first unit is called "Genesis", the second "Passion" and the third "Glory".

In the "Genesis" unit, the poet identifies his destiny with the destinies of his people. In the second unit which is the most expanded, the poet views the suffering his people underwent throughout the centuries of Greece's long history, and ends with the sufferings they endured during the Axis occupation. The "Glory" is an optimistic vision for a better future for Greece and for all mankind.

The above poem earned Elytis the "National Prize in Poetry" the highest honor in literature his country could offer. A few years later, the poem was set to music by the well-known Greek composer Mikis Theodorakis.

Finally, "The Crazy Ship", is another masterful allegorical poem. The poem is divided into two units, each consisting of four parts. Greece is represented by a ship that journeys through the centuries in rough waters and future storms - the latter representing its turbulent history.

In the first part, the ship (Greece) sails proudly counting on the unexcelled achievements of its ancient civilization. But the commanders of the ship, (the rulers of Greece), are not all worthy thus making the ship go at times forward (progress) and at times backward (regression).

In the second part, Greece is shown in a position between the Eastern and the Western world always choosing from the world that would contribute to its progress.

The third part describes the nature of the Greek soul, its ups and downs, in the long history of the Greek people.

The fourth part uses two crewmen of the ship – an innocent boatswain and a deceiving sailor – to represent the virtuous and evil people who throughout history try to prevail.

In all four parts of the second unit, the poet is no longer an outside observer of the unfolding events, but he is in the ship with his people sharing with them the calms and the tempests, that is, the good years of Greece's history in the 20th century and the bad ones, such as those that were marred by wars, civil wars, foreign occupation, or those during which the country was ruled by dictatorial governments.

Yet despite this unstable history, the poet happily affirms that Greece managed to survive and that its future would be one of progress and success.

In 1979, Odysseus Elytis received the much-coveted Nobel Prize in Literature. His high reputation is now internationally recognized. He died in 1996.

61
THE MONARCH OF CONDUCTORS

His name was Herbert von Karajan and he was the most famous conductor of the twentieth century. He was a conductor whose great accomplishments in the art of music performance have become legend.

This most famous conductor was of Greek and Austrian ancestry. His great-grandfather, George John Karajannis, was a Greek immigrant who came to Austria from the town of Kozani, Greece in 1760. He was only seventeen years old when he came to Vienna seeking a prosperous future.

Not long after he arrived in Vienna, young George was hired to work in a fabric store. He tried to learn the German Language as best as he could as well as the many aspects of trading. In ten years, he had saved enough money to start his own business as a cotton importer. At that time, Austria was importing great amounts of cotton from abroad and his cotton import business became very successful. Karajannis now had enough capital to begin his own spinning industry. Having made this decision, he moved to the town of Shemnich, about fifty miles southwest of Vienna and founded his own spinning industry. Again, having become very successful in the output and sale of his product, he was able to acquire two more factories. Thus, thanks to his vigilance and wise direction of his industry, Karajannis in three decades, had become one of the leading figures of his trade in Austria. Recognizing his tremendous success, the Austrian government awarded him the much coveted title of Von.

Herbert von Karajan

In 1800 and at the age of fifty-seven, he settled permanently in Vienna. By now, his seven children - three sons and four daughters had grown. The oldest son assumed leadership of the business, the second became a colonel in the Austrian army, and the third, Theodore, who was the grandfather of Herbert von Karajan, became a professor of German literature at the University of Vienna and assistant curator of the National Library of Vienna.

Theodore had four children - two daughters and two sons. The younger son - Ernst, became a surgeon, and after his marriage he settled in the historic and romantic city of Salsburg, the birthplace of Austria's most famous composer - Amadeus Mozart. Ernst Karajan, owing to his excellent surgical skills, soon became the chief surgeon in Salsburg. Of his marriage to Martha Cosmac, two sons were born to them - Michael and Herbert. The latter was born on April 5, 1908.

When only three years old, Herbert began taking piano lessons. His progress was so rapid, that at the age of five he was able to present his first public piano recital. To that point only Mozart had achieved such a feat. While Herbert attended elementary and high school, his father, following the advice of the child's first piano teacher, hired Bernhard Paumgartner. He was the director of the famous "Mozarteum Conservatory of Salsburg". Soon the expert teacher diagnosed correctly his very young student's future, real musical interest - conducting. Years later, and, to be more exact, in 1923, when Herbert saw the famous conductor Arturo Toscanini conduct the orchestra at the Salsburg Music Festival, the young adolescent spectator made up his mind to become a conductor.

Following his graduation from high school, Herbert enrolled at the Academy for Music and the Performing Arts in Vienna in order to specialize in the study of conducting under Klemens Krauss. Simultaneously, he took courses in philosophy and music at the University of Vienna.

December 17, 1928 was for Herbert a milestone in his life. On that day, he made his conducting debut with a student orchestra for the Academy of Music and the Performing Arts. A month later, while still a student, upon hearing that the Opera House of the German city of Ulm needed a new conductor as its present one was ailing, Herbert immediately seized the opportunity. After raising the necessary funds needed for such an undertaking from relatives and friends, he hired Mozarteum Conservatory's Orchestra and arranged to conduct this orchestra in Salsburg on January 23, 1829. Prior to that date, he sent out invitations to many people and made sure that the director of the Ulm Opera House would definitely receive one. He marvelously succeeded in this effort, as the most desired guest did attend and was very impressed by young Herbert's conducting. As a result of his success, Herbert was asked to come to Ulm. There, on March 2, 1929 he conducted a superb performance of Mozart's opera "La Nozze di Figaro"

(The Marriage of Figaro), a performance that insured his retention as a conductor.

Ulm's opera house was a typical provincial small one. The number of orchestra members and those of its chorus were small. Any other conductor would have been discouraged with such a limited number of staff. But not Karajan! He accepted the situation as a challenge and did the best with what he had available. With a tireless energy he sought to improve orchestra and chorus - forcing them to bring out the best they could. Moreover, by attacking this problem in this way, he himself gained tremendous experience, an experience that would eventually make him famous.

Improving significantly the opera house's orchestra and chorus were not his only objectives. He also supervised the staging and lighting. He would also go to his native city to assist Richard Strauss and Arturo Toscanini, and he would even go as far as Milan, Italy to watch Toscanini direct, and thus learn from him what he considered to be a priority in directing an orchestra - directional control.

As he gained experience and progressed, his fame also increased, and, in 1934, he was hired to present a concert by conducting a major symphony orchestra - the famous Vienna Philharmonic.

The young conductor's next post was at Aachen, Germany. Here he was able to achieve something that no other conductor had ever accomplished - conducting forty different symphonic programs annually. By now, he had become so firmly established as a first rate conductor that offers and invitations arrived from many cities and countries.

In 1937 he guest-conducted Wagner's opera "Tristan and Isolde" at the Vienna State Opera and at the Berlin State Opera. Commenting on his conducting, an opera analyst wrote: "The sensation he created in Berlin marked the beginning of his celebrity. With his handsome appearance, his dash and elegance, and his reputation for always getting what he wanted he would ultimately become a 'kulturidol' (culture idol)."

From this time on and despite the hard and difficult years created by the Second World War and the years that followed thereafter, Herbert von Karajan's reputation as a top and much sought after conductor would never wane. To mention briefly the fine orchestras he conducted - they include those of the Berlin State Opera, the Berlin Philharmonic, the Milan La Scala Opera's Orchestra, London's Philharmonia Orchestra, the Edinburgh Festival's Orchestra, the Salsburg Festival's orchestra, the New York Philharmonic, the Athens Symphony Orchestra, which he directed at the annual summer festival many times in the decades of the sixties and seventies, and the Bayreuth Festival orchestra.

He made a tour of the Soviet Union with the La Scala orchestra, a tour of the United States with the Berlin Philharmonic, and a tour of many capitals around the world with the Vienna Philharmonic. His last tour in the United States with the Berlin Philharmonic took place in 1985.

Over the years, a large number of his symphonic and operatic performances have been recorded on records, on video tapes, videodiscs, CD's, and on regular cinematic film. Karajan even founded his film company in 1980 called "Telemondial" based in Monaco. Its purpose was to film the Salsburg Easter Festival Concerts which he conceived and founded as well as many other concert and operatic performances in order for them to be preserved and seen in posterity. Throughout his career, he made more than 800 recordings that sold more than 100 million copies.

Regarding the physical appearance and other facts of the personal life of the magnificent conductor, these could be summarized as follows. He was five feet six inches tall, of slight build and had blue eyes. Besides German, his native language, he also spoke French, English and Italian. His annual income exceeded $2 million. Being exceedingly affluent, he owned houses in St. Moritz, Switzerland and Buchenhof, Austria and others in France and Austria. He also owned a large yacht, a racing car and an airplane. He loved nature and sports, and in his younger days, he enjoyed skiing and mountaineering. Throughout his long career, he loved his work and was not very eager to attend social functions. For his masterful performances in his native country, he received countless honors and numerous high awards. Included in these are the Gold Medal of the Royal Philharmonic Society, the Order of the White Rose and Finland's Commander, First Class.

During most of his career he was considered by most to be the "Generalmusikdirektor" of Europe. In all his performances, he demanded that players strive for precision, clarity of tone and perfection. Last, but not least, when one listened to the Berlin Philharmonic directed by him, one could not help but feel the overwhelming power of his orchestra's sound.

62
DYNAPOLIS

The continuous growth of the earth's population has had as a concomitant the growth of many cities and towns. Cities, which during the first quarter of the nineteenth century had a population of fifty or more hundred thousand, by the end of the twentieth century, had a population approaching a million. Even cities, that for centuries if not millennia had remained "static" in the number of their inhabitants, since the middle of the nineteenth century, had a phenomenal population growth. Athens, Greece is a case in point.

The growth of heavy industry as well as many kinds of light industry, which usually are located in average and large cities, is one significant factor that contributes to a city's growth in population and area. Job opportunities in factories and related facilities are far more available in cities than in small towns. Besides, cities offer more attractions to an individual that has a family, or plans to have one. Cities have better schools of primary and secondary education, colleges and universities of higher education. A large variety of companies are either based or have branches, thus offering many office job opportunities for a small business enterprise, all kinds of professions, better hospitals, and lastly, a variety of entertainment.

Although cities that were founded in the last three centuries followed a plan, and in the United States mostly a grid plan, in most of them the main administrative, shopping and other civic and professional facilities remained at their core, causing traffic congestion and other problems.

The daily movement of thousands of people from the suburban residential areas to the cores of the big cities and back again, has been more dramatic in cities whose pattern was radial. In such a radically expanded city, where the main avenues converge toward the center, highly enervating traffic jams were daily occurrences. And, although in large cities mass transportation, whether underground or surface, carries a very large number of the city's population to and from work, traffic jams still hinder easy movement of people.

Constantine Doxiades, a twentieth century Greek city planner, devoted most of his life to improving or eliminating the above mentioned urban problems. He labored to conceive an urban pattern in that these problems would either be eliminated or reduced to a minimum.

Doxiades was born in the late 1920s in a small town of Greece. He was a graduate of the National Polytechnic of Athens, and, after furthering his studies in the Berlin Polytechnic of Germany, from which he had graduated with honors, he returned to Athens to establish his architectural firm.

During his long and very successful career, Doxiades succeeded not only in becoming a highly respected city planner in his own country, but in many foreign countries as well. He was asked to draw plans for the expansion of many cities in the United States, including Washington D.C., Detroit and Chicago. He did the same for cities in Spain, Brazil, Syria, Iraq, Iran, and India. He also earned distinction for solving the housing problems of other cities around the world.

The crowning achievement of his life, however, was the fulfillment of a request that involved the designing of a new capital for the nation of Pakistan.

The ever-ambitious architect, capitalizing on his experience of having seen the problems that already existing cities have experienced as they expanded with the passing of time, was determined to design a capital that would facilitate future expansion and would not experience the problems of older cities.

What was the shape of the city that his resourceful mind conceived? It was neither circular nor square, but rectangular. Its square blocks would form a grid, thus causing the streets and avenues to crisscross. The rectangular city would have, in the middle, the main avenue that would extend from the one narrow end of the rectangle to the other. On this main wide avenue, that would be the main thoroughfare of the capital, the government and other administrative buildings, the main shopping outlets, and some of the small industries would be placed. Easy access to this main and most vital artery of the capital would be made possible by way of the many smaller avenues that intersected the main thoroughfare at right angles. Other wide avenues would also run parallel to the main thoroughfare of the capital. Professional offices, small businesses and stores would be located on these avenues and other streets. Heavy industries would be placed outside the residential blocks that would lie on both sides of the main artery. There would be parks in many spots of the city in order to provide outdoor restful places, and whose green trees would remind one of the countryside.

Future expansion of the city, due to the growth of its population, would be limited to the one narrow end of the rectangle, extending the grid of the city to the predetermined new boundary. Thus, the city would continue growing uniformly in one direction, never causing any problems to the already existing one. There would be easy access to any point of the city, and traffic would move undisturbed.

His plan was accepted, and soon, Islamabad, as the new capital of Pakistan was named, began to rise.

Doxiades had reached the peak of his professional career. His "Dynapolis", as he called his rectangular design, that was to grow only in one direction without causing any problems, rendered the city a dynamic and well-functioning organism – a concept that represents a stepping-stone in the march of architecture.

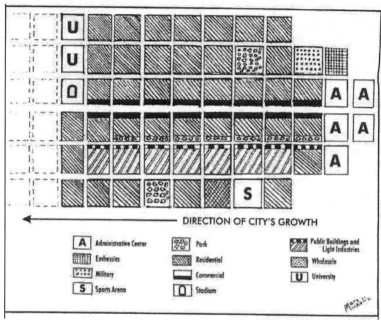

Doxiades' Concept of Dynapolis

63
A MOST CELEBRATED DIVA

She was the world's most celebrated diva for almost a decade and one of the three most famous divas of the twentieth century thrilling opera audiences with her superb soprano voice in both the old and the new worlds. There were two other fields for which she had the potential to equally excel had she chosen to do so. She could have been a motion picture actress of the highest repute, or a stage actress of the highest caliber, either in dramatic or comic roles, capable of winning the highest awards in both fields.

Maria Cecillia Sophia Anna Kalogeropoulou, better known to the world as Maria Callas, was born of Greek immigrant parents in New York City on December 21, 1923. She spent the first fourteen years of her life in her native city attending school, and while only eleven years old, won a medal in a children's voice contest. This was the first indication of what was to come later in her life.

In 1937, her mother, together with her two daughters, returned to Greece. They settled in Athens where Maria was encouraged by her mother to enroll at the National "Odeum (conservatory) of Athens". She studied voice under the soprano Elvira de Hidalgo and showed great enthusiasm for all other curricula. At the age of fifteen, she appeared in Pietro Mascagni's "Cavalleria Rusticana" (Rustic Chivalry) in the role of Santuzza, giving with her superb singing, the first hints of a future brilliant soprano career.

During the Second World War, Maria Callas continued her musical studies and made periodic appearances in soprano roles. On July 4, 1941, she made her debut at the Athens Opera in Puccini's "Tosca" in the soprano role of Florida Tosca. She scored a memorable success.

When the Second World War ended, Callas decided to return to the United States. Upon arriving in New York, she sought interviews at the Metropolitan Opera Company and other minor companies. She was not successful. But when she was interviewed by the famous tenor Givanni Zenatello, he engaged her for Ponchielli's opera "La Gioconda" in the soprano role of La Gioconda. The opera was staged in Verona, Italy and so Maria Callas traveled to that country. Her very successful appearance at this opera, whose premiere was held on August 2, 1947, was definitely the start of her real career and from that point she was in demand by many Italian Opera Houses for very serious roles such as Aida's, Turandot's, Isolde's and many others. Thus, in a short time, Callas had achieved a rare accomplishment. She had become one of the top operatic singers in the country where opera had originated. It was an admirable feat.

An appearance that showed Callas' rare versatility was her decision to replace an ailing colleague to sing in bel canto role of Bellini's "I Puritani", when only three days before, she was singing in the role of

Brunnhilde in Wagner's opera "Die Gotterdamerung". It was a feat only a handful of divas had achieved in the history of Wagnerian operatic singing.

At the suggestion of her guide, Tulio Seraphin, Callas began to abandon the "heavy roles" she had been singing, and began concentrating on lighter Italian and non-Italian operas. Her success thereafter was truly legendary. She would sing the leading roles of at least a dozen different Italian operas, some of which had not been performed for decades, plus non-Italian operas such as Gluck's "Alceste" and "Iphigenie en Tauride", Haydn's "Orfeo and Euridice" and several others. Italian operas that were resuscitated were Cherubini's "Medee", Rossini's "Armida" and "Il Turko in Italia", Spontini's "La Vestale", Donizetti's "Anna Bolena" and "Lucia di Lammermoor".

In 1949, she married the Milanese entrepreneur Giovanni Meneghini who truly loved her and was devoted to her. He had many connections with the trustees of the La Scala Opera House – the world's most famous opera house. And so, on April 12, 1950, Maria Callas appeared in the role of "Aida" – Giuseppe Verdi's most popular and best-known opera. This appearance by Maria was another memorable stepping stone in her life. As usual, she continued to make regular appearances in different

Maria Callas

opera houses of London, Chicago and New York.

It was in the decade of the 50s that Maria Meneghini Callas, as she was now professionally known, had reached the pinnacle of her career. She had become known the world over for exceptional voice, the effortless way in which she sang, the marvelous vocal inflections she was able to effect, and the wonderful control of her voice. At this stage of her life, there was none in the operatic world to match her unique talents. She was the most outstanding diva.

Fate had it that she would meet the Greek magnate Aristotle Onassis. She fell in love with him and hoping to marry him, divorced her husband who throughout their married life adored her. She never understood, however, that Onassis neither loved her nor wished to marry her. Actually, it was her fame that made Onassis seek her company. In fact, when he later met Jacqueline Kennedy – widow of the late president John F. Kennedy, Onassis' interest in the famous diva ceased.

The marriage of Aristotle Onassis to Jacqueline Kennedy shattered the diva. She even contemplated suicide. But she managed to recover, and renewed operatic appearances in England, Germany, and Japan in 1974. She was accompanied by former colleague Giuseppe di Stefano. But in all these appearances, she was no longer the diva of the fifties. The effectiveness of her talents that made her past performances universally admired had now somewhat diminished, thereby robbing them of the high quality that always characterized them.

In despair, she decided to spend the remainder of her life in an exclusive apartment in Paris. There, she frequently listened to recordings of her operas dreaming that she might resume appearances in the future.

On September 16, 1977, she suffered a heart attack and died. Summing up Maria Callas' career, a musical analyst wrote: "Of Callas' artistic pre-eminence there can be no doubt. Among her contemporaries, she had the deepest comprehension of the classical Italian Style, the most musical instincts and the most intelligent approach, together with exceptional dramatic powers. Her first appearance on a stage aroused immediate excitement, and while she remained there she riveted the attention of the house. There was authority in all that she did, and in every phrase that she uttered. Her voice, especially during the early 1950's, was in itself an impressive instrument, with its penetrating individual quality, its rich variety of color, and its great agility in florid music."

64

THE CAPSTONE OF FRANCE'S EDUCATIONAL PYRAMID

When a person is born into a rich family, grows and matures, takes over his father's prosperous business and manages to steer it successfully, we say of him: "He does well."

When a person is born into a well-to-do family, and, having grown up, able to start a business or pursue some professional career thanks to his father's financing his business venture or his studies, again we say: "Good for him."

However, when a person is born to a very, if not an extremely poor family, and, when he or she grows up reaches the pinnacle of the academic structure, the academic edifice of a foreign country, that person's achievement deserves our utmost admiration, for he or she has achieved against all odds a rare, most commendable success.

It is about the rare academic success of a person that belonged to the third category this chapter deals with.

Back in August 28, 1926, there was born to the very poor family of Nicholas and Calliroe Glykatzi who lived in a poor suburb of Athens, a baby girl who they named Helen. She was not their first child but their sixth.

Although the parents rejoiced in the birth of Helen, actually, they were not that happy because they knew that the addition of the new child would cause further financial strain to their family. Little did poor Nicholas and Calliroe know how immensely God had blessed them; God had enriched them with the addition of that little baby girl. It would take years for them to find out. Presently, it was impossible to think what wondrous surprises, and what honor and fame little Helen – their sixth child – would bring to them, and even to her native country.

Like all other boys and girls of her country, little Helen, at the age of six started attending school. She would walk daily, in the morning, to her suburban grammar school, and, early in the afternoon, she would walk back home. Right from the start Helen loved school and after returning home she always did her homework alone. She easily absorbed everything the teachers taught, a fact it did not take the latter long to notice. Even in those early days little Helen had made the teachers aware that she was very gifted. All through grammar school and later high school she managed to be tops in her class thus proving to her teachers and her parents that a potentially brilliant academic career lay ahead.

She graduated from high school in 1944 and decided to enroll at the University of Athens where she would major in Byzantine (Medieval Greek) History and Civilization. Again, she was a top student all through the years of study graduating with top honors and with a "PhD", the most advanced degree possible.

Possessing such a degree many a graduate would be content to end all studies at this level and eventually become a professor in any of the higher institutions of learning in Greece. But, not Helen! She was determined to continue her studies doing post-graduate work in France.

With scholarships granted to her, she was off to Paris. She first attended the University of Paris and then began working as a member of the Committee on Science Ethics. She worked in this committee for twelve years eventually becoming its head for three years. Then, another coveted post was offered her. She became a professor at the University of Sorbonne, which is part of the University of Paris, and then, president of the same university for the period of 1976-1981

Helen who by now was known as Helene Ahrweiler (pronounce Arveler) due to her marriage to Jaques Ahrweiler in 1958, had indeed traveled a very long way, longer than any other fellow Greek intellectual in the 20th century. She had managed to become the president of the most prestigious university of France and one of the most prestigious in the world, a feat she achieved only twenty-one years after her arrival in France. Moreover, she was the first non-French academic to hold such a most distinguished position. Then, from 1982-1989 she was the chancellor of the same Institution, while at the same time, and to be more exact from 1980-1990, she was the Secretary of the International Committee of the Historical Sciences.

More top academic positions were offered to her – positions she did not hesitate to take, like Vice-President of the George Pompidou Centre from 1975-1989, Head of the National Education of France from 1983-1989, President of the University of Europe, located in Paris, and President of the Committee for Science Ethics.

Her astonishing, meteoric career encouraged the academies of certain nations to include her as a member. And so, she became a member of the Greek, British, Belgian, German, and Bulgarian academies. Moreover, the following universities conferred on her honorary doctorates. They were the Universities of Harvard and of New York (U.S.A.), London (England), Belgrade (Serbia), New Brunswick (Canada), Lima (Peru), Athens' Social Science University, and the American University of Paris.

Very few academics have been so honored as was this lady from Athens, Greece. Her fame had spread far and wide. By now, she was famous not only in her native Greece, but in France – a foreign country where she went as a young girl to do post-graduate work, and eventually, thanks to her perseverance, rose to the highest rung of the academic ladder of her adopted country. She now enjoyed very high esteem from her French peers as well as from those of many other countries. She had achieved the near impossible.

Despite her extremely busy schedule, being a member and president of so many academic institutions and committees, Helen managed to find time to write five books all of which relate to Byzantine History and Civilization – her original specialty. Her books bear the following titles: "Byzantium and the Sea", "Studies on the Social Structures of Byzantium", "The Political Ideology of the Byzantine Empire", The Regions and the Territories of Byzantium", and the "Geographica".

Every summer, Helen, with her family, husband and daughter, visited Greece. Helen, being President of the European Cultural Center of Delphi, would miss no opportunity to use its intellectual symposiums as means of projecting the significance of Greek Civilization.

Throughout her long and extremely successful academic career, Helen Ahrweiler never stopped loving her native country – Greece. She has always supported the rights of her native country whenever she saw that those were either overlooked or not recognized. Toward this end, she also used the tremendous reservoir, the awesome depository of her knowledge of Greek History and of Greece's role of being the Mother of Western Civilization, to defend this role whenever it was questioned. And, in doing this, she didn't do it with loud emotional patriotic exclamations, but with quiet, soft arguments based on unshakable historical facts of which she is an inexhaustible fountain.

What a meteoric, astonishing ascent Helen has achieved from obscure and poor beginnings to dazzling academic limelight, an honor to France and to her Native Country.

65

A DASTARDLY PROVOCATION
AND A HUMILIATING DEFEAT

An event remembered by elderly Americans and well known by young Americans is the dastardly attack on Pearl Harbor by the Japanese on December 7, 1941. On that "Day of infamy", as President Roosevelt called it in his special address to the Congress, carrier-based Japanese bombers suddenly attacked the American Naval Base in Hawaii in the early morning hours. As a result, many warships of the American Pacific Fleet were sunk, or were heavily and irreparably damaged, naval installations were severely hit, and many United States servicemen were killed or severely wounded. The attack, moreover, was made without Japan formally declaring war against the United States.

A similar smaller scale dastardly and provocative act of war took place on the Greek Island of Tenos on August 15, 1940. It involved the torpedoing and sinking of a Greek light cruiser by an unknown submarine.

At this time the Second World War was well on its way. Since September 1, 1939 when it had started, Germany had conquered Poland, Denmark, Norway, Holland, Belgium, and France. Now, she was ceaselessly bombing England, while the army was preparing for an invasion of that country – an invasion, however, that never materialized.

Allied to Germany was Italy, then governed by the fascist government of Benito Mussolini. Like his partner, Hitler, Mussolini too, craved for expansionist conquests. In 1938, he had conquered Albania, and now was preparing his armies in Libya – an Italian colony, to march against the British who occupied Egypt. The fascist dictator had one more great ambition, an ambition he had as yet kept secret. He craved to conquer one more country, and to provoke that country, he staged the following incident.

Every year on August 15, the Feast of the Assumption of the Virgin Mary, a great celebration, is held on the Greek Island of Tenos. Thousands of people come by ship to Tenos to venerate the miraculous icon of the Virgin, to attend the impressive Divine Liturgy celebrated by many bishops and priests and to participate in the procession which winds through the main streets of the city. Those who were sick, lame, paralyzed, mute or suffered from like diseases also came to Tenos fervently hoping that God's healing Grace might heal them through the icon.

The celebration of August 15, 1940 was not to be any different from those of the previous years. From the day before, pilgrims kept arriving in large numbers from various parts of the country, eager to witness the solemn celebrations.

Shortly after sunrise, the Greek Navy's light cruiser "Elli" arrived in the harbor and dropped anchor some five hundred yards from the quay. A warship's visit to the island on this date was an annual event. Its crew would participate in the litany of the miraculous icon through the streets while the ship would fire the customary gun salute.

At about 8 A.M. an airplane flew over the town. Although its markings were not clear, the people thinking it to be of the Greek Air Force cheered and waved. The plane made a circle over the town and later disappeared over the horizon.

By this time also, a group of Elli's crew that was to participate in the litany of the icon was boarding one of the cruiser's motorboats to go to the quay. Minutes later, a second group was assembling on deck to board the next boat and become part of the on-shore celebrations.

Suddenly and most unexpectedly at 8:30 A.M., a tremendous explosion occurred in the middle of the ship shaking it violently. Smoke and flames were now coming from below as fragments of the ship's engines were also hurled up in the air. Fire was also burning on the side corridors of the ship's deck.

Some members of the crew who happened to be on the deck at the time of the explosion died instantly as they were severely hit by heavy iron fragments that were hurled from the engine room. Those who were alive instantly began to perform firefighting procedures to extinguish the fire, provided care to the wounded, and to get below to rescue the wounded engineers.

In the confusion, some began asking; "Was it really an explosion in the engine room, or had the ship been hit by a torpedo?" Minutes after the explosion, two additional explosions occurred in the quay and on the jetty of the harbor. People on the pier to observe the litany of the icon became casualties. One was killed and dozens of others were wounded.

Motorboats and all kinds of small craft rushed toward the burning ship in order to rescue the surviving wounded and those who were not wounded. By 9:45 AM, the ship capsized and began to sink.

Such an atrocious act, committed under the circumstances described above, forces one to ask the following questions:

Which civilized nation's government would authorize one of its submarines to carry out such a criminal act in time of peace?

Which Navy's regulations consider the torpedoing of harbor quays and jetties, and the killing and wounding of unarmed civilians during peacetime, a justifiable act?

Which Navy's regulations consider it a justifiable act to torpedo, during peacetime, an anchored warship that was there to accord honor during a religious holiday?

And, if the unknown submarine's captain did not intend that the two extra torpedoes that he fired hit the pier and the jetty, it is natural to ask: "Which navy's submarine commander would fire two torpedoes to hit an anchored, stationary warship? Evidently, he had no confidence in his expertise. If all three torpedoes were aimed at Elli, then the submarine's commander proved to the world that he was most unworthy, most incapable, most inept, and one of the least capable captains that was ever invested with such a task. Truly, an act without honor!

Although John Metaxas – the then Prime Minister of Greece, upon being informed, only minutes later of this criminal act immediately divined which nation's government had crafted such a hideous act, he wisely decided never to publicly incriminate that government. He had correctly sensed that if he had made such a disclosure, the guilty government would have denied it, and, in retaliation, it would have declared war. He was absolutely right for that's what Italy's dictator – Benitto Mussolini was hoping Metaxas would do. A public incrimination of Italy's government would be a most welcomed pretext for Italy to declare war on Greece. Thus, Metaxas, by remaining silent, escaped the trap his enemy had set. Moreover, he gained precious time to properly prepare for the forthcoming war with Italy.

Following the end of the Second World War, the Greek Admiralty sent divers to the bottom of the sea where Elli had sunk in order to find fragments of the torpedo that had hit the ship. On one of the many fragments that was brought up, was the name of the Italian factory that had manufactured the torpedo. Today, these fragments are exhibited in the Naval Museum of Greece, which is located in the Passalimani Harbor.

As for Benito Mussolini, seeing that his dirty scheme had not succeeded, and having lost all patience, he ordered the Italian ambassador in Athens to visit the premier of Greece John Metaxas at three o'clock in the morning of October 28th. He was to tell him that, if at six o'clock in the morning he did not allow the Italian Army to enter Greece and take it over in order to use it as a military, naval and airforce base in its war against England, there would be a war between the two countries.

Premier Metaxas ignored the Italian ambassador's threat and said to him: "No! I will not permit the Italian Army to enter my country. There will be war between us in which the Greek Army, the Greek Navy and the Greek Air Force will do their best to defend our country." On hearing such a reply that amounted to a flat "no", the Italian ambassador bid goodbye to the Greek premier and went to his embassy to telephone Mussolini to tell him the sad news.

When the Italian ambassador left the Greek Premier's home, Metaxas called the generals of the Greek Army and ordered them to let the Greek Army at the front know that at six in the morning, the Italian Army would march against Greece. Mussolini, on the other hand, furious and angry, ordered his generals to attack at six in the morning.

And so, on October 28th and at the early morning hour, the war between Greece and Italy began. Hundreds of Italian big guns began pounding continuously the Greek defenders while 135,000 Italian Soldiers with their rifles, machine guns and many tanks added more fire against the Greek defenders. Faced by such a large enemy army, the 35,000 Greek Army began to retreat from the borders. In fact, during the first ten days, the

Italian Army somehow managed to work its way into Greece for some 18-22 miles. But that was the farthest enemy penetration.

On the tenth day since the war began, as fresh Greek soldiers arrived at the front and not only were they able to stop the Italians, but now they were also able to make a counter attack. It was a turning point. From then on the Greek Army would be marching against the enemy. The Italians were overtaken by panic and began to pull back.

In one week, the Greek Army had pushed the enemy back to the border and by the third week of November, the Greek Army was making its way into Albania – an Italian occupied country from which Italy had attacked Greece. In fact, by the middle of February, 1941, one third of the country of Albania had been taken over by the Greek Army. Most large cities of Albania were now in Greek hands, along with warehouses full of Italian guns, rifles, machine guns, ammunition, and all kinds of weapons, food, and thirty-five thousand Italian prisoners.

The whole world was now admiring the small country of Greece whose small but very brave and strong army was defeating the enemy, and had won the first victory against the hitherto undefeated Axis.

Mussolini, who now was laughed at by all people, decided to try again. He gathered new armies, guns, tanks, and airplanes and on March 11th, 1941, made another attack. It was his last hope and effort to regain the prestige he had lost. In vain, his army could neither break through the Greek lines nor force the Greeks to pull back. By March 20th, seeing that even this effort had failed, in disgust and desperation he returned to Italy. Later, he asked Hitler, the leader of Germany and his ally, to make war against Greece and conquer it. And Hitler, who always wanted to take Greece, declared war against the small country on April 6, 1941. By the middle of May the country had been conquered.

Besides the Greek Army, which in that unforgettable war had fought bravely, the small Greek Air Force and the very small Greek Navy (consisting of only ten destroyers and six submarines) also caused destruction to the enemy. Greek submarines sank eighteen large transport ships carrying guns, ammunition and food from Italy to Albania while the small Greek Air Force continuously bombed the enemy at the front.

The only country that came to the help of Greece was England. England, which was at war against both Germany and Italy, sent a few squadrons of fighters and bombers to help the small Greek Air Force. The victorious battles were fought in snow-covered ravines and passes of mountains seven to eight thousand feet high. It was the victory of a small nation's armed forces against those of a large one. It was the first victory won by the Allies against the up to now undefeated Axis Powers – Germany, Italy and Japan.

66
OPERATION "MARITA"

By the end of March 1941, the Italian General Staff was convinced that the war against Greece had failed. Mussolini's dream of proudly standing by the Parthenon on the Acropolis of Athens at the end of November of 1940 with the Italian flag waving on the same eternal hill had by now dissolved. With his Spring counteroffensive ending in total disaster he had made himself, his armed forces and his country the laughing stock of the entire world. Moreover, for the first time the hitherto undefeated Axis had suffered a serious blow. Its reputation as being invincible – a reputation it had gained and held since September 1, 1939 due to Germany's spectacular victories over Poland, Denmark, Norway, Holland, Belgium, and France, had now received a most unexpected setback.

While the world laughed and Mussolini brooded, Hitler was now fuming. He could not endure his partner's failing him so miserably. So, before his next major operation, which was to be the attack on Russia, he decided to clean up his inept partner's mess. By April, he would attack both Greece and Yugoslavia and so, even these two, still free southeastern European Countries would come under the domination of the Axis.

With great speed, Hitler transferred, through Hungary, Romania and Bulgaria – countries that were partners with the Axis, whole divisions to the Yugoslavian and the Greek borders. As for the attack, that had been set for Sunday, April 6, 1941.

For the conquest of Yugoslavia and Greece, Germany had placed on the borders eighteen mechanized divisions consisting of two thousand tanks and armored vehicles, two thousand cannons and eight hundred bombers of various types.

On Sunday, April 6, at 5:30 A.M. Prince Erbach – ambassador of Germany to Greece visited the Greek Prime Minister, Alexander Koryzis, to inform him that at precisely this time the German divisions that had been placed along the Greek – Bulgarian border were attacking both Yugoslavia and Greece. The reason why Nazi Germany was attacking Greece, it was claimed, was because Greece had become a British military and air force base. Some fifty-five thousand British troops were in Greece at this time as well as many squadrons of bomber and fighter planes to aid the very small Greek Air Force in its defense against Italy.

Against such an awesome ultimatum, the Greek Prime Minister calmly answered: "My people will never allow the sacred land of their country to be taken by a foreign aggressor without defending it." And with this laconic answer, Greece was prepared to fight another enemy. Now, Greece was fighting against two big nations – the nations that made up the "Axis". Greece, a small nation of only eight and-a-half million, was fighting two nations totaling one hundred and thirty million people.

At 5:30 A.M. of April 6, General Maximilian Von List attacked with his troops at the Greek-Bulgarian border. His main target was the "Metaxas Fortification Line", consisting of twenty-one large forts, which commanded twenty-one strategic positions along the Greek-Bulgarian border, more specifically between the Axios and Nestos rivers. These almost impregnable forts had a complement of ten thousand soldiers and officers. They were armed with heavy cannon and machine guns whose continuous firing made passage or approach lethal.

For three continuous days and nights, the enemy kept relentlessly shelling and bombing the twenty-one forts using heavy batteries and "Stuka" diving planes. He also used specially trained commandos to approach the forts and destroy them with heavy explosives. All these attempts failed. The superbly built forts not only withstood the aerial and cannon bombardment, their firing took the lives of countless German soldiers.

Since the beginning of the Second World War, that is, during the past nineteen months, never before had the Nazi Army met such resistance. It was a defense the Nazis were facing for the first time. Neither in the Belgian Fort of Eben Emael nor in the French Maginot Line had they met such a fantastically unbelievable resistance.

In two days, the Yugoslavian defense line broke down allowing the German armored divisions to pour into Yugoslavia and then head south toward Greece, since the Greek-Yugoslavian border was not defended, they passed into Greece and soon they entered into the strategic city and Port of Thessalonica. The Greek Army now found itself encircled and cut-off from the rest of the country, without a port to get supplies to continue the defense, and its General concluded that any further resistance would be pointless.

Since the forts of the Metaxas Line were well stocked with ammunition and food, the resistance continued for days. And they continued it until most of their ammunition had been used.

And, when finally, German soldiers were able to penetrate the corridors of the forts, even there the Greek soldiers put up a gallant fight. In the end, when their last bullet had been fired, with faces dark from the smoke of the firing and of the flame throwers, the Germans had used in the corridors, and with tattered uniforms, one-by-one, those modern Greek heroes raised their hands and surrendered.

With admiration, the Germans accepted their surrender. In fact, they did something here, they had never done in earlier battles when they conquered the Belgian and the French forts. The German officer-in-charge lined up a platoon in front of the fort's entrance, and as the defenders came out; the platoon saluted the defenders with present arms. Moreover, they would not raise the German flag over the fort until the last Greek defender had come out – a courtesy they had not extended when they captured the Belgian and French forts.

Since northern Greece was now in the hands of the new invader in less than a week and with only a small part of the Greek Army able to fight, the main defense of the remaining Greek territory was taken up by the British Expeditionary Force. They were fifty-five thousand strong, well-equipped, and fully-mechanized with heavy cannons.

But the Germans were superior in many ways. They had complete mastery over the Greek air space enabling them to relentlessly bomb harbors, airports, railways, ships, bridges, supply lines, and military targets. They had a vast superiority in cannon and all types of arms and they had superior numbers of men thus making their thrust southward unstoppable.

In only two regions were the British able to resist the enemy for a few hours. They were the area of Platamon near the legendary Mt. Olympus, and in the narrow pass of Thermopylae, where almost two and-a-half thousand years before, three hundred Spartans had successfully resisted the vastly superior Persian Army when the latter was on its way to Athens.

On Sunday, April 26, 1941, the German Army entered Athens. No people were on the streets on that morning. The people of the capital had been ordered from the previous day to remain in their homes until the sirens would sound for them to go out to the streets. That occurred at 2:00 P.M.

Until the people left their homes, the only sign that indicated that the enemy was already in the capital was its flag, which was now waving on the Northeastern corner of the Hill of the Acropolis where the Greek flag always waved. There, the enemy's flag would wave for the next three and-a-half years.

The conquest of Greece did not end with the occupation of the capital. The enemy would have to fight for at least another week to make himself the master of southern mainland Greece known as "Peloponessos".

During their retreat, the British destroyed the strategic bridge of the Corinth Canal, hoping in this way to delay the Germans' southward advance. Their plan, however, proved to be fruitless as the efficient German engineers, in a few hours, had constructed a pontoon bridge over which their mechanized divisions passed without delay into the Peloponessos. Within a week they had conquered all major cities of that region reaching at last the southernmost harbors from which the British were frantically and hastily trying to board the ships that would ferry them to Crete.

From two harbors, namely, those of Calamata and Gythion, the retreating British were boarding their ships while under heavy attack by pursuing German forces and the rain of bombs coming from the enemy's bombers. It was under such indescribably hellish conditions that twenty-seven thousand British, Australians and New Zealanders – all members of the "British Expeditionary Force" to Greece, managed to escape. They headed toward the big Island of Crete. There, together with some ten thousand Greek armed men, who escaped with them, they were determined to continue the resistance as the enemy prepared to invade.

And so, in only one month, mainland Greece and most of its islands in the Ionian and in the Aegean Seas had been conquered by the armies of Hitler. For Hitler, it was yet another "Blitz" victory - a victory that gained him yet another country (except Crete), a victory that somehow dampened the inglorious defeat of his partner Mussolini.

Before closing this account, mention must be made about an enemy air raid that caused much havoc and destruction during the night of April 6-7.

During most of Sunday, April 6 – the day Germany attacked Greece - German planes kept flying over Athens at high altitudes leaving behind the usual white streaks. What was their intention? It wasn't to bomb the capital because, first, Athens was an historic city, and, secondly, the Greek Government from the beginning of the war with Italy had declared it an "Open City" which meant a defenseless city.

It was during the night of April 6-7 that the people of the capital and of the Port of Peiraeus found out. At half past midnight, the sirens sounded the coming of an air raid. About one o'clock in the morning, a tremendous blast shook the entire capital. What had happened?

Enemy bombs had raided the Harbor of Peiraeus. Their reconnaissance planes that had flown over Athens during the previous day, spotted British tankers and a British ammunition ship berthed close by and decided to destroy them. As the oil tankers blew up from the direct hit of the "Stuka" diving bombers, the fire soon engulfed the ammunition transport whose tremendous explosion not only shook Athens, it razed to the ground much of Peiraeus along the roadstead to the harbor and broke the window panes of most of the houses around the harbor. The result? A great number of people were left homeless. Many of them were rehabilitated in homes of Athens. Others were rehabilitated in churches where for two weeks they slept and cooked their meals.

67
OPERATION "MERCURY"

Some sixty miles south from the southernmost point of mainland Greece lies the country's largest island – Crete. It is almost one hundred and sixty miles long by thirty-five at its widest. The island is girded by an indented coastline of serene coves and small bays, enjoys a balmy climate during most of the year, and has rich farms and orchards.

The earliest Greek civilization known as the "Minoan" flourished here from the twenty-fifth century BC to the fourteenth B.C. Today, its ruined but still impressive palaces located at Knossos, Phaestos, Malia, and Zacros are visited annually by thousands of tourists.

Extensive commerce with countries of the eastern and western Mediterranean was the Minoans' one source of wealth. The other was the abundant harvest produced by the island's rich soil.

When by the first week of May, 1941, the Nazi Germany's Army had conquered all of mainland Greece and nearly all its Aegean and Ionian islands, Crete was the next most obvious target.

As twenty-seven thousand British, Australian and New Zealand troops had escaped from the mainland and had safely arrived in Crete along with ten thousand Greek troops, their presence made the German commanders, who were now preparing for an attack on Russia, believe that Crete's conquest ought to have top priority.

There were other reasons for such a decision. The Germans figured if Crete had remained in British hands, the latter would convert it into a powerful naval and air force base. British bombers taking off from Crete would raid German military installations in Greece and in the other Balkan Countries, in Eastern Europe and, especially, the rich oil fields of Ploesti, Romania, that were the biggest source of energy for the Axis armed forces.

Lastly, if Crete had remained in British hands, British naval units and air force planes would seriously harass the Axis air and sea supply lines needed to support their troops which were fighting against the British in North Africa.

The operation against this big island was code named "Mercury" by the German High Command. The planners decided that twenty-two thousand and seven hundred and fifty men would suffice. Of these, ten thousand would be paratroopers, seven hundred and fifty would be transported by gliders, five thousand would be carried by air-transports, and seven thousand by sea. For their transportation and protection, the German Air Force committed one thousand and two hundred planes.

On May 19, 1941, hundreds of German bombers began a relentless bombardment of three airfields, namely, of Maleme in western Crete, Rethymnon in central Crete and Heracleion in eastern Crete. The bombardment would be succeeded by drops of paratroopers whose aim would be the capturing of those three vital airfields to be used thereafter as bases to bring in supplies for the army.

When the relentless bombardment ceased, waves of transport planes dropped some three thousand and five hundred paratroopers that flew over the targets. They saturated the sky with descending paratroopers whose white parachutes resembled, from the distance, the falling of snowflakes.

Although the descent of the paratroopers was uneventful, a fierce and stubborn resistance awaited them when they touched ground. British and Greek soldiers began firing at them taking a heavy toll. Even Cretan civilians, using very old rifles, joined in the defense shooting the invaders as they landed in orchards, farms and in the open country.

Despite the defenders' initial successes, the enemy kept bringing more and more paratroopers determined to capture those three key airfields. Slowly, they gained the upper hand. Thus, after fierce fighting and by the end of the first day, the Maleme airfield was captured. Maleme, having now become a German base, would hence make the bringing of troops and supplies an easy and fairly safe process.

The continuing influx of German troops and supplies to the island soon enabled the invaders to take the offensive, attacking the main targets, and the big cities of Chania and Heraclion. Eventually, the British defensive lines broke down resulting in the capturing of those two key cities by the invader.

Bernard Freyberg – the supreme commander of the British and Greek troops on the island, realizing that the loss of those two key cities and three airfields signaled the final defeat of the defenders, ordered all his troops to begin evacuation.

Under continuous bombardment by the German Air Force, the British and Greek troops began boarding warships and army transport ships that were in the seaports of Rethymnon and Sfakia for this purpose. It was a hasty, and often confusing, if not chaotic evacuation.

As a result, of the twenty-seven thousand British troops that were initially on the island, fourteen thousand managed to escape along with most of the Greek troops. They sailed to Egypt. The rest were captured or killed by the pursuing German troops, while the protecting British naval units lost seven warships sunk by German "Stuka" bombers – a loss that considerably weakened the Mediterranean British Fleet.

In military history, never before had such a massive air-assault operation taken place. For the Axis, it was the biggest ever undertaken. It was also the last as its toll was heavy in both men and equipment. Never again would the German High Command commit paratroopers for the capturing of so large a target.

Descending on Crete

68

THREE AND-A-HALF YEARS OF UNBEARABLE SUFFERING

When on April 27, 1941, the German Army entered Athens initiating an occupation that was to last three and-a-half years, the people of the capital, along with the rest of the people of the country, were to suffer one of the greatest dramas in the long history of their country.

An old saying goes: "To the victor belong the spoils." The following paragraphs plainly show how the occupation forces exploited this saying to the fullest – a saying that is as old as war and conquest.

Almost since the first week of his entry into the capital, the victorious invader began to impose, on the inhabitants of Athens and all of Greece, a series of restrictive measures – measures that intended to make the occupation of the land easier and safer for his troops. Transgressors of such measures would meet severe punishments, and, in some cases, death.

Radio Athens, a hitherto nationally owned broadcasting agency, would henceforward broadcast censored news relating to the Axis War as handed out by the occupation authorities. All other programs were also censored. The same rule applied to all the newspapers of the country. As for motion picture theaters they too would hence show only German and Italian films.

The surrendering of light firearms to police stations by the inhabitants of the capital and by the inhabitants of all Greece was another early restrictive measure. Pistols, rifles, hunting rifles, any type of automatic weapons, even antique arms that had been passed down for generations as heirlooms; these too had to be surrendered. One can imagine the pain people felt on surrendering such heirloom weapons.

Confiscation of privately owned vehicles was another early restrictive, painful measure that the invader imposed. It included the surrender of new cars, trucks, small buses, and motorcycles. We can easily imagine what a serious blow this measure was to businessmen who relied heavily on trucks to carry their goods.

A most burdening measure the occupation authorities imposed on Greece was the payment of all expenses required by the forces of occupation out of the Greek National Treasury. Moreover, the Germans reserved the right to arbitrarily appropriate as many tons of crops they needed as well as raw materials. The raw materials would be used to support their war efforts.

Mass transportation of civilians also faced restrictions. As the invader would now use most of the available gasoline for is own purpose, it follows that the remainder would not be sufficient to keep all buses going. As a result, only a minimum of buses was available in the capital for the mass transportation of civilians. Thus, walking to and from their place of work became the daily habit of most people.

What, however, made the Greek people suffer the most? During those dreadful years of occupation was the lack of food, especially during the years of 1941-1942.

A month after Athens was occupied; the shelves of all grocery stores in the capital and all other cities and towns of Greece were empty. There were no more cereals, legumes, cheese, butter, olives, olive oil, salt, pepper, cocoa, chocolate, milk, coffee, sugar or other such basic foodstuffs. All these had disappeared not to be seen again in grocery stores until three and-a-half years hence. The only things that could now be found in grocery stores were mustard, toilet paper, etc. Foodstuffs such as beans, lentils, olive oil and like items would hence be available on certain days and only through rationing in minimum quantity.

Vegetable markets had hardly anything to sell. The only items available were such things as endives, cabbage, lettuce, lemons, garlic, and some greens. Vegetables were usually so stale and hard that even after protracted boiling they required much chewing.

Meat and fish markets were likewise mostly empty. Meat was rarely available and only through rationing. Occasionally one would find small fish at exorbitant prices.

Those who went to restaurants to eat lunch or dinner, regardless what they chose to eat, in the end, they were almost as hungry as when they sat down. If, for example, they had ordered chick-pea soup, the waiter would bring them a bowl that would contain thirty or forty boiled chick-peas swimming not in broth that would contain oil, but in hot "crystal clear" water. It was literally a tasteless soup. If the customer had ordered boiled vegetables, his order would come without the usual accompanying bottle of oil. If he had asked for oil, the waiter would rarely furnish it.

The only time people had bean, or lentil soup at home, or a little coffee and sugar was when these were available in groceries through rationing. The only basic foodstuff available daily through rationing, and in a very small amount, was bread. The amount available was a small loaf for a family per day. If there were children in the family parents would deny themselves their portion in order to give it to their children. Often the bread's flour was mixed with corn or lupine flour. The result was bread hard to digest with limited flavor.

During February of 1942, the bakeries distributed bread, whose crust had a cinnamon color. When people asked why the bread had such an unusual color, the answer was that it had been made from seeds of the plant from which brooms were made. This bread was the hardest ever sold. It would take the stomach several hours to digest it.

During the winter of 1941-1942, starvation was rampant and the people began to look like skeletons. It was a most disheartening sight to see people gaunt, emaciated, pale, as though suffering from tuberculosis. Some being utterly weak could hardly walk slowly shuffling their feet and ready to collapse on the sidewalk or on the street. They were a most pitiful sight.

Some became scavengers and would resort to looking into trashcans to see if they could retrieve something that was edible. Starving children would do the same often getting into the trashcans to find something to eat. Hunger reduced young and old to the level of stray cats and dogs.

According to national statistics, during the winter of 1941-1942, some two hundred and sixty thousand Greek men, women and children died in Athens and in the other cities of Greece from this terrible starvation. Rarely in its long history had Greece lost so many of its people. And, this high number was only the beginning, the preamble of the drama that was to follow in the subsequent years of occupation.

Something had to be done to lessen this tremendous loss, and the one who initiated positive action in these critical times was Archbishop Damaskinos – Archbishop of Athens and of all Greece.

After coming in contact with the International Red Cross from which he requested food aid, and, with the occupation authorities having received assurances from both sides, he organized the "National Organization for Christian Solidarity". Two and-a-half thousand men and women volunteers would cook food, and, from many relief centers, they could distribute it to seventy thousand children ages two to seven and to an additional number of children ages seven to twelve. This most commendable effort not only provided meals to thousands of starving, growing children, it even prevented their certain death.

Another task that befell this organization was of a macabre nature. Every day they would pick up the dead who had died of starvation in the different sections of Athens and would bury them in mass graves.

The winter of 1941-1942 was very cold, rather unusually cold. As firewood was very scarce, people were freezing. Some whose strength had not totally abandoned them would go to the nearby hills and mountains and chop down trees in order to heat their homes.

An old Greek saying goes: "Need is the mother of discovery," and another states: "Poverty forces one to invent ways to obtain things." During those harsh years of foreign occupation many young and very daring men called "jumpers", to obtain bread, did the following thing at the risk of their lives:

Whenever a German or Italian truck carrying bread to the barracks was passing through a byway, some daring "jumpers" would jump from the rear into the truck's bed that was loaded with bread, and immediately begin tossing loaves to their friends who were running behind the truck. Then, when all had caught one or two loaves each, the "jumper" would jump from the truck and all of them would disappear in narrow alleys. Pedestrians who happened to be near the scene would always covertly approve the courage of the "jumpers".

The above accounts by no means ended the suffering of the Greek people during those dreadful years. The following "nightmares" daily tormented the hard-pressed people of the capital and of every other city and town.

The first nightmare was the continuing inflation that went on from April 1941 to October 1944, that is, from the beginning to the very end of this Axis occupation. The inflation, which almost daily kept devaluing the drachma, greatly worried the Greek people who could not be sure if on the morrow, or on the following days they would have enough money to buy food or other badly needed things. And so, as inflation, with the passing of weeks, months, and years, kept increasing, by the time Greece was free again, people would have to pay six billion drachmas for a single cigarette, forty-five billion drachmas for a loaf of bread, fifty billion drachmas for a shoeshine, and one hundred and eighty-six trillion drachmas for a man's suit. It is unthinkable what fantastic sums, amounting to trillions and quadrillions of drachmas people would have to pay in order to buy more expensive items.

The other nightmare the people of Greece faced during those very hard years was the "Black Market". Totally depraved individuals looking for a quick gain, quick lucre at the expense of their fellow Greeks, their fellow starving and deprived compatriots, would sell foodstuffs in clandestine places at outrageous prices. The spectacle of emaciated children and haggard parents would in no way move their insensible hearts to lower their prices. The urge to become rich was uppermost in their minds. It was their golden opportunity and nothing would dissuade them from achieving their goal.

Many people who desperately needed oil, sugar, butter or other such expensive edibles and had enough money to buy them, brought their gold and silver jewelry or other heirlooms with them in order to exchange for two, three, or more pounds of oil or other expensive foodstuffs. Heirlooms that had been handed down by ancestors, and, as such, had great sentimental value, not counting their value of being antiques, were now given up for the survival of the family.

During the months preceding the liberation of Greece, as more foodstuffs became available for rationed distribution to the people, thanks to the International Red Cross, the black marketers noticing that their sales were dropping were now furious. Seeing that their filthy lucre, their filthy profiteering was slowly coming to an end, they lamented the fact that the Allies were winning the war. The Axis would soon be forced to evacuate Greece.

The hitherto mentioned dreadful deprivations the Greek people suffered for three and-a-half years were not the only ones these unfortunate and hard-pressed people endured. There were more.

In the summer of 1942, fearless, courageous young men from every walk of life led by pure patriotic feelings took to the mountains and became guerrillas in order to fight and harass the enemy in whichever way they could.

Aided by the Allies who frequently dropped them arms, ammunition and explosives, they would often come down from their mountain hideouts to sabotage bridges, railroads, trains, tunnels, truck convoys, and installations of the enemy. Many times they would even engage in fierce battles against enemy regiments killing and wounding many of their combatants. When the battle was over, the Greek guerrillas would easily escape to their mountain hideouts.

But the enemy retaliated. In order to lessen the attacks and the harassments of the Greek guerrillas the enemy would resort to horrific reprisals. Entire villages would be surrounded, the male inhabitants would be arrested, and, in the presence of the wives and children they would line up the men up against a wall and execute them.

In other cases, the enemy's rage was so savage that after surrounding a village, all the inhabitants were arrested – men, women and children, and executed them all. Then, after sprinkling the homes with flammable material dropped by an airplane, they would set fire to the village thus destroying it totally. Two villages that were so destroyed were the "Distomo" and the "Calavrita". Other small villages also met with the same fate.

The countryside was not the only area where the guerrillas fought and harassed the enemy. Many numbers of the two organizations that took to the mountains, and which were known by the acronyms EAM (National Liberation Front) and EDES (National Democratic Liberation Army), were living in Athens and in other cities of Greece always seeking an opportunity to harass the enemy.

To counteract these activities, the occupation forces would execute prisoners who they held in various prisons, most notorious of which was "Haidari", a suburb of Athens. Hundreds of prisoners who the occupation forces had captured in battles against the guerrillas, or had arrested them as suspects, or as political extremists, were executed in revenge.

The Greek people who died during the years of the Axis occupation as a result of starvation, diseases, guerrilla warfare, and executions by the enemy numbered in the hundreds of thousands. Adding to these, the ones killed during the war of 1940 to 1941 on land, in the sea and in the air, and those who were killed serving alongside the Allies until the end of the war in 1945, according to an official statistic, the total number of military and civilian losses amounted to from 800,000 to 1,000,000 dead.

What an awesome sacrifice of human life offered by a small nation for the cause of freedom!

69
FIRST IN THE REALM OF POSEIDON WORLDWIDE

As far back as the first quarter of the second millennium B.C. Greek merchant ships of the Minoan Age were already plying the blue waters of the Mediterranean Sea. They were carrying wine, fruit and oil from their island-kingdom to other ports that dotted the Mediterranean coastline from Gibraltar to the west to the coasts of Syria and Phoenicia to the east.

Owing to the Greek mercantile mind, the Minoan Trade was thriving. Despite the hard competition they faced from the Phoenicians who were at that time the masters of the Mediterranean, the Minoans continued the race, and when, by the fourteenth century B.C. their civilization declined due to a most violent eruption of the volcano of Thera which virtually destroyed the Minoan cities, the Mycenaeans who succeeded them continued the competition with the same fervor.

By the seventh century B.C., the Phoenicians, unable to continue the trade race, slowly conceded. In the end, Athens and Corinth, along with many coastal colonial cities in the West, emerged as mistresses of the ancient sea. Their ships were bigger, faster and sturdier and, with the use of some rudimentary navigational instrumentation, carried Greek products not only in the Mediterranean and the Black Sea, but even beyond the Straits of Gibraltar – to England, which was known at this time as the "Tin Island". From there, they would return to their ports carrying this much needed metal.

When Alexander the Great conquered the Middle East as far as India, the ports of Asia, hitherto never visited by Greek mariners, now became accessible. Since there was no Suez Canal to avail passage to Greek ships that wanted to sail from the Mediterranean to the Indian Ocean at this time, Greek ships would leave from ports along the Red Sea and sail east to India and beyond.

During the long Byzantine Era (330 AD – 1453 AD) Byzantine ships continued the trade that had been begun by the Hellenistic Greeks. Greek products were now sold in the markets of many Indian cities while fabrics, spices and other items were now available in the markets of Constantinople and in the other Byzantine cities.

Constantinople was conquered by the Turks in 1453 A.D. The entire Greek nation was subjugated by 1460 AD and unfortunately, activities of the Greek merchant marine declined. The "Serene Republic" of Venice had now succeeded the former Byzantine mercantile supremacy.

The decline, however, which during the early seventeenth century had attained a period of "doldrums", did not last forever. By the eighteenth century, although Greece was under harsh Turkish occupation, its merchant shipping had revived. Greek shipowners could again be found in every port of the Mediterranean ready to carry cargo to any port in the Mediterranean, the Black Sea and in Northern Europe. Greek cargo ships, mostly of the frigate and barge type, numbered in the hundreds owing, of course, to the traditional Greek mercantile spirit.

During most of the seventeenth, eighteenth and early nineteenth centuries, the Mediterranean Sea was infested by piracy. In order to defend themselves, the Greek ships had mounted cannons on both sides of their ships. The arming of Greek ships with cannons proved beneficial in two ways. It effectively protected them against the pirates' attacks, and, when in March of 1821, the Greek Revolution broke out, Greece had available a sizable fleet to challenge the Turks. Moreover, as the Greek merchant ships had very frequently engaged in battle with pirate ships, the crews of the Greek merchant ships had gained much battle experience which, oddly enough, the crews of the Turkish ships did not have.

In nineteenth century England, a revolution occurred in the shipbuilding industry. Sails were replaced by steam engines for propulsion, and wood was replaced by iron for construction. As a result, ships no longer depended on wind currents to propel them. Their steam engines enabled them to attain a desirable speed that could be maintained throughout the trip irrespective of the change of wind currents. On the other hand, their iron construction made them sturdier. Eventually, as bigger and more powerful steam engines were built, shipbuilders could now build bigger and faster ships whether they were carrying passengers or freight.

Greek ship owners were not late in the effort to modernize their merchant fleet by buying steamships built of iron. As it happens in most initial stages, Greek ship owners bought few steamships. They were small and usually second hand. Then as their trade proved more lucrative, they began buying more and more steamships from England, America, Germany, and France, thus increasing their merchant fleet to a respectable size.

Although Greece, for many decades, lagged behind such countries as the United States, United Kingdom, France, Italy, Japan and other maritime countries, by the last decade of the nineteenth century and the first decades of the twentieth, Greek ship owners had purchased so many freighters that Greece, slowly but surely, found itself among countries that were in the forefront.

During the Second World War that lasted from 1940-1945, the Greek merchant fleet joined the Allied side. Hundreds of Greek-owned small and large freighters were routinely used by the Allied convoys in the Atlantic, Indian and Pacific Oceans for transporting troops and material. As the war went on, many Greek ships were sunk by German submarines in the Atlantic Ocean and by Japanese ones in the Indian and the Pacific. Needless to add, the resulting casualties and loss of Greek crews was high.

When the Second World War ended, many leading Greek shipowners – men like Niarhos, Onassis, Livanos and others, bought many "Liberty" and "Victory" freighters built in the United States and in Canada respectively. These large freighters were used during the war to carry troops, material and food to England for the eventual invasion of Europe, and as well, for the same purpose in the Indian and the Pacific Oceans for the defeat of Japan. As these ships were sold by the American and the Canadian Governments at a very low price, Greek ship owners immediately seized the opportunity and bought them by the dozens.

In the decades that followed, the Greek shipowners continued to buy more and more new ships of all types – bulk freighters, oil tankers, chemical products tankers, ore carriers, liquefied gas tankers, container ships, passenger ships and other types built for them in Japanese shipyards and in shipyards of other countries. This phenomenal increase of the Greek-owned merchant fleet brought it, by the early years of the last decade of the twentieth century, to third place among the merchant fleets of the world.

As Greek shipowners register only a portion of their ships under the Greek flag, by March 1997, the Greek flag fleet included 987 out of a total of 3,204 Greek-owned ships. By March 1998, it included 946 ships of a total of 3,358 Greek-owned. The remainder of 2,412 ships has been registered in some thirty-four different countries like Panama, Liberia and others whose registry fees are low.

And so, by March of 1998, the small country of Greece owned the largest merchant fleet in the world. Today, some twenty-eight Greek shipping magnates each own ships whose collective tonnage is over a million. To mention the top five, they are – G. Livanos 4,719,890 tons, A. Martinos 3,901,040 tons, A. Polemis 3,600,000 tons, Empiricos 3,454,376 tons, and Latsis 3,394,044 tons.

What a marvelous accomplishment for a small European country! What an unbelievable miracle!

70
THE GOLDEN GREEK

Descendants of a people, who more than twenty-seven centuries ago originated sports and Olympics, would not abstain from participating in sports especially having been born in America where sports have been so popular in the life of its people. And that's what happened with many first generation American born Greek-Americans. From the fourth decade of the twentieth century, a large number of young and ambitious Greek-Americans entered the arena of professional baseball and other games.

Consider, for example, Alex Kampouris born in Sacramento, California in 1912. He made his first professional appearance when he played in 1932 for the Solons, and in 1938, he began playing for the New York Giants. His next contracts were with the Yankees and then with the Brooklyn Dodgers, and by 1943, he was sold to the Washington Senators. He was the first Greek-American to reach the major leagues thereby becoming an inspiration to countless Greek-American sports lovers. He won many honors for his excellent performance as a second baseman, exceptional fielder and a hitter of the long ball.

Alexander Sebastian Campanis was the only native-born Greek baseball player to play in the major leagues. He was born on the Greek Island of Cos in 1916. He was six years old when he and his mother came to America and settled in New York City. When as an adolescent he told his mother that baseball would be his future career, she attached a stipulation. He would not become a player unless he earned a college degree first. He did exactly as his mother wished, and by 1940, he graduated from New York University with a degree in education.

At the university, he was a star in baseball and football, and had served as captain of both teams. By 1943, he was playing for the Brooklyn Dodgers, a team with which he distinguished himself. He had an excellent throwing arm, great speed and excellent body coordination. Three years later, he played for the Montreal Royals. In 1950, he retired as a player and joined the Brooklyn Dodger's scouting staff. By 1957, he became the team's scouting director. In this capacity, he directed the activities of one hundred and two subordinates who scouted in many Latin American countries. As director, he had the final word in every selection, and was very successful in this crucial endeavor. He wrote three books, of which one is his autobiography entitled "Once a Dodger Always a Dodger". Today, his picture hangs in the Baseball Hall of Fame in Cooperstown, NY.

Milt Pappas, born in Detroit, Michigan in 1939, was another widely known Greek-American baseball player. After graduating from high school in 1957, he joined the Baltimore Orioles where he made a name for himself as a superb pitcher. During the first three years of his employ with the Orioles, two other well-known Greek Americans belonged to the same team

- Bill Loes and Gus Triandos. By 1962, Pappas, aged only twenty-three, led Baltimore pitching with the best record and became an All-Star. Seven years later he made the All-Time Team of the Orioles.

During the same year, the Chicago Cubs decided to acquire Pappas. His acquisition greatly benefited the Cubs. Both Pappas and the team had a new beginning. He had become such an excellent batter that when, in 1970, Pappas went out to bat, thousands of spectators at Wrigley Field of Chicago gave him a standing ovation.

In September of 1972 Pappas had the greatest game in which he had ever pitched, a no-hitter. He had no-hit the Padres 8-0 on field. Thirteen days later, he became the sixty-seventh pitcher in major league history to win two hundred games. Milt had also won fame as one of the most powerful hitting pitchers of all time. He hit twenty career home runs including two in one game in 1961. Today, Milt Pappas' name is on the list of the two hundred victory pitchers in the Cooperstown, NY Hall of Fame.

Indisputably, twentieth century's most famous Greek-American was Harry Agganis.

From a small town located near Sparta, ancient home of the brave, indomitable heroes, hailed the parents of New England's greatest all-around athlete and all-around Greek-American athlete ever - Aristotle George Agganis, better known as Harry Agganis.

Upon arriving in the United States, Harry's parents settled in Lynn, Massachusetts. It is a small town compared to nearby Boston, but it thrived with small industries until G.E. built a large industrial complex in the nineteen fifties.

The Agganises had seven children. Harry was the youngest of them. While attending high school, he began showing unmistakable signs of the indescribable success he was to achieve in the future. He was a three-sport high school star at Lynn's Classical High School, performing so expertly, that his coach once said that "If Harry were to take up golf or tennis, he would have been great in those sports, too."

With such a dynamic player on its team, Lynn Classical achieved high records resulting in Harry Agganis' receiving in 1946 his first major award, whereby he was recognized as the outstanding high school baseball player in the state. On Christmas Day of the same year undefeated Lynn Classical with Harry Agganis won the national high school championship by beating Gramby High School of Norfolk, Virginia.

When time came to attend college, Harry had eighty college football offers. He chose Boston University in order to be near home and because B.U.'s coach was Aldo Donelli - one of the country's best. By 1949 Harry was on the field playing for B.U. causing his school's team to win unprecedented victories. Recognizing Agganis' invaluable contributions to B.U.'s team, the Washington Post wrote: "By birth, he is Greek-American, by performances he is All-American."

When the Korean War broke out, Harry was drafted by the Marine Corps. He was soon placed on the football and baseball teams at Camp Lejeune. As a result of his brilliant performance in every game, he was voted Most Valuable Player and earned All-Marine and All-Navy honors in football and baseball. Agganis returned to Boston University and found the university team's record embarrassingly low. With Agganis' addition, however, conditions soon changed. Whenever the B.U.'s team played, it always won. In fact, at a game of B.U. versus Camp Lejeune, Agganis helped B.U. win 16-0. Recognizing his invaluable contribution, B.U. inducted him in its Athlete Hall of Fame.

On April 4, 1954 Harry signed a contract with the Red Sox, and on the 15th of the same month, he made his debut at Fenway Park playing against the Washington Senators. Some seventeen thousand fans went to the stadium to see the "Golden Greek". It was a 6-1 victory. During the next year, Harry played for the Red Sox helping the team win many victories.

On June 3, 1955 while out with two friends, Harry complained that he did not feel good. He was immediately driven to a hospital where the doctor found that he had a fever. Two days later, he was flown to Boston and was hospitalized, being taken care of by the Red Sox's three doctors. Harry remained in the hospital for twenty-one days during which time the doctors tried to treat him for severe pulmonary infection as well as phlebitis. Then, on the 27th of June the famous player, after feeling an unbearable pain in the chest resulting from a massive blood clot in his leg, which having broken loose had entered his lung causing pulmonary embolism, Harry died.

The reaction that followed was unbelievable. Everybody in Boston, in New England and in many other parts of the country was stunned. Both Americans, and especially Greek-Americans, found the news shocking. He was too young, only twenty-six, too soon for him to die.

Upon learning the shocking news the Red Sox manager commented: "We have lost an outstanding athlete and a young man of great character," while the Boston mayor said: "Agganis epitomized the strength of the old Greek warriors."

On June 30, 1955 the funeral service for Harry was held at the Saint George Greek Orthodox Church in Lynn, Massachusetts. It was an unprecedented funeral. According to newspaper statistics, one thousand and four hundred people filled the church, while outside, an additional ten thousand throng followed the service through speakers. Many more thousands had lined both sides of the streets that led to the cemetery.

At the same time, memorial services for Agganis were held at the Griffith Stadium in Washington prior to the game between the Red Sox and the Washington Nationals. In eulogizing the great athlete, the representative of the Red Sox said: "Harry you have been, and ever will be, an inspiration to us. We all sorely miss you as well as your family and your thousands of friends. We have been lucky to have known you and to have been associated with you. We have suffered a tremendous loss and your fellow players all join in a silent prayer of tribute to one of the greatest guys ever to swing a bat, field a ball, or run a base. God rest you."

The words of broadcaster Curt Gowdy were equally moving as they addressed relationships with his family and his friends. He said: "They called him the 'Golden Greek.' His athletic feats were golden and shining and so was Harry Agganis personally. Devotion to his mother and family, extremely loyal to his friends, teammates and coaches, these were personal habits of Harry, which could be copied by every youngster. These are the things which made Harry 'Golden' to those who knew him well."

Finally, a grieving mother, emerging from the initial shock that followed the most painful news of having lost a most prized and beloved son, was able to utter the following thoughts: "Harry's work is done. He is where he belongs - in the arms of God. God gave me that boy to watch over, but he never really belonged to me. He belongs to the people who loved him and to Christ. God has taken him at this time, to bring home to young people everywhere how high they can go from nothing if they work hard and live good lives."

Many honors came to Agganis posthumously. The Harry Agganis Memorial Foundation was established for scholarships, and a wooden statue of him was carved and was placed in the Sports Museum of New England.

71
THE TENNIS WORLD CHAMPION

He was only nineteen when this hitherto little known Greek-American tennis player became, in 1990, the youngest man to win the United States Open Title, one of the four annual tournaments that make up the grand slam; The others are the Australian Open, the French Open and the All-England (Wimbledon) Championship. The stunning championships that he won were the U.S. Open in 1993, 1995 and 1996; the Wimbledon in 1993, 1994 and 1995, becoming the first American to win the title three years in a row, plus those he won at Wimbledon in 1997 and 1998; and the Australian Open in 1994 and 1997.

Who is this legendary Greek-American who has dazzled tennis fans and colleagues all over the world? It is Pete Sampras. He was born in Washington D.C., on August 12, 1971. He was one of four children born to Sam (Soterios) and Georgia Sampras. His father, an aerospace engineer, was employed by the Department of Defense. The family lived in Potomac, Maryland until 1978, at which time, his father was hired by a California-based aviation industry and the family moved to Rancho Palos Verdes, California.

Pete's love for tennis began while he was still a very young child in Potomac, Maryland. At the basement of the house he would hit the ball against the wall for long periods every day. But when the family moved to California, Pete joined the racquet club, and all four children began receiving regular lessons in tennis.

At the age of eight, Pete was showing a tremendous enthusiasm for the sport, as well as an unusual aptitude for it. His father did not fail to notice this, and, wishing to help his son move in this direction, asked Peter Fischer - a pediatrician and amateur tennis player, to coach the young aspirant. Fischer volunteered to coach the young fellow for ten years free of charge. Nineteen years later, following a championship victory, a grateful Sampras told a reporter: "Fischer taught me how to play the game. He taught me how to serve and volley; he taught me strategy."

By the time Sampras was twelve, he had decided to become a tennis player. Determined to achieve that goal, he stepped up his daily practices during three junior years, being able to eventually place himself among the top twenty-five. When he was only fifteen, he was the youngest player on the United States Junior Davis Cup Team.

The first victory that brought Pete to the limelight was the one he scored in 1989 at the age of eighteen in the borough of Queens, New York City, "knocking off" his opponent, Matts Wilander, who was defending his championship. Commenting to a friend, Pete said that he couldn't believe he was still in the tournament, because everyone expected him to lose. He had not yet realized that he was already one of the top tennis pros of America.

What was Sampras' special skill that catapulted him to U.S. and world fame? It was his serve that could reach 130 miles per hour. Such powerful serves that he made throughout the duration of each game put his opponents on the defensive and allowed him "to call the shots", and thus "command" the game's momentum.

From 1990 on, the young Greek-American tennis player managed to win often. His repeated victories in the U.S. and abroad made him the undisputed national and world champion - a record that is truly astonishing. Once he played doubles with President George Bush, and not long after that he won the inaugural Grand Slam Cup which was an event for the top sixteen performers in the year's Grand Slam tournaments. By defeating Brad Gilbert in three easy sets in the finals, Sampras earned $2 million - the largest single paycheck ever in tennis. He received the check composedly, and, unhesitantly, donated $250,000 of that paycheck to Cerebral Palsy Research for the discovery of a cure.

Another exceptional year for Sampras was 1993. In that year, he earned $3.6 million in prize money; he had scored eighty-three match wins, and, having scored 1,011 unreturnable serves, he became the first player in tennis history to record more than one thousand aces (serves the opponent could not return) in a year.

As the twenty-first century began, it found Sampras still very young, only twenty-nine years old, effervescent, robust, very healthy, in top shape to pursue and win championships.

While still a youngster, Sampras said "I want to be a good role model so that kids will say that they want to grow up to be like Sampras." His wish materialized.

In bringing this brief biographical sketch to a close, the following words made by a reporter and printed in the September 13, 1993 issue of New York Times, are most befitting to the high stature of this famous Greek American. He wrote "It is just possible we have a latter-day classic on our hands."

72
THE SILVER SCREEN

The Master Director

Among the thousands of Greek immigrants who arrived in the United States in the early decades of the twentieth century were the Kazanjoglous. Prior to coming to the United States, they lived in Constantinople, Turkey - a city that was still the home of over one hundred thousand Greeks.

On September 7, 1909, a son was born to the family of Kazanjoglou whom they named Elia. Two years later, the father, who was a successful rug merchant decided to move with his family to Berlin, Germany. But he did not stay there too long. The family returned to Constantinople, and, a year later, they were off again to New York City where Elia's father became a successful carpet merchant.

Elia was not like his father. He had no desire to be a businessman. Early in life he had shown a preference toward the performing arts - a field in which later he was to distinguish himself. In fact, what he actually pursued and eventually triumphed in was directing theater plays and movies. And to realize his dream, he first enrolled at the Yale University Drama School and then continued his studies at Williams College from which he graduated in 1930.

In 1931, Elia Kazan, as he came to be hence known, had his "first crack" at directing - the art he was to pursue all his life. He directed "The Second Man" at the Toy Theater in Atlantic City. Although a beginner, his directing was so good, that in the following years he had scores to direct plays in New York and in other cities. He directed Pulitzer Prize plays such as Kingsley's "Men in White", Thorton Wilder's "The Skin of our Teeth", and Tennessee William's classic "A Street Car Named Desire" with such outstanding stars as Marlon Brando, Jessica Tandy, Karl Malden, and others. The play was a box-office success for months. Needless to say that his persistence to direct every play with artistry, made him, in less than six years, the most celebrated director of Broadway. His name had now become known from coast-to-coast.

The year 1945 marks another milestone in the life of Elia Kazan. A director of so wide a fame could not be overlooked in Hollywood - the center of the motion picture industry. At a prominent studio's invitation, he went to Hollywood where his talent would be indelibly stamped on nineteen movies that are of the finest ever made. Moreover, being an already acclaimed director, he was given the opportunity to work with some of the best known actors and actresses that the studio of Twentieth Century Fox, Paramount, Warner Brothers, Columbia, and United Artists availed to him.

"A Tree Grows In Brooklyn", was the first motion picture he directed in 1945. In 1947 there followed "The Sea of Grass", "Boomerang" and "Gentleman's Agreement" - a story of anti-Semitism, which earned him his first academy award.

In 1949, he directed "Pinky", a moving story on racial prejudice, and in 1950, "Panic in the Streets"- a first rate thriller dealing with a possible breakout of plague in New Orleans.

In 1951, he directed an assignment dear to his heart - "A Street Car Named Desire", in which the cast was the same as that he had used in the Broadway production. The movie received twelve Academy Award Nominations, and was awarded five. As for Kazan, this movie earned him his second Oscar.

Other outstanding films that Kazan directed include "Viva Zapata" in 1952, "Man on a Tightrope" in 1953, and, in 1954, "On the Waterfront" which included such actors as Marlon Brando, Lee J. Cobb, Eva Marie Saint, Rod Steiger and others.

In 1955, he directed "East of Eden", based on John Steinbeck's namesake-novel; in 1956, "Baby Doll" - another Tennessee William's novel; in 1957, "A face in the Crowd"; in 1960, "Wild River", with such select stars as Montgomery Clift and Lee Remick; and in 1961, "Splendor in the Grass", with Natalie Wood and Warren Beatty.

In 1963, Elia Kazan directed his "America, America", written, directed and produced by him. The film, almost three hours long, in the words of a contemporary movie analyst: "Is an eloquent tribute to Elia Kazan's Greek uncle, who was the first of his family to immigrate to the United States." The tribute is expressed entirely in vivid, vigorous motion picture terms, to the courage, tenacity and foresight that drove the young man to fight his way out of a land of bondage in Turkey at the turn of the century and on to this land of freedom where his strength and his spirit might have full play. And since the recipient of the tribute might be any young immigrant of that day, the film indeed is not only a tribute but also a ringing ode to the whole great surging immigrant wave.

"An ode - that is what it is, precisely, for the story conveyed in this film, is a minor odyssey that has the major connotations of a rich lyric-epic poem. It has a story as ancient as Homer, as modern as the dossier on the kid who has tried three times to enter this country as a desperate but clumsy stowaway. And in it is of the tireless wanderer who seeks and finally finds his spiritual home."

Commenting on the performance of the cast, the same analyst wrote: "We must also be thankful to him for selecting a splendid cast to perform his colorful characters and for directing all of them so well. A Greek lad, Stathis Giallelis, is incredibly good as the determined hero, putting fire and spirit into the role, as well as a poignant relevant of the naiveté's and gentleness of the youth." As for the other characters, he wrote, "They are stand-outs in a cast that offers gem-like performances in even the smallest roles."

In 1967, Kazan directed "The Arrangement", a film based on an autobiographical novel dealing with his own mid-life crisis, and in 1976, he directed "The Last Tycoon", based on a novel by F. Scott Fitzgerald that dealt with the life of a disillusioned Hollywood director. "The Last Tycoon" was the last film he directed.

While in Hollywood, Kazan would shuttle to New York to direct Broadway plays - a task he enjoyed as much as directing movies. Needless to add, in both instances Kazan contributed the best and the most of his inimitable artistry to make his cinematic and theatrical productions real gems. Hence his name as a director will remain unforgettable.

In 1999, the Academy of Motion Pictures Arts and Sciences honored him with the Life Achievement Award. He more than deserved it.

In addition to Elia Kazan, eleven more Greek nationals and Greek-Americans have likewise won Oscars. They include: Hermis Pam for choreographing the film "A Damsel in Distress"; Katina Paxinou for being best supporting actress in the film "For Whom the Bell Tolls". Basically a distinguished stage actress, Paxinou has also performed in eleven other films; the Greek composer Manos Hatzidakis for composing the music for the film "Never On Sunday", and who also has composed music for forty-five other Greek and foreign films; Vagelis Papathanasiou for composing the music for the film "Chariots of Fire"; dress designer Theone Aldrich for designing the garments for the film "The Great Gatsby"; Angelo Graham of Warren, Ohio and Dean Tavoularis from Massachusetts for best art direction for the film "Godfather 2"; George Chakiris for being best supporting actor in the film "West Side Story"; Robert Zemeckis for directing the film "Forrest Gump"; Olympia Dukakis for being best supporting actress in the film "Moonstruck". Last but not least, Costas Gavras is recognized for directing the film "The Ignored". Gavras, who is a native of Athens, Greece, while still a young man emigrated to Paris, France, where he has resided ever since. He has directed the film "Z" and many other French films. For his excellence in directing, France's President Francois Mitterand appointed Gavras President of the French Cinematographic Academy, the equivalent to the America's Academy of Arts and Sciences.

On Top of Twentieth Century Fox

In 1910, three brothers named Charles, George and Spyros Skouras arrived in New York along with thousands of other Greek immigrants. They were three of the ten children of a very poor family. The father was a farmer and a shepherd and lived in the small town of Skourohorion in northern Peloponnesus.

Of the three brothers that had come to America, Spyros was the most entrepreneurially aggressive. He had been born on March 28, 1893, and, when in 1910 he immigrated to America, he was seventeen. Young, healthy and vigorous and with hopes to succeed in life, Spyro devoted himself to hard work, goading his brothers to do the same. All three worked long hours as pages, and bus boys at a St. Louis hotel, saving their money to invest in some business venture later on.

Having worked at the hotel for four years, by 1914, they decided to invest their money by buying the St. Louis Olympia Theater. Purchasing a theatre after four years of hard work in a major city of the United States was the brothers' first and very successful milestone. Twelve years later, that is, by 1926, the brothers owned thirty-seven theaters in St. Louis. Actually, they owned almost all the theaters which in 1929, they sold to Warner Brothers. After this deal, Spyros assumed the role of general manager of the Warner's Theater Circuit.

Spyros' road to success continued. In the 1930's, he assumed the role of general manager of the "Paramount" affiliated theaters, and later he assumed control of the "Fox Metropolitan Group" which he led from bankruptcy. Leading this company out of bankruptcy was another significant plus in the chain of his entrepreneurial achievements.

Then in 1935, Spyros scored another successful move that has lasted to this day. He orchestrated the merger of Fox Metropolitan Theaters with the Twentieth Century Movie Studios, thus creating one of the largest movie studios in America as well as in the world. With the aid of Darryl Zanuck, a production genius, Twentieth Century Fox began producing some of the finest films ever made, such as: "The Black Swan" in 1942, "A Walk in the Sun" in 1945, " The Keys of the Kingdom" in 1947, "All about Eve" in 1950, and "The Diary of Anne Frank" in 1959.

At the end of the Second World War, Spyros, having never forgotten his old country, which during that war had suffered all sorts of deprivations, humiliations and devastations by the Axis Powers, organized and became the head of a nationwide Greek War Relief organization that sent food, clothing and other items to needy Greek people. He put a lot of energy into this philanthropic effort thus earning the gratitude of the Greek people and of their government.

The advent of television and its fast and successful penetration into the American homes became a threat to the movie studios of Hollywood. Former regular theater-goers that filled the theaters every evening, now found it more convenient, relaxing and inexpensive to stay home and comfortably watch news, serials and very old movies.

Skouras, who throughout his life had been aggressive, would not give in to the threats of television. He began an aggressive marketing campaign for movies, and was the first to perceive the advantages made by a new wide lens invented by Henri Gretien in France, whereby motion pictures could be projected on a wider screen known as "Cinemascope". Skouras bought the patent, and soon afterwards, after having the theaters install wide screens, began producing cinemascope pictures.

"The Robe", a religious motion picture released in 1954 and based on a novel by Lloyd C. Douglas, was the first picture filmed in the Cinemascope innovation. It elicited very favorable remarks from spectators all over the country and the then free world, as they were most impressed by the visual and sound effects of the wide screen.

Twentieth Century Fox continued producing many other motion pictures based on this novel innovation, pictures such as musicals, adventure and romance, often set in foreign countries. Then in 1963, Skouras decided to produce one of the longest (four hour) most spectacular, and, up to that time, most expensive movie ever made - "Cleopatra" with Elizabeth Taylor as the charming Queen of Egypt and Richard Burton as Mark Anthony. But this thirty million dollar super production nearly wrecked the financial structure of the studio resulting in Spyros Skouras' resigning as president, and assuming the position of the studio's board chairman.

In 1969, Skouras resigned from Fox to concentrate on other interests. One of these was international shipping. He moved from Hollywood to New York City where he died in 1971.

Spyros Skouras, along with Elia Kazan, exemplifies that an individual can succeed when he has the will, the tenacity, the vision, and right thinking. Skouras in particular, being an immigrant and with no higher education, with ample common sense became a super-achiever. He was ready to meet adversity by seizing opportunities when they appeared.

73
GREEK SCHOLARS & U.S. PRESIDENTS

As stated in previous chapters, five hundred years ago, an artistic and cultural movement, known as the "Renaissance" (meaning "Rebirth") swept Italy. The movement spread gradually to other countries of Europe such as France, Spain, Portugal, England, Germany and others.

What this movement did was to turn the attention of artists, architects, writers, philosophers, and scientists to the artistic and intellectual achievements of the ancient Greeks and Romans. People began to learn the ancient Greek and Latin Languages, in order to study and profit from the writings of the ancient Greek poets, philosophers and scientists. Also, architects began designing buildings that resembled those of the ancient Greeks and Romans. Painters made paintings with classical scenes and sculptors made statues very much like those of the Ancient Greeks. The Greek Language was introduced in the universities of Europe so that those who were studying the arts and sciences could easily read and understand better the writings of the Ancient Greeks.

When late in the fifteenth century Columbus discovered America and universities and colleges were built in many cities of the US, the Ancient Greek and Latin Languages were taught to most students who attended them. It has become such a common practice that nine of our American presidents learned the Ancient Greek Language. They were: John Adams – our second president; Thomas Jefferson – our third president; James Madison – our fourth president; John Quincy Adams – our sixth president; James Polk – our ninth president; Franklin Pierce – our fourteenth president; James Garfield our twentieth president; Woodrow Wilson our twenty eighth president; and Calvin Coolidge our thirtieth president.

A very famous American president who not only knew the ancient Greek Language but had also studied the writings of the ancient Greeks was Thomas Jefferson. He was born in 1743 in Albermarle County, Virginia, and at the age of seventeen he entered the College of William and Mary in Williamsburg, VA, to study law. But besides law, Jefferson studied languages, literature and science. In fact, science became the hobby of his life. He also invented many things such as the swivel chair, a revolving music stand, a letter copying machine, and a pedometer – an instrument used to measure walking distance.

Jefferson also loved politics. He served in the Virginia Legislature and in the Continental Congress. He was Governor of Virginia, a US Congressman, Minister to France, Secretary of State, and Vice-President, and, in 1800, was elected President. He served two terms.

History, poetry, literature, art, and architecture, as well as the democracy, invented by the Ancient Greeks, were his prime interests. He would read Greek literature, poetry and the plays in the original ancient Greek Language which he had mastered.

When the thirteen American Colonies rebelled against Great Britain, Jefferson soon became one of the most ardent revolutionaries. It was at this time that he wrote the "Declaration of Independence", a document in which he so well expressed the ideals of liberty and individual freedom that go back all the way to ancient Athens. Later, when the thirteen colonies won their independence, he was one of the "Framers of our Constitution" and of the "Bill of Rights", two documents that strongly echo the democratic principles developed in Athens twenty-three centuries earlier.

While he was our Minister in France, he visited Marseilles, Nice, Antibes, and Monaco - four cities that in ancient times had been founded by Greek colonists. It was in these cities, that, for the first time, he saw ancient Greek ruins – remnants of a culture he always admired. Later in his life, when he would design his home (Monticello), the Capitol of the State of Virginia, and the University of Virginia in Charlottesville, elements of Greek architecture dominated these buildings.

Jefferson loved the two poems of Homer, which he always read in the Ancient Greek text. In a letter to Dr. Joseph Priestley, an eminent classic scholar from Philadelphia, he wrote: "I enjoy Homer in his own language infinitely beyond Pope's translation of him. I thank on my knees, him who directed my early education, for having put into my possession and I would not exchange it for anything which I could then have acquired, and have since acquired."

Lehman, a biographer of Jefferson, in describing the influence of the Greek Language on Jefferson, wrote, "Jefferson frequently praised the sound of the Greek Language" to which the biographer has attributed the "vigorous, rich and beautiful" in Jefferson's writing style "never scrupulous about words when they are once explained." Jefferson so loved the sublime poetry of Homer that, when his wife died in 1782, he wrote on her tombstone the following excerpt from Homer:

"Nay if even in the house of Hades the dead forget their dead, yet will I even there be mindful of my dear comrade."

When he heard Patrick Henry's speeches before the Revolution he recalled years later: "He appeared to me to speak as Homer wrote." He considered likewise no more pure delight than escape into a foreign world of the imagination of Homer's Greece. "It was distant, heroic, poetic life."

When the University of Virginia, which he had designed, was completed, Jefferson had a marble statue of Homer, playing his lyre and attended by a young boy, placed at one and of the quadrangle (rectangular courtyard) of the school, and in front of one of the two main buildings of the University which he had designed in Classical Greek Style. On the upper part of the façade and below the pediment, he ordered the following Greek inscription to be chiseled in large Greek capital letters. It reads: "Know the truth, and the truth shall make you free."

Jefferson was one of the greatest presidents that our country ever had. Liberty and democracy were his most cherished ideals – ideals he had learned from studying the writings of the Ancient Greeks.

Another distinguished American who was a Greek scholar before he became President of the United States was James Garfield.

He was born on November 19, 1831 in a log cabin. His parents named him James. His father's name was Abraham and his mother's Elizabeth.

It didn't take long for James' mother to find out that James was a very smart little fellow and, therefore, a promising child. In fact, she was amazed that her toddler, when only three years old, was able to read without difficulty. He attended a school in the district of Orange Township, Ohio, was an "A" student, thus earning the admiration of his teachers. In his free time, he would do any kind of job in order to earn some money to someday pay for college.

When James came of age, he enrolled at the Geauga Academy of Chester, Ohio, where he studied Ancient Greek, Latin, English Literature, Algebra, Botany, and Geography. Young James found the language, history, and civilization of Greece fascinating. The Greek ideals about democracy, justice, freedom, and truth as well as Greece's literary and scientific achievements made a deep impression upon him. He studied these things with fervor in the original Greek Language.

Upon completing his studies at the Geauga Academy, he enrolled in Hiram College at Hiram, Ohio. After that, he attended Williams College in Massachusetts. To earn money necessary for his tuition and other expenses, he would work as a carpenter and janitor at the colleges he attended and would tutor students in Ancient Greek.

When James completed his studies, he returned to Hiram to become a professor of Ancient Greek and Latin. Later, he was elected president of Hiram College. This poor boy from Orange County was now the head of one of the leading colleges in Ohio.

James' aspirations did not stop there. James studied law on his own for two years and was admitted to the Ohio Bar in 1860. Now, he turned his attention to politics. He became an Ohio State Senator and a US Representative. During the Civil War, he joined the Union Army and rose to the rank of Major General. He had considered slavery an inhuman and repulsive institution totally contrary to the ideals of freedom and equality that the American Constitution held so high.

In 1880, James decided to run for President of the United States. He won the election thus becoming the 20th President of the US.

President James Garfield had come a long way. From Mentor, Ohio to Washington D.C.! From a log cabin, to the White House! And, from a poor boy to the highest office of our country! How proud his mother must have felt as she watched her son's presidential inauguration. She was the first mother to attend her son's inauguration.

Unfortunately, President Garfield did not finish his four-year term. On July 2, 1881, Charles Guiteau fatally wounded the President. He was angry because he was not appointed to the US Embassy in Paris. And so, a prominent American, who was a Greek Scholar and a US President, died very early.

74
A DISTINGUISHED ASTROPHYSICIST

In October of 1957, the former Soviet Union surprised the world by sending a rocket into space to orbit the earth which carried a small sized artificial satellite called "Sputnik". This feat signaled a new era, an era in which man could now launch artificial satellites. Through its instrumentation, information could be transmitted back to earth which was very useful to scientists of various fields as well as to the military.

Within weeks after the launching of Sputnik, the American Government realized the beneficial as well as the dangerous consequences that artificial satellites would incur.

It took this immediate measure to form the National Aeronautics and Space Administration (NASA) to rigorously pursue programs that would benefit scientific fields and the military.

From the very start, NASA planners concentrated on a comprehensible program to probe all of the planets and the natural satellites of our solar system. Also, another program of equal priority was the landing of an American astronaut on the moon and his safe return to earth. Other vital missions of NASA's satellites were the investigation of the forces of the earth, its atmosphere, geomagnetism, volcanism and others.

Another very vital department of NASA's formation was the "Applied Physics Laboratory" of the Space Department of the John's Hopkins University whose scientists were responsible for much of the planning, the designing, construction, instrumentation, and launching of the satellites.

The Applied Physics Laboratory was directed by Stamatios (Tom) Krimigis from the year January 1991 through April of 2004. Some 600 scientists and high technology experts worked under his direction.

Krimigis was born in the town of Vrontado on the island of Chios, Greece. Upon completing his secondary education in his native town, he came to the U.S. to pursue studies in physics. He enrolled at the University of Minnesota from where he graduated with a Bachelor in physics degree. He then enrolled at the University of Iowa from which he received an MS in 1963 and PhD in physics in 1965. Subsequently, he served on the faculty of the physics and astronomy department at Iowa U. and in 1968 he joined its Applied Physics Laboratory. At first he led the Space Physics and Instrumentation Group where by 1980 he became its Chief Scientist. By the year 1991 he became Head of the Space Department, a position he held until April of 2004. Thereafter, he continued as Head Emeritus still doing research work.

For thirty years Dr. Krimigis worked in the above mentioned positions in the Applied Physics Laboratory. He managed the many stages of preparation for the launch of the unmanned satellites to the nine planets of our solar system. In all, he was responsible for about 60 satellites.

Our astronomical and astrophysical knowledge greatly increased due to the planetary data that was transmitted through the satellite's instrumentation back to earth. It showed us the physical conditions that existed in space. Never before had so much valuable information been gathered.

Satellite "Voyager 1" was programmed by Dr. Krimigis to travel beyond the interplanetary space entering the interstellar space. This meant that Voyager 1 raced 8 billion miles reaching the outermost boundary of our Solar System where the sun's magnetic field lessens. Upon entering the interstellar magnetic field, the satellite would experience perturbations. On December 16, 2004 Voyager 1 successfully crossed the outermost boundary continuing its voyage into fathomless space, a feat that is a first in man's history.

Aside from his daily routine in the laboratory, Dr. Krimigis still found time to contribute 380 papers in books and in journals. He has also lectured many times to Space associations on all five continents.

Dr. Krimigis has received numerous awards for his conscientious and professional accomplishments. Topping these highly deserved recognitions are the "NASA Medal for Exceptional Scientific Achievement" which he received twice in 1981 and in 1986. The "COSPAR Space Science Award" which is the highest honor that the world space science community bestows. Also, the "Johns Hopkins Applied Physics Laboratory Life Achievement Award" and the "Golden Cross of the Order of Phoenix" by the President of the Greek Republic.

Finally, in 1999 the International Astronomical Union honored him by naming Asteroid 8323 "Krimigis".

In retrospect, Urania, the ancient Greek muse of Astronomy, must have rejoiced immensely at the marvelous accomplishments of Dr. Tom Krimigis.

75
EPILOGUE

Greece's present population numbers a little over 10,000,000. As it has not significantly increased due to wars and large scale emigration to other countries, Greece is still a small country. Yet, what is amazing about its people is their consistent ardor in intellectual and entrepreneurial pursuits throughout their long recorded history that covers more than three millennia.

As we have already noted, throughout antiquity and especially during the Fifth Century, three generations of citizens created an intellectual wellspring of a civilization from which the Western World drew and still draws.

Greece's philosophical thought searched every area of speculative inquiry, finding its culmination in Socrates, Plato and Aristotle, and became the legacy of Western thinkers both academic and ecclesiastic. Ancient Greek political ideals, especially democracy, are still regarded as the most viable of governmental systems, while mathematics and the sciences trace their foundations to the ancient Greeks.

Fanciful Greek mythology has been the inspiration of secular European and American artists. Ancient Greek tragedy and comedy still hold first place. Its stature is owed to its inimitable, masterful plays. Greek sculpture and painting, that sought to explore and create the ideal human physique, is still admired and imitated by sculptors and painters around the world. Like Euclid's geometry, their intellectual achievements will forever have an inestimable, enduring value.

In Byzantine times, ancient Greek thought, particularly philosophy, significantly aided the great Church Fathers to define the dogmas of Christian theology and other matters in ecclesial and ecclesiastical areas. Simultaneously, literature, art, architecture, and the sciences continue to evolve.

In recent times, and especially following the struggle for independence, the literary, artistic, scientific and commercial pursuits, that for four centuries, had received limited attention due to the harsh restrictions imposed by the foreign occupiers. They have since been pursued with renewed energy and vision, thus enabling the people to emulate the latest advances in every area of Western progress.

Today, Greeks who live in Greece, in the United States, in Canada, in Western Europe, in Russia, in Australia and elsewhere, continue to forge ahead in every professional, civic or entrepreneurial field. Possessed with an unwaning ambition for professional and business success, they have succeeded admirably wherever they live. They continue to recognize that high achievement levels are attained and maintained only by insuring with an almost passionate zeal, that Greek youngsters proceed religiously to some field of higher education. Greek youngsters are, per capita, among the greatest achievers in post secondary studies in the United States of America. Proceeding to college after high school is expected of the vast majority of youngsters of Greek descent, and families plan for and make necessary sacrifices to facilitate the process.

Like their ancestors who always exhibited phenomenal excellence, the Greeks of the Twenty-first century continue with the same fervor to attain that excellence. The spirit of Hellenism still shines brightly.

BIBLIOGRAPHY

Balanos, D., The Byzantine Church Writers, Athens, Greece, 1951 (in Greek)

Botsford, G. W., and Robinson, C.A., Jr., Hellenic History, New York, NY 1950

Burton, R., Cavendish R., Stonehouse B., Journeys of the Great Explorers, New York, NY, 1992

Bury, J. B., A History of Greece, London, England, 1912

Carpenter, R., The Esthetic Basis of Greek Art, Bloomington, IN, 1959

Diehl, C., Byzantium: Greatness and Decline, New Brunswick, NJ, 1957

Cavarnos, W. A., Byzantine Sacred Art, New York, NY, 1957

Constantelos, D., Byzantine Philanthropy and Social Welfare, New Brunswick, NJ, 1968

Cunliffe, B., The Extraordinary Voyage of Pytheas the Greek, New York, NY, 2001

Dieter, A., Temples of the Pharaohs, Oxford, England, 1999

Gillespie, C. C., Dictionary of Scientific Biography, New York, NY, 1970

Hartt, F., Art, New York, NY 1976

Jurgens, W., The Faith of the Early Fathers, Collegeville, MN, 1970

Murray, G., The Literature of Ancient Greece, Chicago, IL 1957

Obolensky, D., Byzantium and the Slavs, Crestwood, NY 1994

Pappas, P. C., The United States and the Greek War for Independence 1821 - 1828, New York, NY 1985

Runciman, S., Byzantine Civilization, London, England, 1961

Sakelariou, A., The Position of Greece in the Second World War, New York, NY, 1944 (in Greek)

Sophocles, S., A History of Greece, Thessalonike, Greece, 1961

Thomas, T. and Solomon A., The Films of 20th Century Fox, Secaucus NY, 1979

Triantafillov, V.K., The Nature of the Operations of Modern Armies, Moscow, U.S.S.R., 1929, Burhans, W. (translator), London, England, 1994

Wakeman, J., World Authors, New York, NY, 1975

Volumes I, II, III, VII, XII, History of the Greek Nation, Athens, Greece, 1980 (in Greek)

Zervos, D., Baseballs Golden Greeks, The First Forty Years, 1934 - 1974, Canton, MA 1998

ILLUSTRATION CREDITS